# Those Not-So-Sweet Boys

7

YOKO NOGIRI

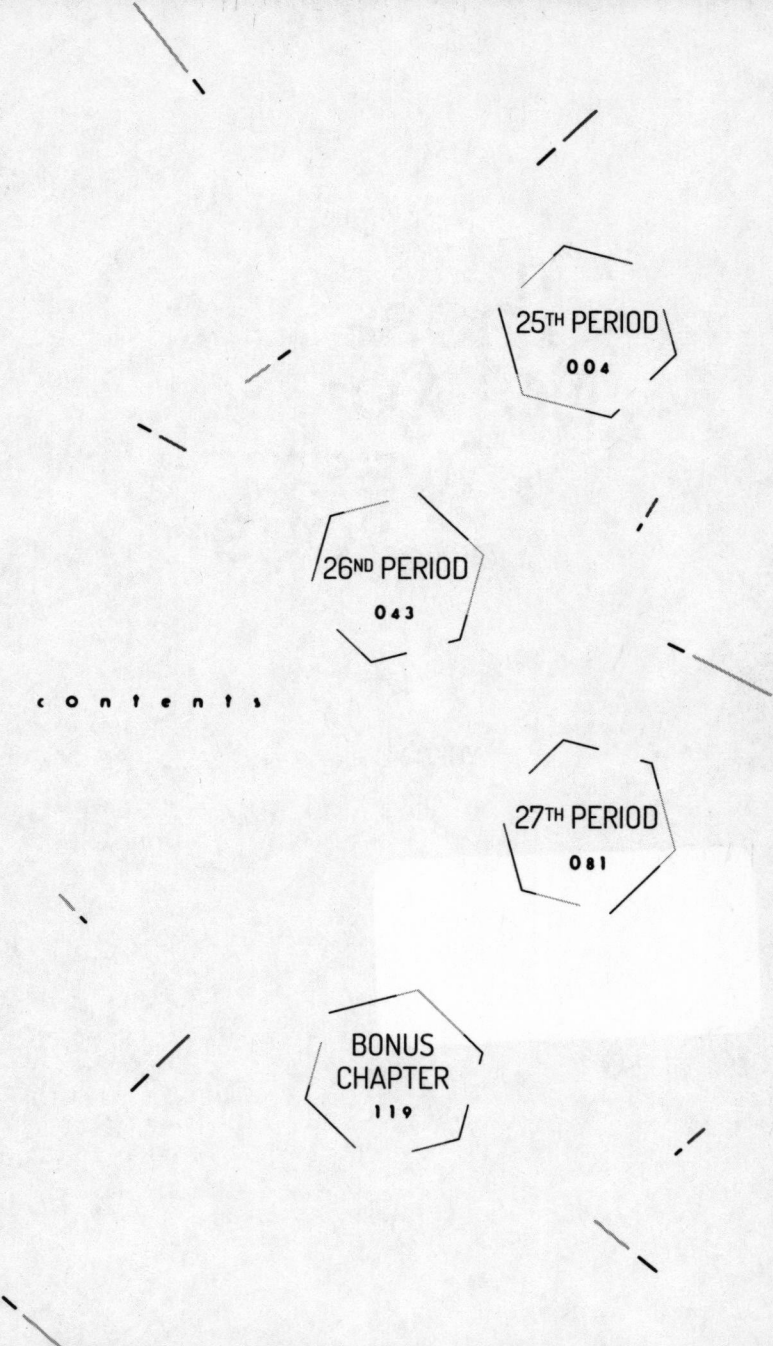

contents

## characters

### REI ICHIJO

Heir to the Ichijo Conglomerate.
Lives alone in a fancy apartment.

### MIDORI NANAMI

Attends high school on a scholarship
to help with her family's finances.
It's sunshine and butterflies with
Rei—the crush is mutual!

### CHIHIRO GOSHIMA

Successor to the Goshima gang.
Is used to the assumptions people
make about him due to his family.

### YUKINOJO IEIRI

Son of a doctor. A good friend to
Rei and Chihiro, and an overall
nice person, but...

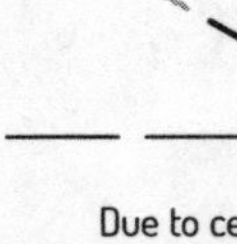

### KEIICHI SUZUKI

Chairman of the
school Midori attends.
Is concerned about Rei
and his friends.

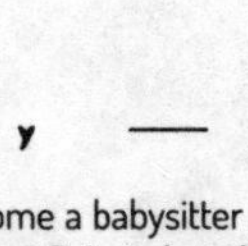

### KON NANAMI

Midori's beloved little
brother who's in junior
high school. A great cook,
and super reliable to boot.

## story

Due to certain circumstances, Midori has become a babysitter of sorts to the truants Rei, Yukinojo, and Chihiro. She develops a crush on Rei, and at the school festival they officially become a couple. One day, Midori is tricked and "kidnapped," and she ends up joining Rei at his grandmother's birthday party! Pressure from Rei's grandmother causes trouble in their relationship, but Rei figures out what he really wants and makes up with Midori. With a supportive push from Midori, he even manages to confront his father for the first time. Then, like a bolt from the blue, Midori gets a call from her own father, who had disappeared and left the family in deep debt. Now Midori doesn't know what to do!!

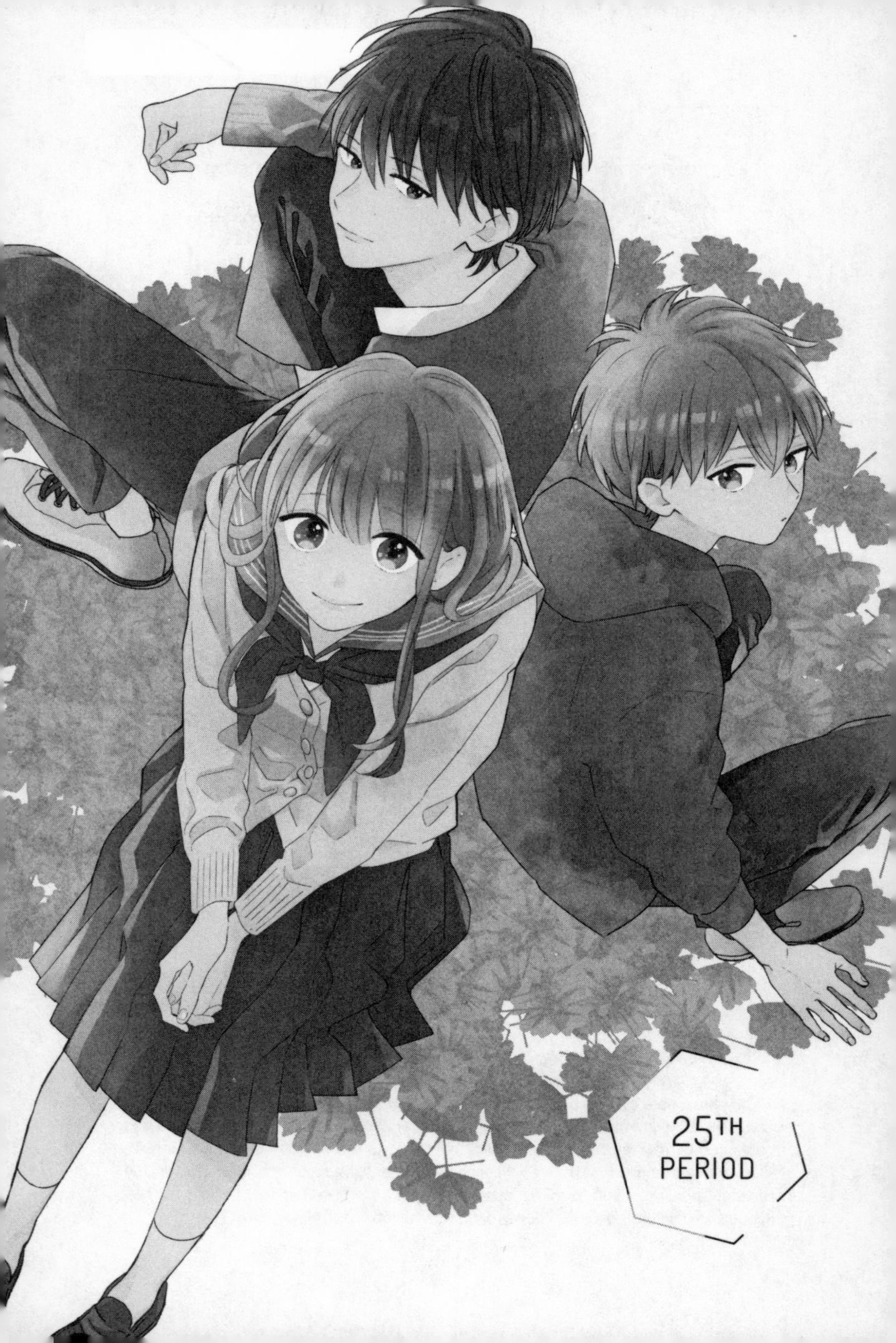
25TH
PERIOD

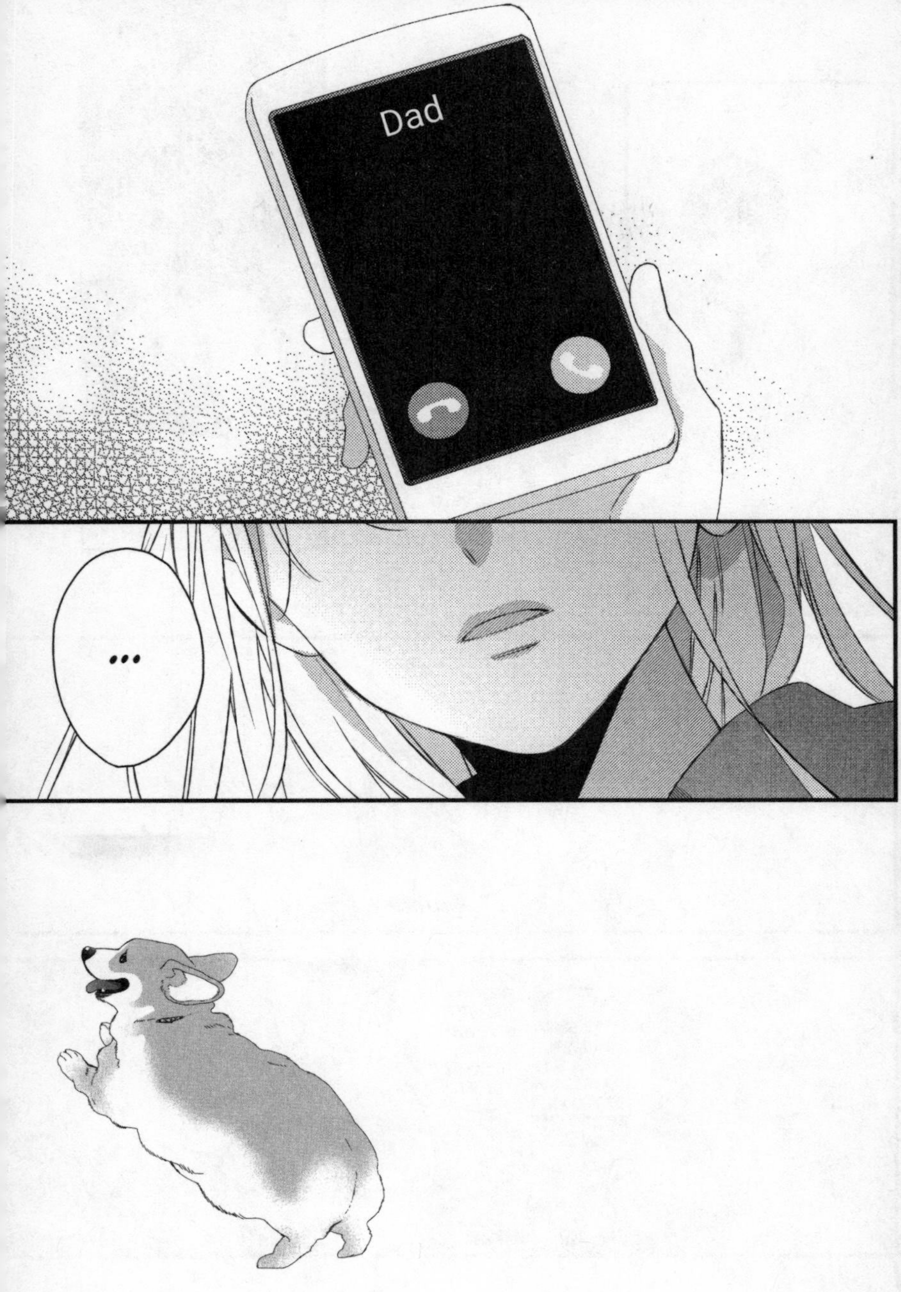
Dad
...

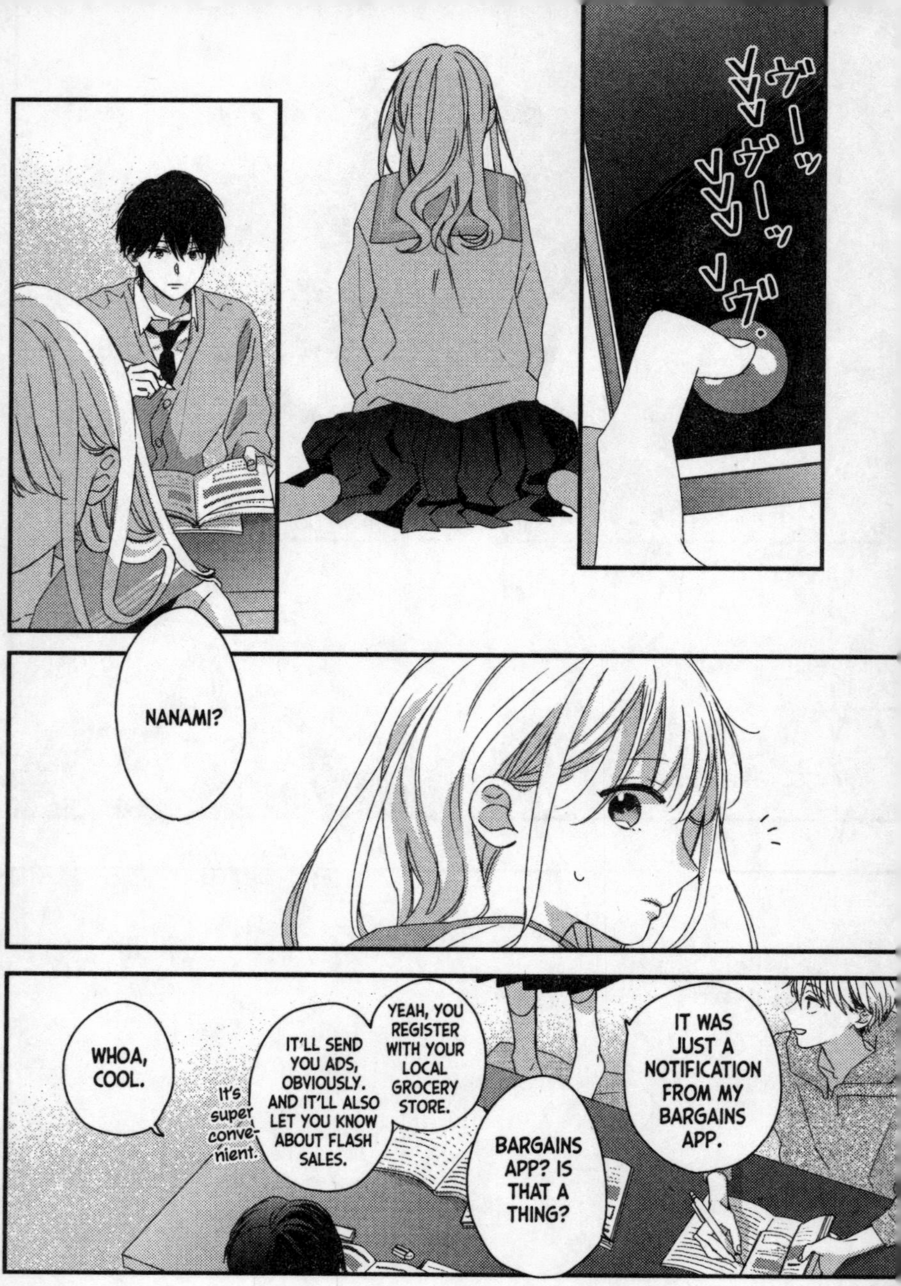
ヴーッ ヴーッ ヴ
NANAMI?
IT WAS JUST A NOTIFICATION FROM MY BARGAINS APP.
BARGAINS APP? IS THAT A THING?
YEAH, YOU REGISTER WITH YOUR LOCAL GROCERY STORE.
IT'LL SEND YOU ADS, OBVIOUSLY. AND IT'LL ALSO LET YOU KNOW ABOUT FLASH SALES.
It's super conve-nient.
WHOA, COOL.

How very domestic of you.

I DIDN'T EVEN THINK.

I JUST HUNG UP.

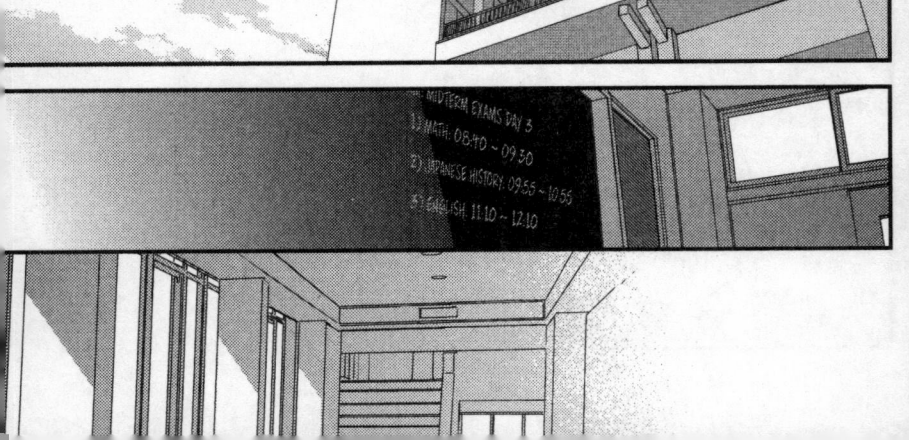

MIDTERM EXAMS DAY 3
1) MATH: 08:40 ~ 09:30
2) JAPANESE HISTORY: 09:55 ~ 10:55
3) ENGLISH: 11:10 ~ 12:10

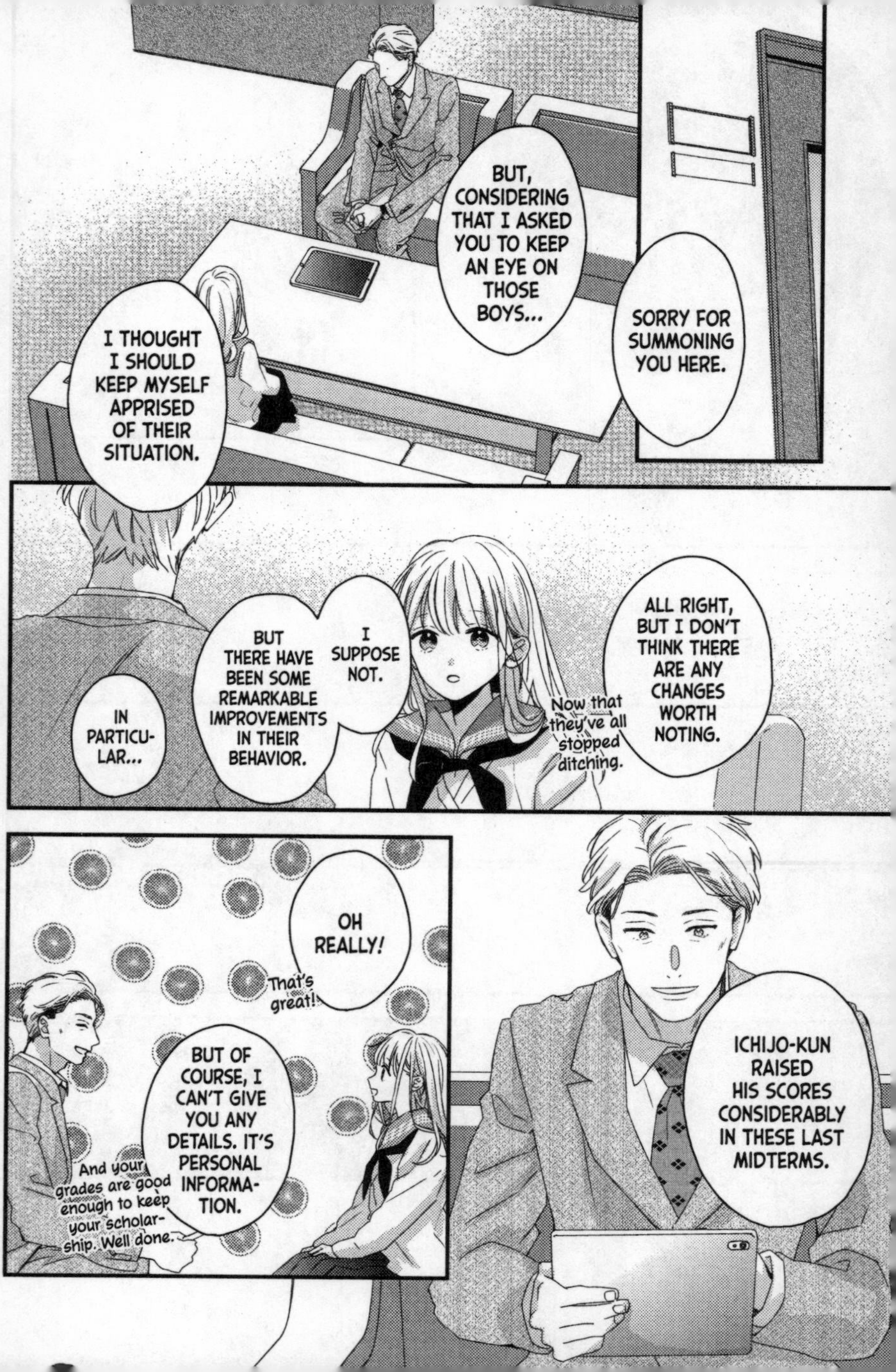
SORRY FOR SUMMONING YOU HERE.
BUT, CONSIDERING THAT I ASKED YOU TO KEEP AN EYE ON THOSE BOYS...
I THOUGHT I SHOULD KEEP MYSELF APPRISED OF THEIR SITUATION.
ALL RIGHT, BUT I DON'T THINK THERE ARE ANY CHANGES WORTH NOTING.
Now that they've all stopped ditching.
I SUPPOSE NOT.
BUT THERE HAVE BEEN SOME REMARKABLE IMPROVEMENTS IN THEIR BEHAVIOR.
IN PARTICU-LAR...
ICHIJO-KUN RAISED HIS SCORES CONSIDERABLY IN THESE LAST MIDTERMS.
OH REALLY!
That's great!
BUT OF COURSE, I CAN'T GIVE YOU ANY DETAILS. IT'S PERSONAL INFORMATION.
And your grades are good enough to keep your scholarship. Well done.

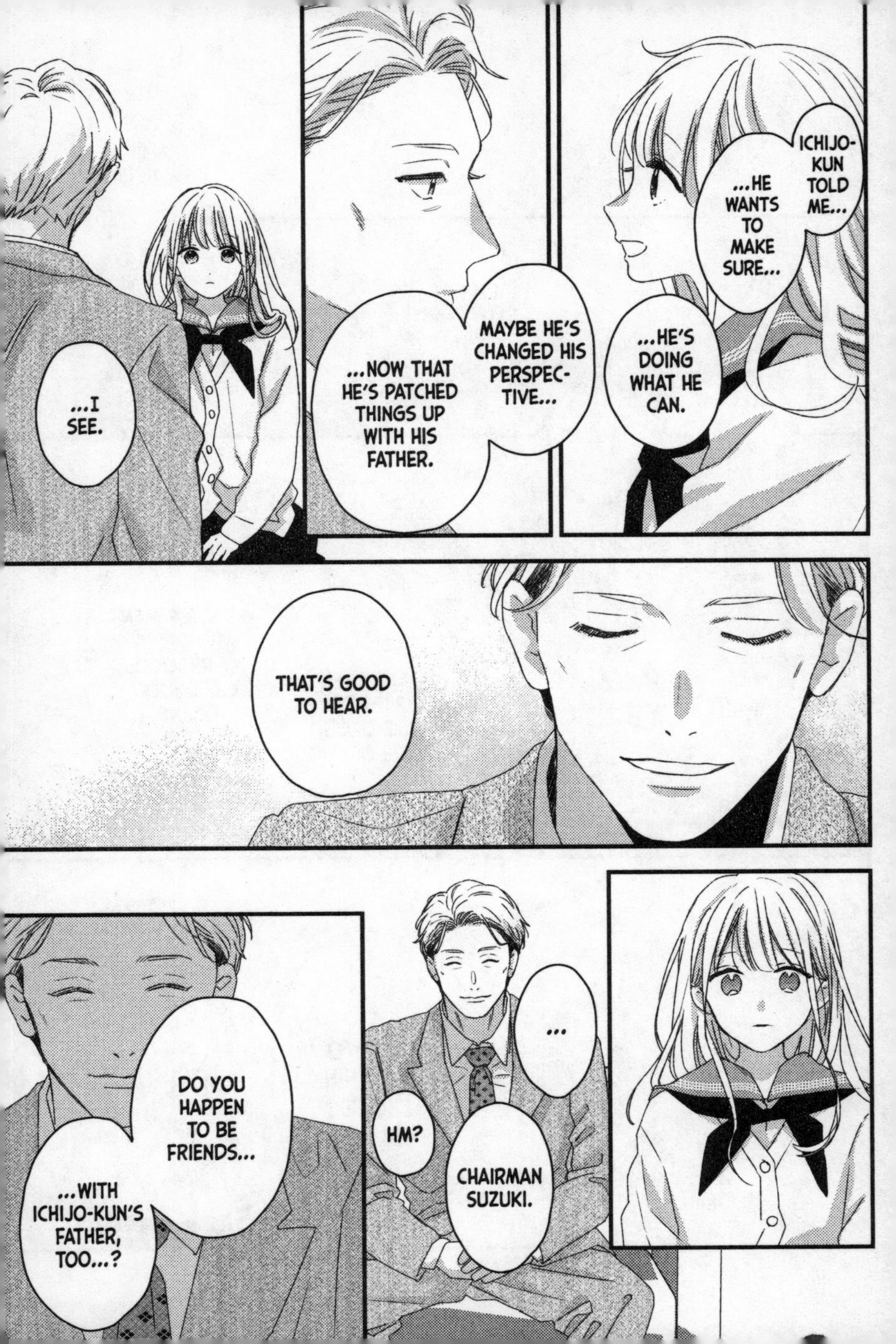
ICHIJO-KUN TOLD ME...
...HE WANTS TO MAKE SURE...
...HE'S DOING WHAT HE CAN.
MAYBE HE'S CHANGED HIS PERSPEC-TIVE...
...NOW THAT HE'S PATCHED THINGS UP WITH HIS FATHER.
...I SEE.
THAT'S GOOD TO HEAR.
...
CHAIRMAN SUZUKI.
HM?
DO YOU HAPPEN TO BE FRIENDS...
...WITH ICHIJO-KUN'S FATHER, TOO...?

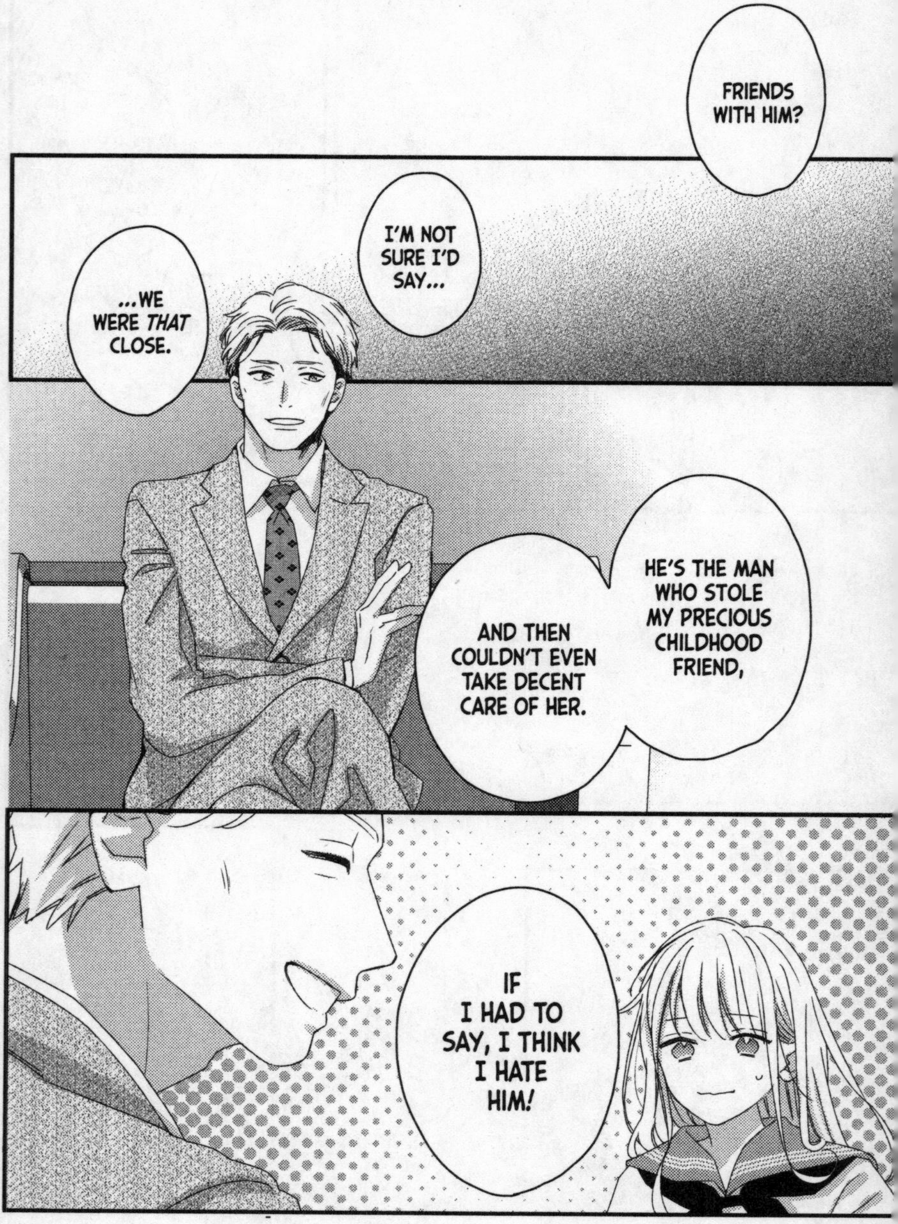
FRIENDS WITH HIM?
I'M NOT SURE I'D SAY...
...WE WERE *THAT* CLOSE.
HE'S THE MAN WHO STOLE MY PRECIOUS CHILDHOOD FRIEND,
AND THEN COULDN'T EVEN TAKE DECENT CARE OF HER.
IF I HAD TO SAY, I THINK I HATE HIM!

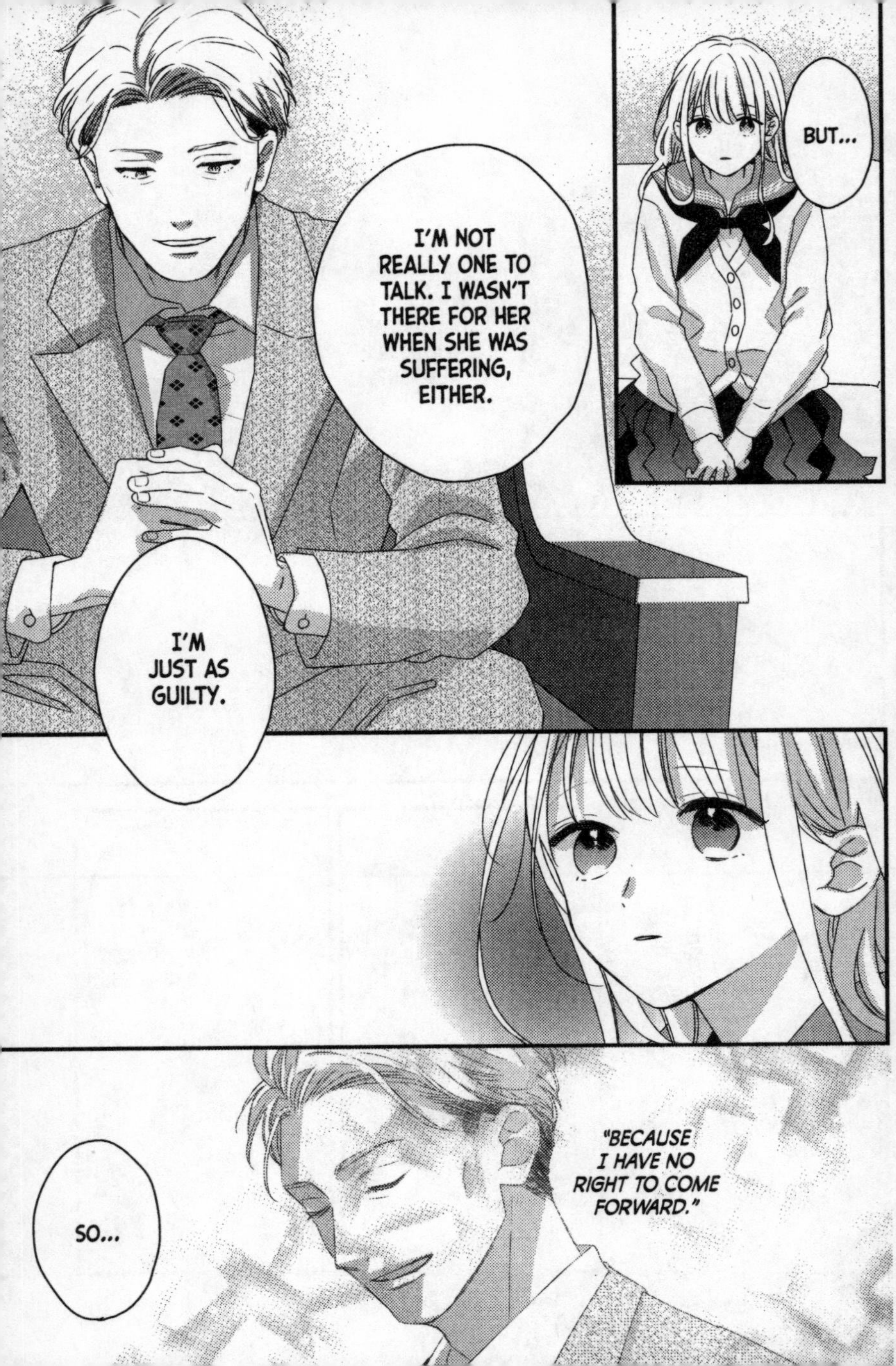
BUT...
I'M NOT REALLY ONE TO TALK. I WASN'T THERE FOR HER WHEN SHE WAS SUFFERING, EITHER.
I'M JUST AS GUILTY.
"BECAUSE I HAVE NO RIGHT TO COME FORWARD."
SO...

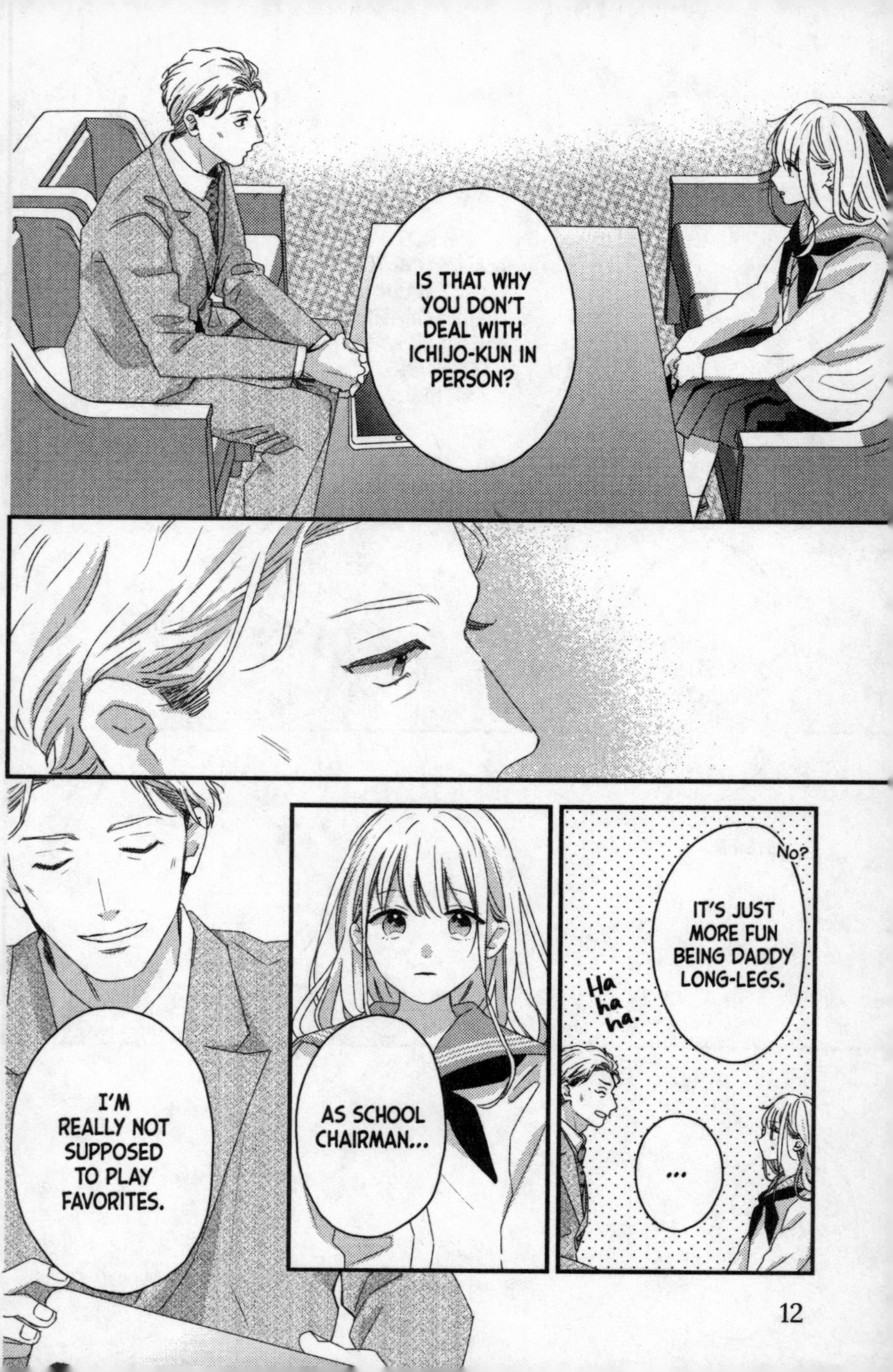
IS THAT WHY YOU DON'T DEAL WITH ICHIJO-KUN IN PERSON?
No?
IT'S JUST MORE FUN BEING DADDY LONG-LEGS.
Ha ha ha.
...
AS SCHOOL CHAIRMAN...
I'M REALLY NOT SUPPOSED TO PLAY FAVORITES.

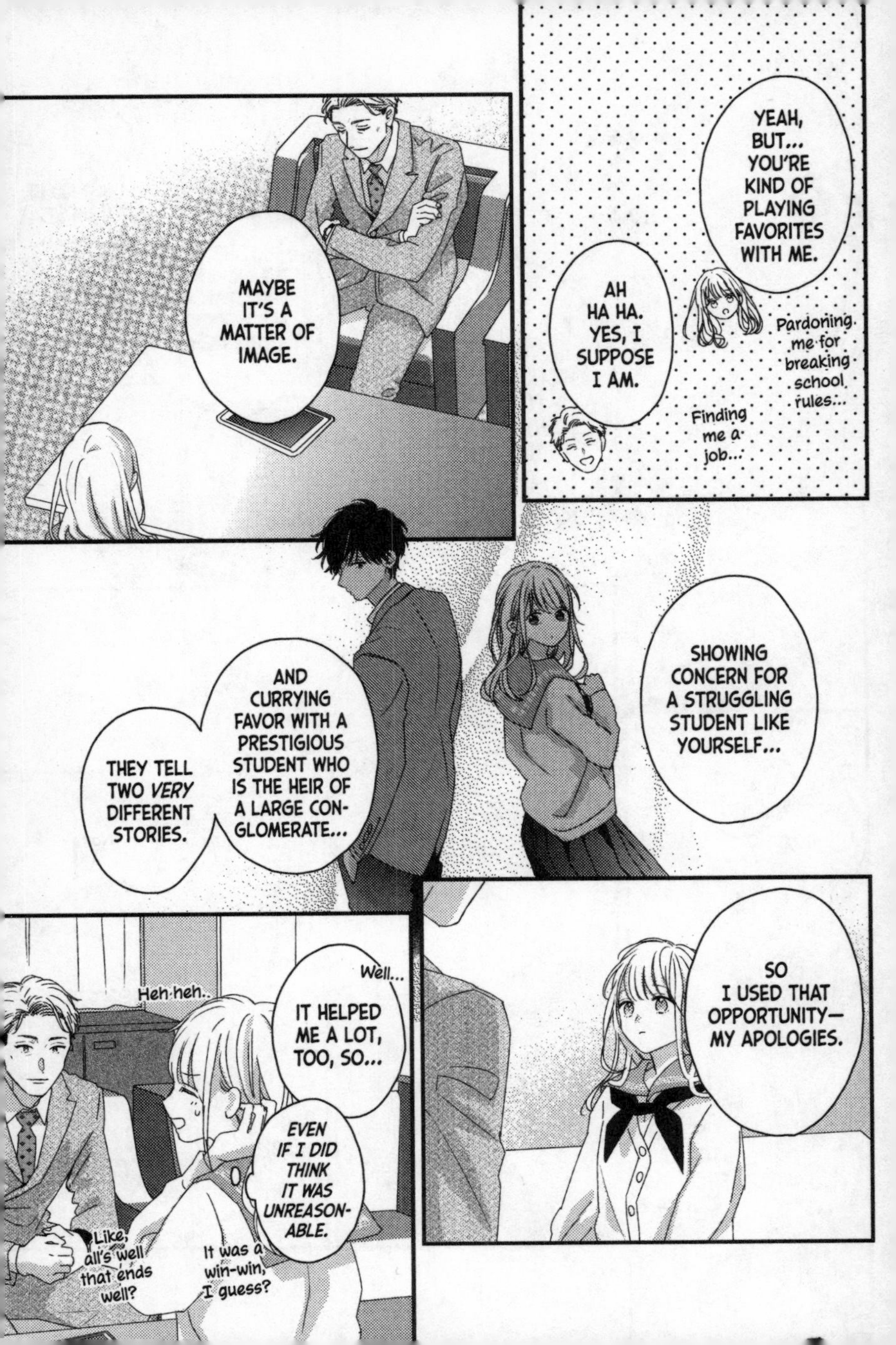
YEAH, BUT... YOU'RE KIND OF PLAYING FAVORITES WITH ME.
Pardoning me for breaking school rules...
Finding me a job...
AH HA HA. YES, I SUPPOSE I AM.
MAYBE IT'S A MATTER OF IMAGE.
SHOWING CONCERN FOR A STRUGGLING STUDENT LIKE YOURSELF...
AND CURRYING FAVOR WITH A PRESTIGIOUS STUDENT WHO IS THE HEIR OF A LARGE CON-GLOMERATE...
THEY TELL TWO *VERY* DIFFERENT STORIES.
SO I USED THAT OPPORTUNITY—MY APOLOGIES.
Well...
IT HELPED ME A LOT, TOO, SO...
*EVEN IF I DID THINK IT WAS UNREASON-ABLE.*
Heh heh..
It was a win-win, I guess?
Like, all's well that ends well?

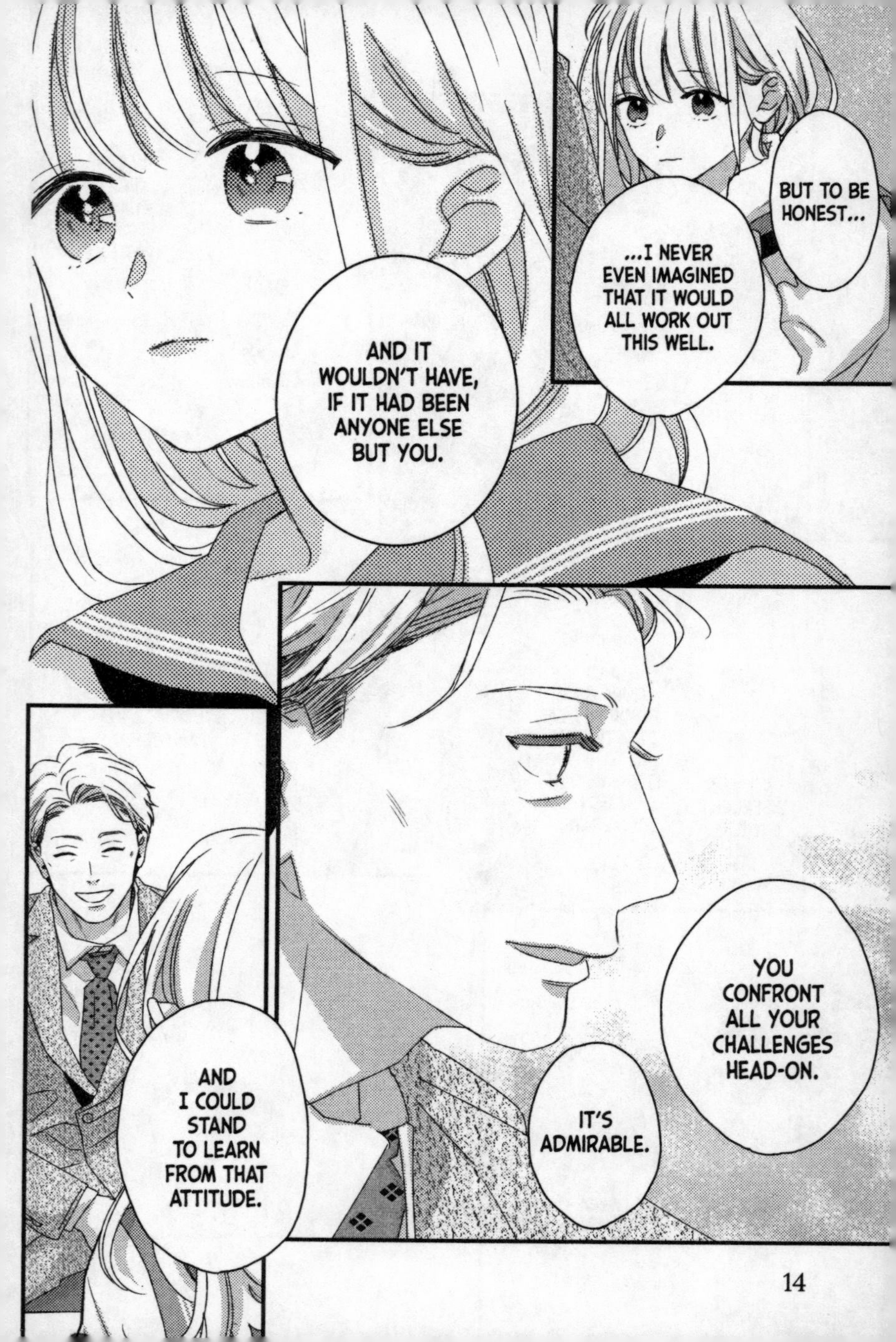
BUT TO BE HONEST...
...I NEVER EVEN IMAGINED THAT IT WOULD ALL WORK OUT THIS WELL.
AND IT WOULDN'T HAVE, IF IT HAD BEEN ANYONE ELSE BUT YOU.
YOU CONFRONT ALL YOUR CHALLENGES HEAD-ON.
IT'S ADMIRABLE.
AND I COULD STAND TO LEARN FROM THAT ATTITUDE.

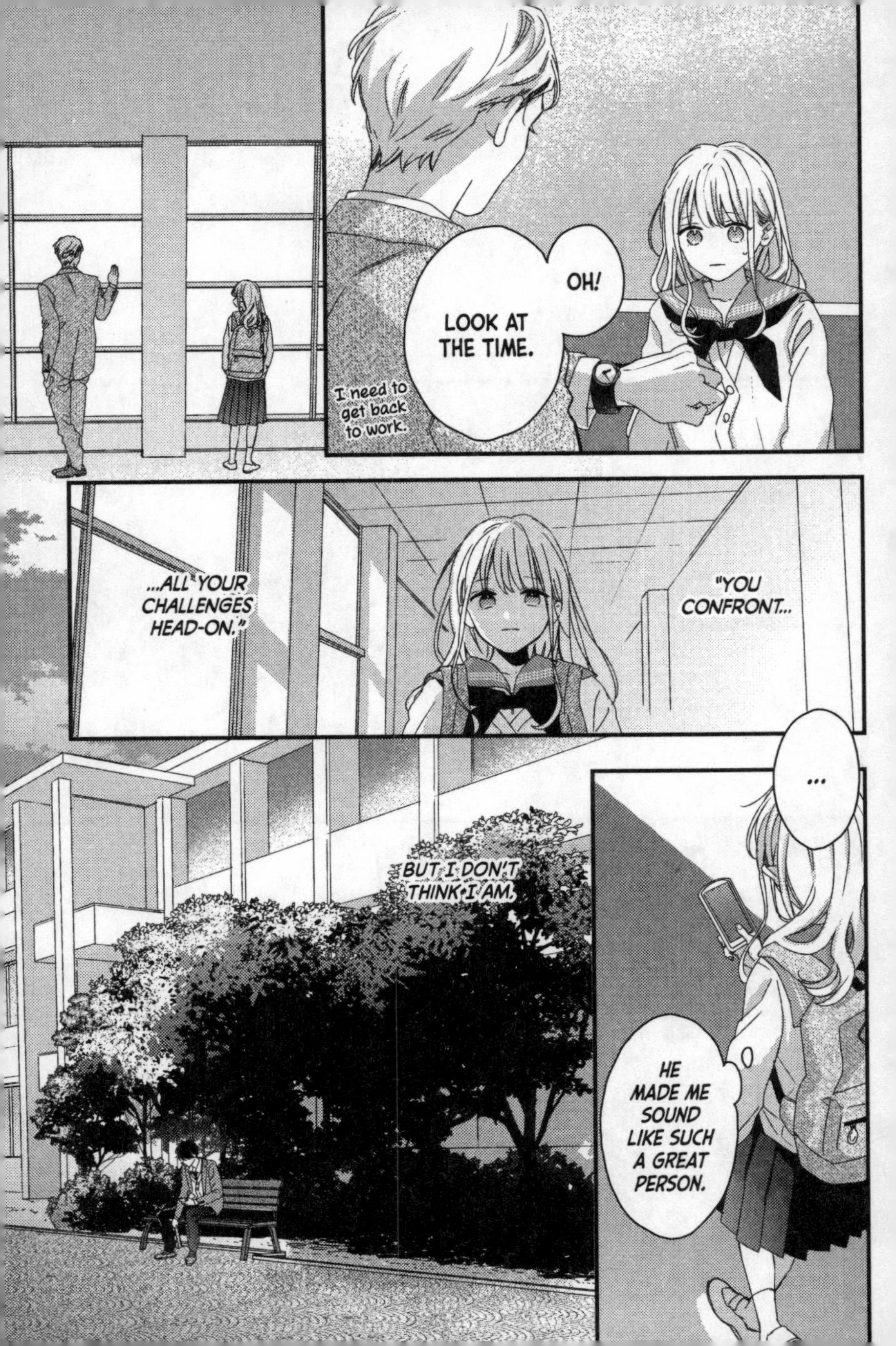
OH!
LOOK AT THE TIME.
I need to get back to work.
"YOU CONFRONT...
...ALL YOUR CHALLENGES HEAD-ON."
...
HE MADE ME SOUND LIKE SUCH A GREAT PERSON.
BUT I DON'T THINK I AM.

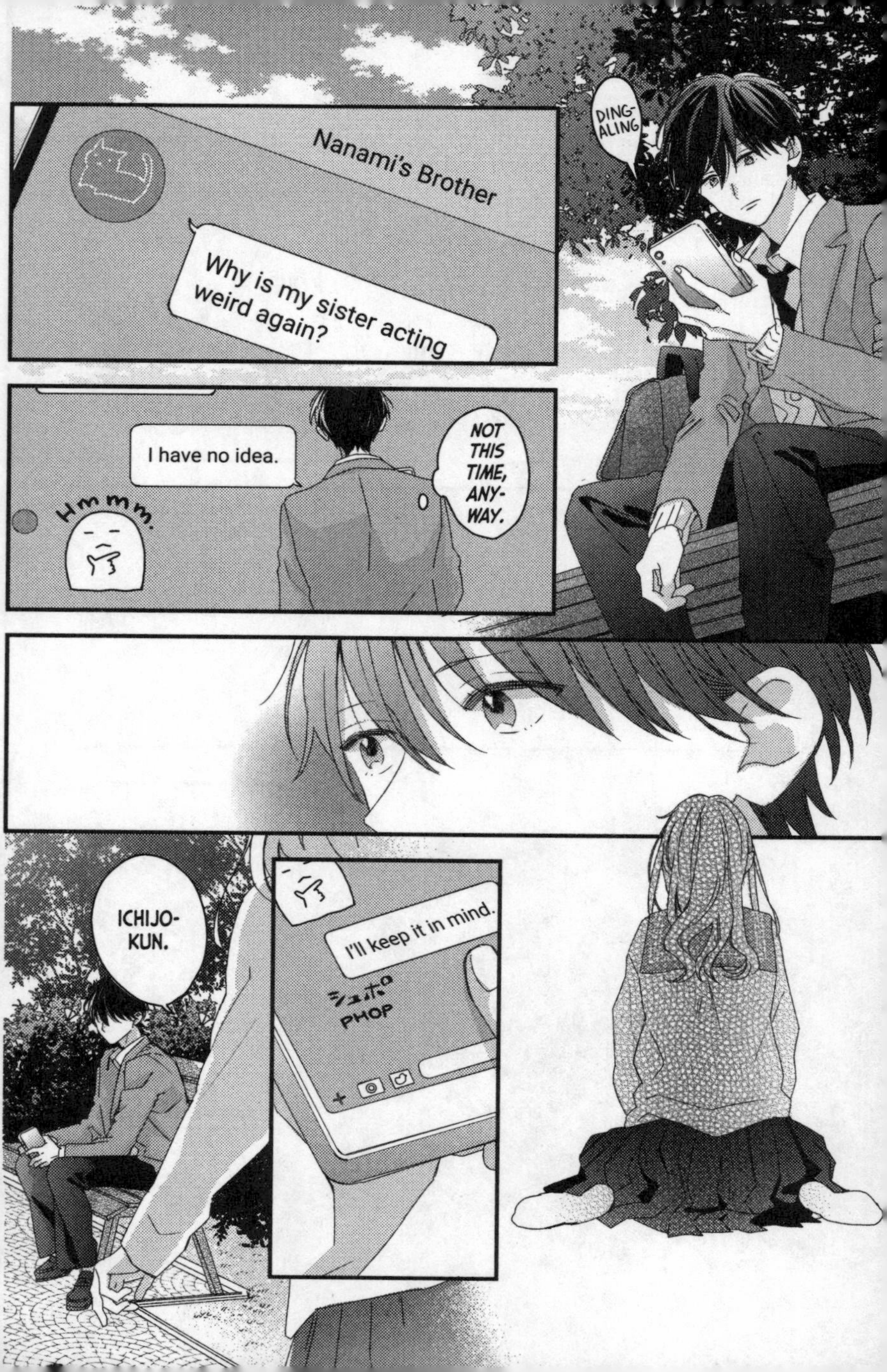
DING-ALING
Nanami's Brother
Why is my sister acting weird again?
NOT THIS TIME, ANYWAY.
I have no idea.
Hmmm.
I'll keep it in mind.
シュポ
PHOP
ICHIJO-KUN.

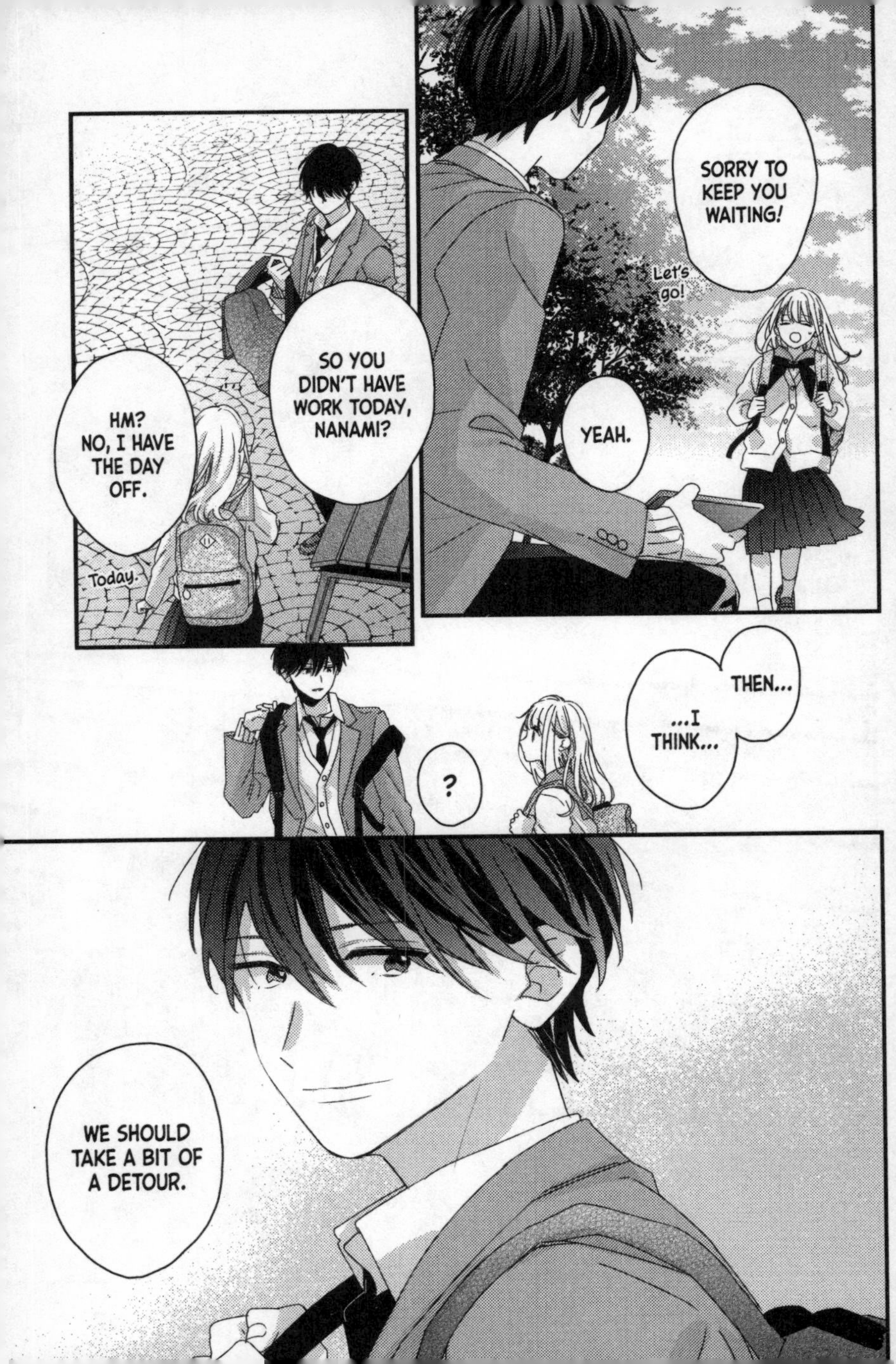
SORRY TO KEEP YOU WAITING!
Let's go!
YEAH.
SO YOU DIDN'T HAVE WORK TODAY, NANAMI?
HM? NO, I HAVE THE DAY OFF.
Today.
THEN...
...I THINK...
?
WE SHOULD TAKE A BIT OF A DETOUR.

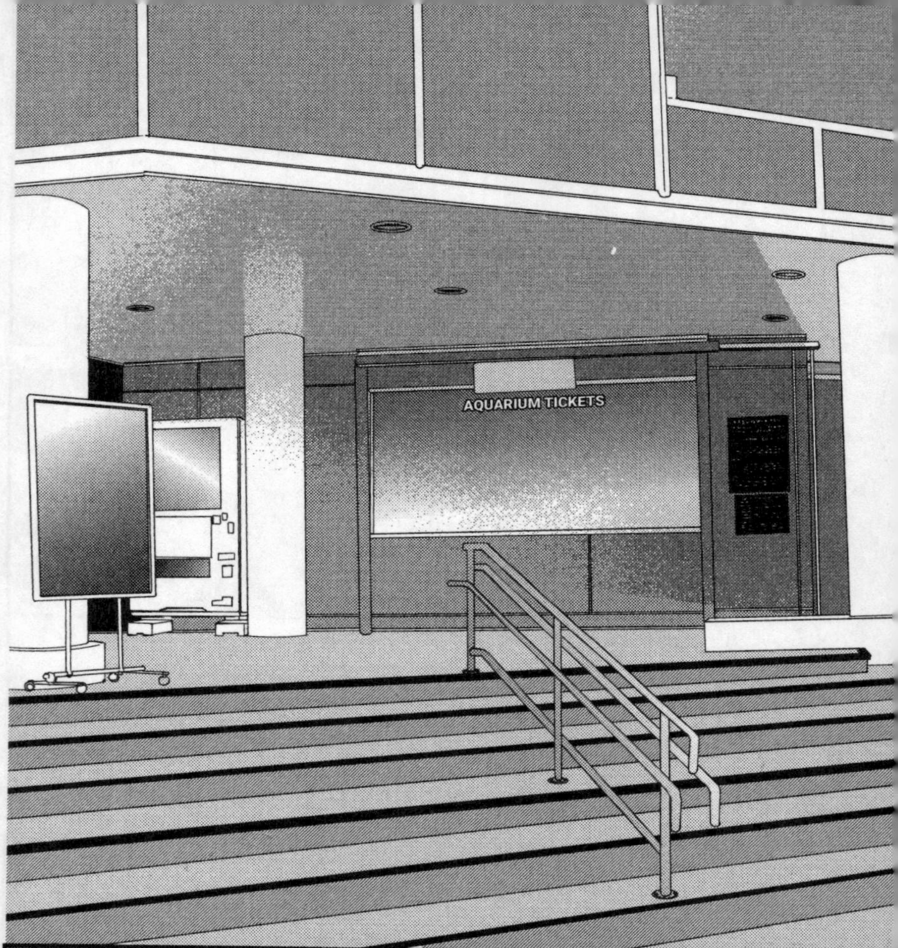
AQUARIUM TICKETS
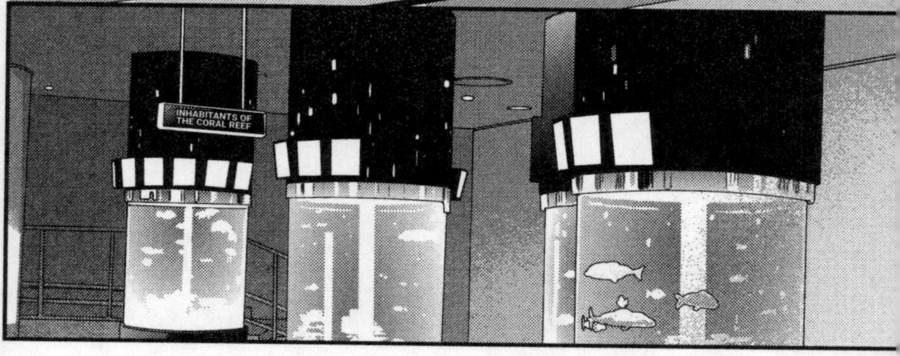
INHABITANTS OF THE CORAL REEF

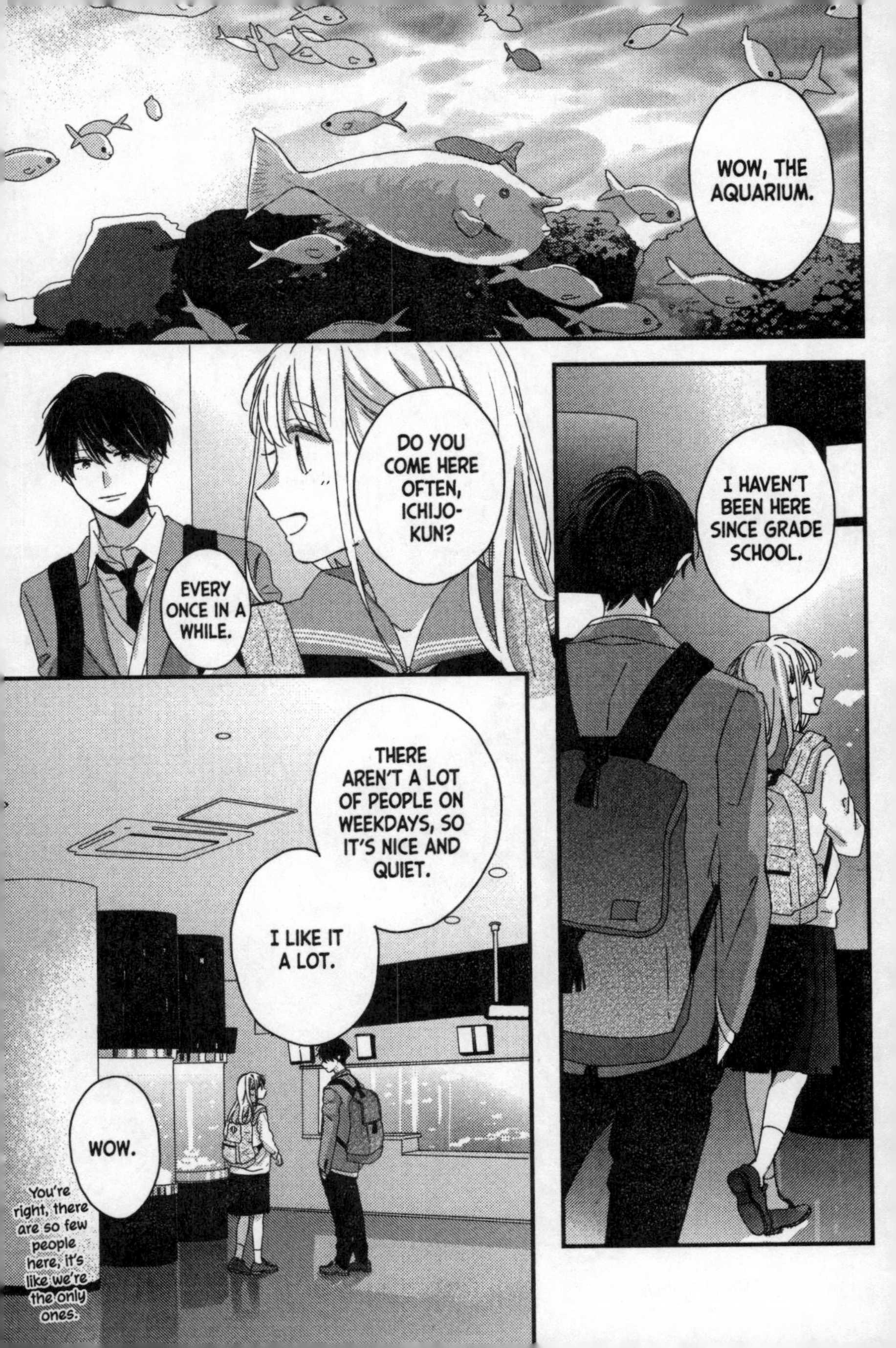
WOW, THE AQUARIUM.
I HAVEN'T BEEN HERE SINCE GRADE SCHOOL.
DO YOU COME HERE OFTEN, ICHIJO-KUN?
EVERY ONCE IN A WHILE.
THERE AREN'T A LOT OF PEOPLE ON WEEKDAYS, SO IT'S NICE AND QUIET.
I LIKE IT A LOT.
WOW.
You're right, there are so few people here, it's like we're the only ones.

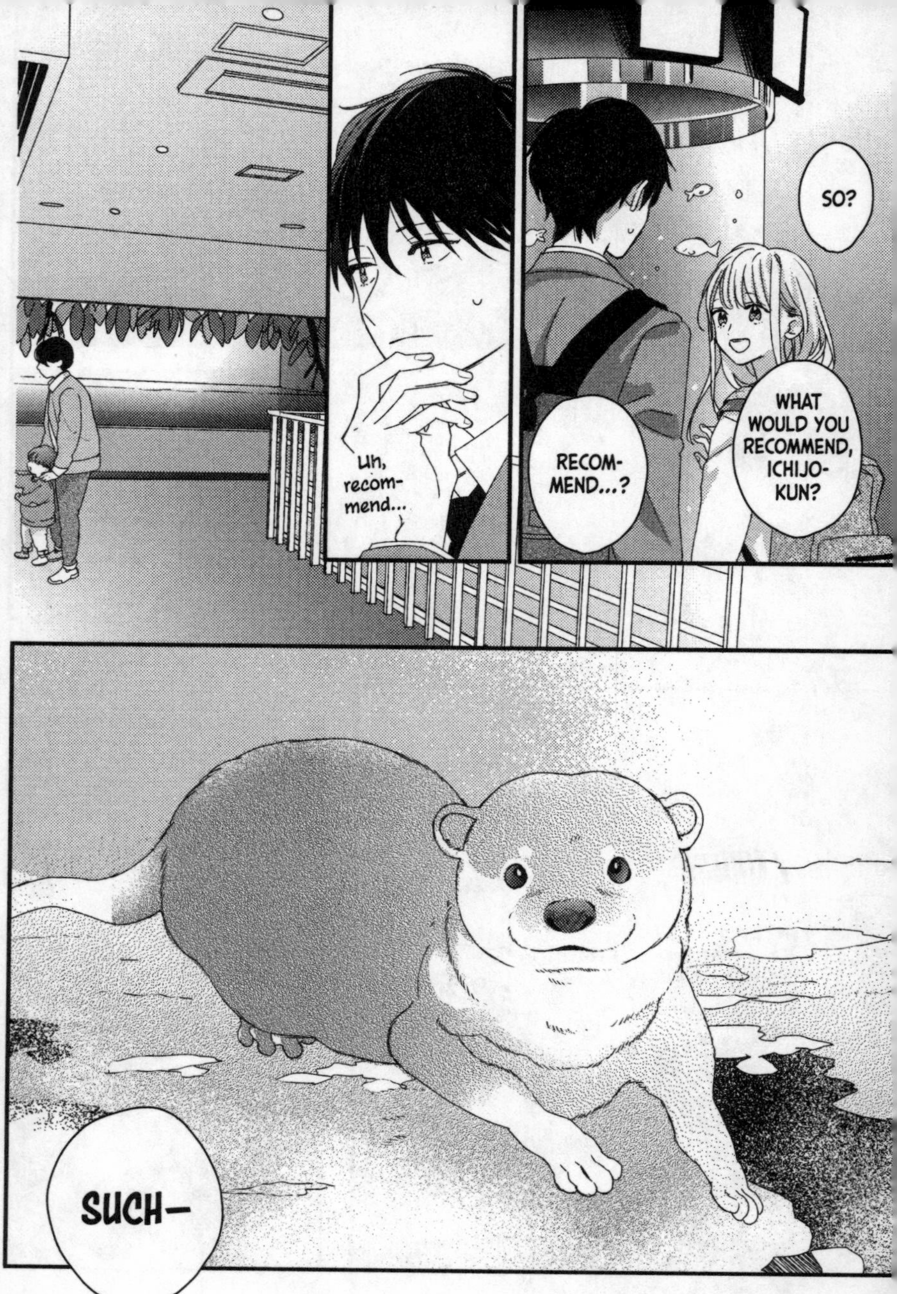
SO?
WHAT WOULD YOU RECOMMEND, ICHIJO-KUN?
RECOM-MEND...?
Uh, recom-mend...
SUCH—

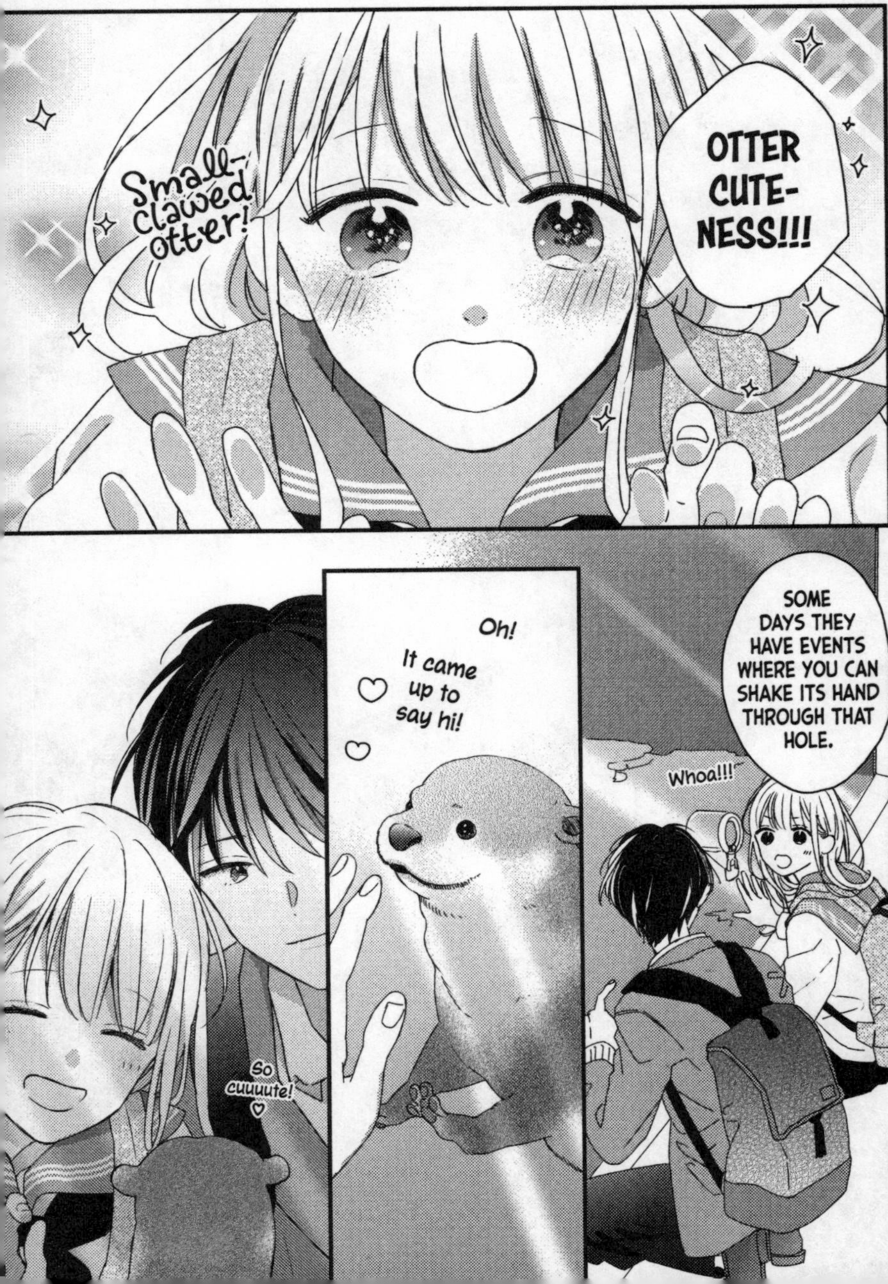
OTTER CUTE-NESS!!!
Small-clawed otter!
SOME DAYS THEY HAVE EVENTS WHERE YOU CAN SHAKE ITS HAND THROUGH THAT HOLE.
Whoa!!!
Oh!
It came up to say hi!
So cuuuute!

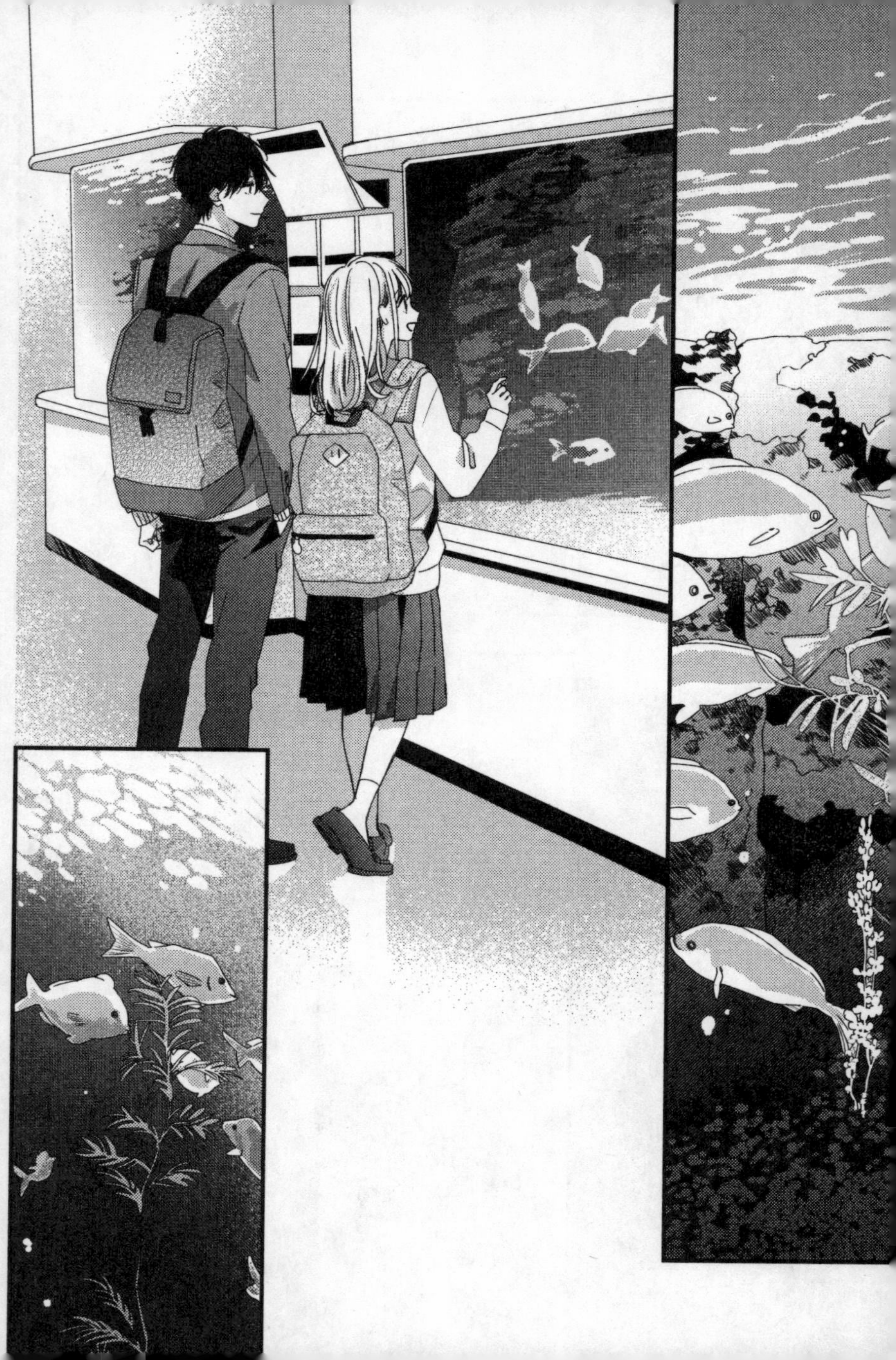

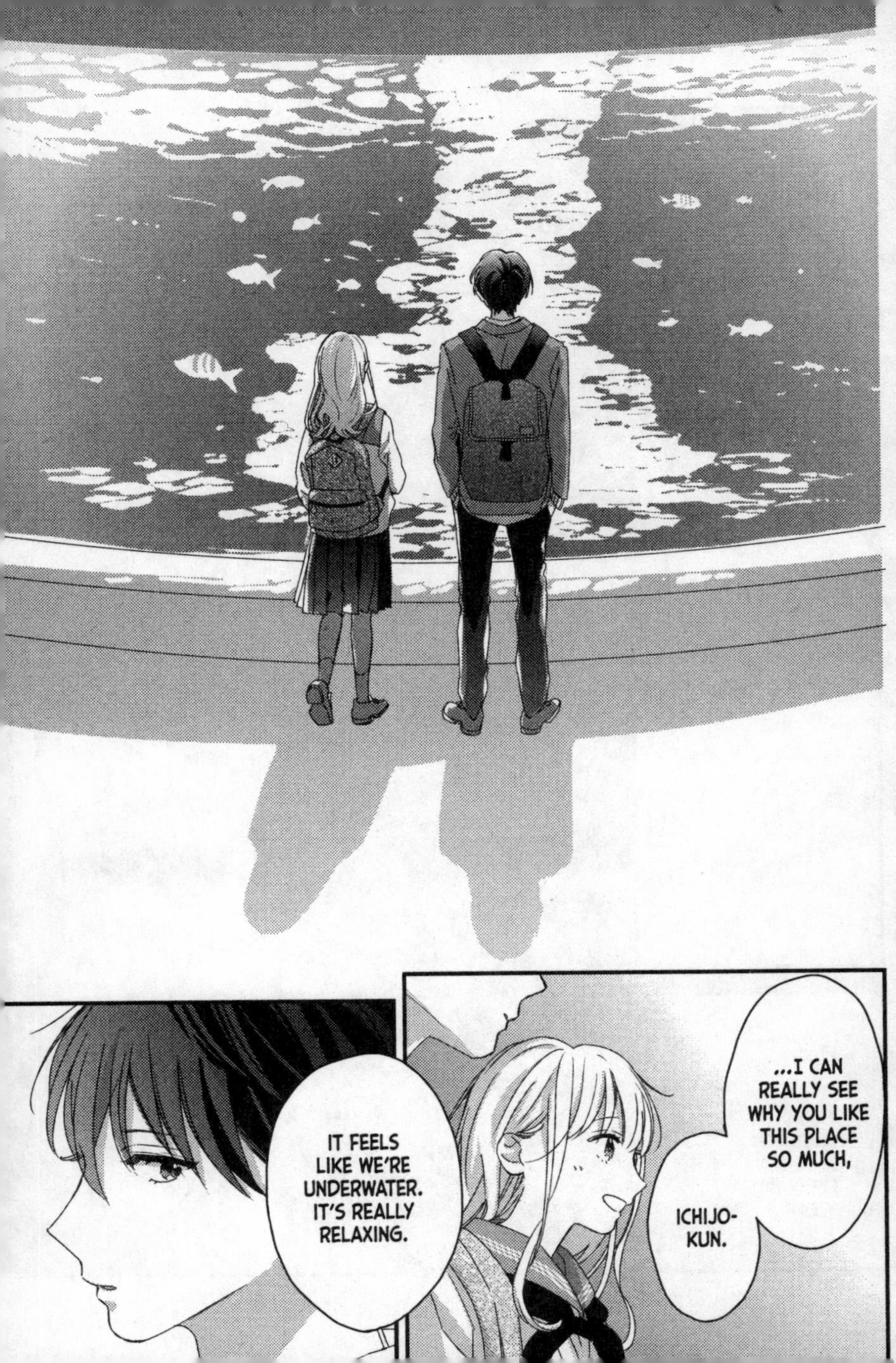
...I CAN REALLY SEE WHY YOU LIKE THIS PLACE SO MUCH,
ICHIJO-KUN.
IT FEELS LIKE WE'RE UNDERWATER. IT'S REALLY RELAXING.

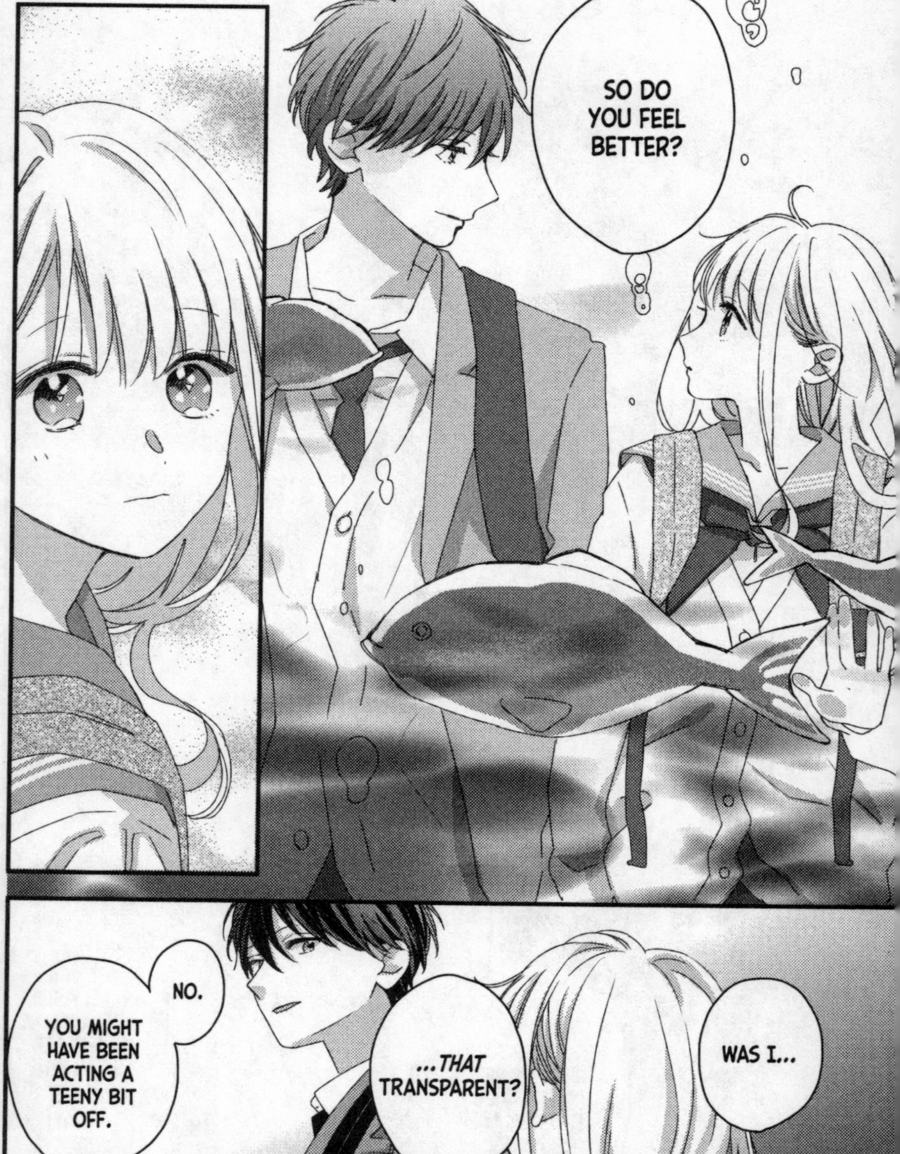
SO DO YOU FEEL BETTER?
WAS I...
...*THAT* TRANSPARENT?
NO.
YOU MIGHT HAVE BEEN ACTING A TEENY BIT OFF.

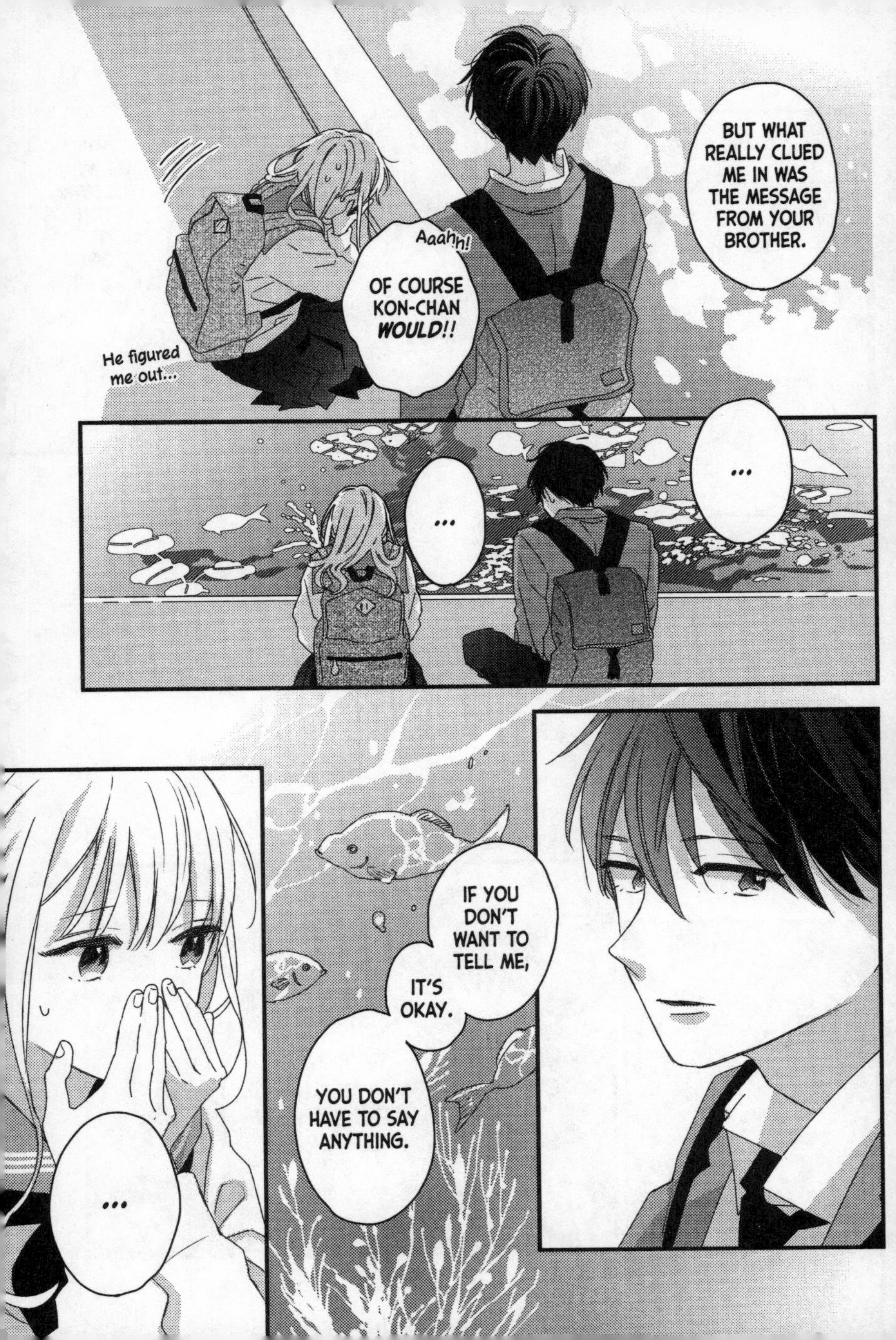
BUT WHAT REALLY CLUED ME IN WAS THE MESSAGE FROM YOUR BROTHER.
Aaahn!
OF COURSE KON-CHAN WOULD!!
He figured me out...
...
...
IF YOU DON'T WANT TO TELL ME,
IT'S OKAY.
YOU DON'T HAVE TO SAY ANYTHING.
...

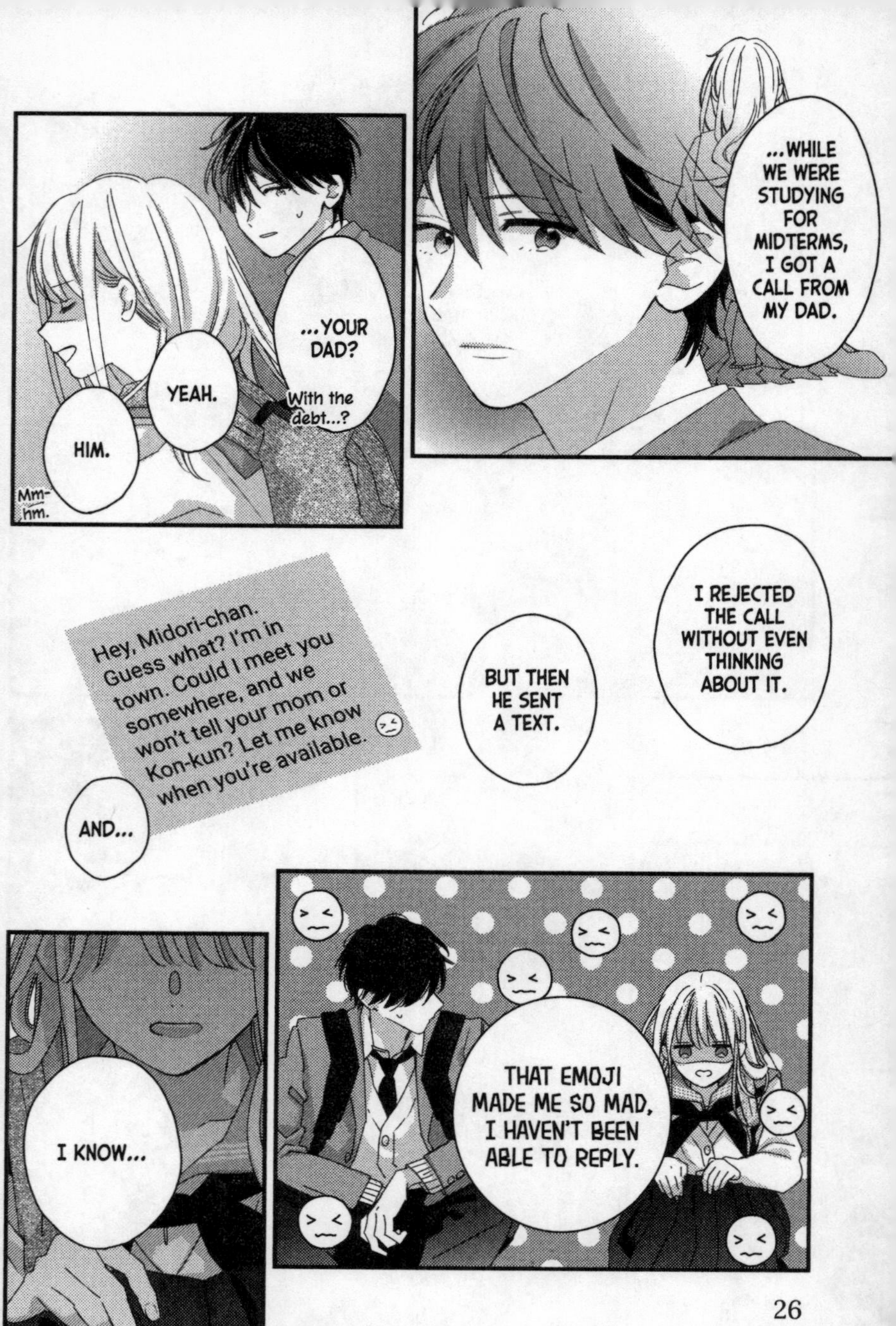
...WHILE WE WERE STUDYING FOR MIDTERMS, I GOT A CALL FROM MY DAD.
...YOUR DAD?
With the debt...?
YEAH.
HIM.
Mm-hm.
I REJECTED THE CALL WITHOUT EVEN THINKING ABOUT IT.
BUT THEN HE SENT A TEXT.
Hey, Midori-chan. Guess what? I'm in town. Could I meet you somewhere, and we won't tell your mom or Kon-kun? Let me know when you're available.
AND...
THAT EMOJI MADE ME SO MAD, I HAVEN'T BEEN ABLE TO REPLY.
I KNOW...

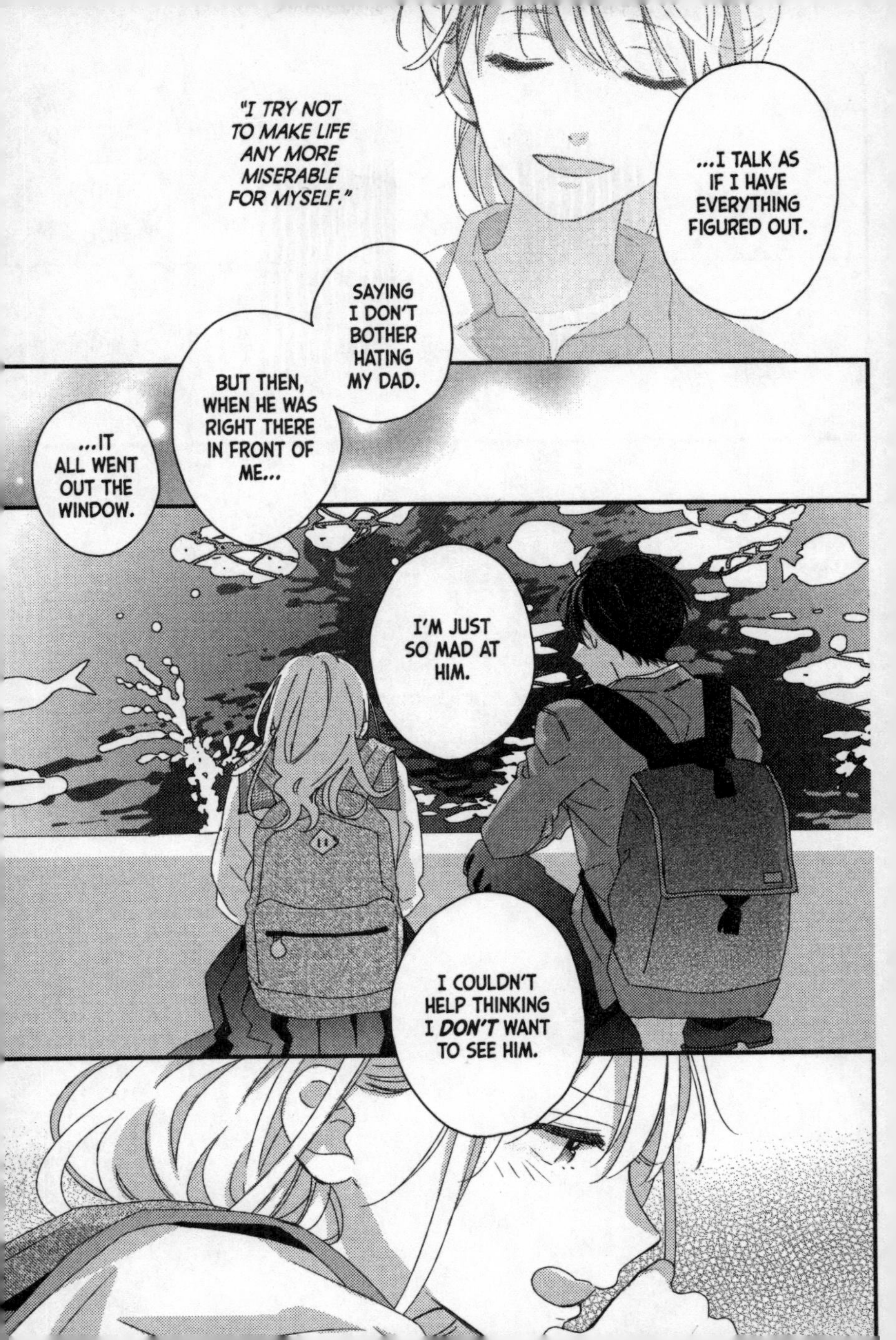
"I TRY NOT TO MAKE LIFE ANY MORE MISERABLE FOR MYSELF."
...I TALK AS IF I HAVE EVERYTHING FIGURED OUT.
SAYING I DON'T BOTHER HATING MY DAD.
BUT THEN, WHEN HE WAS RIGHT THERE IN FRONT OF ME...
...IT ALL WENT OUT THE WINDOW.
I'M JUST SO MAD AT HIM.
I COULDN'T HELP THINKING I ***DON'T*** WANT TO SEE HIM.

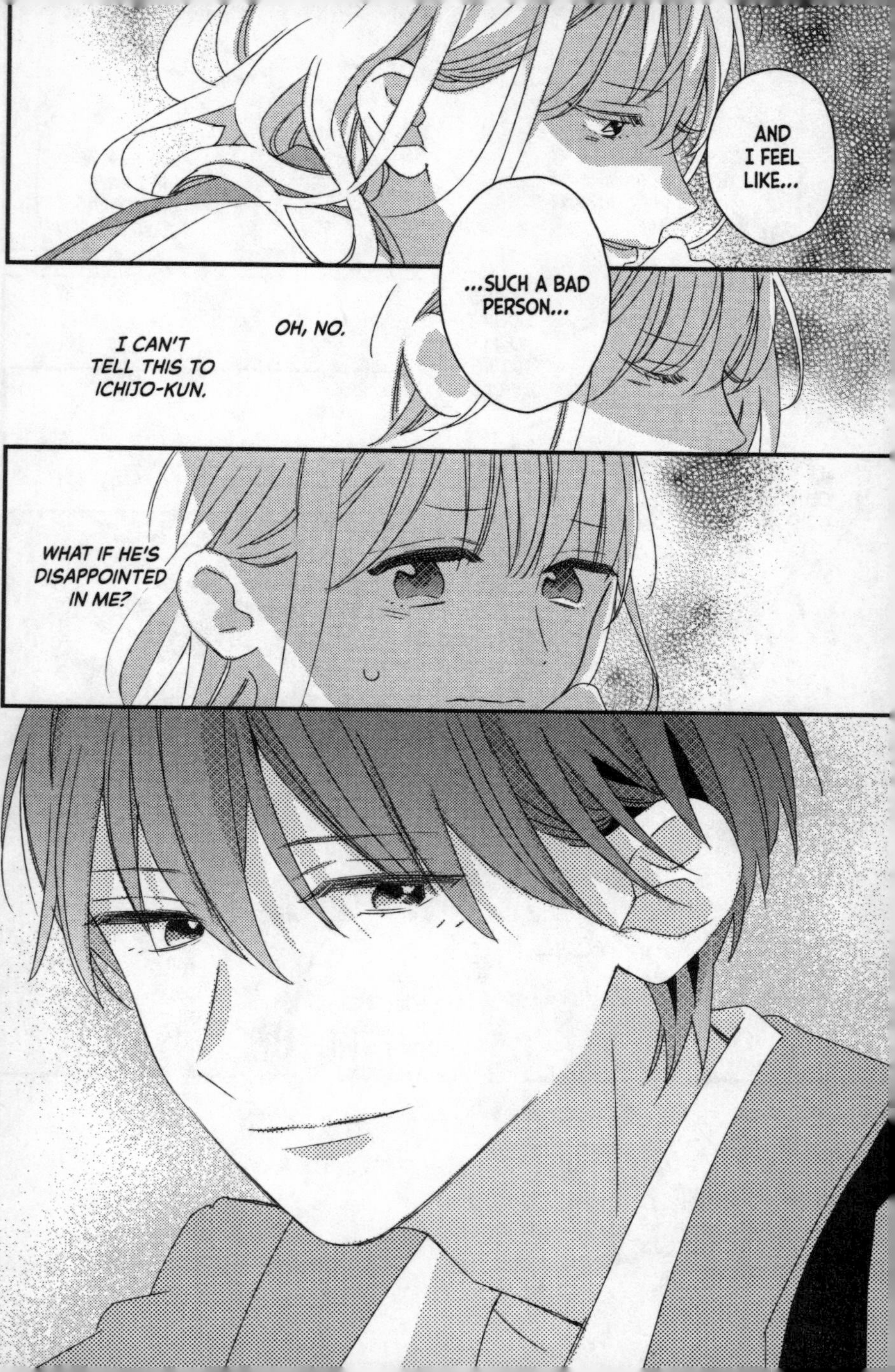
AND I FEEL LIKE...
...SUCH A BAD PERSON...
OH, NO.
I CAN'T TELL THIS TO ICHIJO-KUN.
WHAT IF HE'S DISAPPOINTED IN ME?

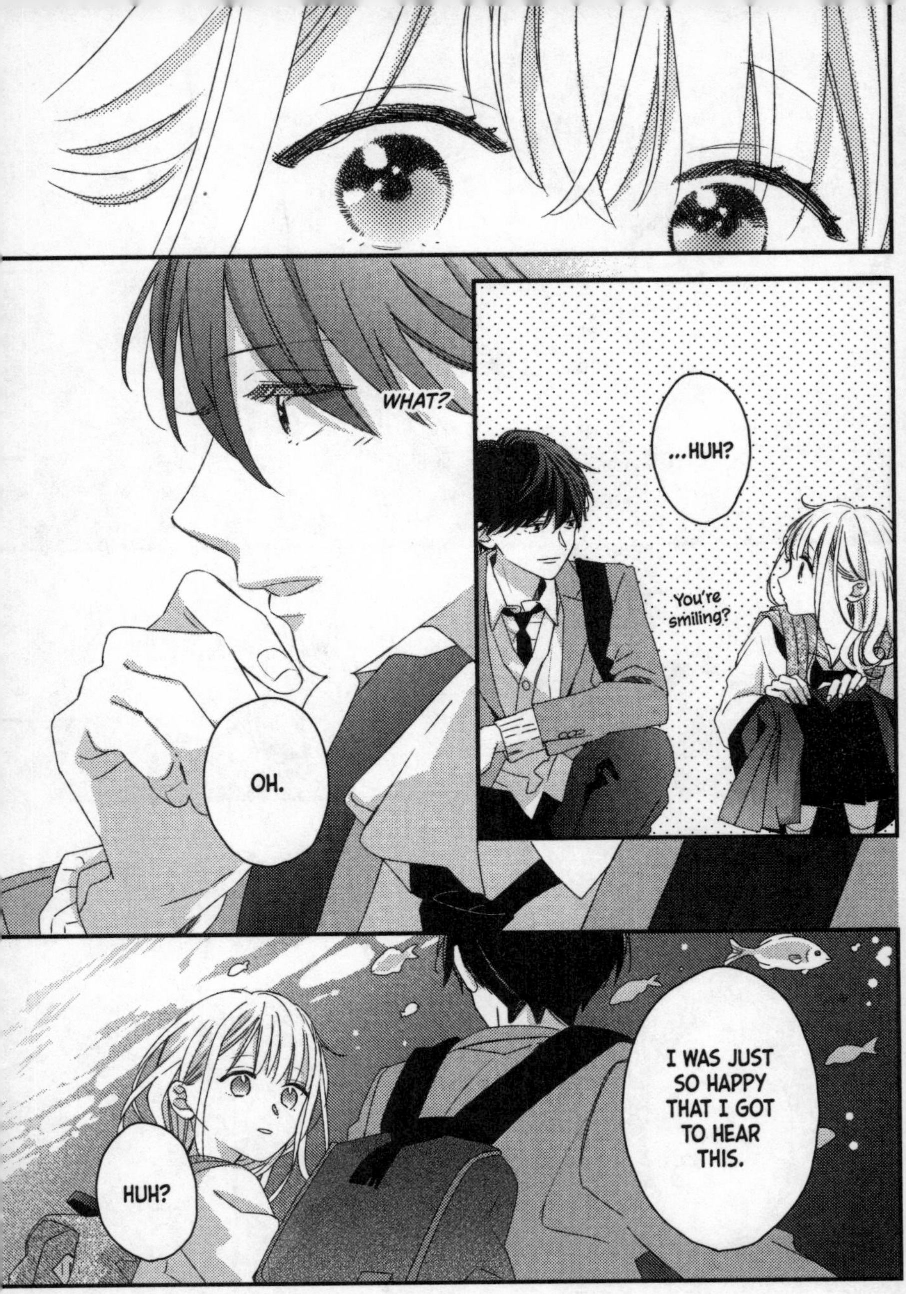
...HUH?
You're smiling?
WHAT?
OH.
I WAS JUST SO HAPPY THAT I GOT TO HEAR THIS.
HUH?

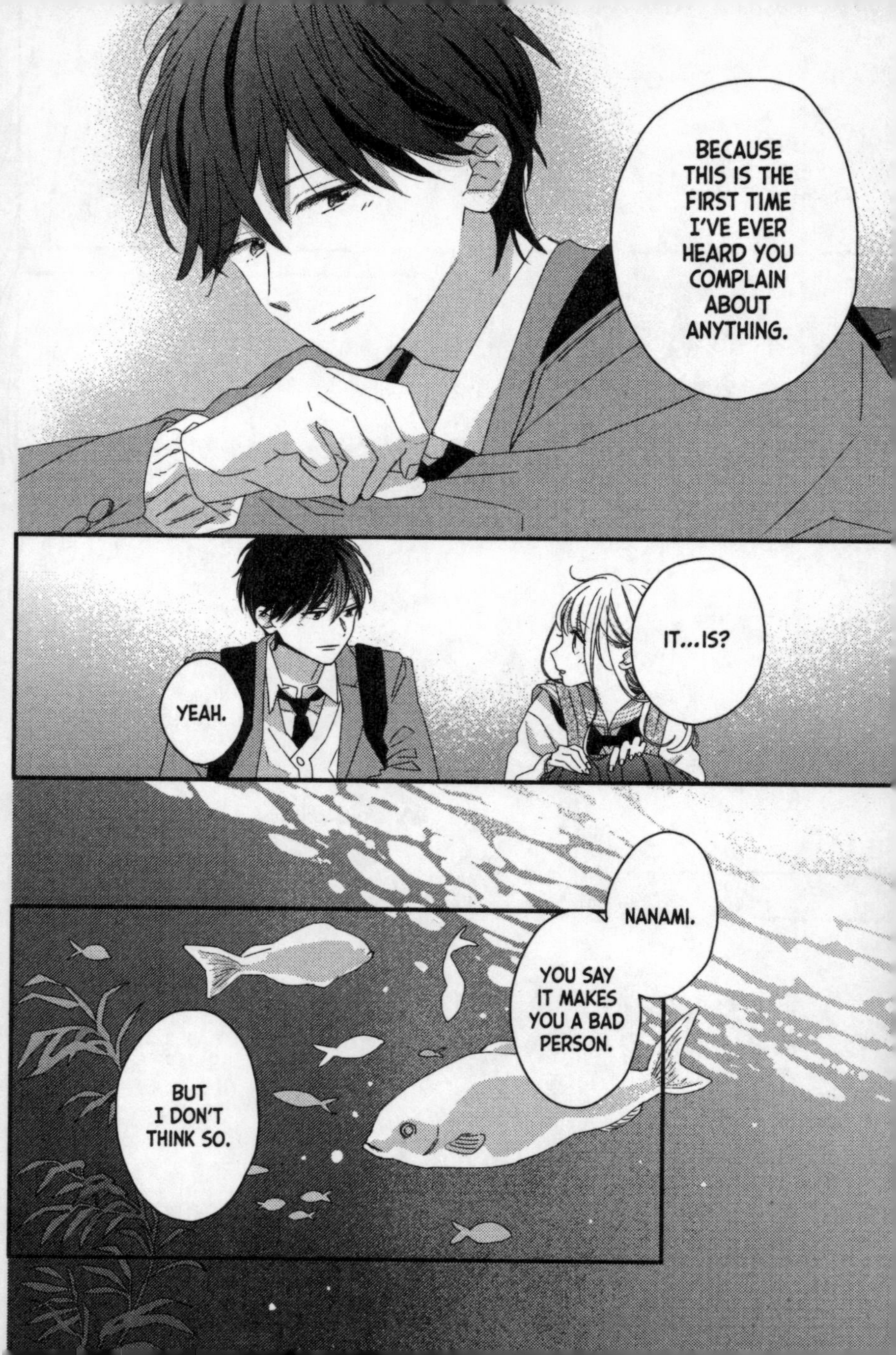
BECAUSE THIS IS THE FIRST TIME I'VE EVER HEARD YOU COMPLAIN ABOUT ANYTHING.
IT...IS?
YEAH.
NANAMI.
YOU SAY IT MAKES YOU A BAD PERSON.
BUT I DON'T THINK SO.

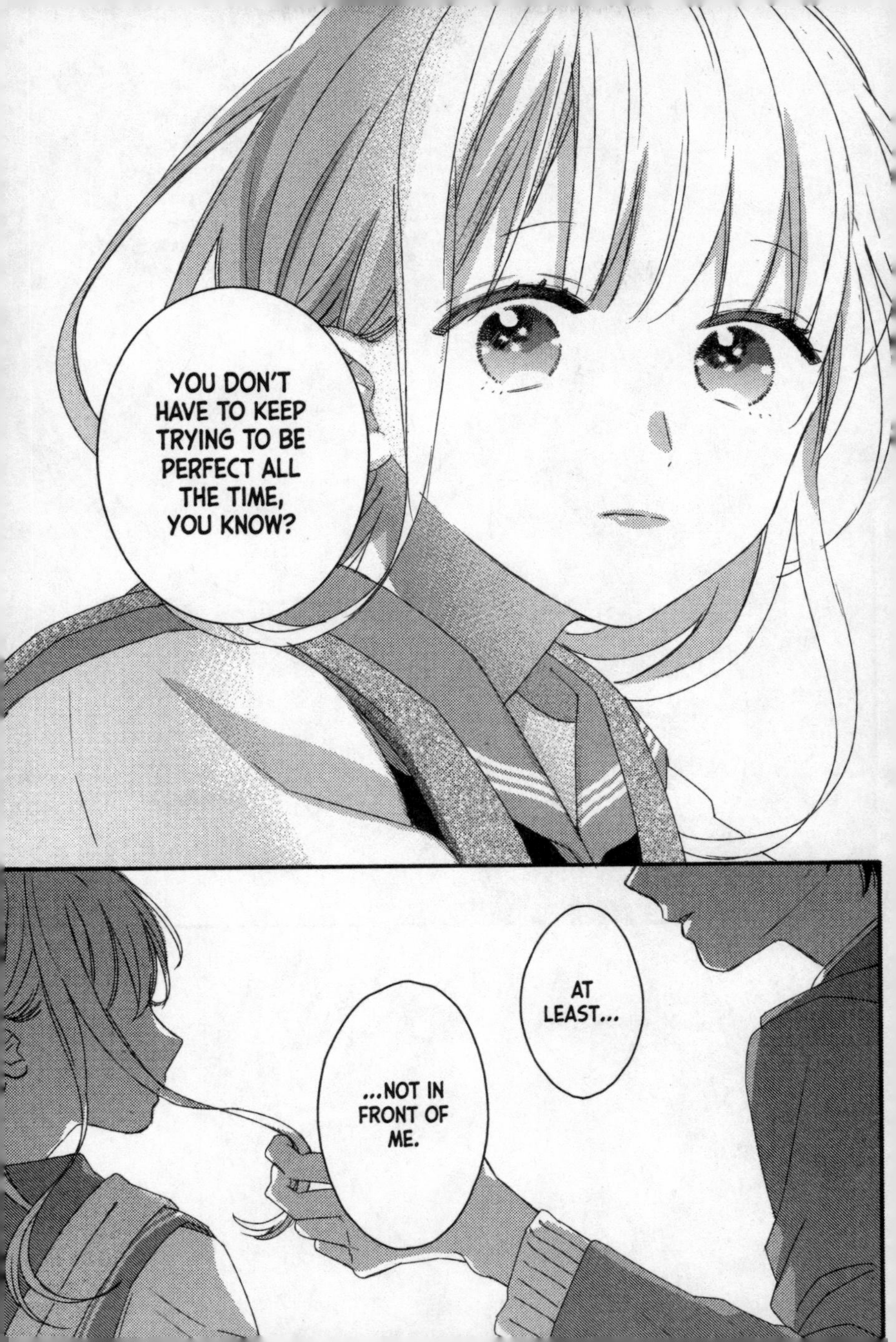
YOU DON'T HAVE TO KEEP TRYING TO BE PERFECT ALL THE TIME, YOU KNOW?
AT LEAST...
...NOT IN FRONT OF ME.

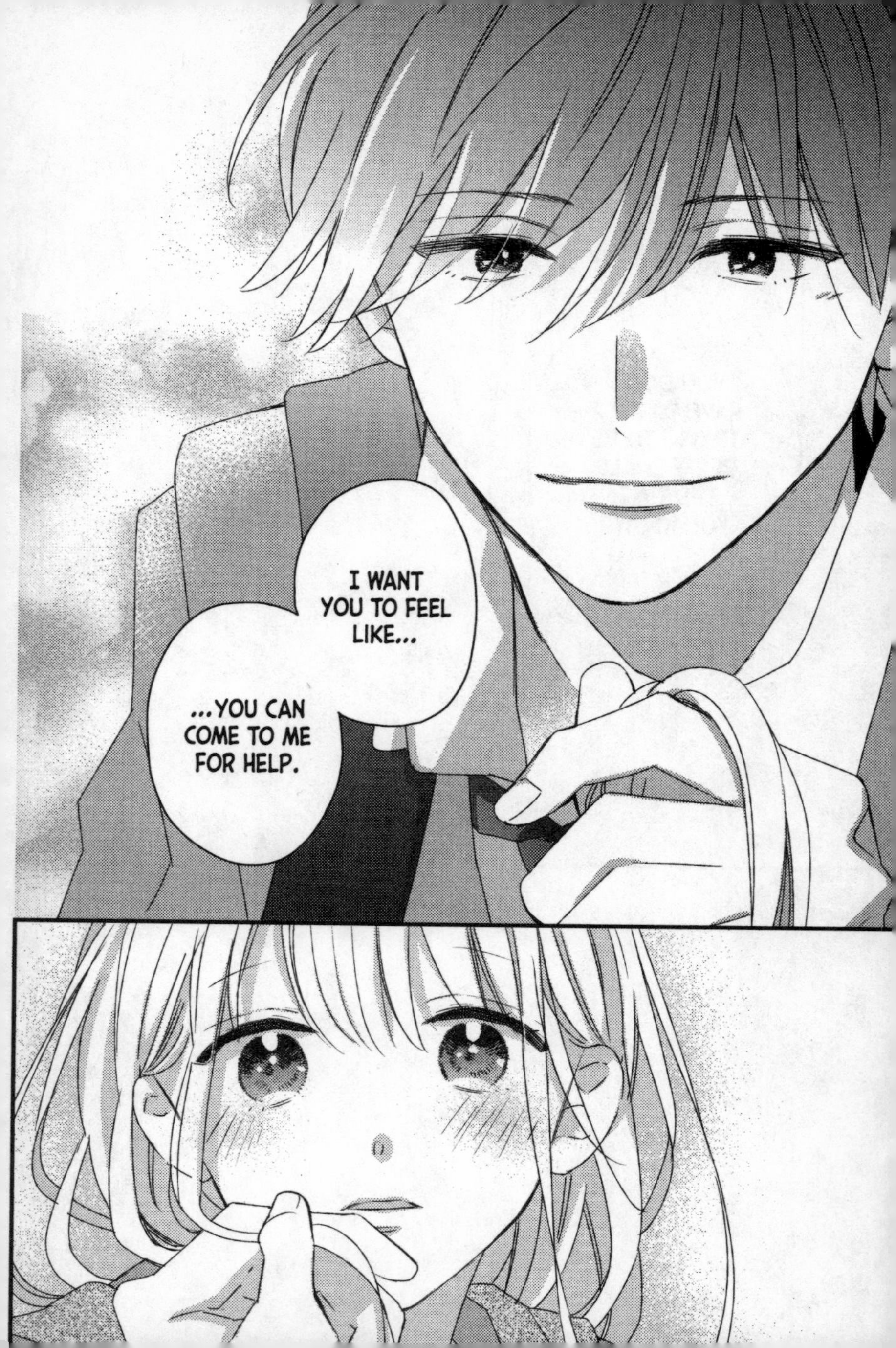
I WANT YOU TO FEEL LIKE...
...YOU CAN COME TO ME FOR HELP.

...THANK YOU.

OH.

IT'S OKAY.

I DON'T HAVE TO TRY DO EVERYTHING PERFECTLY.

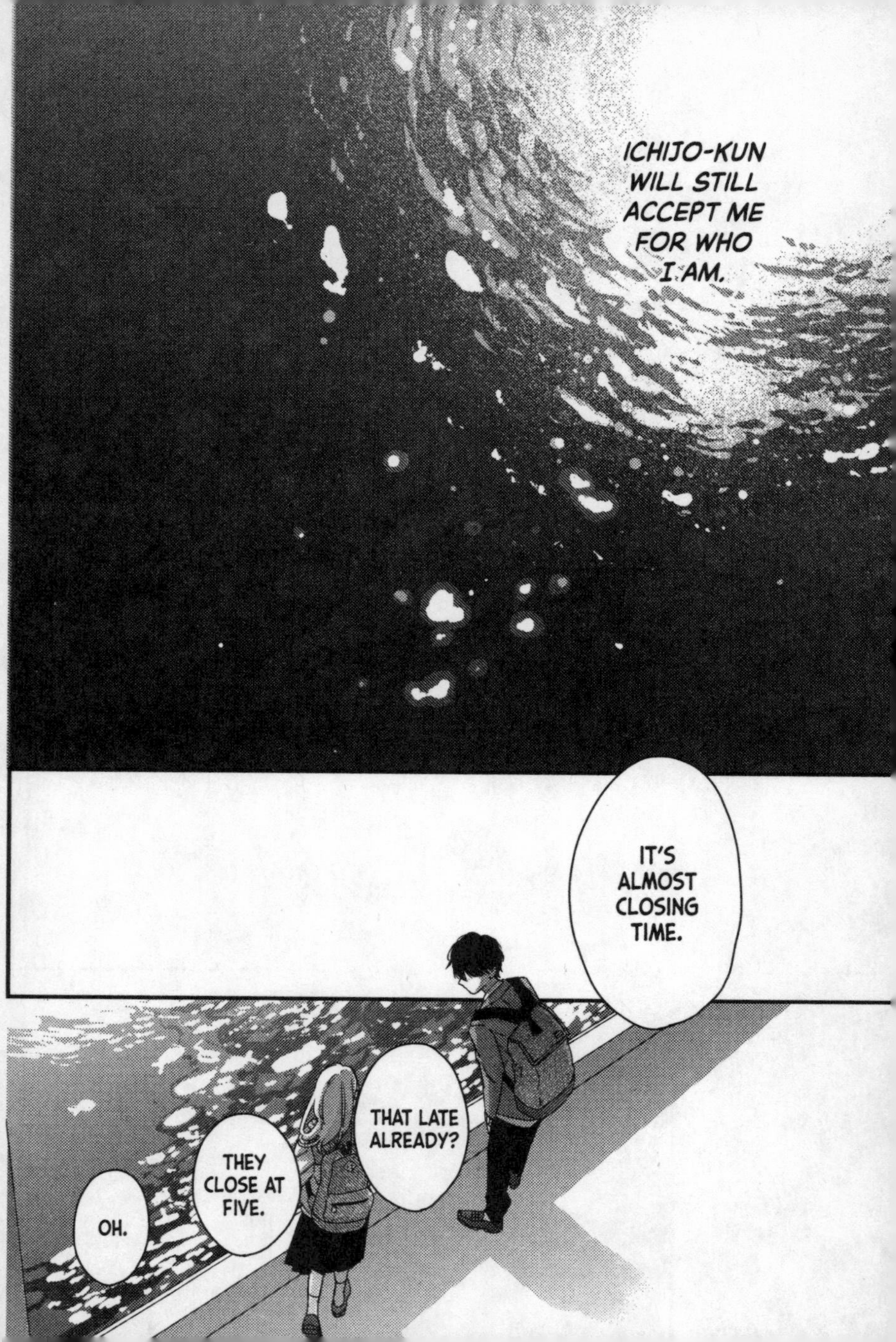
ICHIJO-KUN WILL STILL ACCEPT ME FOR WHO I AM.
IT'S ALMOST CLOSING TIME.
THAT LATE ALREADY?
THEY CLOSE AT FIVE.
OH.

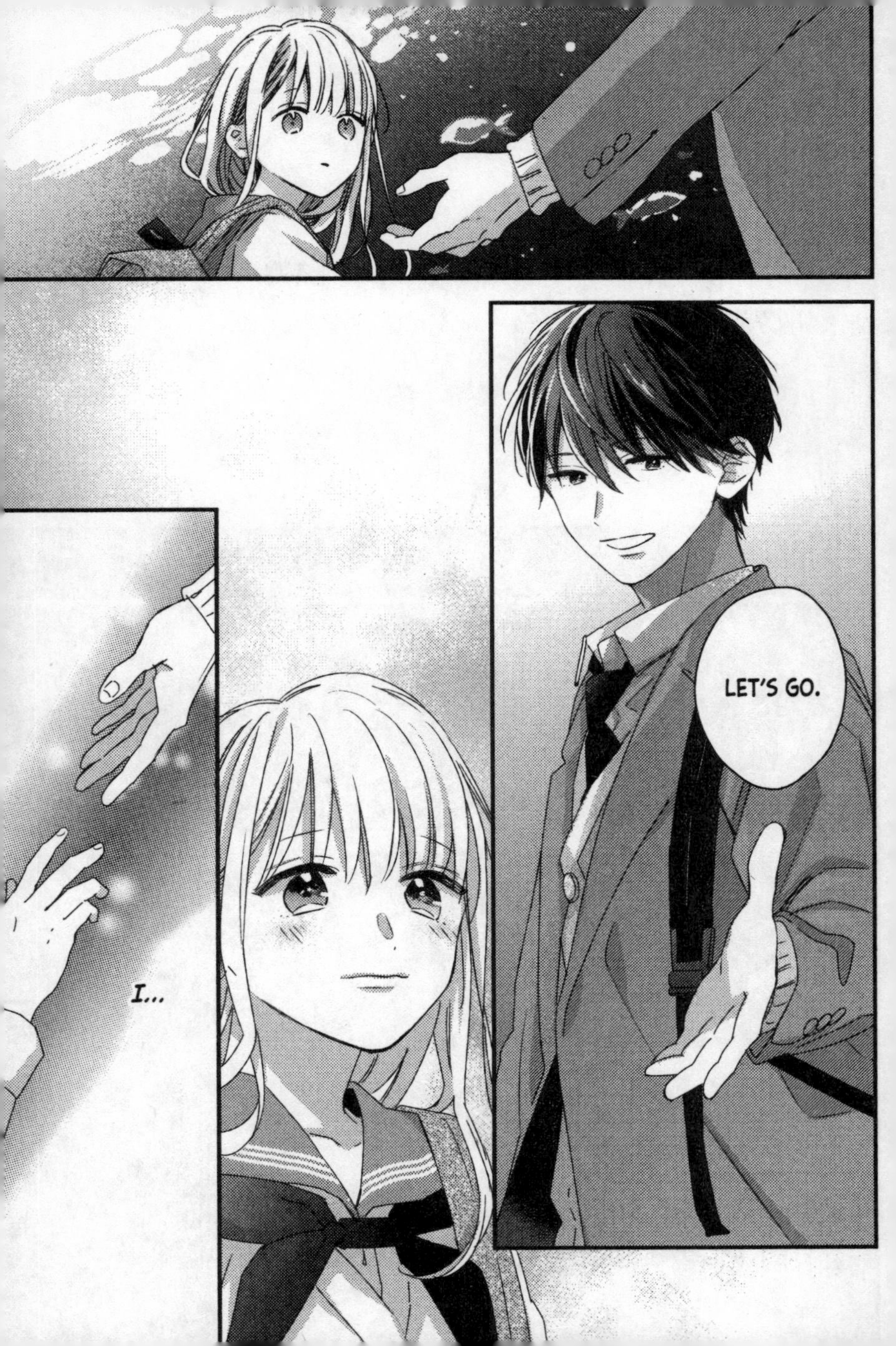
LET'S GO.
I...

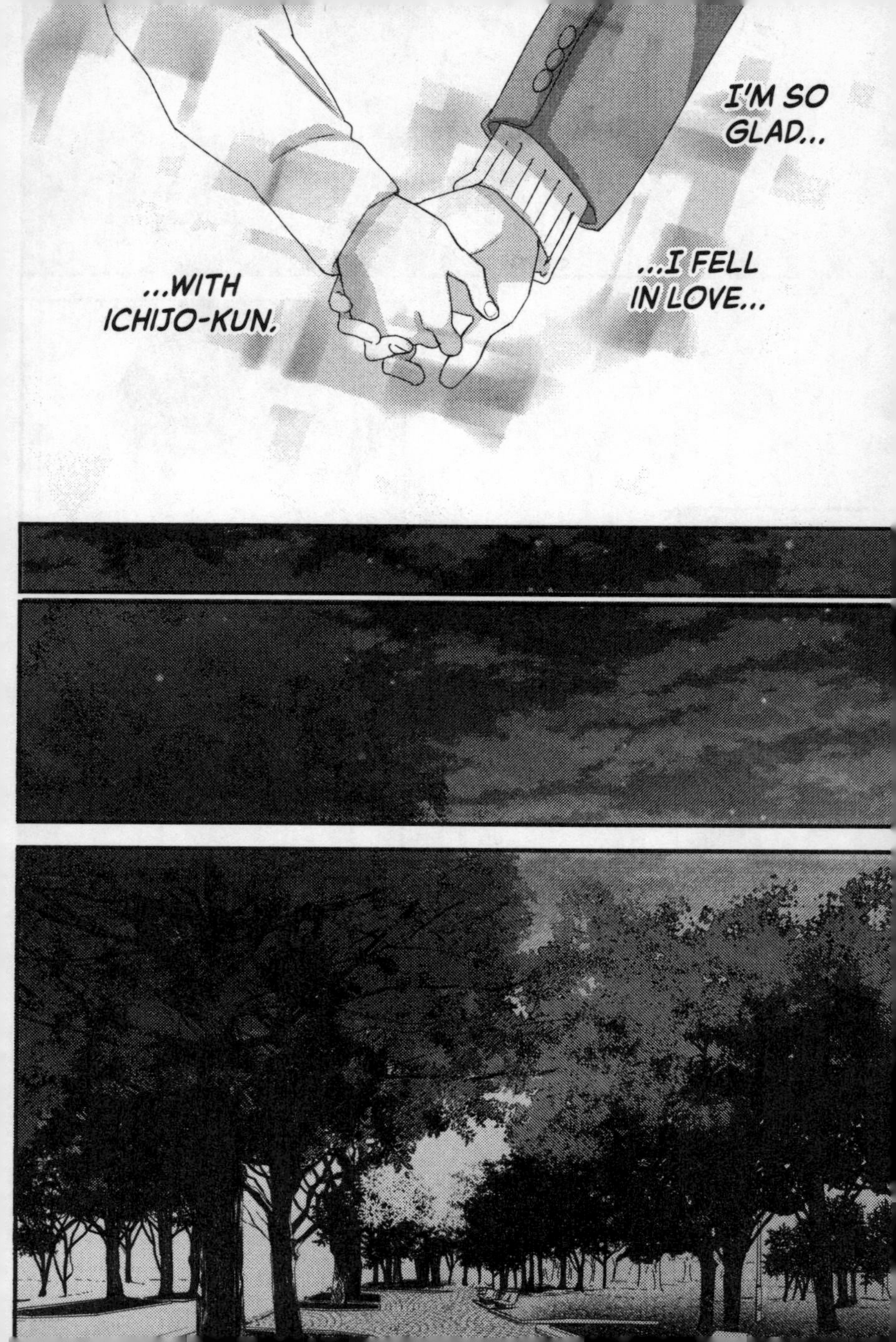
I'M SO GLAD...
...I FELL IN LOVE...
...WITH ICHIJO-KUN.

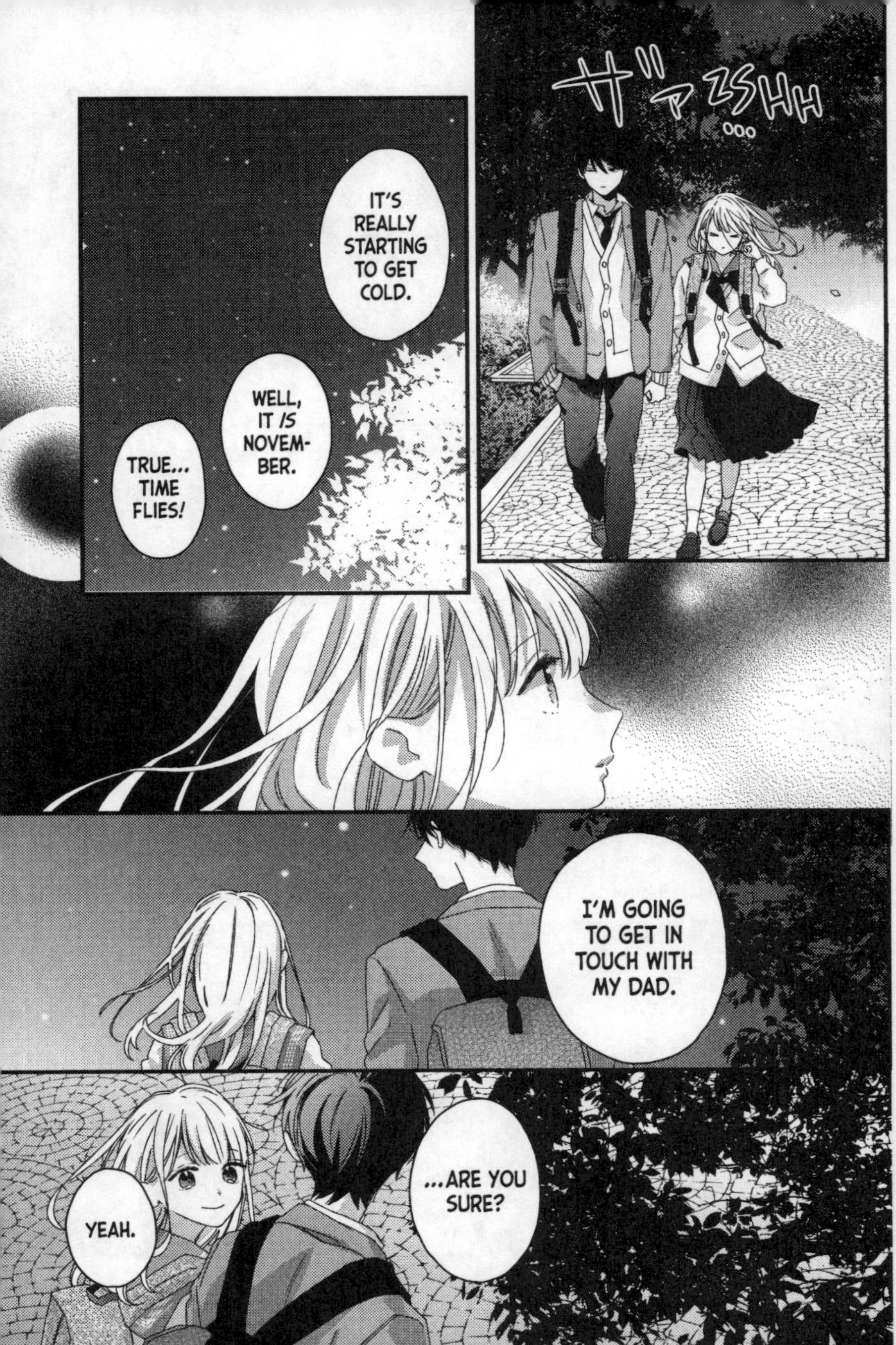
ZSHH...
IT'S REALLY STARTING TO GET COLD.
WELL, IT *IS* NOVEMBER.
TRUE... TIME FLIES!
I'M GOING TO GET IN TOUCH WITH MY DAD.
...ARE YOU SURE?
YEAH.

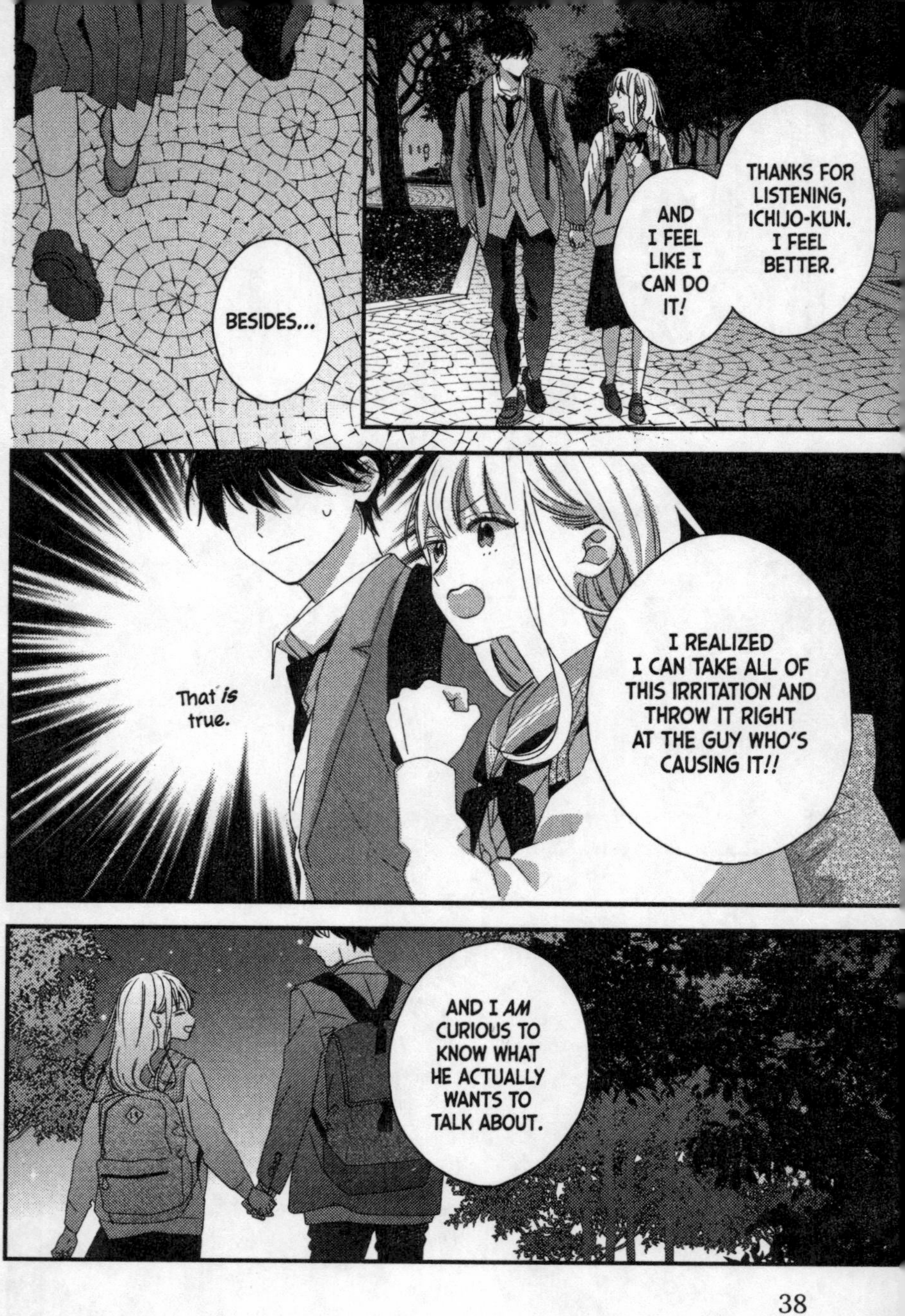
THANKS FOR LISTENING, ICHIJO-KUN. I FEEL BETTER.
AND I FEEL LIKE I CAN DO IT!
BESIDES...
I REALIZED I CAN TAKE ALL OF THIS IRRITATION AND THROW IT RIGHT AT THE GUY WHO'S CAUSING IT!!
That *is* true.
AND I *AM* CURIOUS TO KNOW WHAT HE ACTUALLY WANTS TO TALK ABOUT.

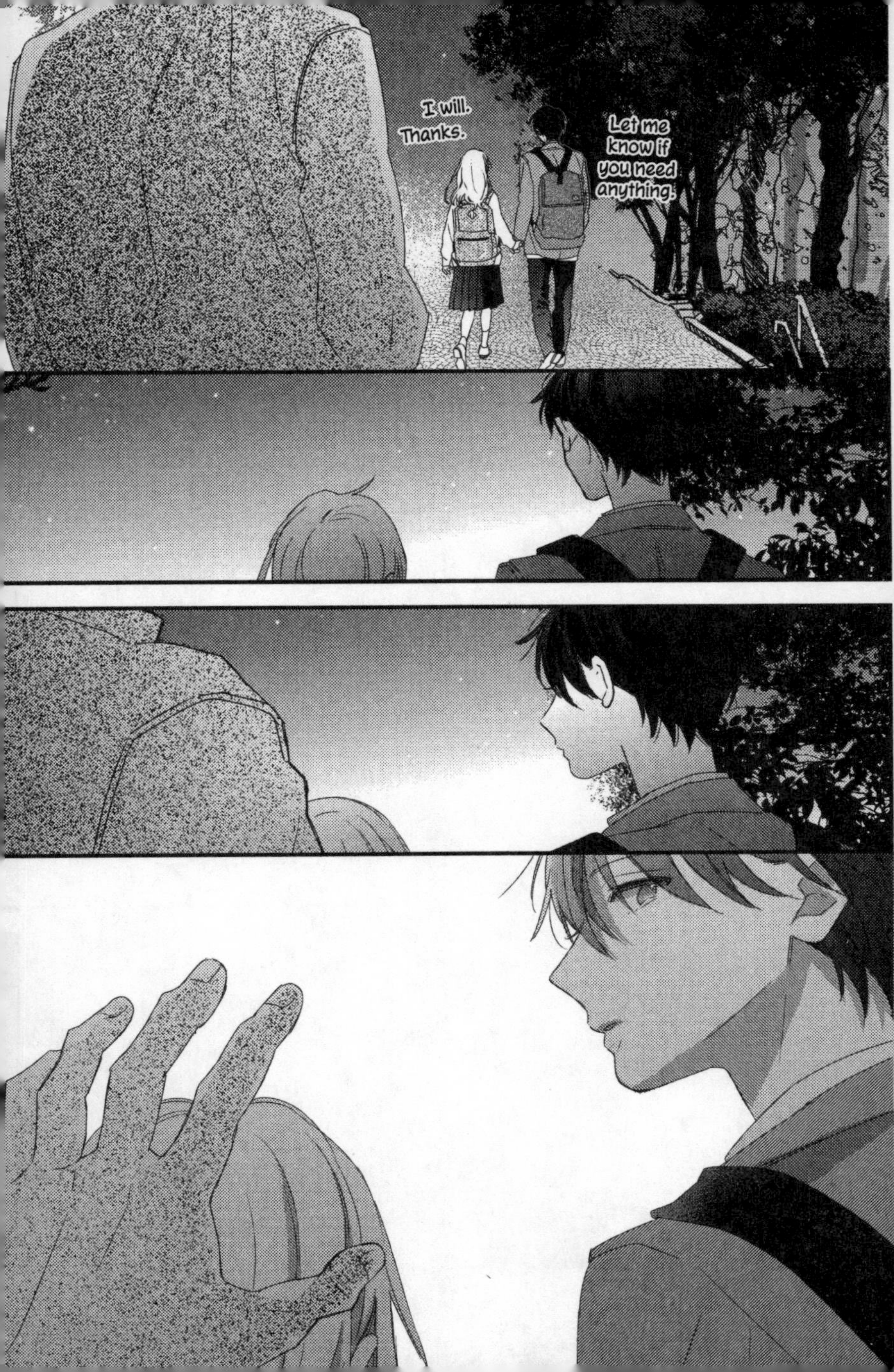
Let me know if you need anything.
I will. Thanks.

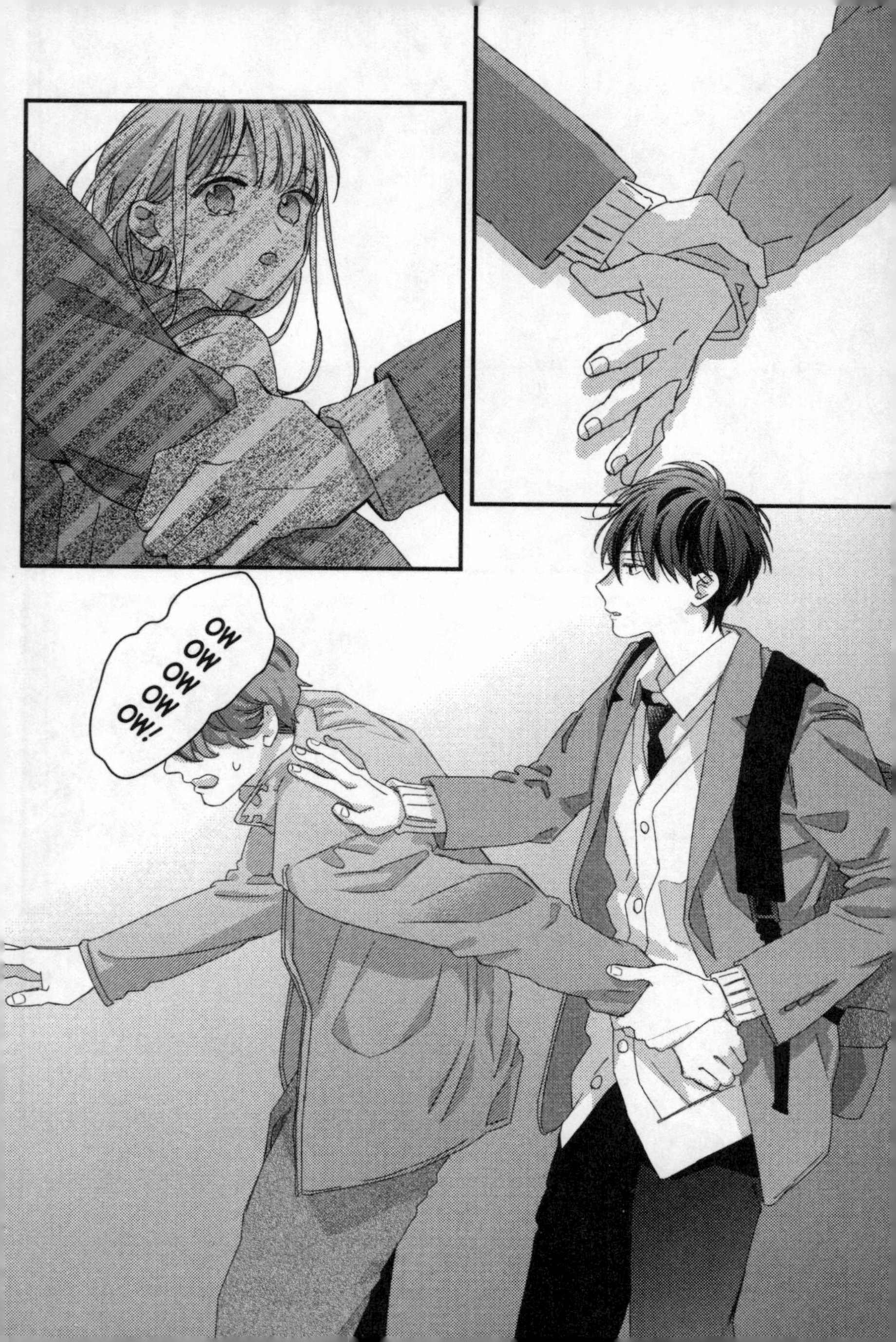
OW OW OW OW OW!

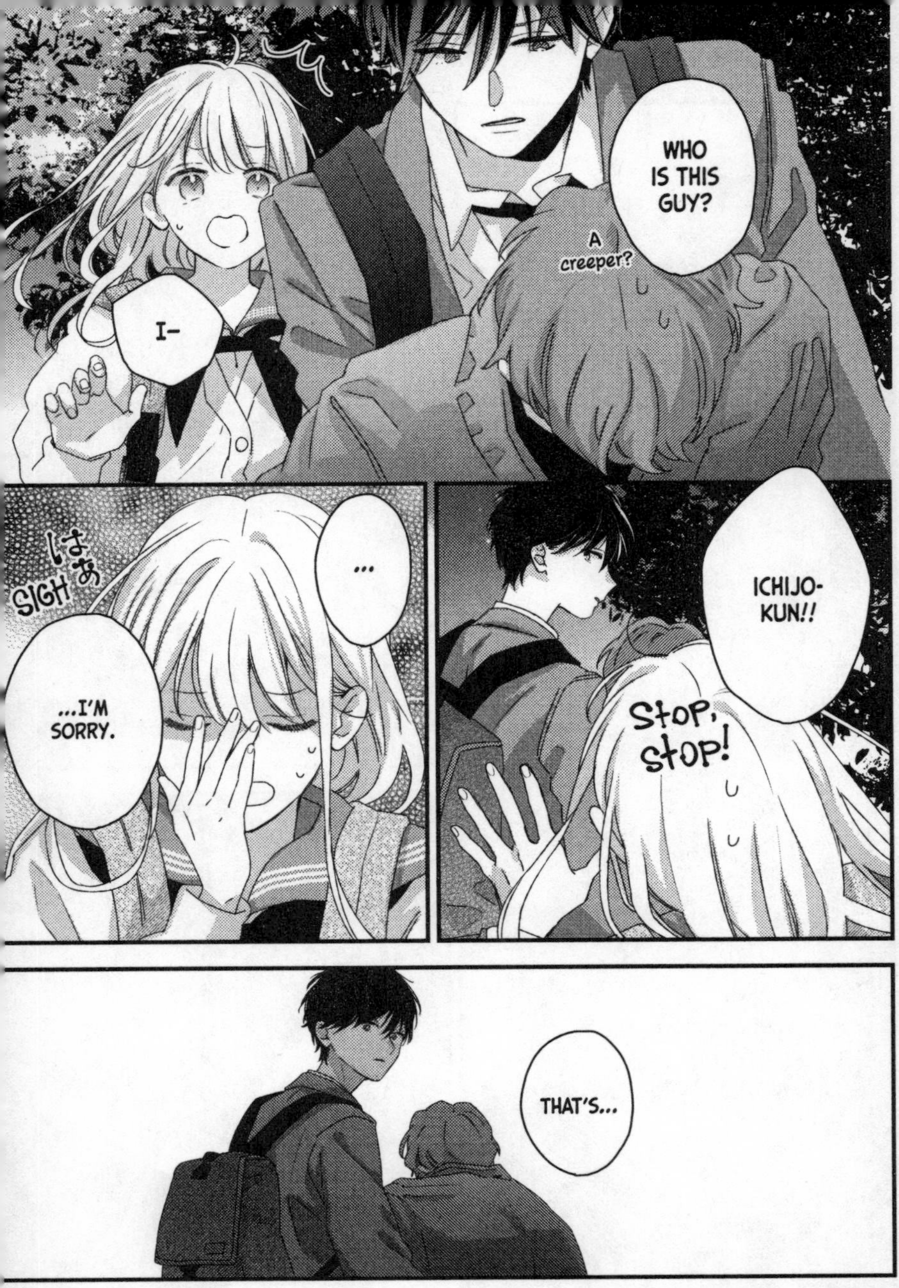
WHO IS THIS GUY?
A creeper?
I–
ICHIJO-KUN!!
Stop, stop!
...
はあ SIGH
...I'M SORRY.
THAT'S...

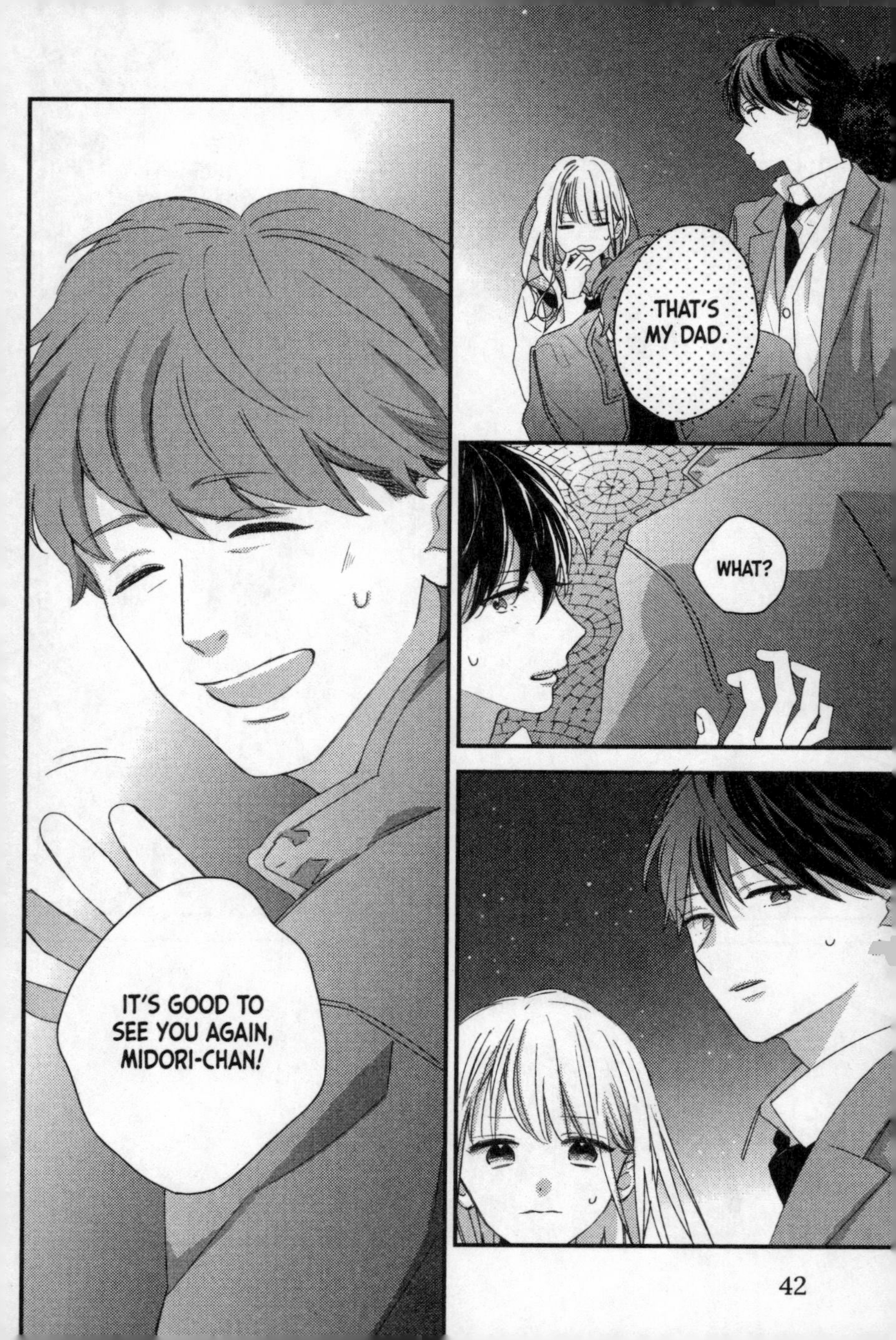
THAT'S MY DAD.
WHAT?
IT'S GOOD TO SEE YOU AGAIN, MIDORI-CHAN!

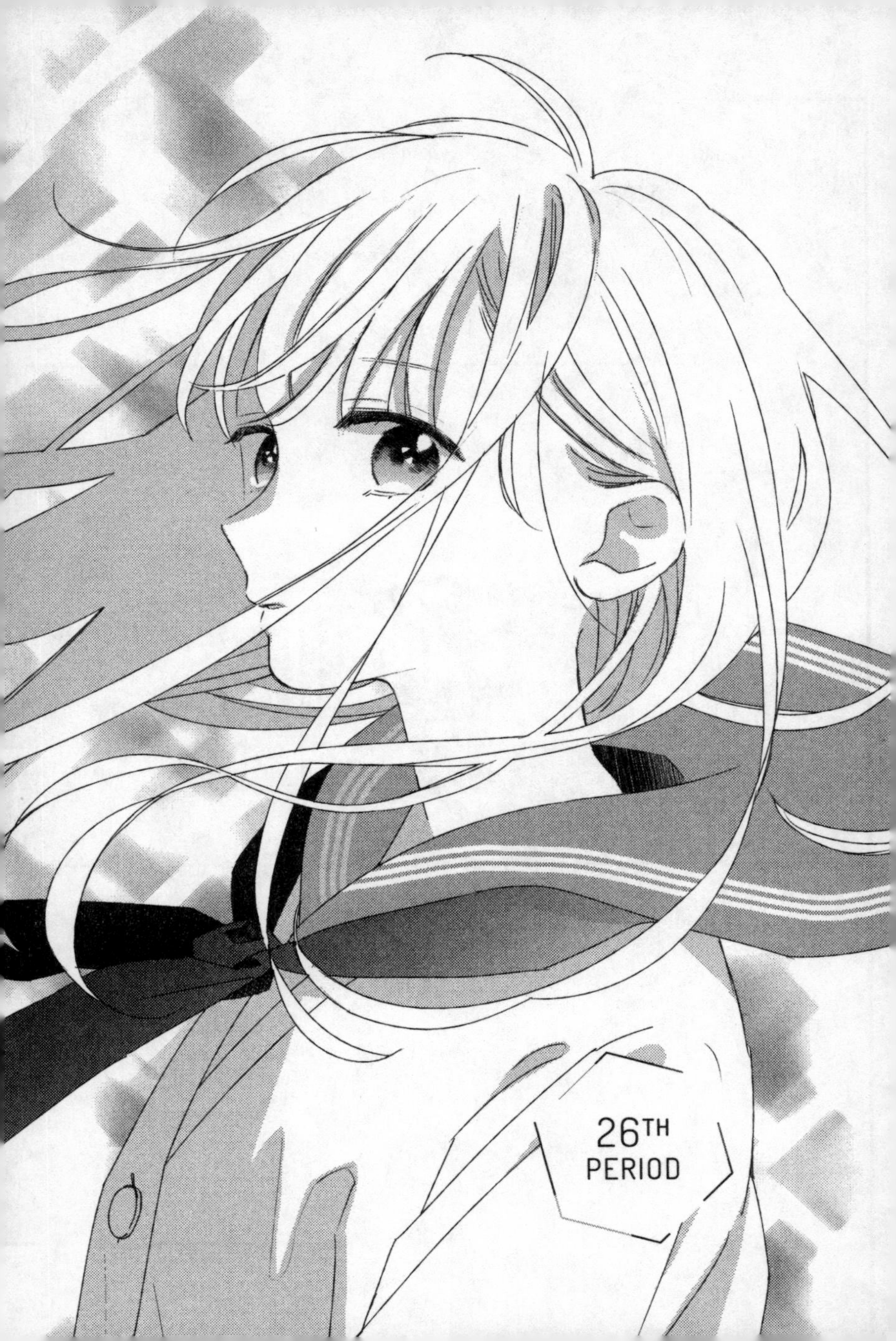
26TH
PERIOD

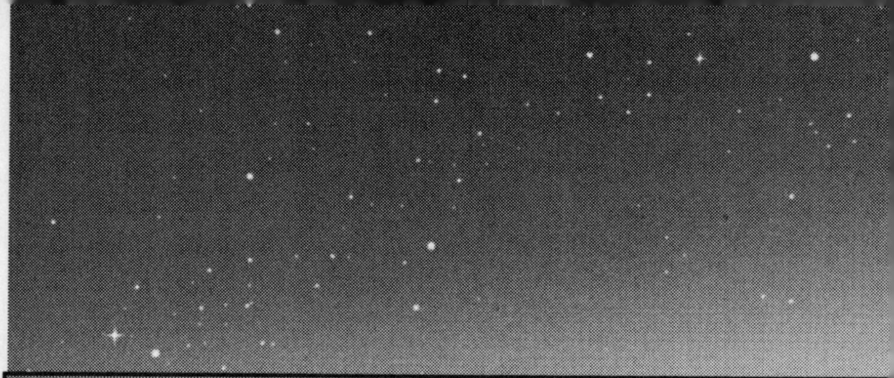
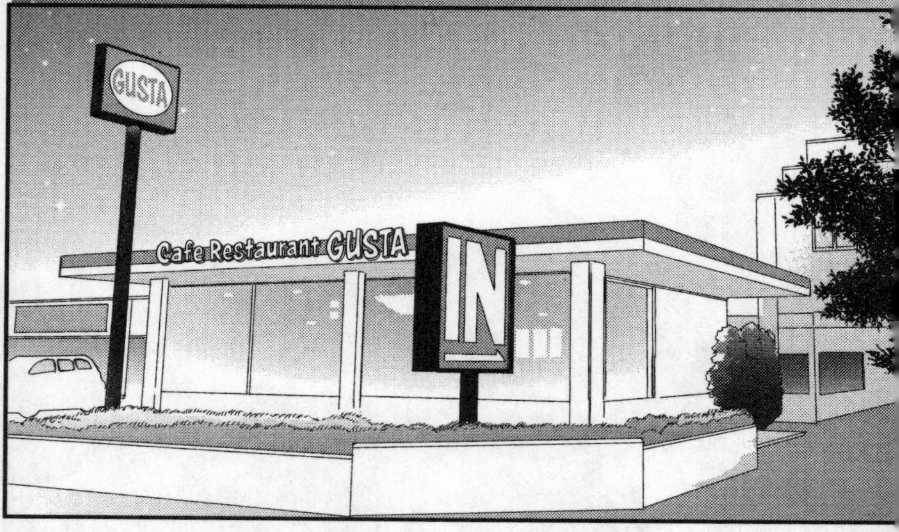
GUSTA
Cafe Restaurant GUSTA
IN
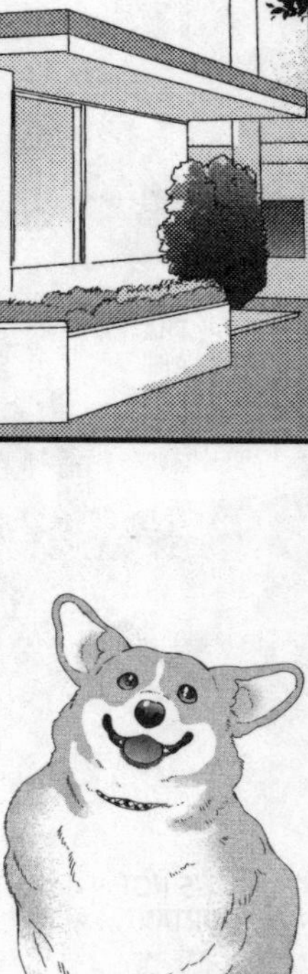

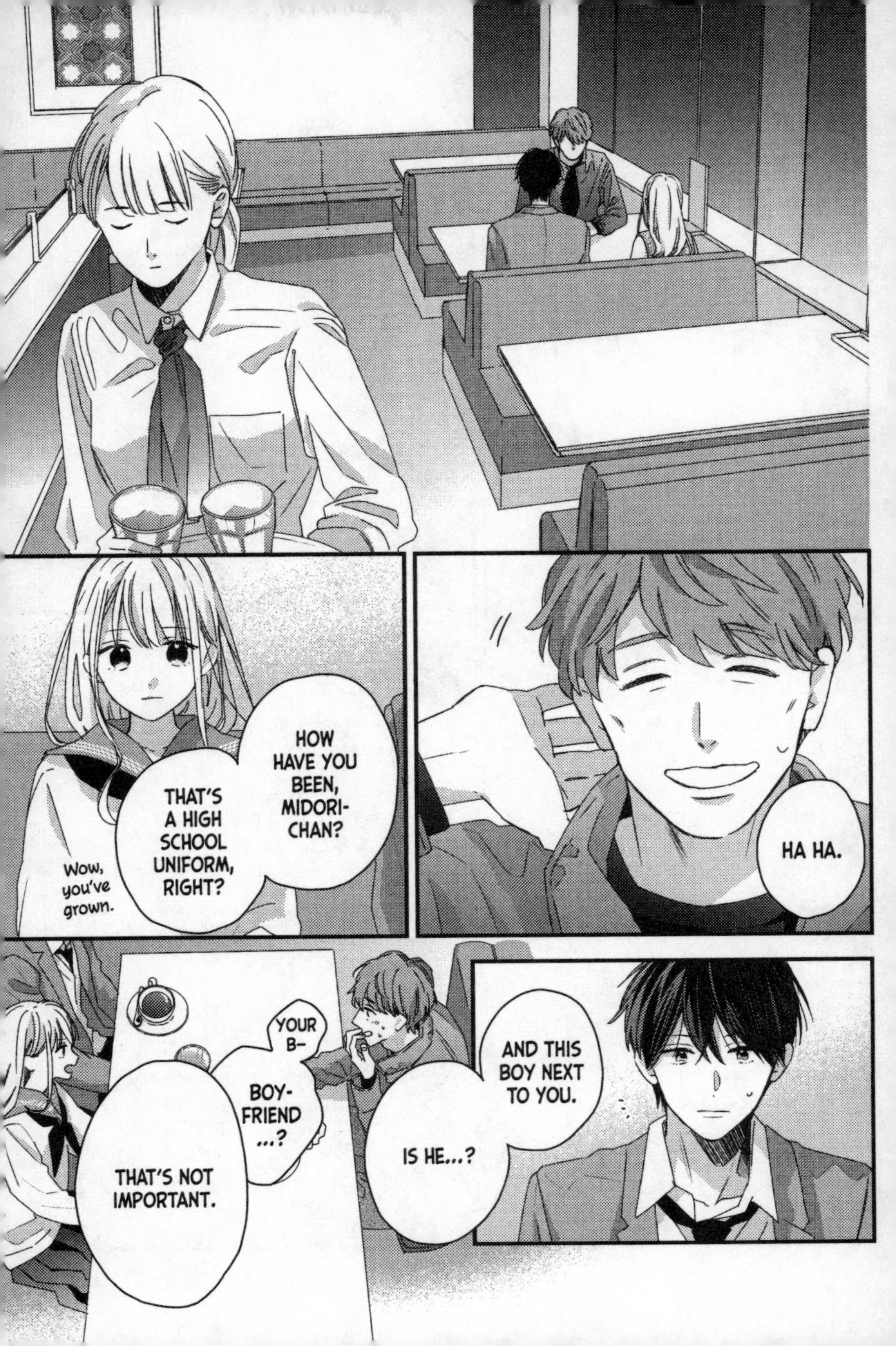
HA HA.
HOW HAVE YOU BEEN, MIDORI-CHAN?
THAT'S A HIGH SCHOOL UNIFORM, RIGHT?
Wow, you've grown.
AND THIS BOY NEXT TO YOU.
IS HE...?
YOUR B-
BOY-FRIEND ...?
THAT'S NOT IMPORTANT.

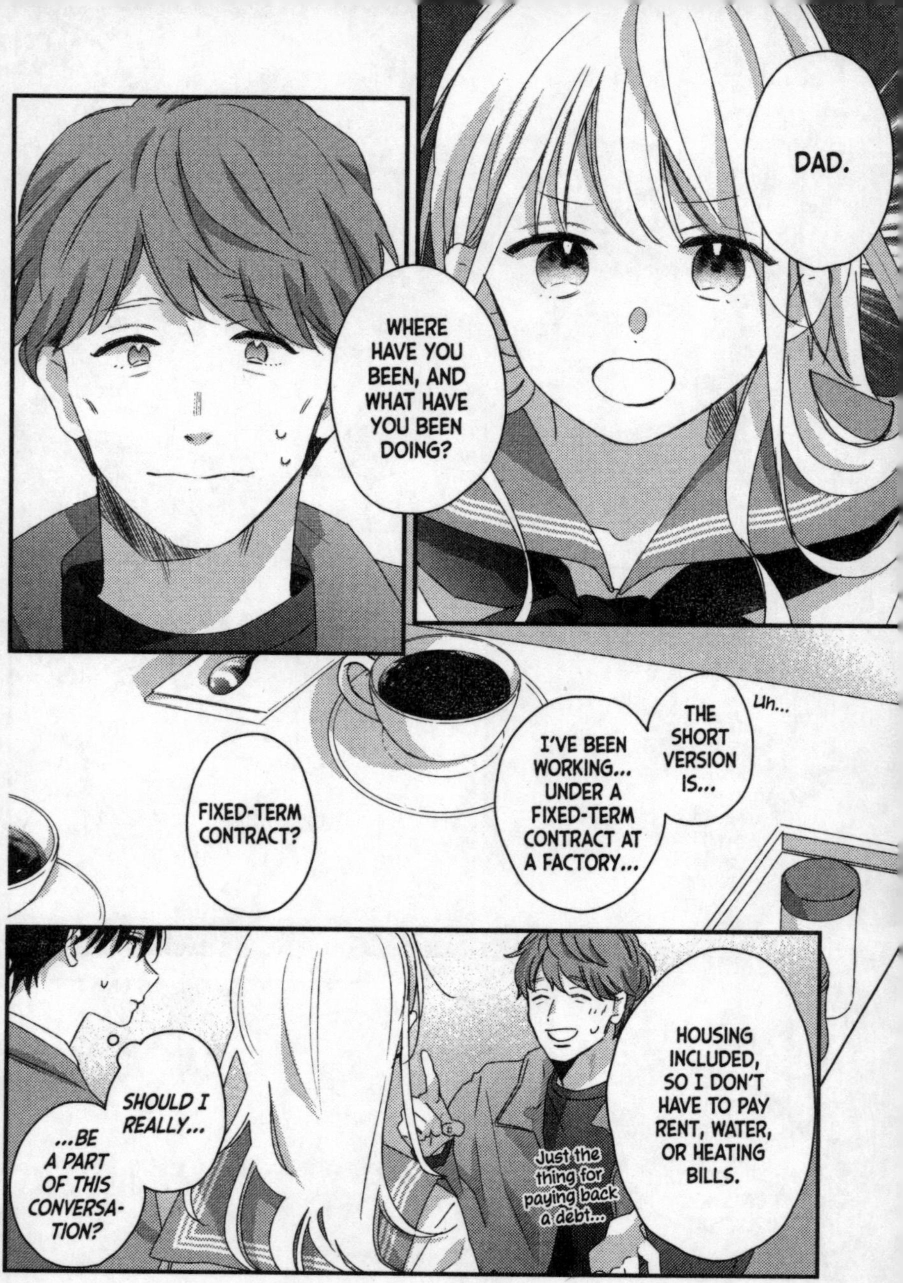
DAD.
WHERE HAVE YOU BEEN, AND WHAT HAVE YOU BEEN DOING?
Uh...
THE SHORT VERSION IS...
I'VE BEEN WORKING... UNDER A FIXED-TERM CONTRACT AT A FACTORY...
FIXED-TERM CONTRACT?
HOUSING INCLUDED, SO I DON'T HAVE TO PAY RENT, WATER, OR HEATING BILLS.
Just the thing for paying back a debt...
SHOULD I REALLY...
...BE A PART OF THIS CONVERSA-TION?

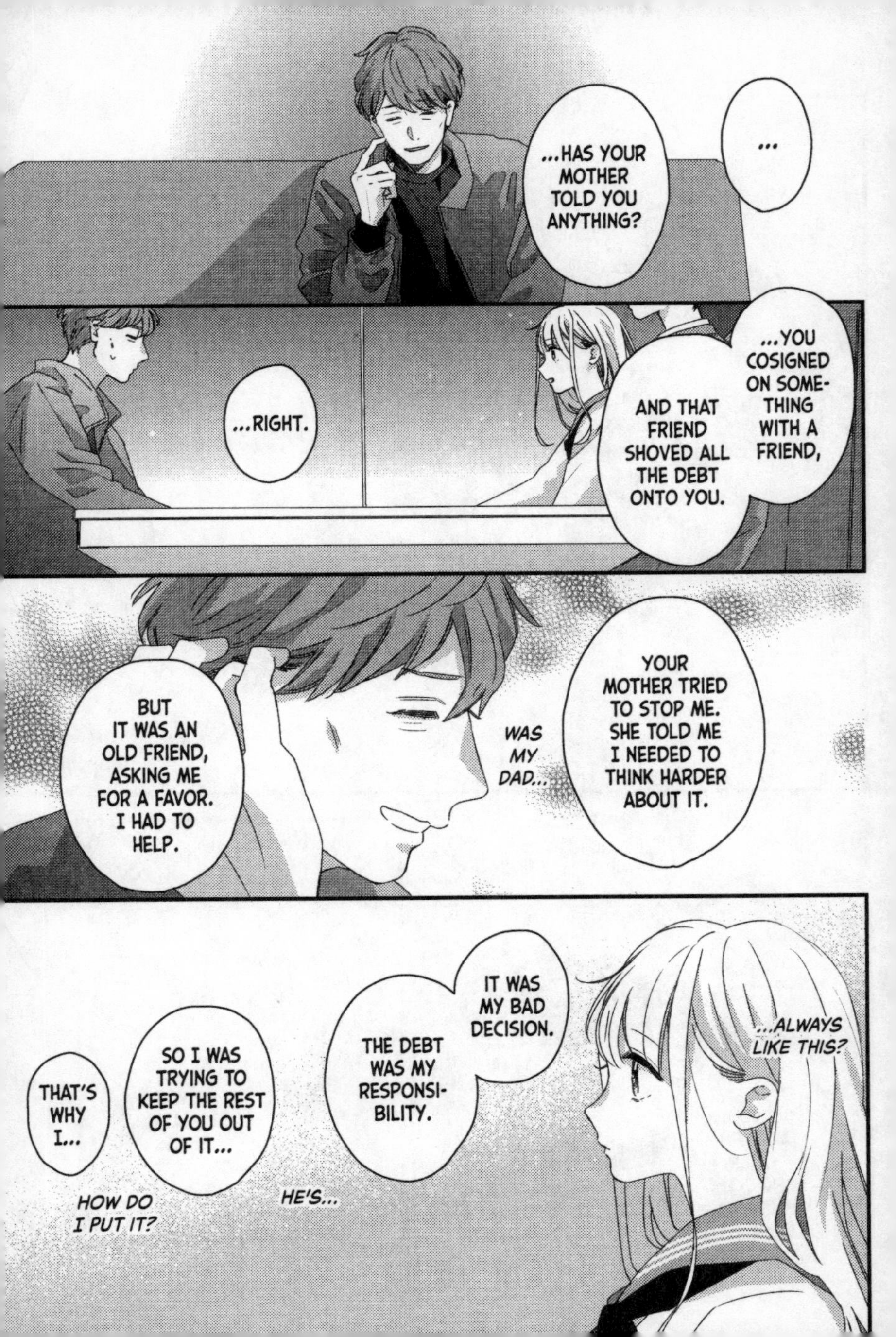
...
...HAS YOUR MOTHER TOLD YOU ANYTHING?
...YOU COSIGNED ON SOMETHING WITH A FRIEND,
AND THAT FRIEND SHOVED ALL THE DEBT ONTO YOU.
...RIGHT.
YOUR MOTHER TRIED TO STOP ME. SHE TOLD ME I NEEDED TO THINK HARDER ABOUT IT.
WAS MY DAD...
BUT IT WAS AN OLD FRIEND, ASKING ME FOR A FAVOR. I HAD TO HELP.
...ALWAYS LIKE THIS?
IT WAS MY BAD DECISION.
THE DEBT WAS MY RESPONSIBILITY.
HE'S...
SO I WAS TRYING TO KEEP THE REST OF YOU OUT OF IT...
THAT'S WHY I...
HOW DO I PUT IT?

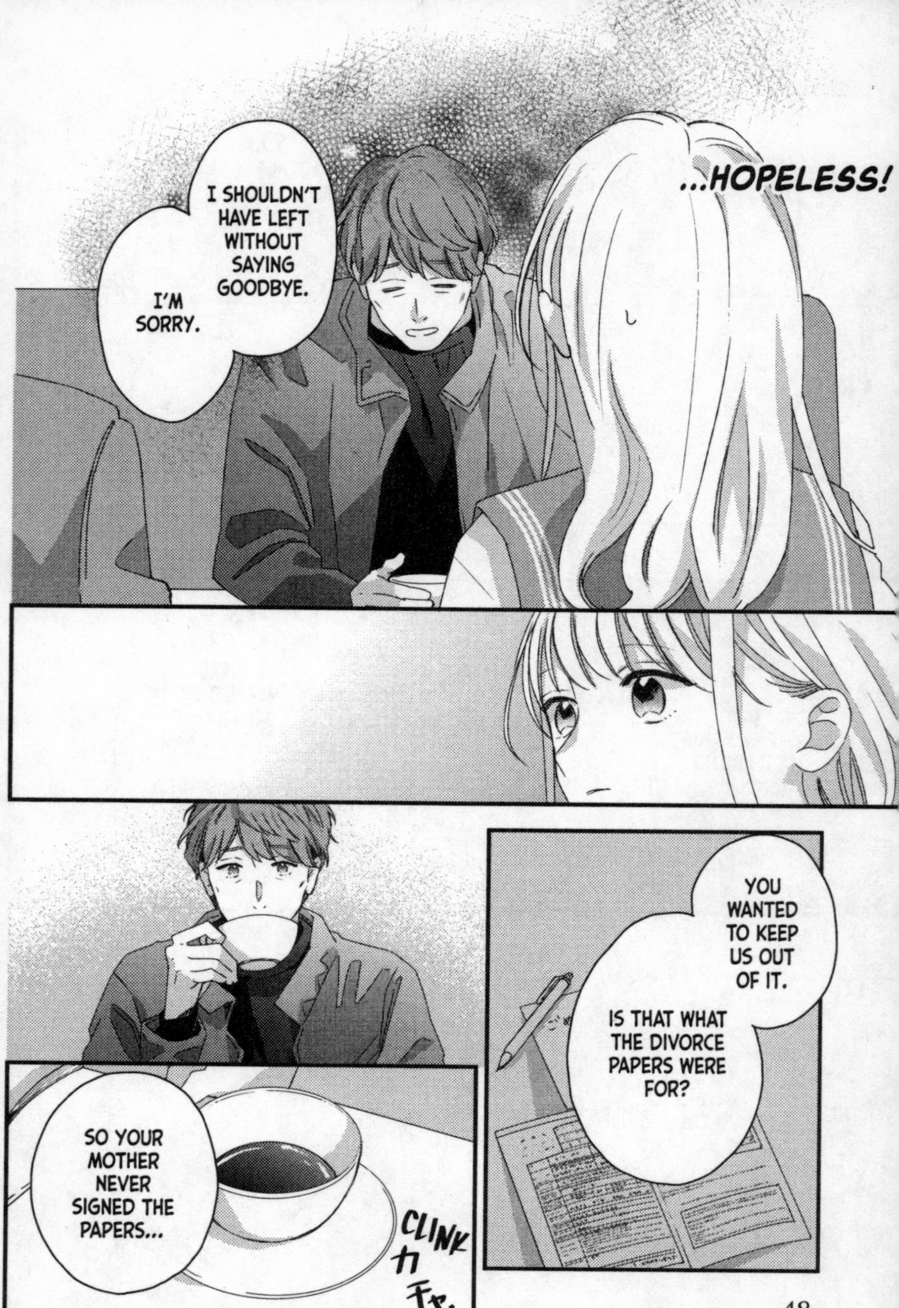
...HOPELESS!
I SHOULDN'T HAVE LEFT WITHOUT SAYING GOODBYE.
I'M SORRY.
YOU WANTED TO KEEP US OUT OF IT.
IS THAT WHAT THE DIVORCE PAPERS WERE FOR?
SO YOUR MOTHER NEVER SIGNED THE PAPERS...
CLINK
カチャ.

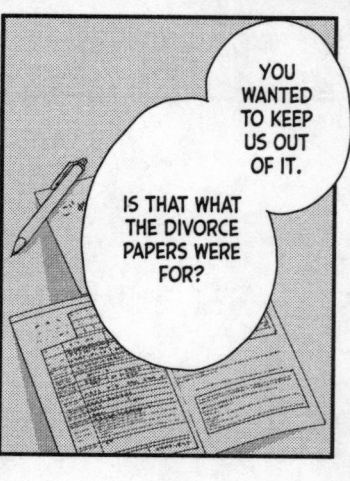

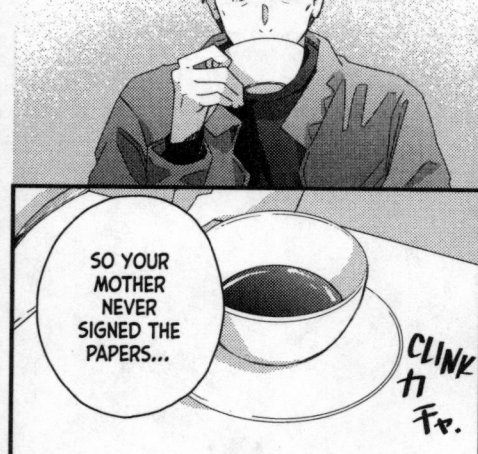

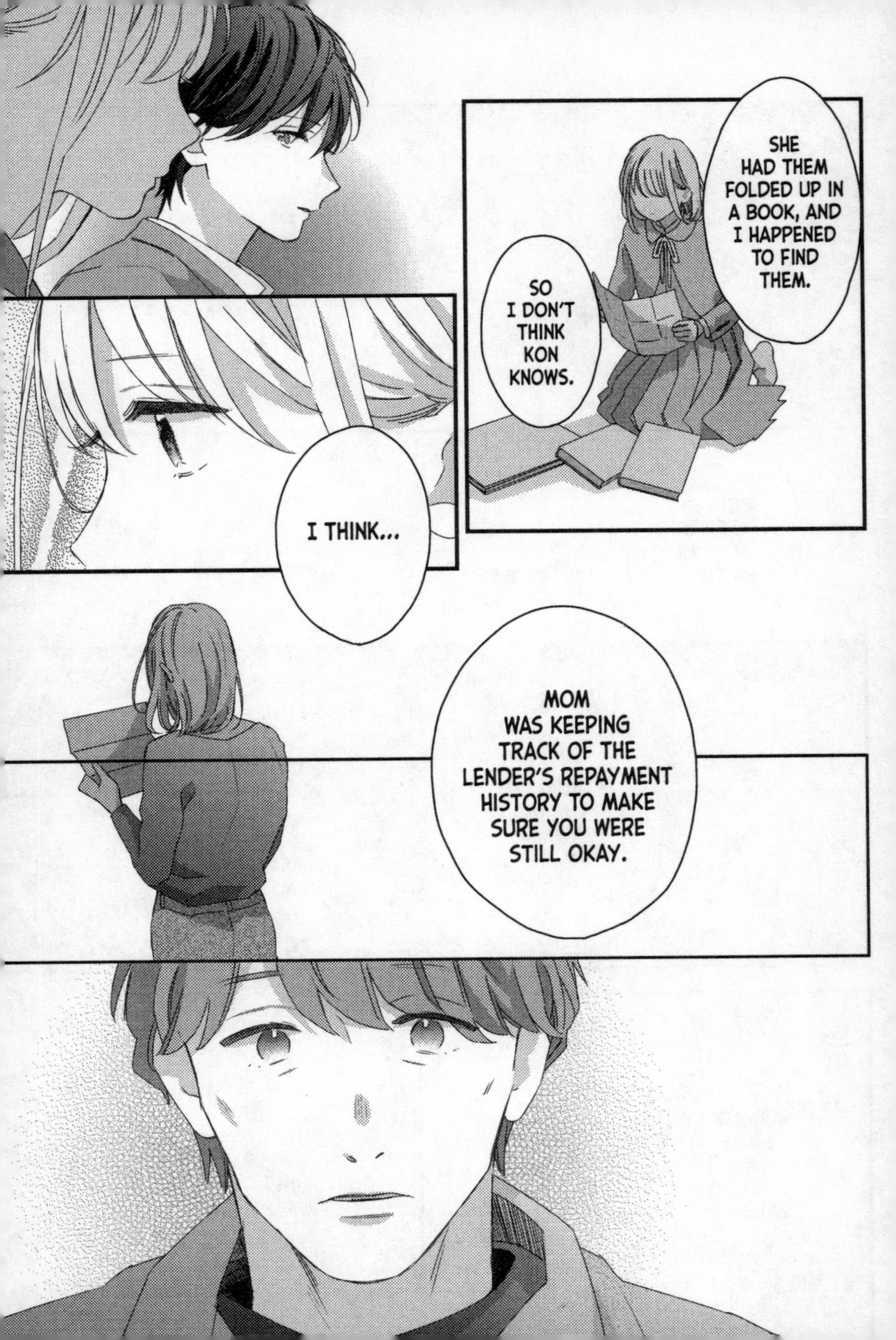
SHE HAD THEM FOLDED UP IN A BOOK, AND I HAPPENED TO FIND THEM.
SO I DON'T THINK KON KNOWS.
I THINK...
MOM WAS KEEPING TRACK OF THE LENDER'S REPAYMENT HISTORY TO MAKE SURE YOU WERE STILL OKAY.

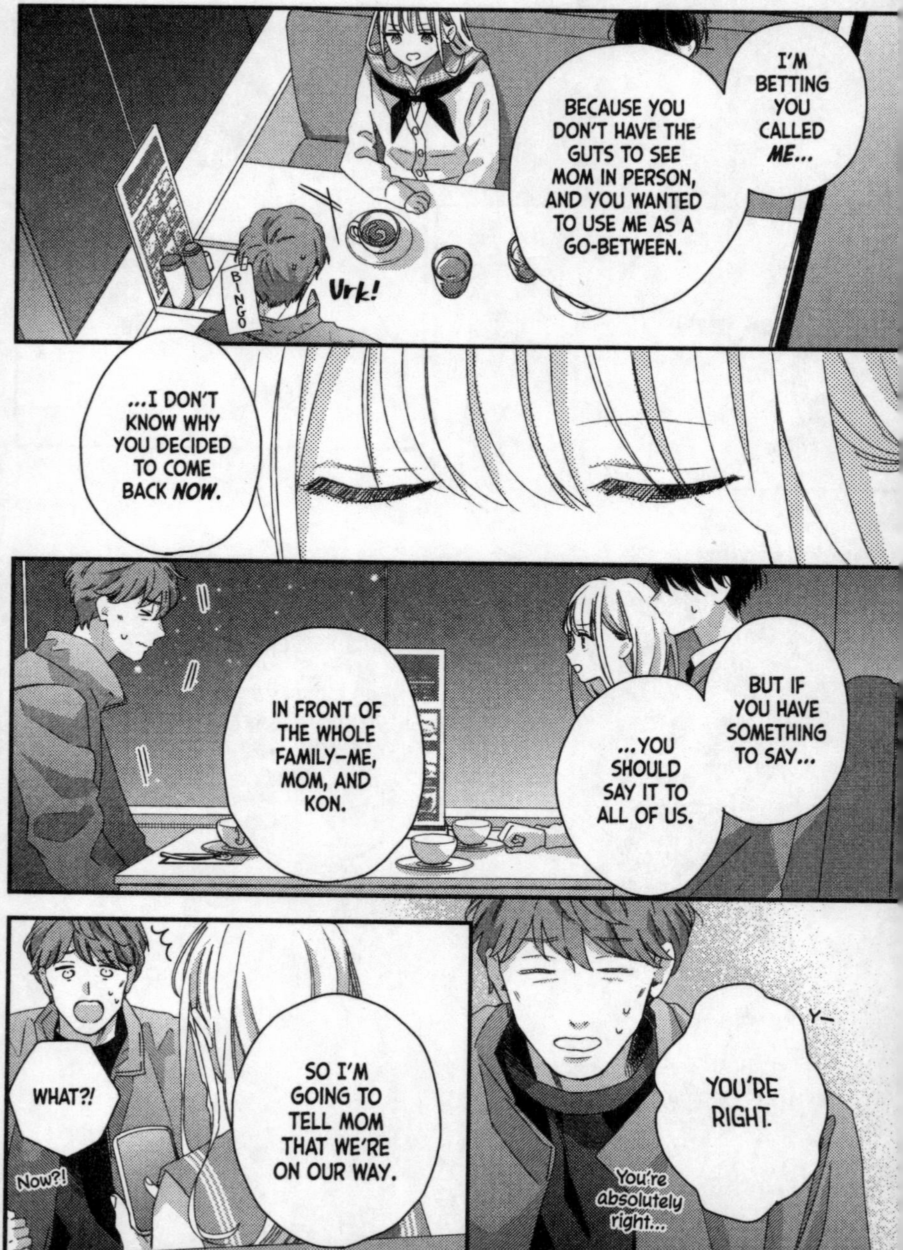
I'M BETTING YOU CALLED *ME*...
BECAUSE YOU DON'T HAVE THE GUTS TO SEE MOM IN PERSON, AND YOU WANTED TO USE ME AS A GO-BETWEEN.
BINGO
Urk!
...I DON'T KNOW WHY YOU DECIDED TO COME BACK *NOW*.
BUT IF YOU HAVE SOMETHING TO SAY...
...YOU SHOULD SAY IT TO ALL OF US.
IN FRONT OF THE WHOLE FAMILY—ME, MOM, AND KON.
Y—
YOU'RE RIGHT.
You're absolutely right...
SO I'M GOING TO TELL MOM THAT WE'RE ON OUR WAY.
WHAT?!
Now?!

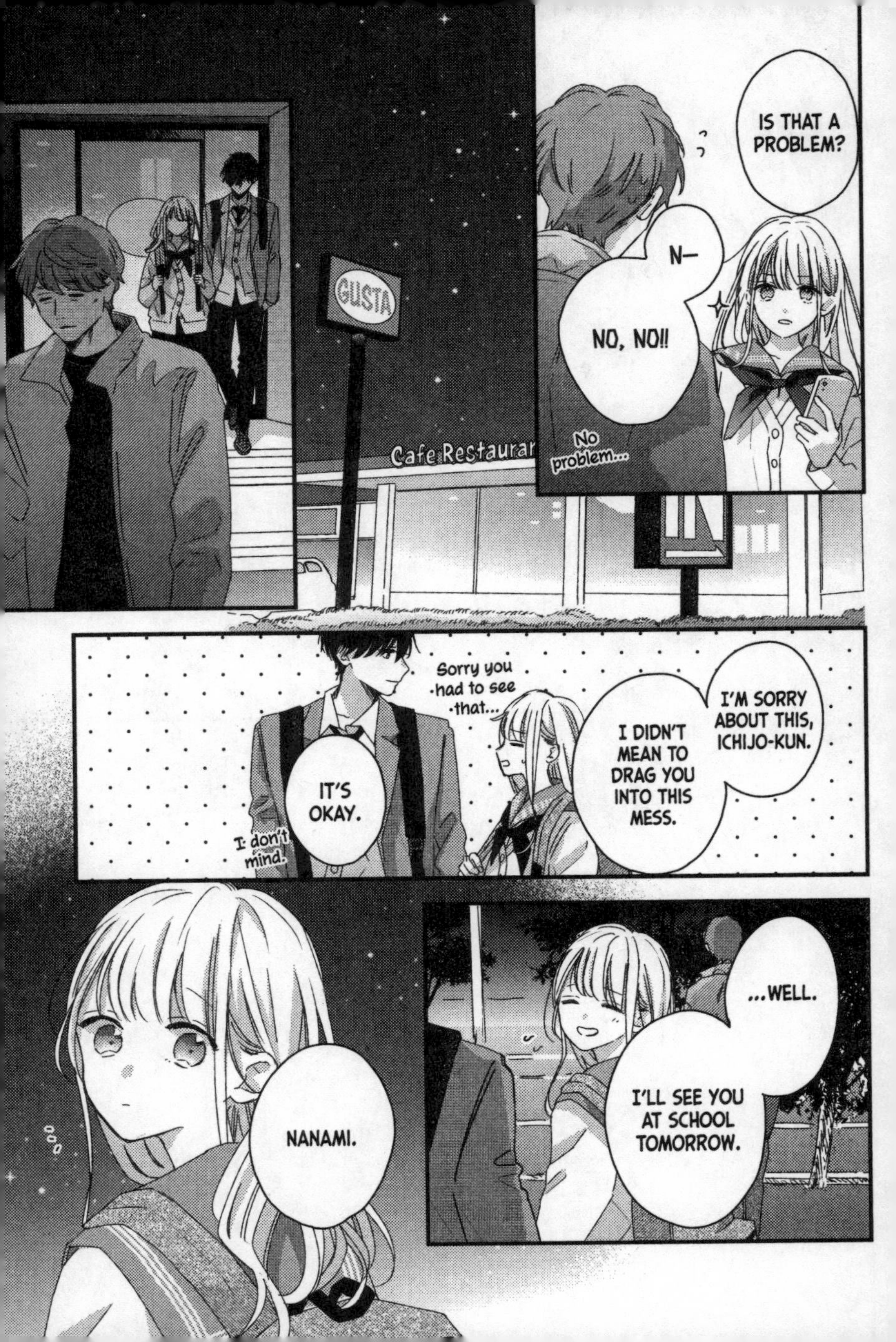
IS THAT A PROBLEM?
N—
NO, NO!!
No problem...
GUSTA
Cafe Restaurar
I'M SORRY ABOUT THIS, ICHIJO-KUN.
I DIDN'T MEAN TO DRAG YOU INTO THIS MESS.
Sorry you had to see that...
IT'S OKAY.
I don't mind!
...WELL.
I'LL SEE YOU AT SCHOOL TOMORROW.
NANAMI.

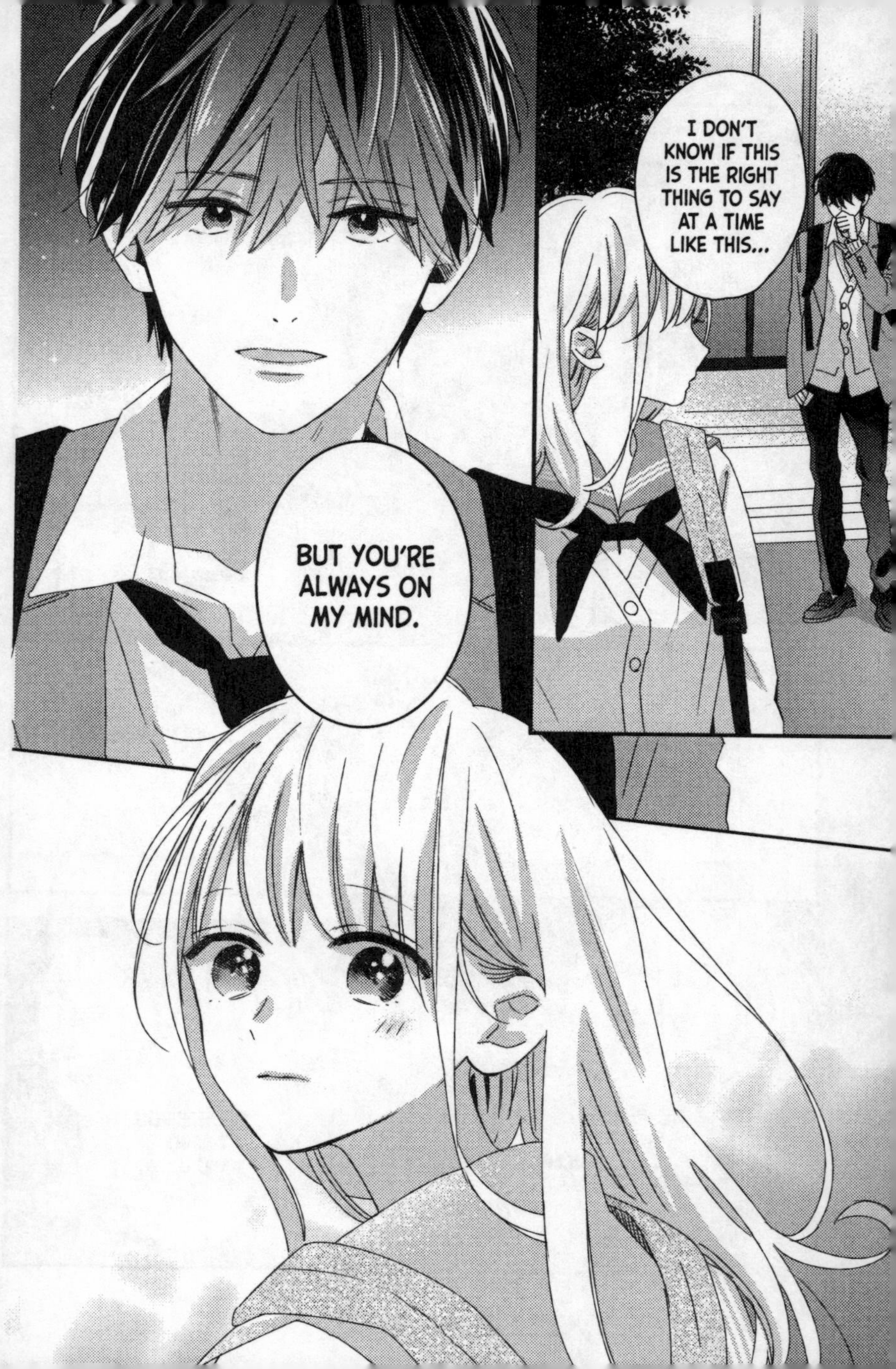
I DON'T KNOW IF THIS IS THE RIGHT THING TO SAY AT A TIME LIKE THIS...
BUT YOU'RE ALWAYS ON MY MIND.

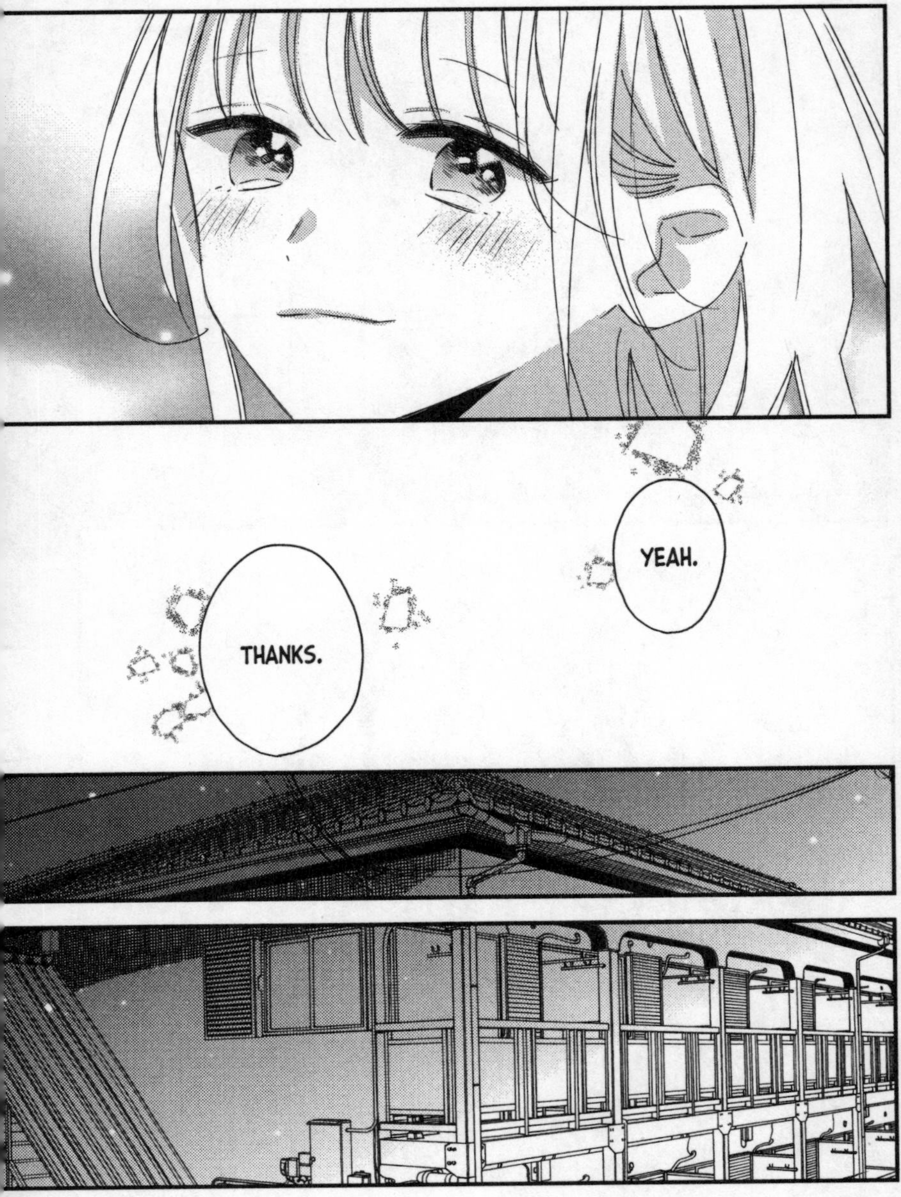
YEAH.
THANKS.

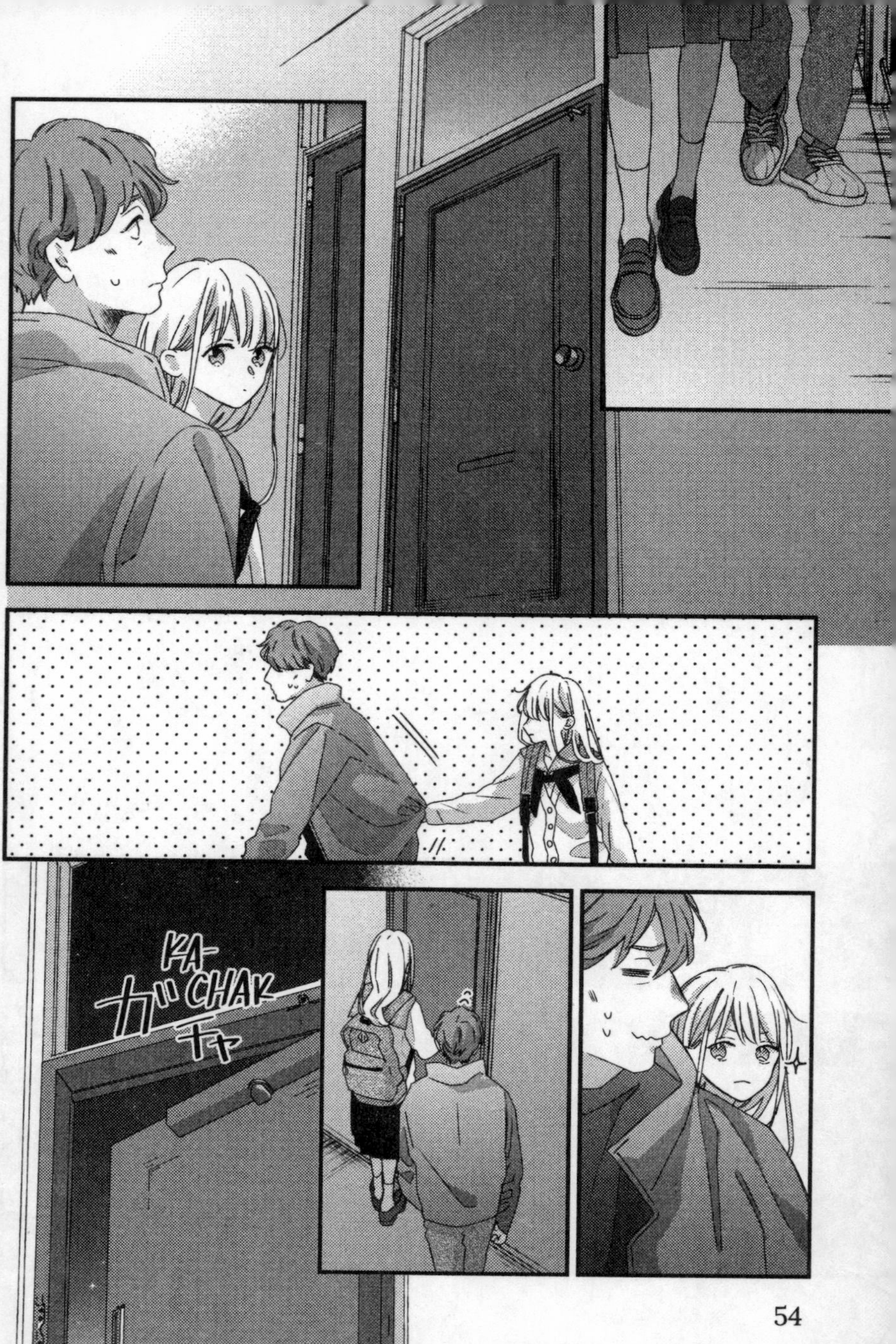
KA-CHAK
ガチャ

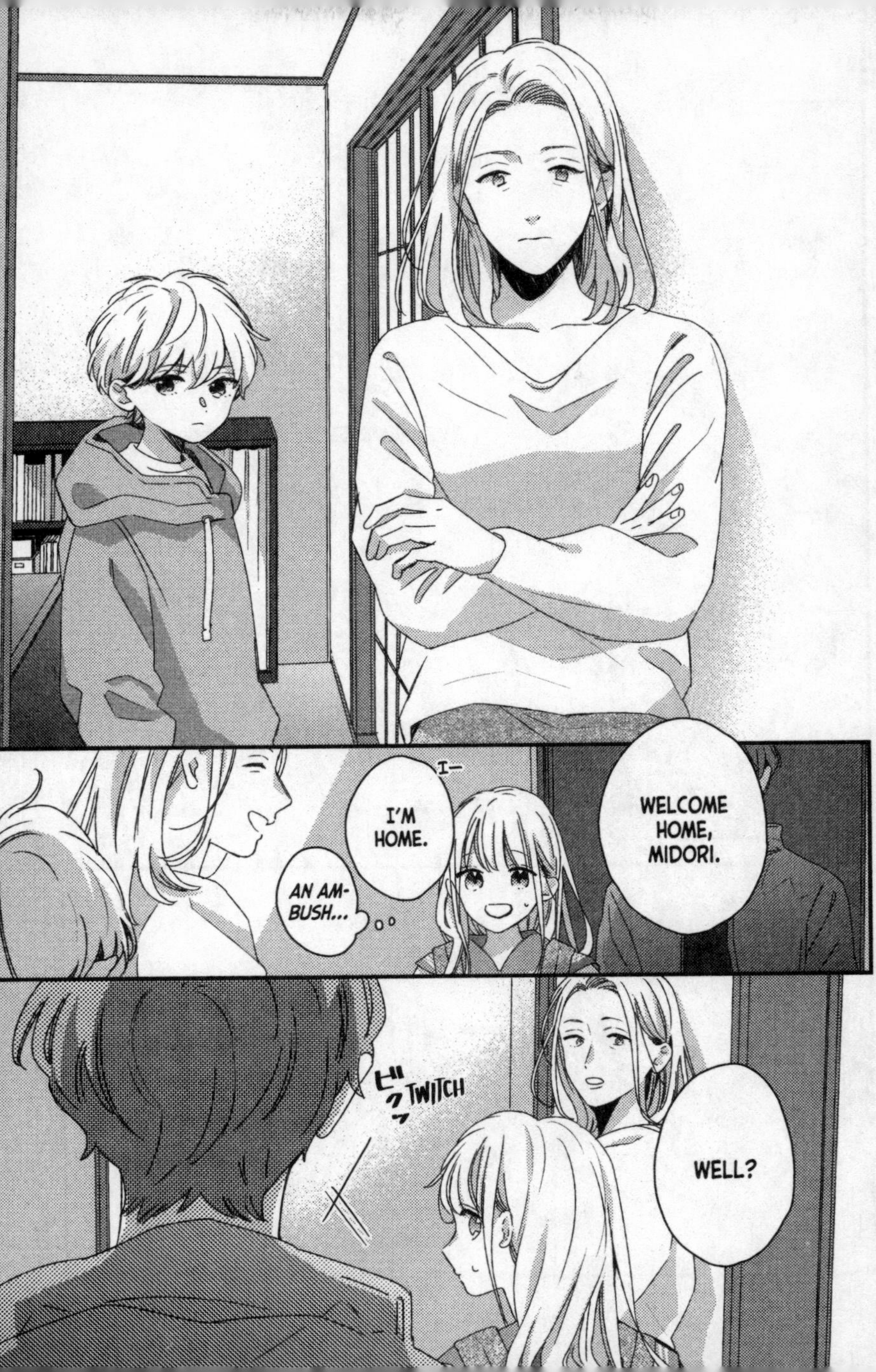
WELCOME HOME, MIDORI.
I—
I'M HOME.
AN AM-BUSH...
ビクッ TWITCH
WELL?

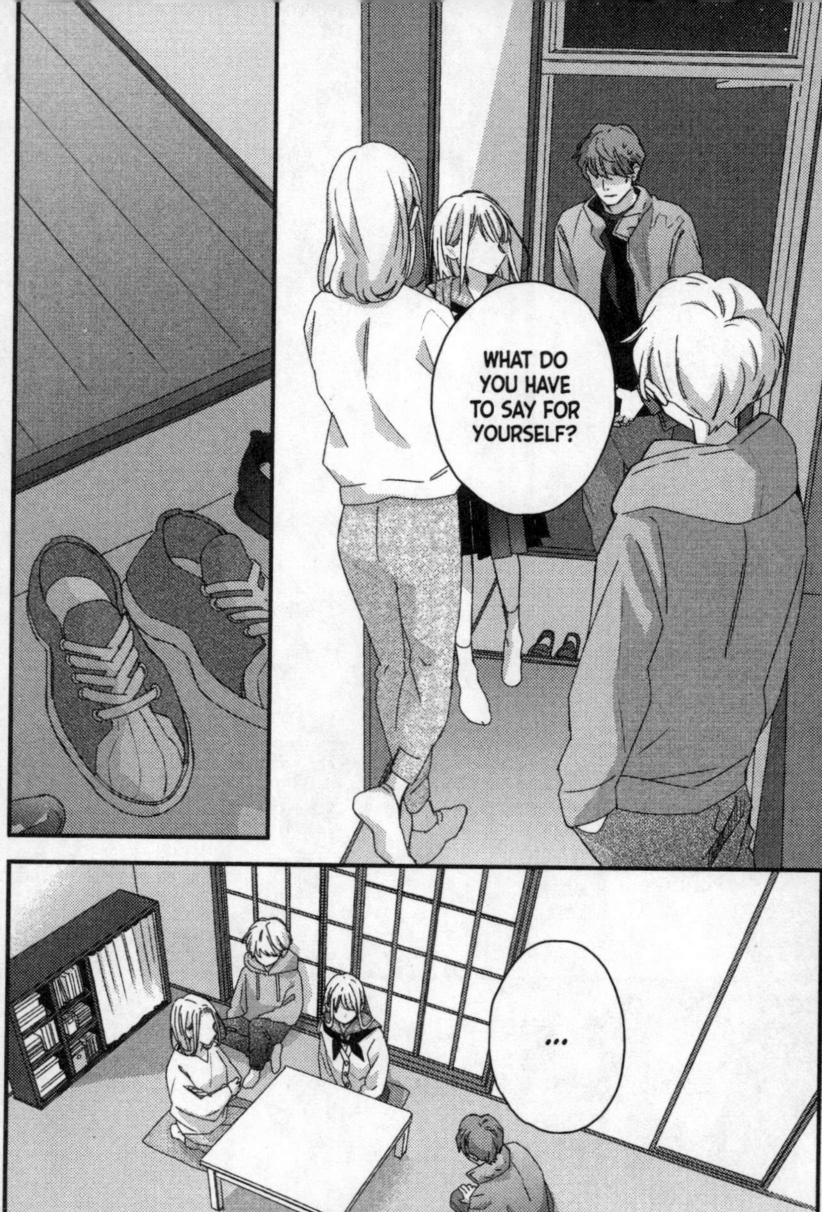
WHAT DO YOU HAVE TO SAY FOR YOURSELF?
...

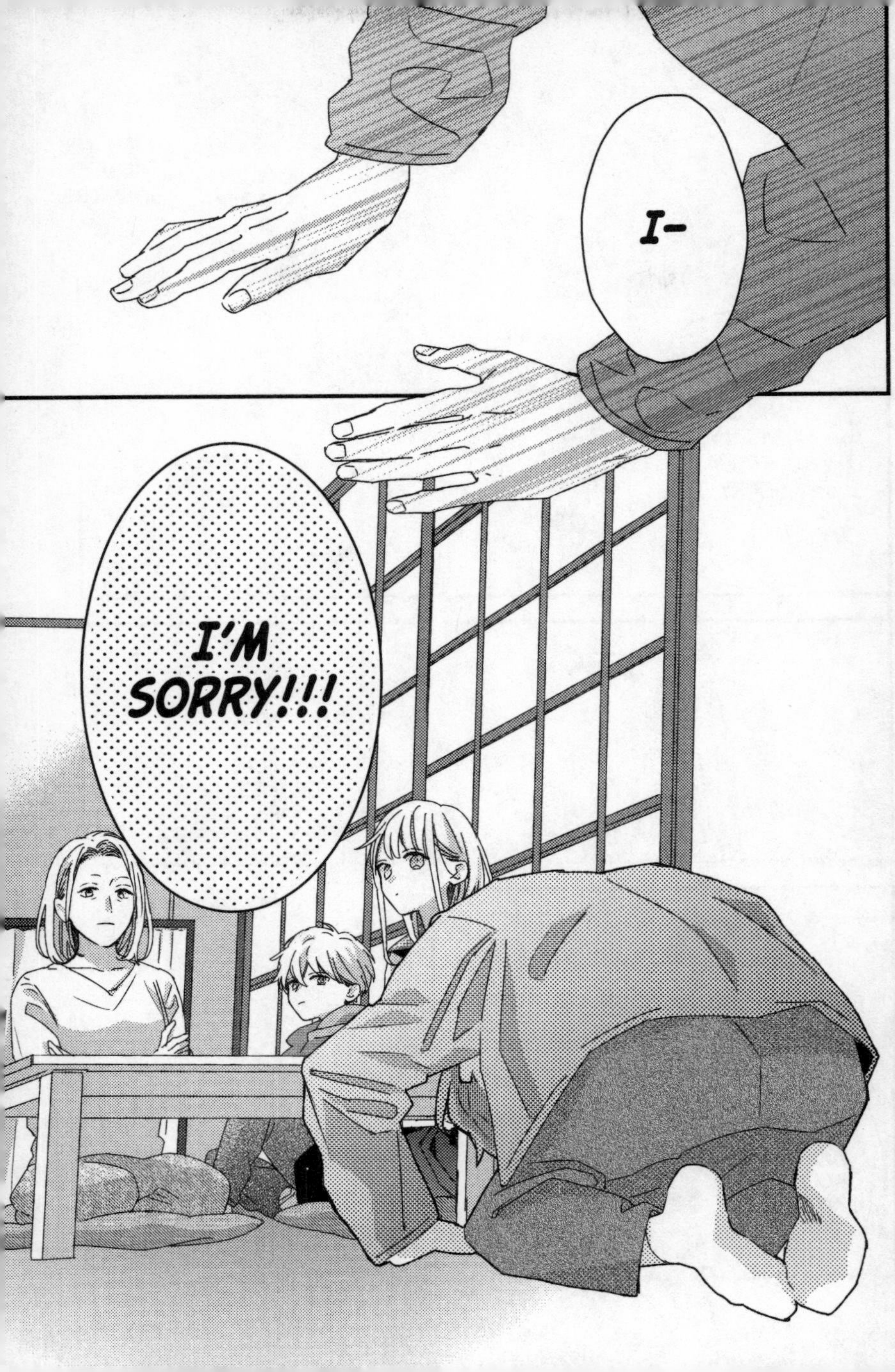
I–
I'M SORRY!!!

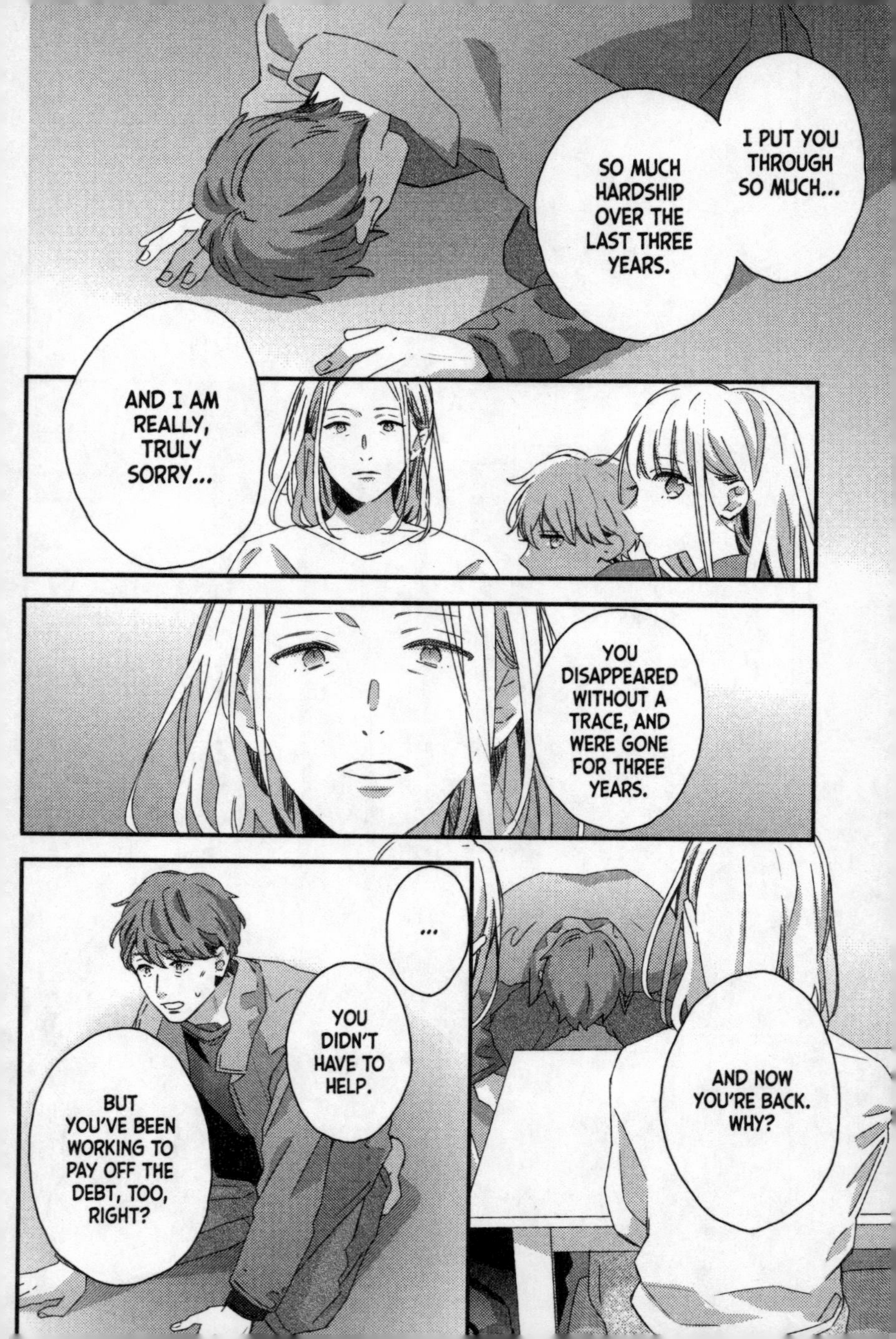
I PUT YOU THROUGH SO MUCH...
SO MUCH HARDSHIP OVER THE LAST THREE YEARS.
AND I AM REALLY, TRULY SORRY...
YOU DISAPPEARED WITHOUT A TRACE, AND WERE GONE FOR THREE YEARS.
AND NOW YOU'RE BACK. WHY?
...
YOU DIDN'T HAVE TO HELP.
BUT YOU'VE BEEN WORKING TO PAY OFF THE DEBT, TOO, RIGHT?

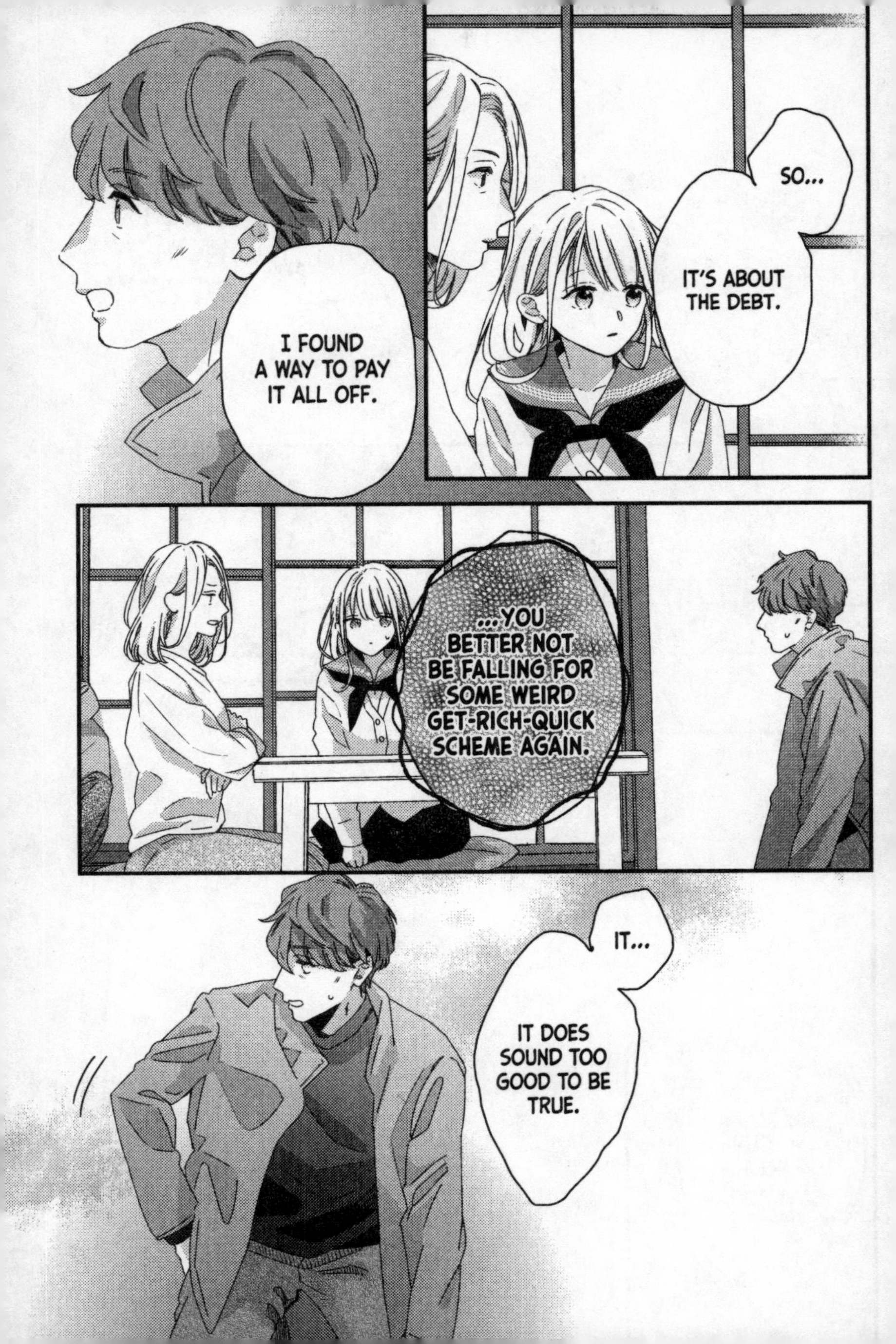
SO...
IT'S ABOUT THE DEBT.
I FOUND A WAY TO PAY IT ALL OFF.
...YOU BETTER NOT BE FALLING FOR SOME WEIRD GET-RICH-QUICK SCHEME AGAIN.
IT...
IT DOES SOUND TOO GOOD TO BE TRUE.

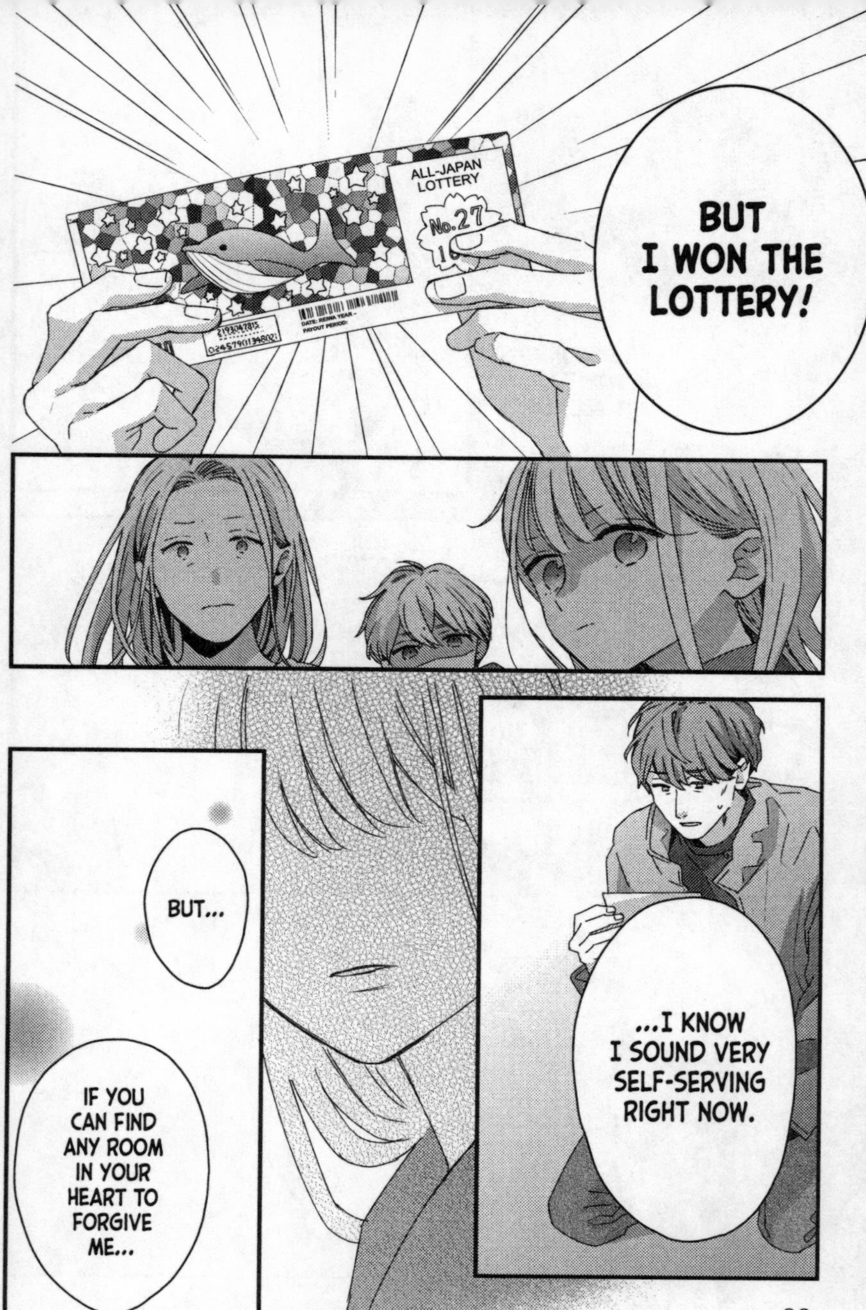
ALL-JAPAN LOTTERY
No.27
BUT I WON THE LOTTERY!
...I KNOW I SOUND VERY SELF-SERVING RIGHT NOW.
BUT...
IF YOU CAN FIND ANY ROOM IN YOUR HEART TO FORGIVE ME...

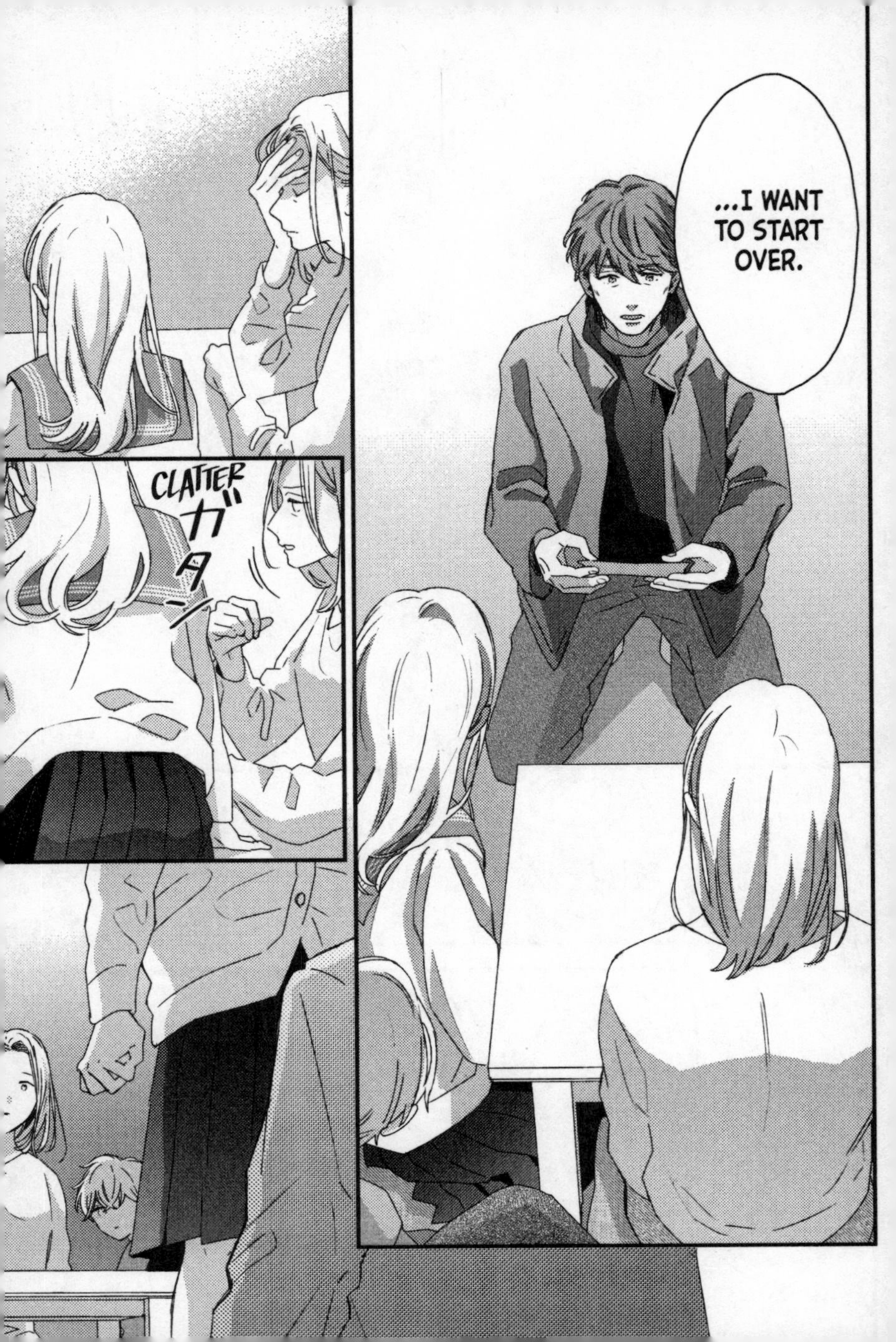
...I WANT TO START OVER.
CLATTER
ガタッ

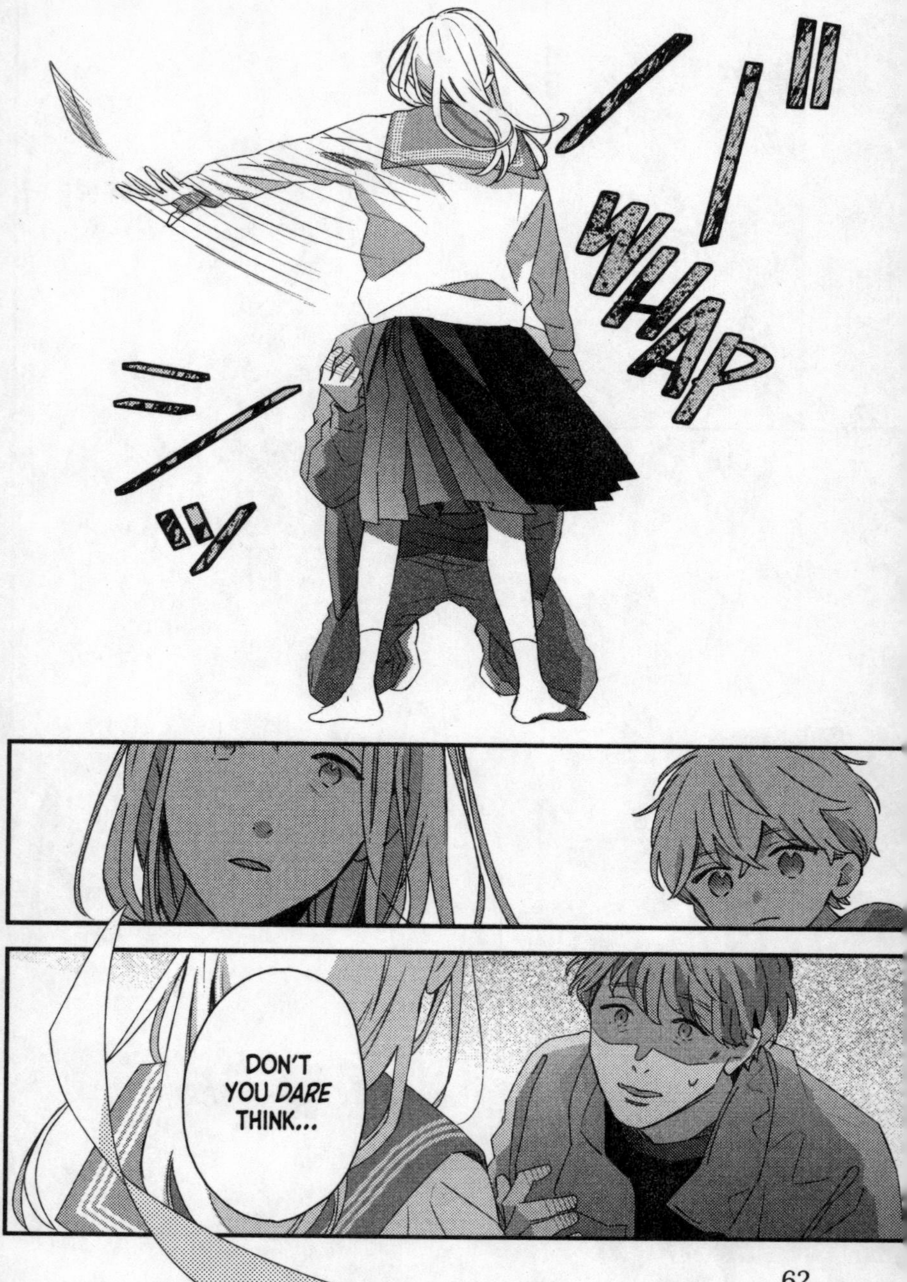
WHAP
DON'T YOU *DARE* THINK...

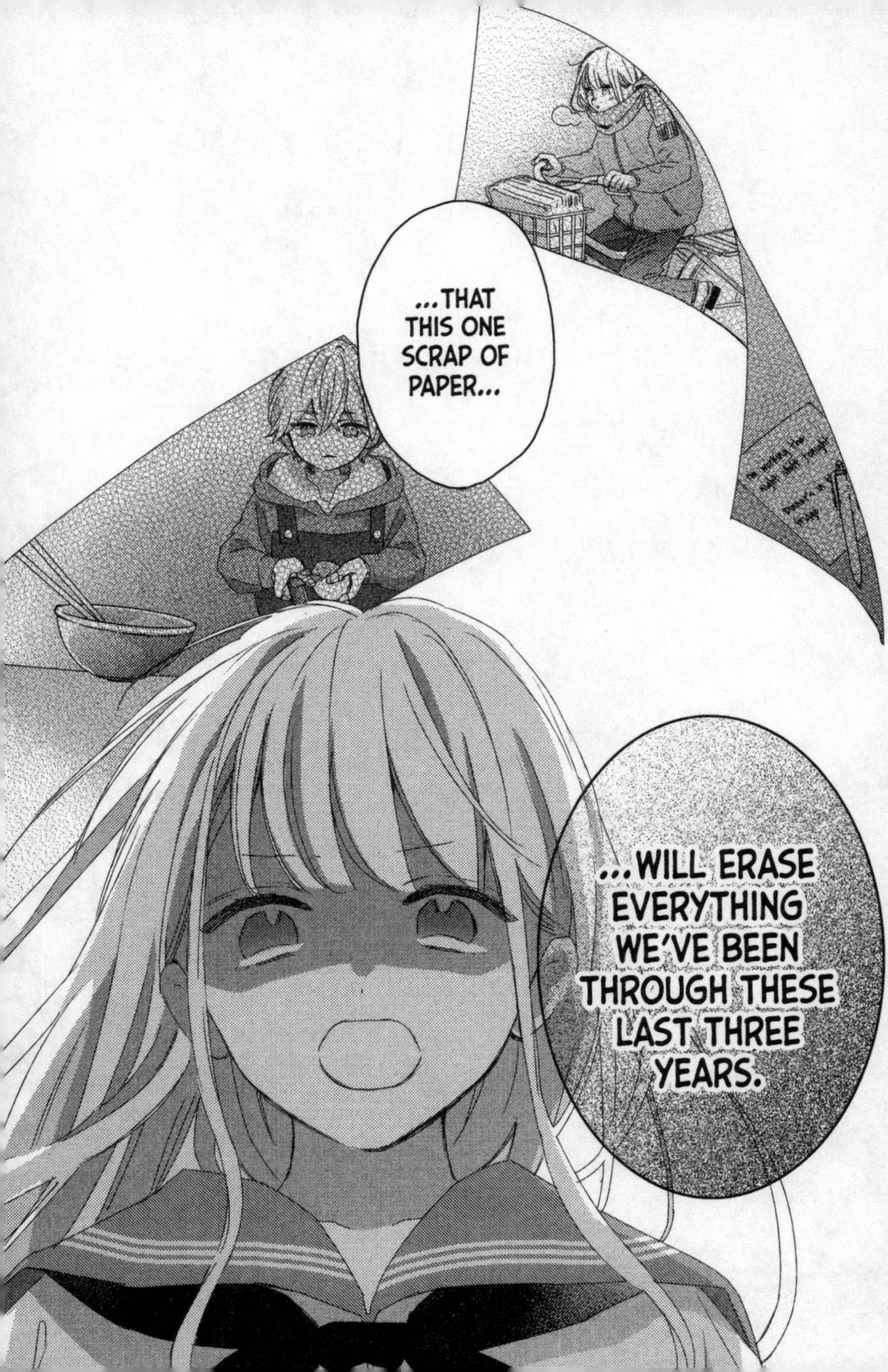
...THAT THIS ONE SCRAP OF PAPER...
...WILL ERASE EVERYTHING WE'VE BEEN THROUGH THESE LAST THREE YEARS.

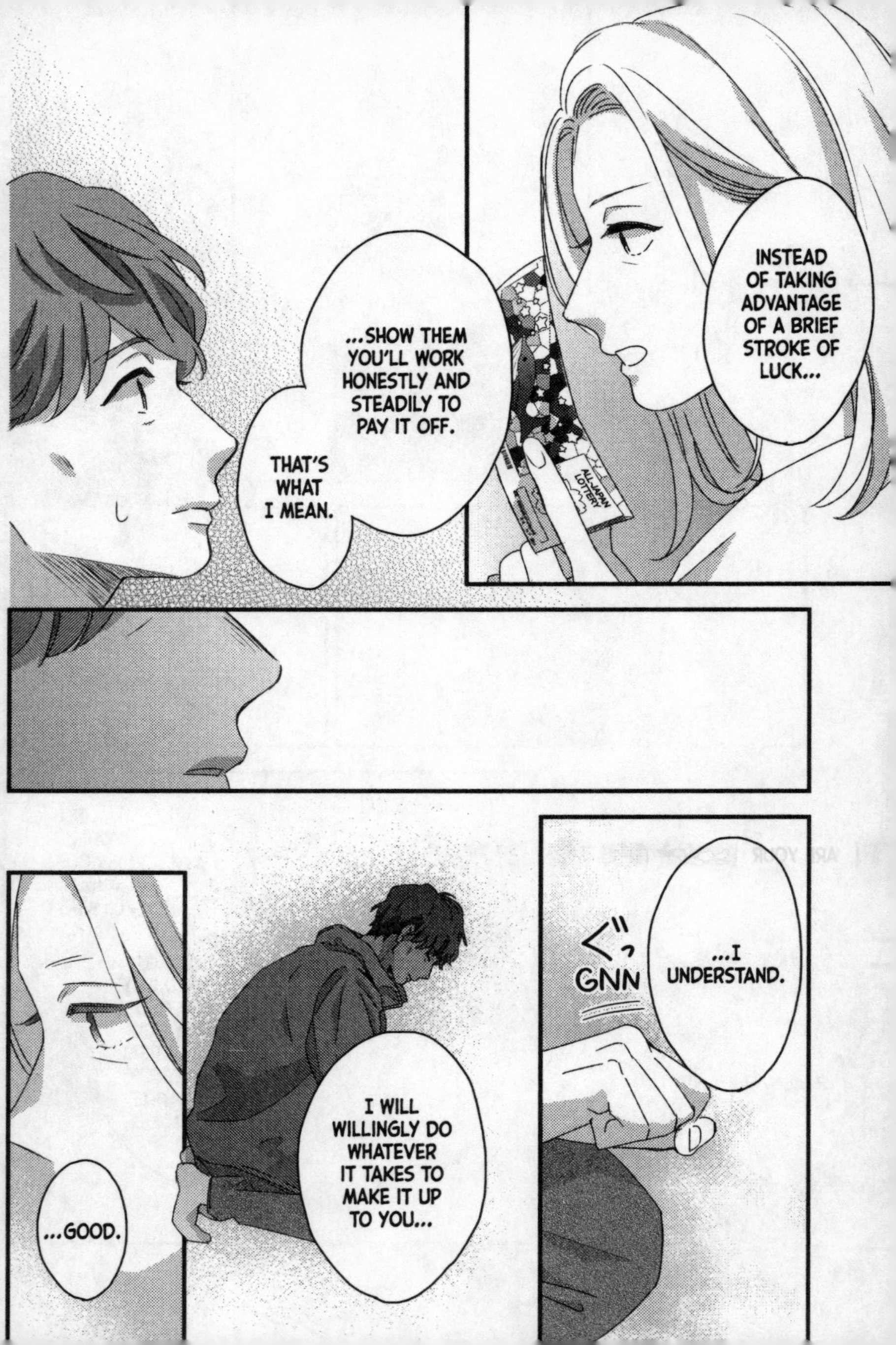
INSTEAD OF TAKING ADVANTAGE OF A BRIEF STROKE OF LUCK...
ALL-JAPAN LOTTERY
...SHOW THEM YOU'LL WORK HONESTLY AND STEADILY TO PAY IT OFF.
THAT'S WHAT I MEAN.
...I UNDERSTAND.
ぐっ
GNN
I WILL WILLINGLY DO WHATEVER IT TAKES TO MAKE IT UP TO YOU...
...GOOD.

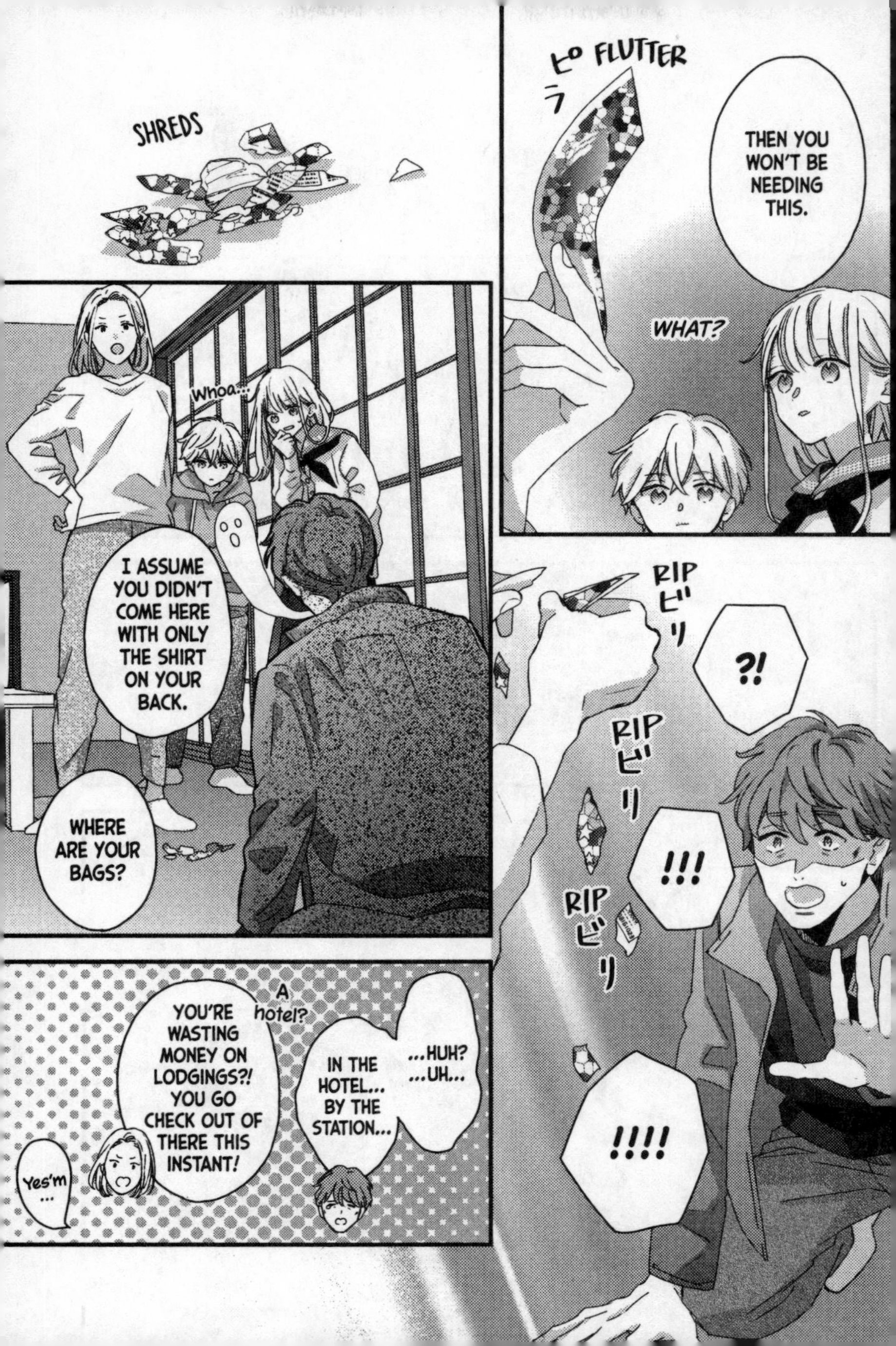
ピラ FLUTTER
THEN YOU WON'T BE NEEDING THIS.
WHAT?
RIP ビリ
?!
RIP ビリ
!!!
RIP ビリ
!!!!
SHREDS
Whoa...
I ASSUME YOU DIDN'T COME HERE WITH ONLY THE SHIRT ON YOUR BACK.
WHERE ARE YOUR BAGS?
...HUH? ...UH...
IN THE HOTEL... BY THE STATION...
A hotel?
YOU'RE WASTING MONEY ON LODGINGS?! YOU GO CHECK OUT OF THERE THIS INSTANT!
Yes'm...

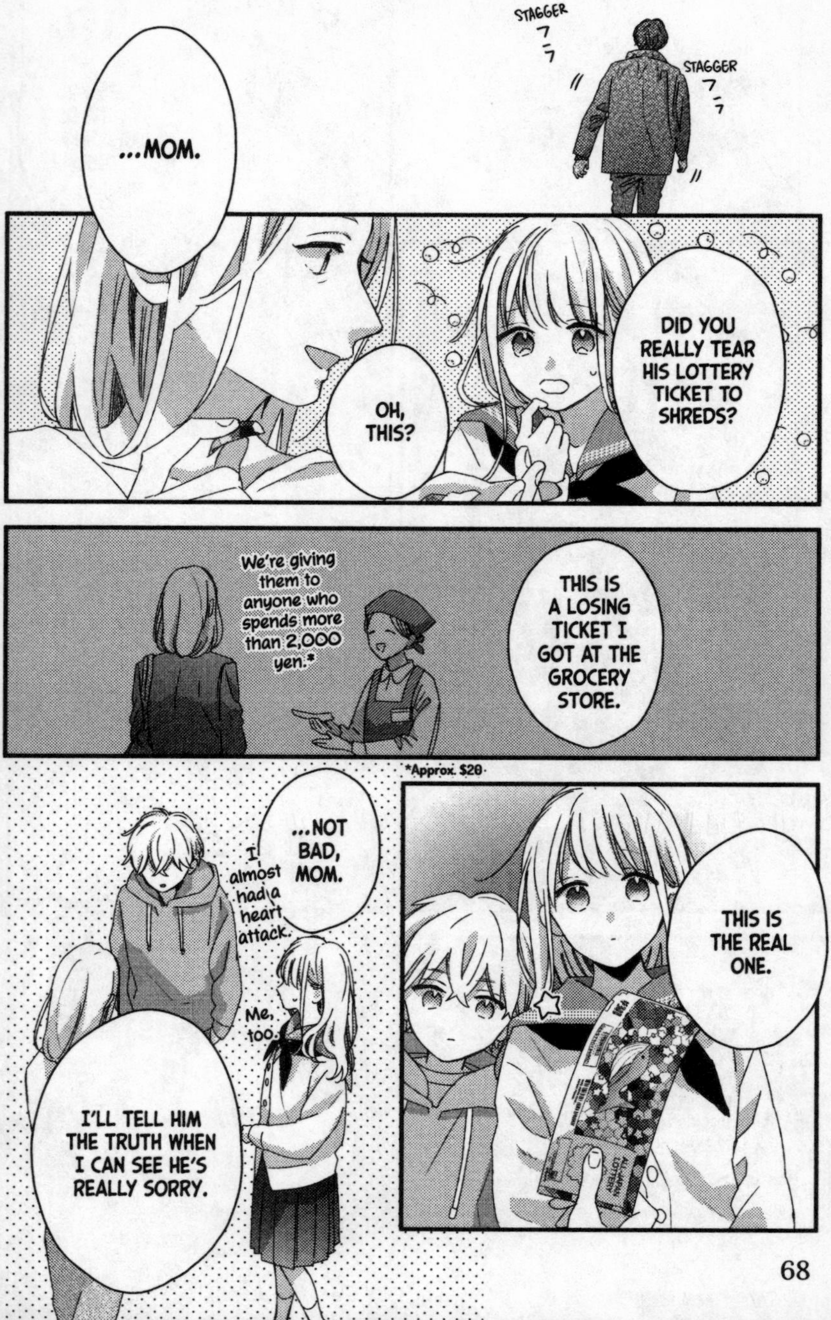
STAGGER
STAGGER
...MOM.
DID YOU REALLY TEAR HIS LOTTERY TICKET TO SHREDS?
OH, THIS?
THIS IS A LOSING TICKET I GOT AT THE GROCERY STORE.
We're giving them to anyone who spends more than 2,000 yen.*
*Approx. $20
THIS IS THE REAL ONE.
ALL-JAPAN LOTTERY
...NOT BAD, MOM.
I almost had a heart attack.
Me, too.
I'LL TELL HIM THE TRUTH WHEN I CAN SEE HE'S REALLY SORRY.

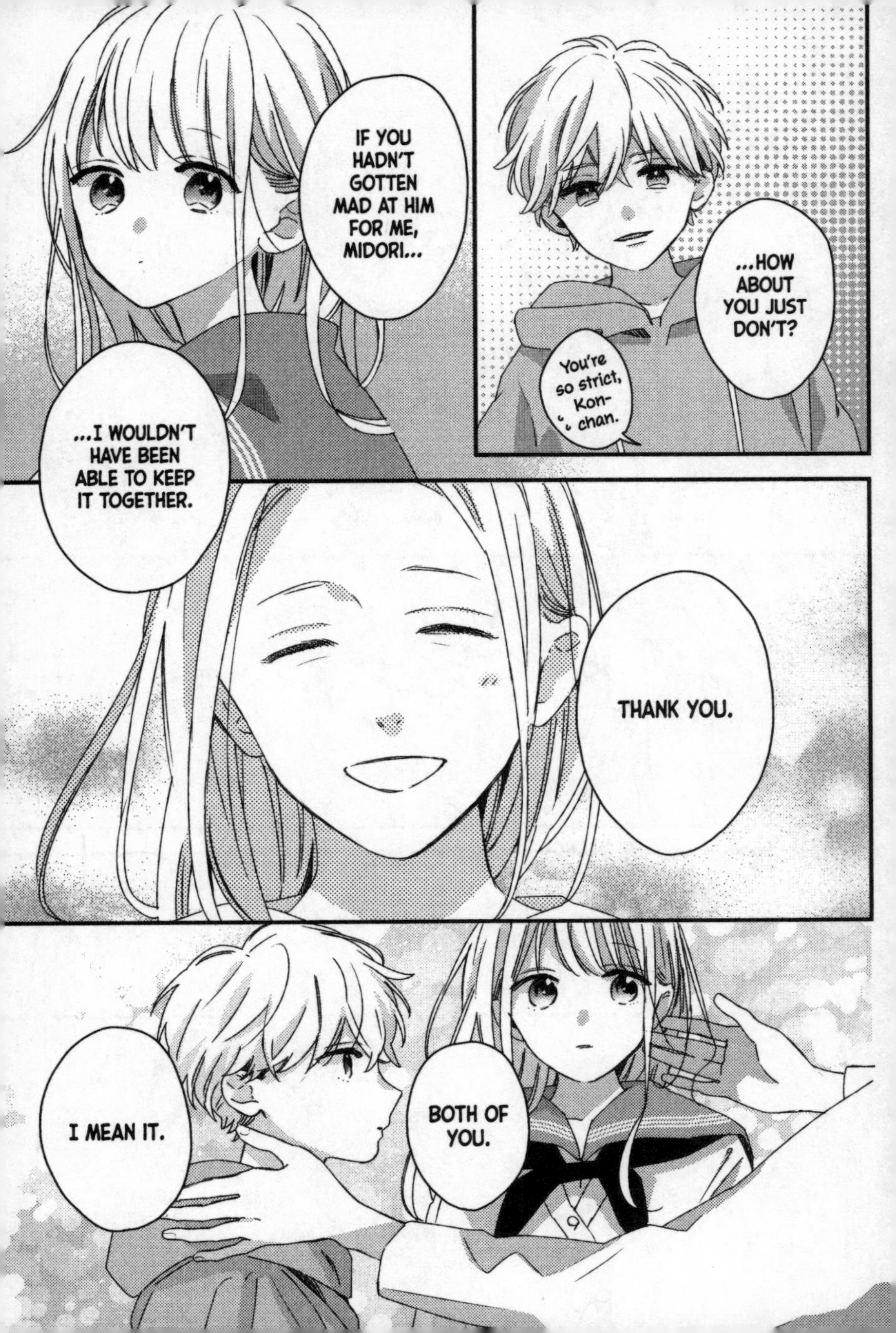
...HOW ABOUT YOU JUST DON'T?
You're so strict, Kon-chan.
IF YOU HADN'T GOTTEN MAD AT HIM FOR ME, MIDORI...
...I WOULDN'T HAVE BEEN ABLE TO KEEP IT TOGETHER.
THANK YOU.
BOTH OF YOU.
I MEAN IT.

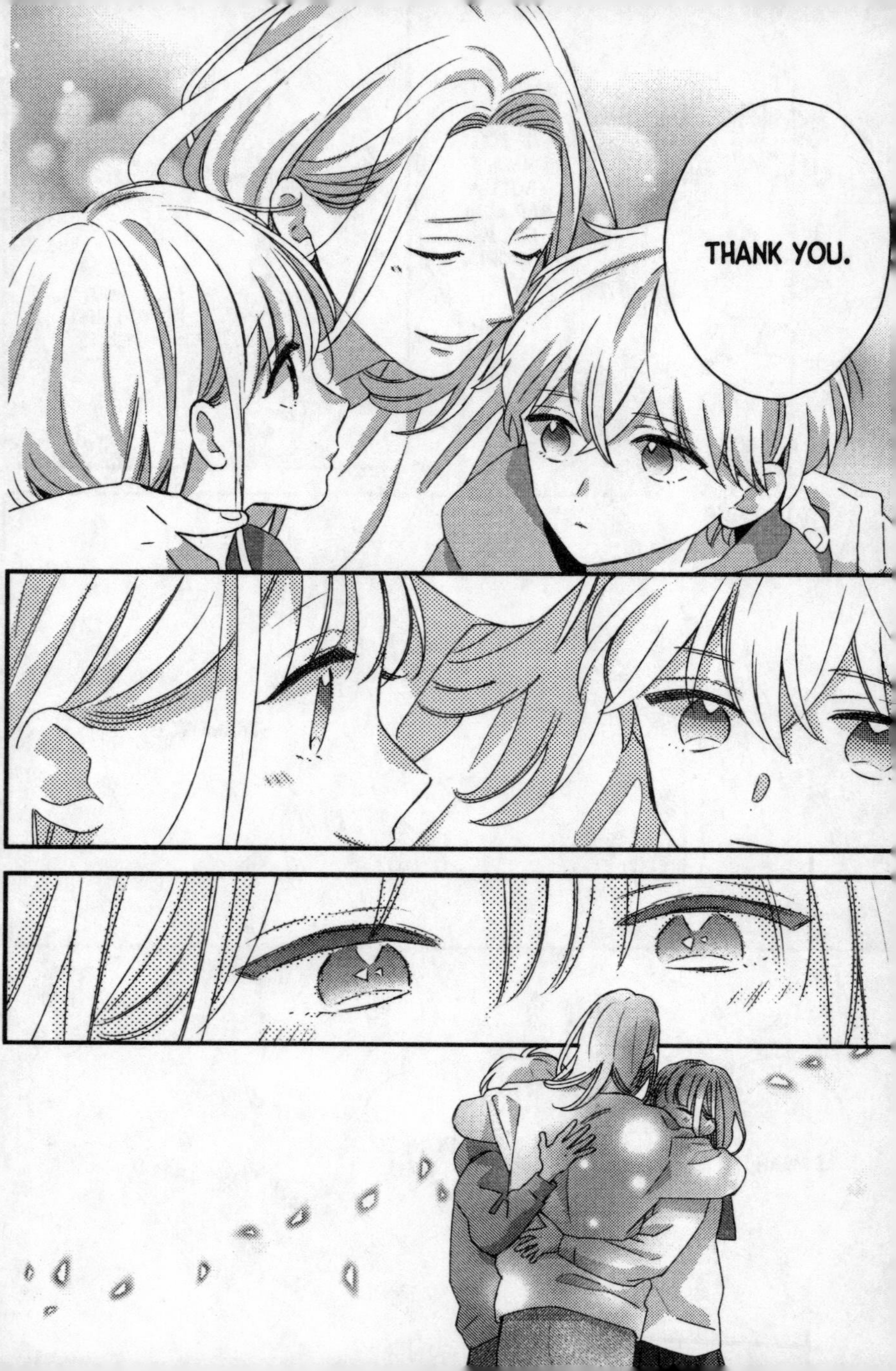
THANK YOU.

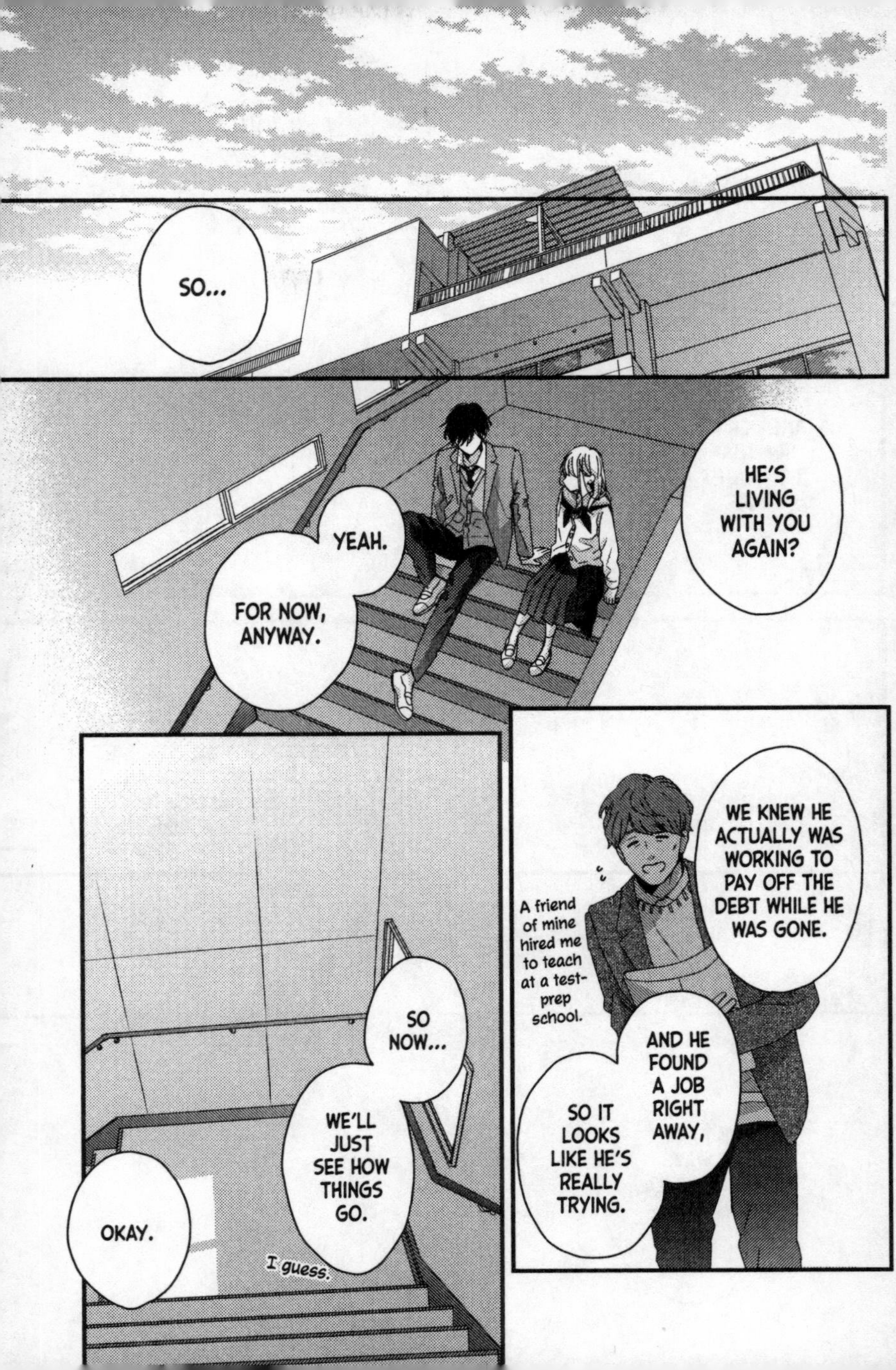
SO...
HE'S LIVING WITH YOU AGAIN?
YEAH.
FOR NOW, ANYWAY.
WE KNEW HE ACTUALLY WAS WORKING TO PAY OFF THE DEBT WHILE HE WAS GONE.
A friend of mine hired me to teach at a test-prep school.
AND HE FOUND A JOB RIGHT AWAY,
SO IT LOOKS LIKE HE'S REALLY TRYING.
SO NOW...
WE'LL JUST SEE HOW THINGS GO.
I guess.
OKAY.

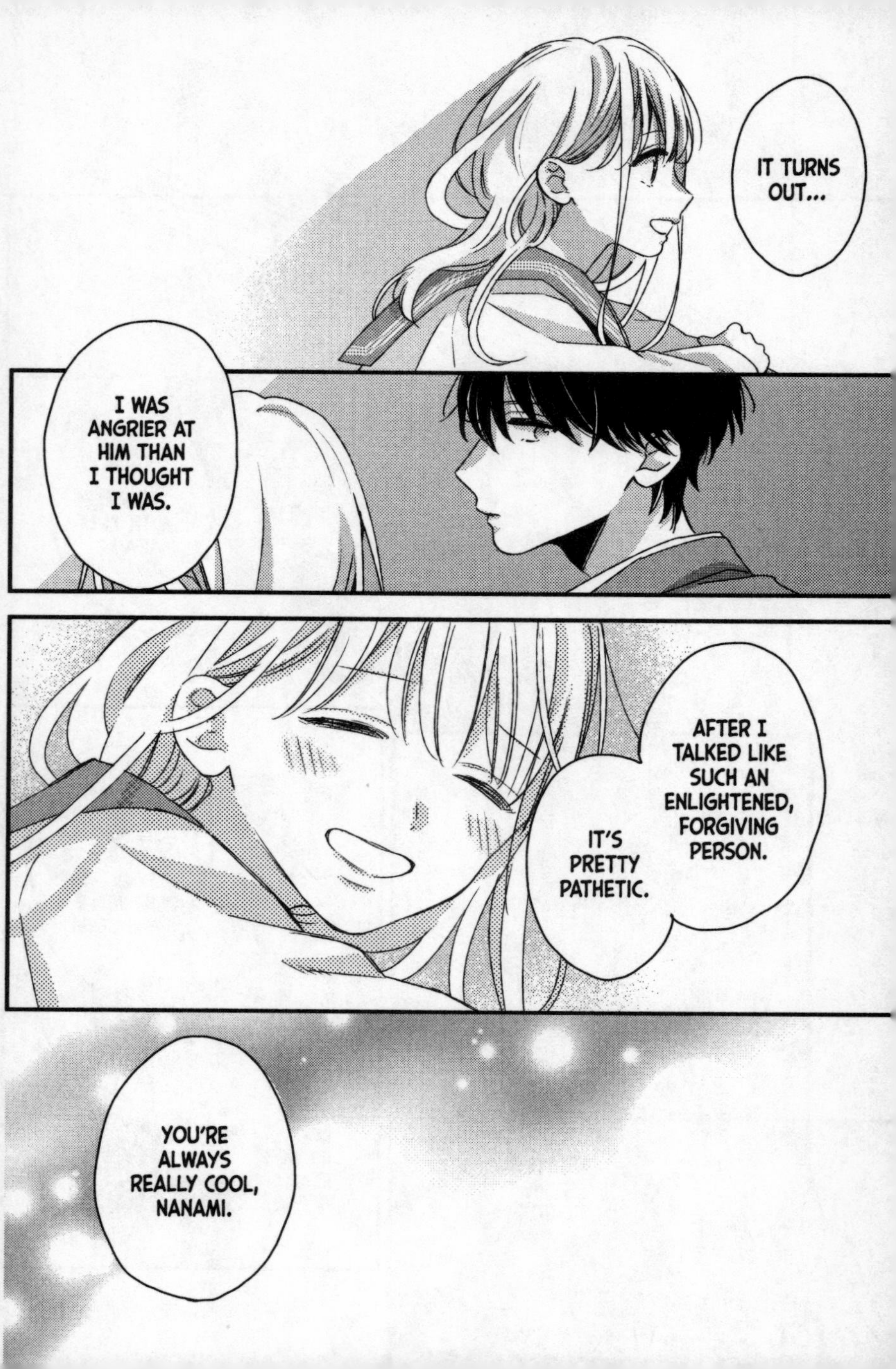
IT TURNS OUT...
I WAS ANGRIER AT HIM THAN I THOUGHT I WAS.
AFTER I TALKED LIKE SUCH AN ENLIGHTENED, FORGIVING PERSON.
IT'S PRETTY PATHETIC.
YOU'RE ALWAYS REALLY COOL, NANAMI.

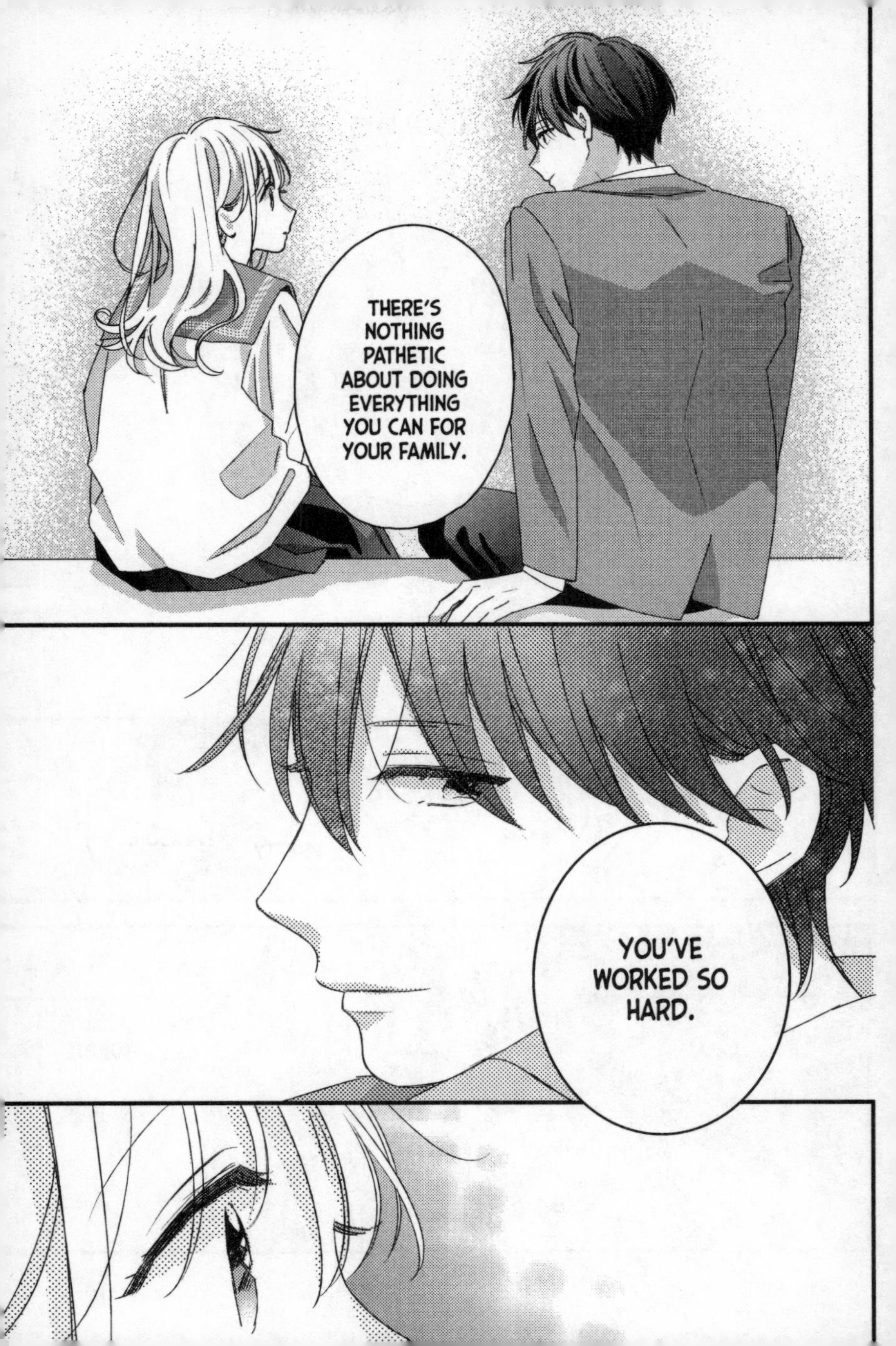
THERE'S NOTHING PATHETIC ABOUT DOING EVERYTHING YOU CAN FOR YOUR FAMILY.
YOU'VE WORKED SO HARD.

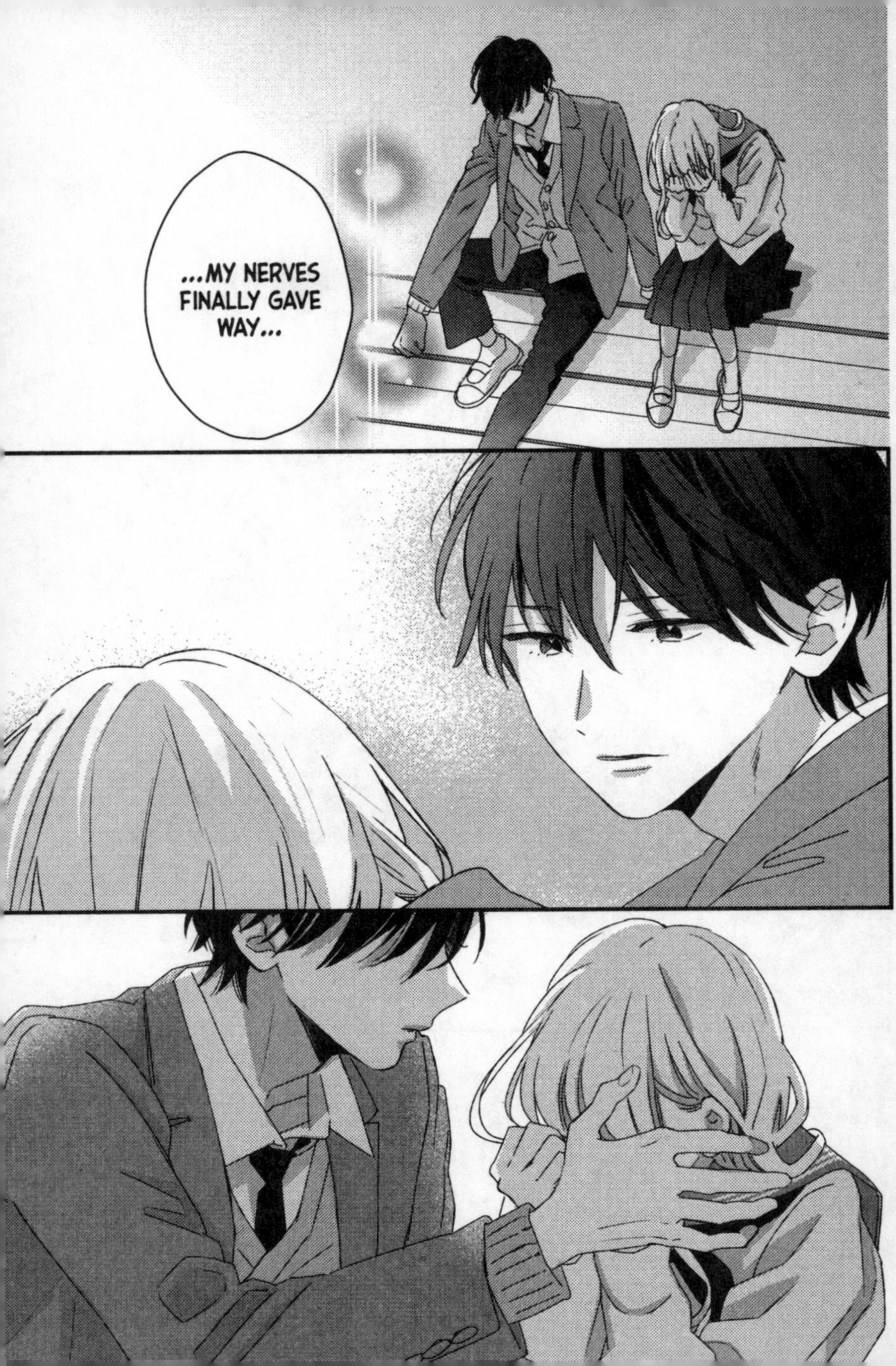
...MY NERVES FINALLY GAVE WAY...

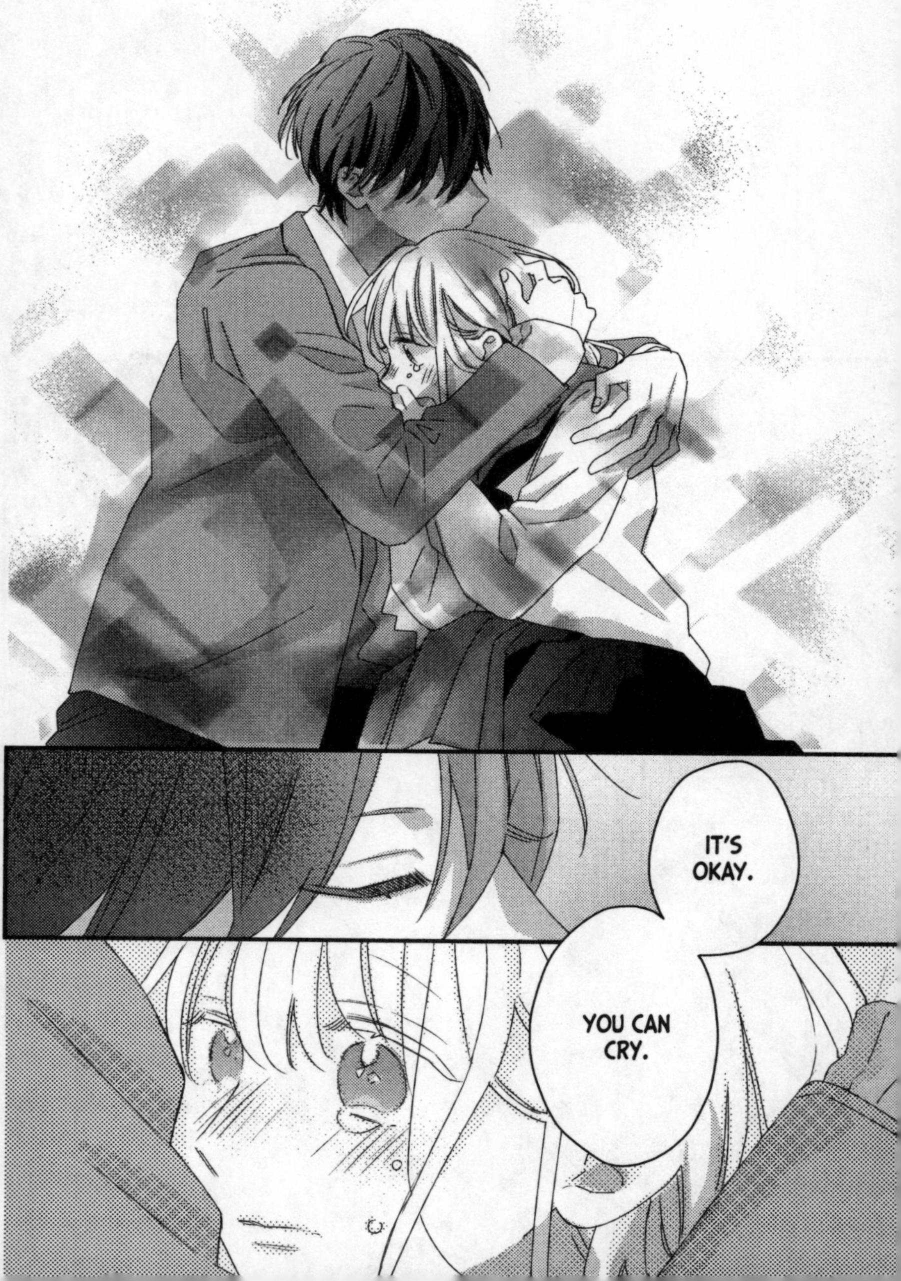
IT'S OKAY.
YOU CAN CRY.

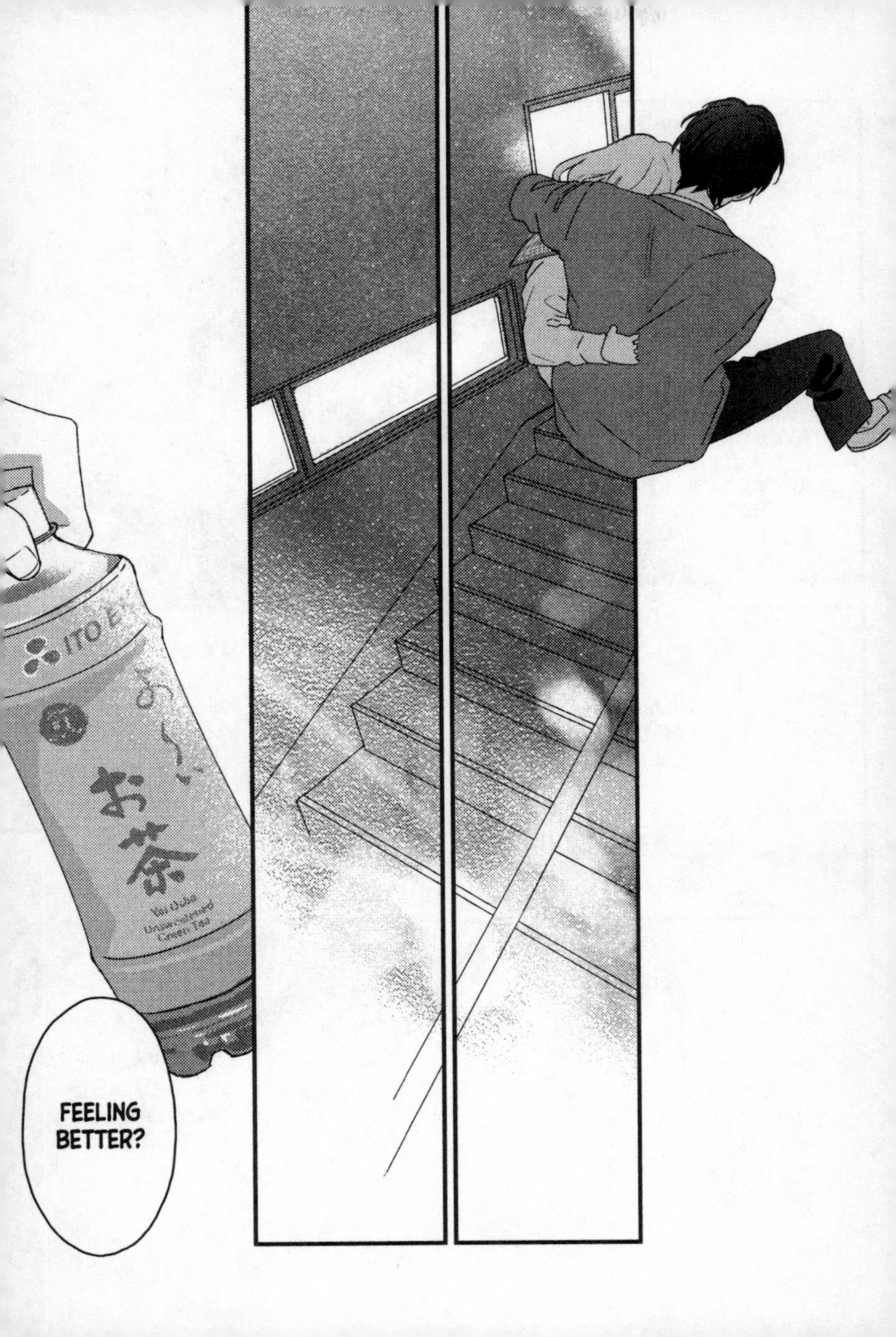
FEELING BETTER?

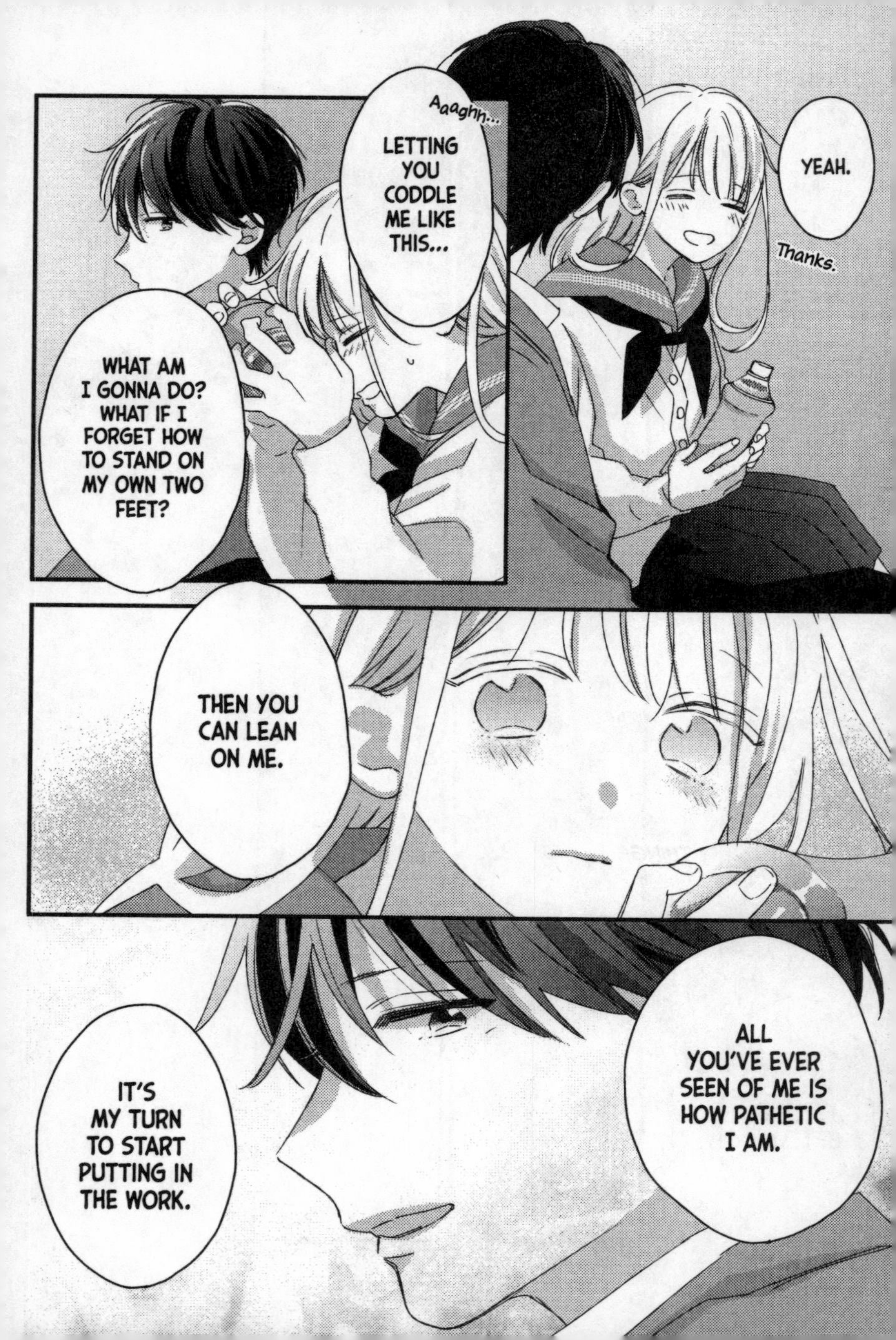
YEAH.
Thanks.
Aaaghn...
LETTING YOU CODDLE ME LIKE THIS...
WHAT AM I GONNA DO? WHAT IF I FORGET HOW TO STAND ON MY OWN TWO FEET?
THEN YOU CAN LEAN ON ME.
ALL YOU'VE EVER SEEN OF ME IS HOW PATHETIC I AM.
IT'S MY TURN TO START PUTTING IN THE WORK.

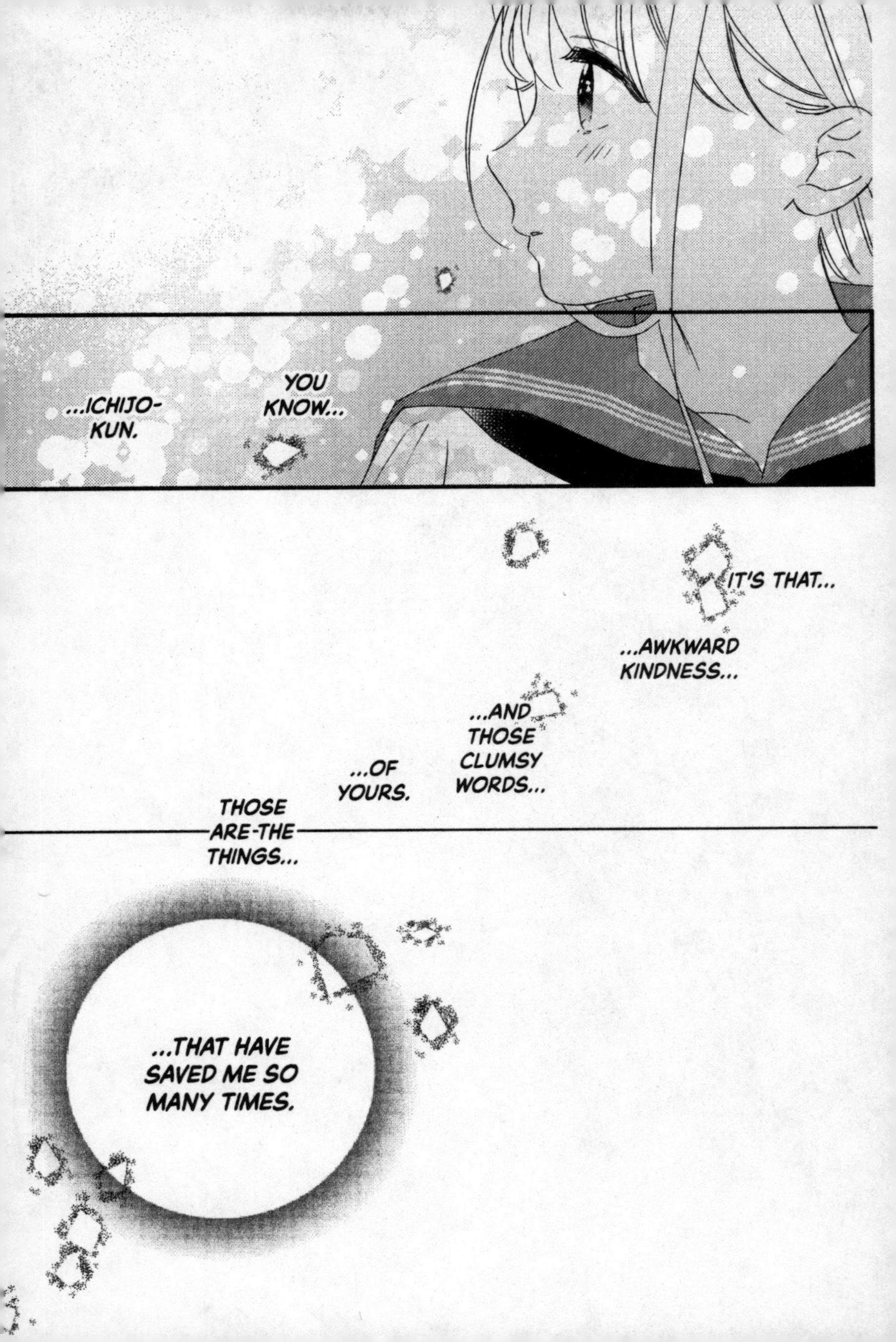
YOU KNOW...
...ICHIJO-KUN.
IT'S THAT...
...AWKWARD KINDNESS...
...AND THOSE CLUMSY WORDS...
...OF YOURS.
THOSE ARE THE THINGS...
...THAT HAVE SAVED ME SO MANY TIMES.

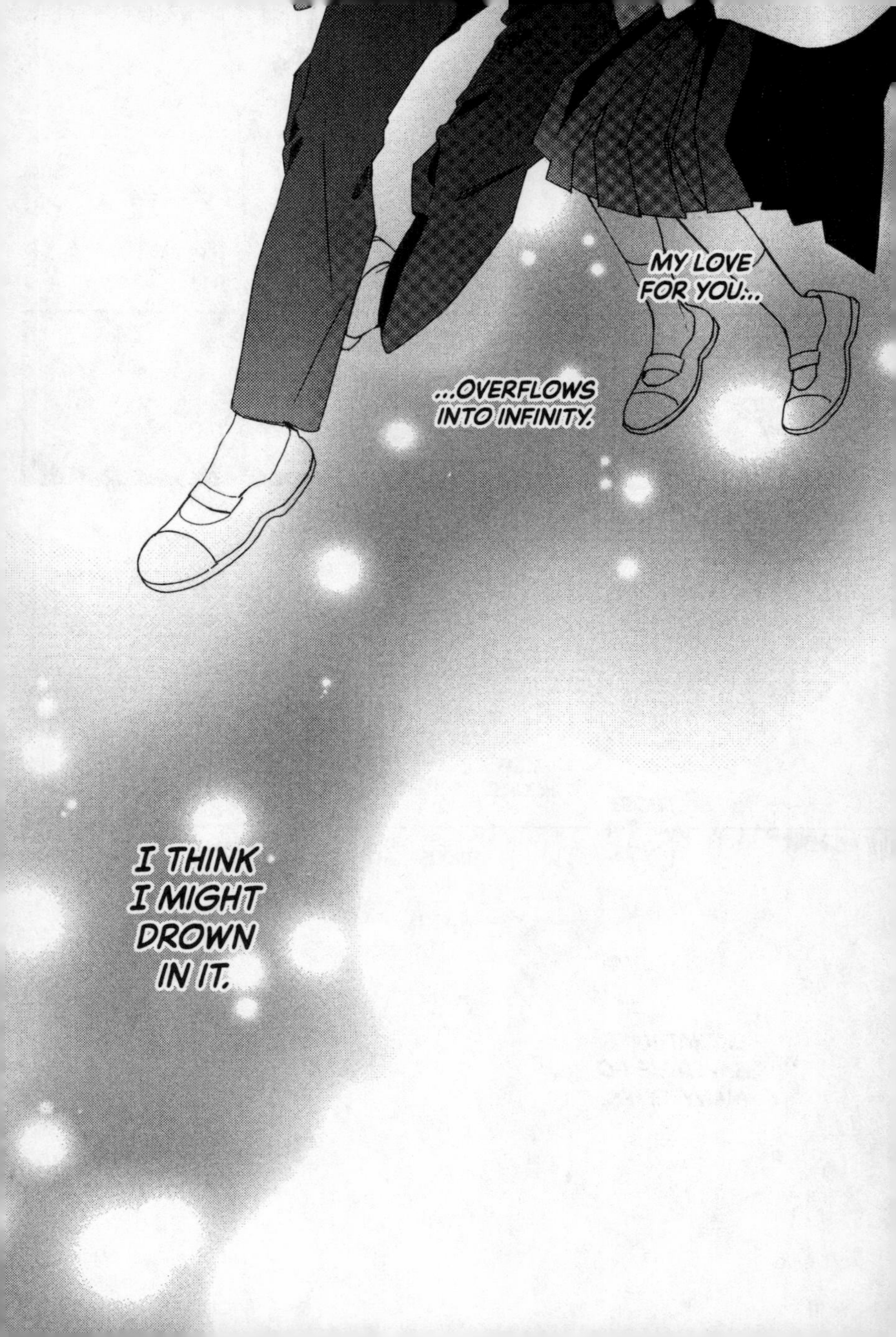
MY LOVE FOR YOU...
...OVERFLOWS INTO INFINITY.
I THINK I MIGHT DROWN IN IT.

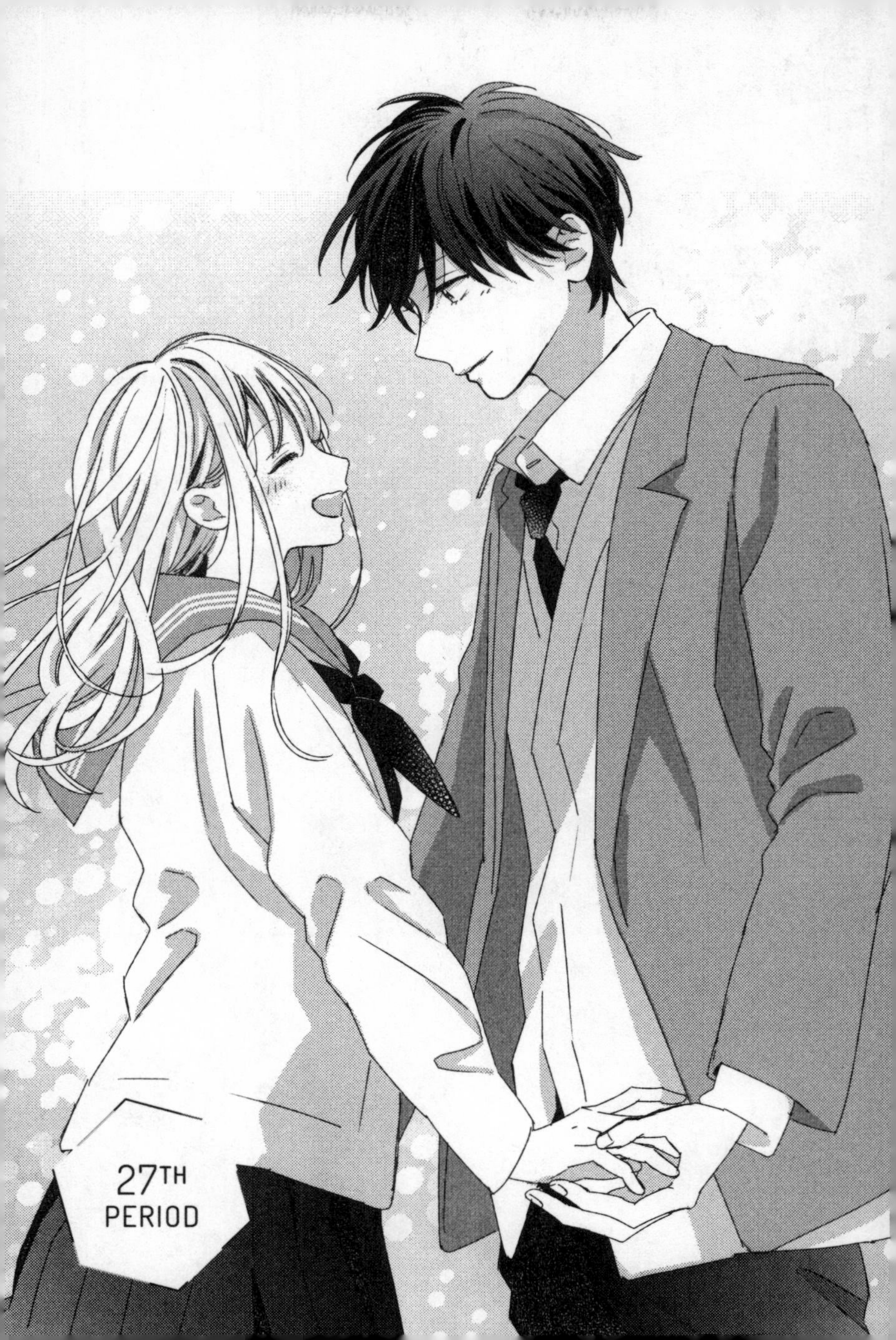
27TH
PERIOD

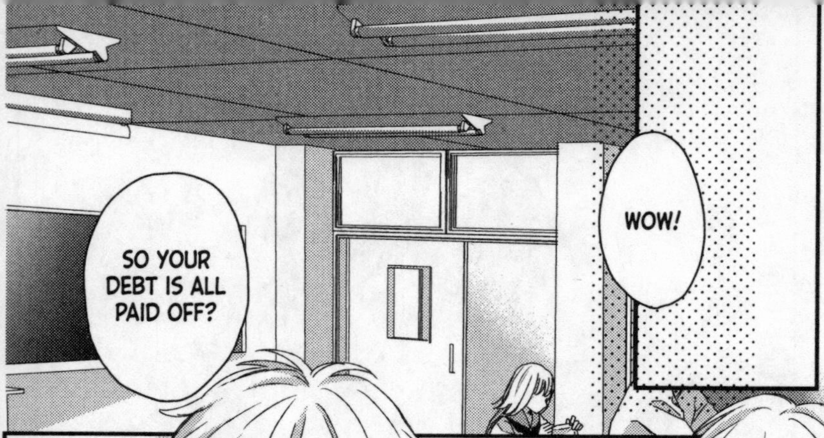
WOW!
SO YOUR DEBT IS ALL PAID OFF?
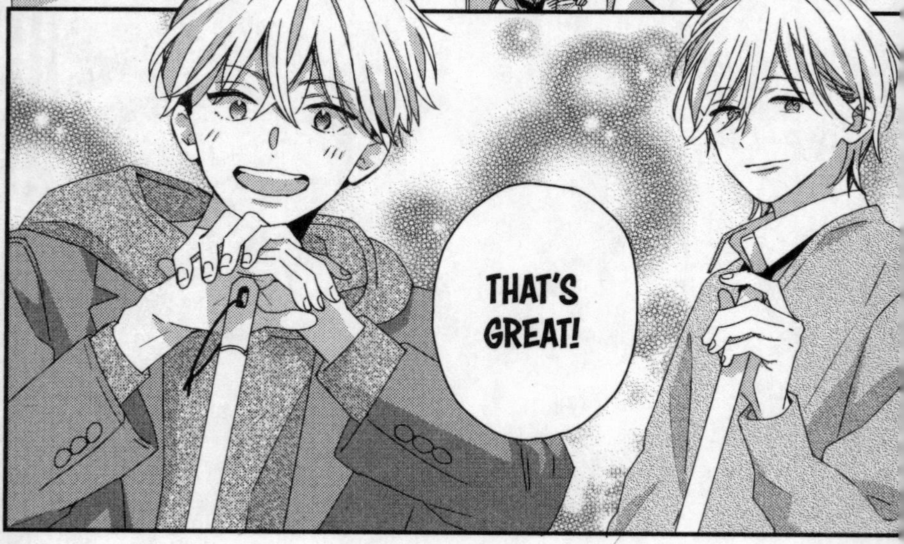
THAT'S GREAT!
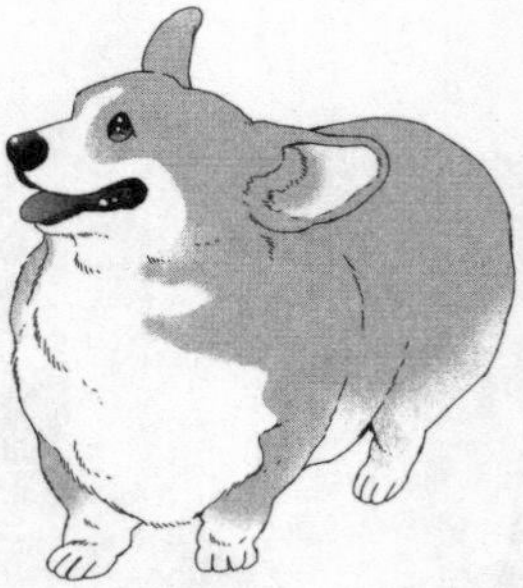

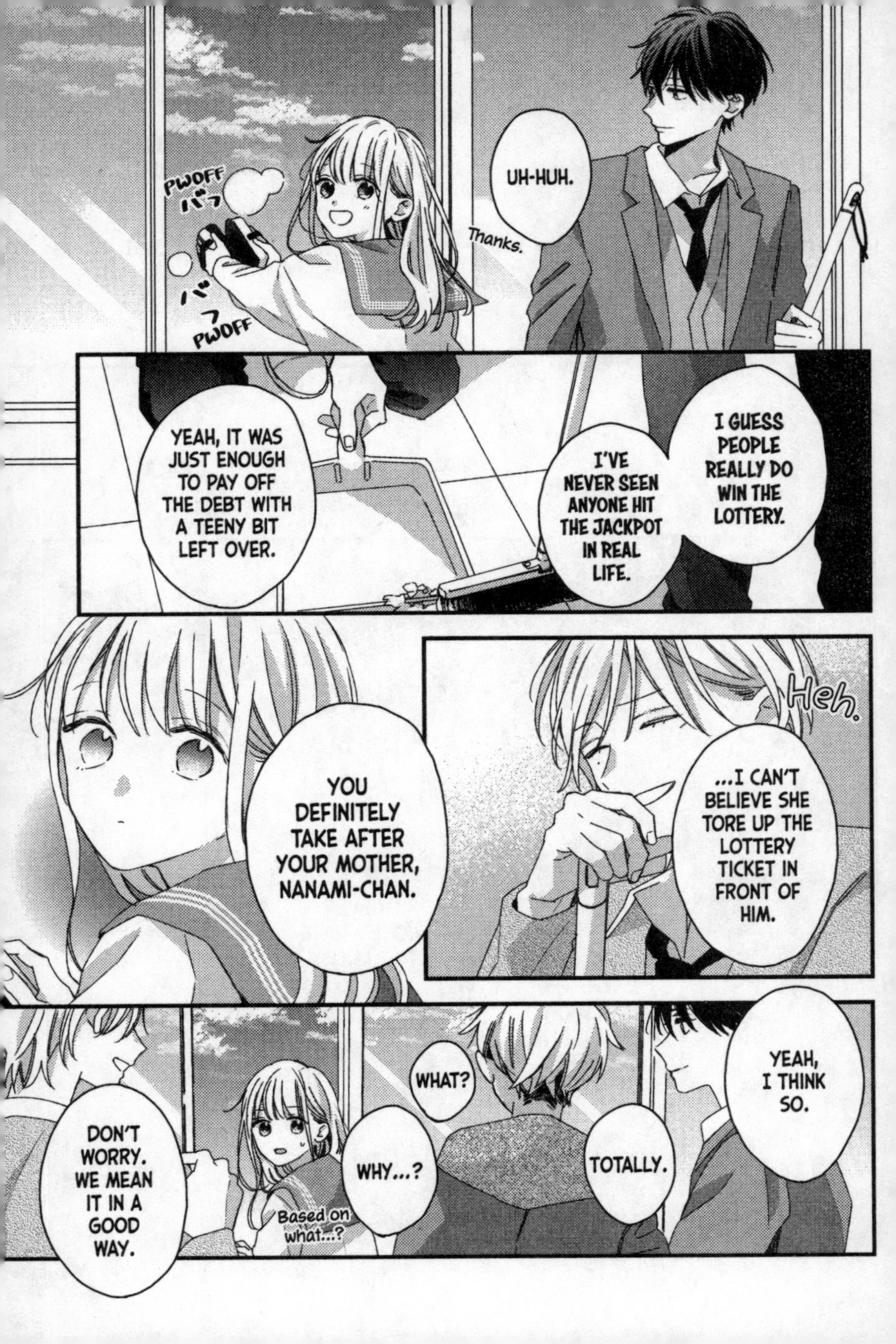
UH-HUH.
Thanks.
PWOFF
バフ
バフ
PWOFF
I GUESS PEOPLE REALLY DO WIN THE LOTTERY.
I'VE NEVER SEEN ANYONE HIT THE JACKPOT IN REAL LIFE.
YEAH, IT WAS JUST ENOUGH TO PAY OFF THE DEBT WITH A TEENY BIT LEFT OVER.
Heh.
...I CAN'T BELIEVE SHE TORE UP THE LOTTERY TICKET IN FRONT OF HIM.
YOU DEFINITELY TAKE AFTER YOUR MOTHER, NANAMI-CHAN.
YEAH, I THINK SO.
TOTALLY.
WHAT?
WHY...?
Based on what...?
DON'T WORRY. WE MEAN IT IN A GOOD WAY.

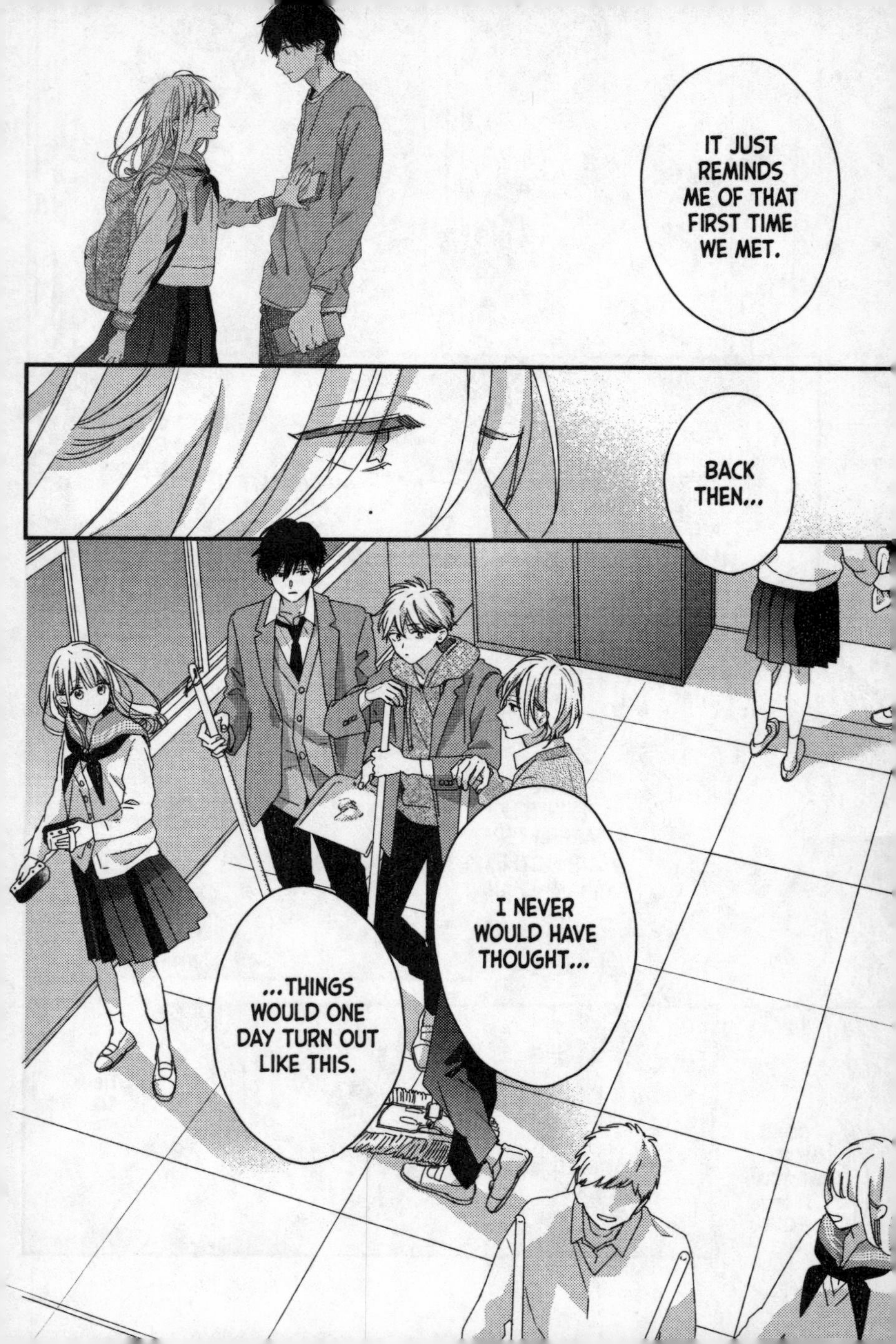
IT JUST REMINDS ME OF THAT FIRST TIME WE MET.
BACK THEN...
I NEVER WOULD HAVE THOUGHT...
...THINGS WOULD ONE DAY TURN OUT LIKE THIS.

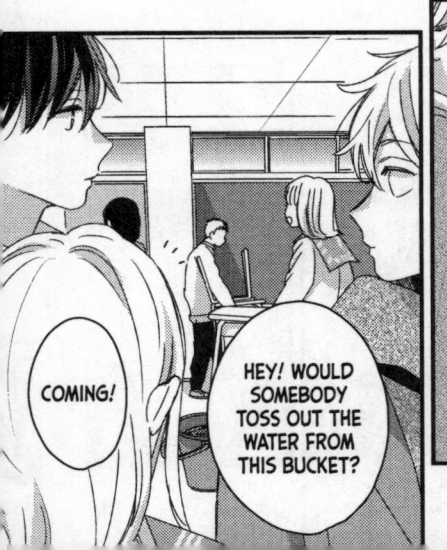

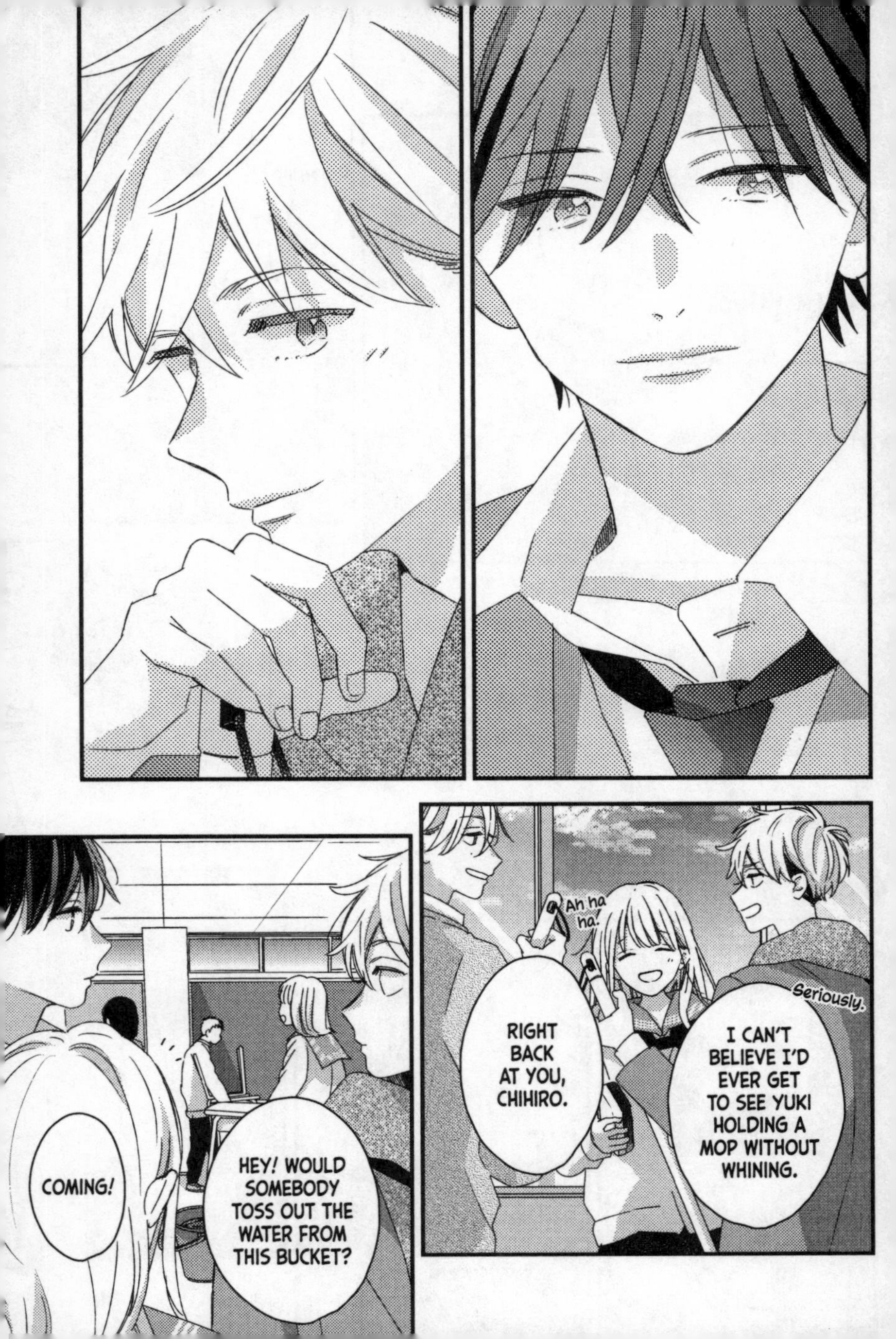
Seriously.
I CAN'T BELIEVE I'D EVER GET TO SEE YUKI HOLDING A MOP WITHOUT WHINING.
Ah ha ha.
RIGHT BACK AT YOU, CHIHIRO.
HEY! WOULD SOMEBODY TOSS OUT THE WATER FROM THIS BUCKET?
COMING!

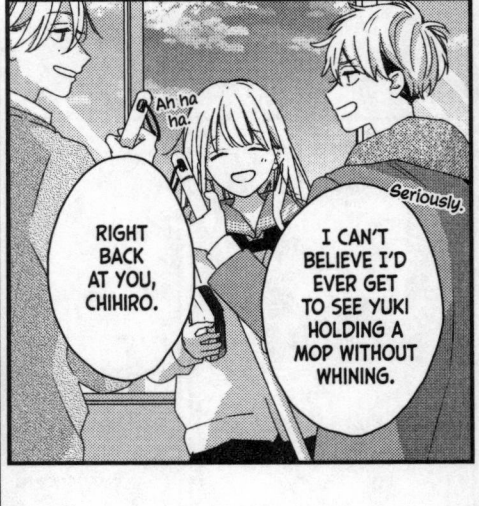

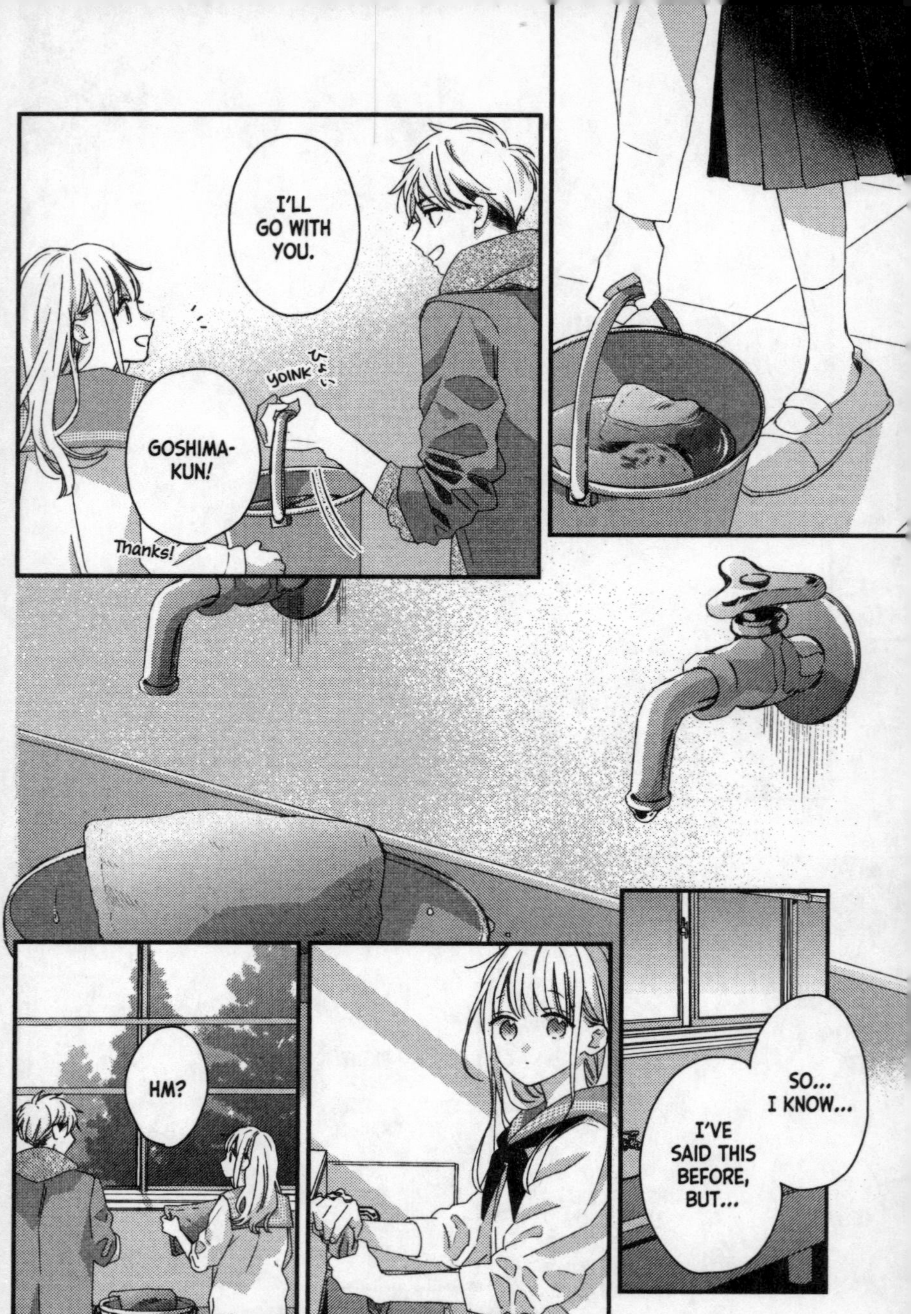
I'LL GO WITH YOU.
YOINK
GOSHIMA-KUN!
Thanks!
SO... I KNOW...
I'VE SAID THIS BEFORE, BUT...
HM?

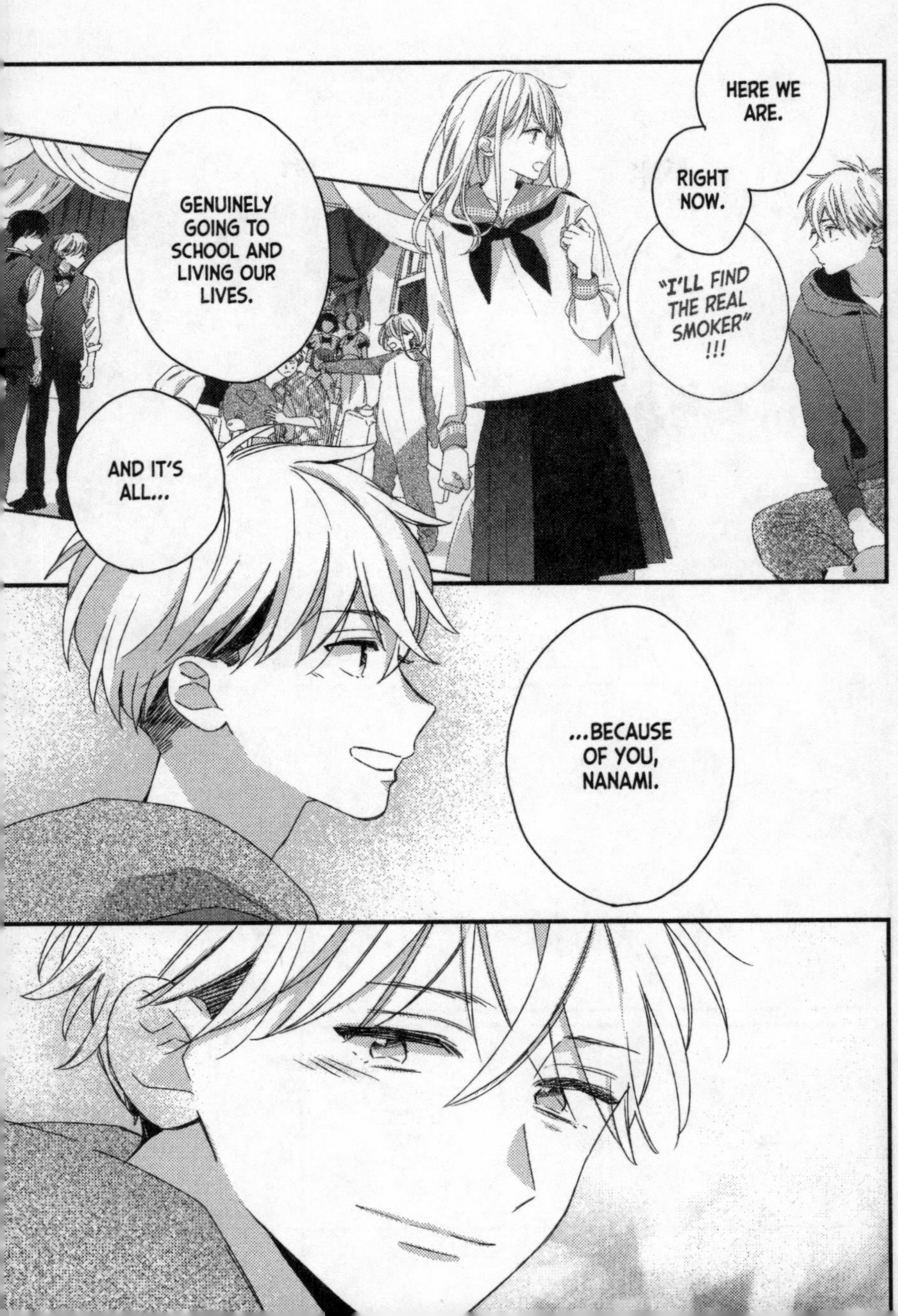
HERE WE ARE.
RIGHT NOW.
"I'LL FIND THE REAL SMOKER" !!!
GENUINELY GOING TO SCHOOL AND LIVING OUR LIVES.
AND IT'S ALL...
...BECAUSE OF YOU, NANAMI.

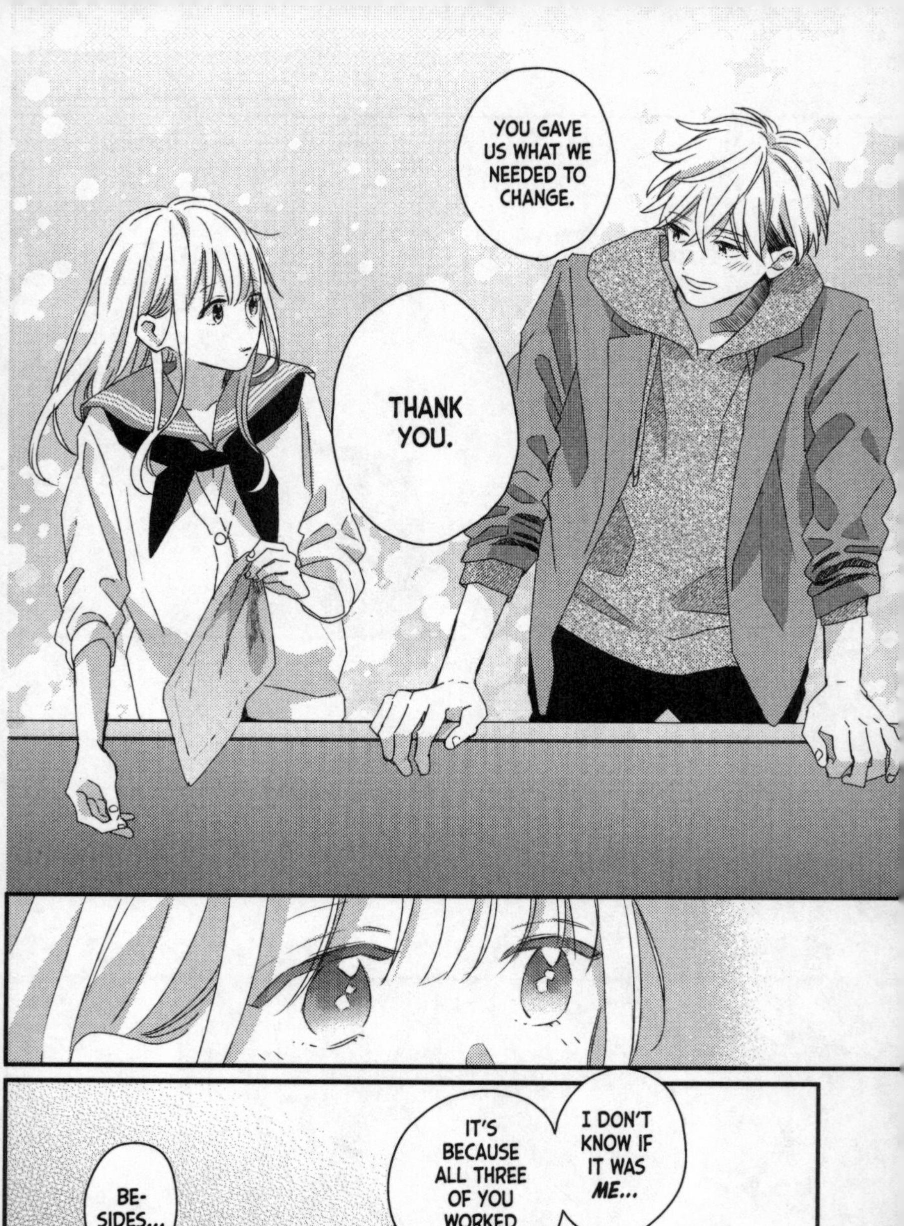
YOU GAVE US WHAT WE NEEDED TO CHANGE.
THANK YOU.
I DON'T KNOW IF IT WAS *ME*...
IT'S BECAUSE ALL THREE OF YOU WORKED FOR IT.
BE-SIDES...

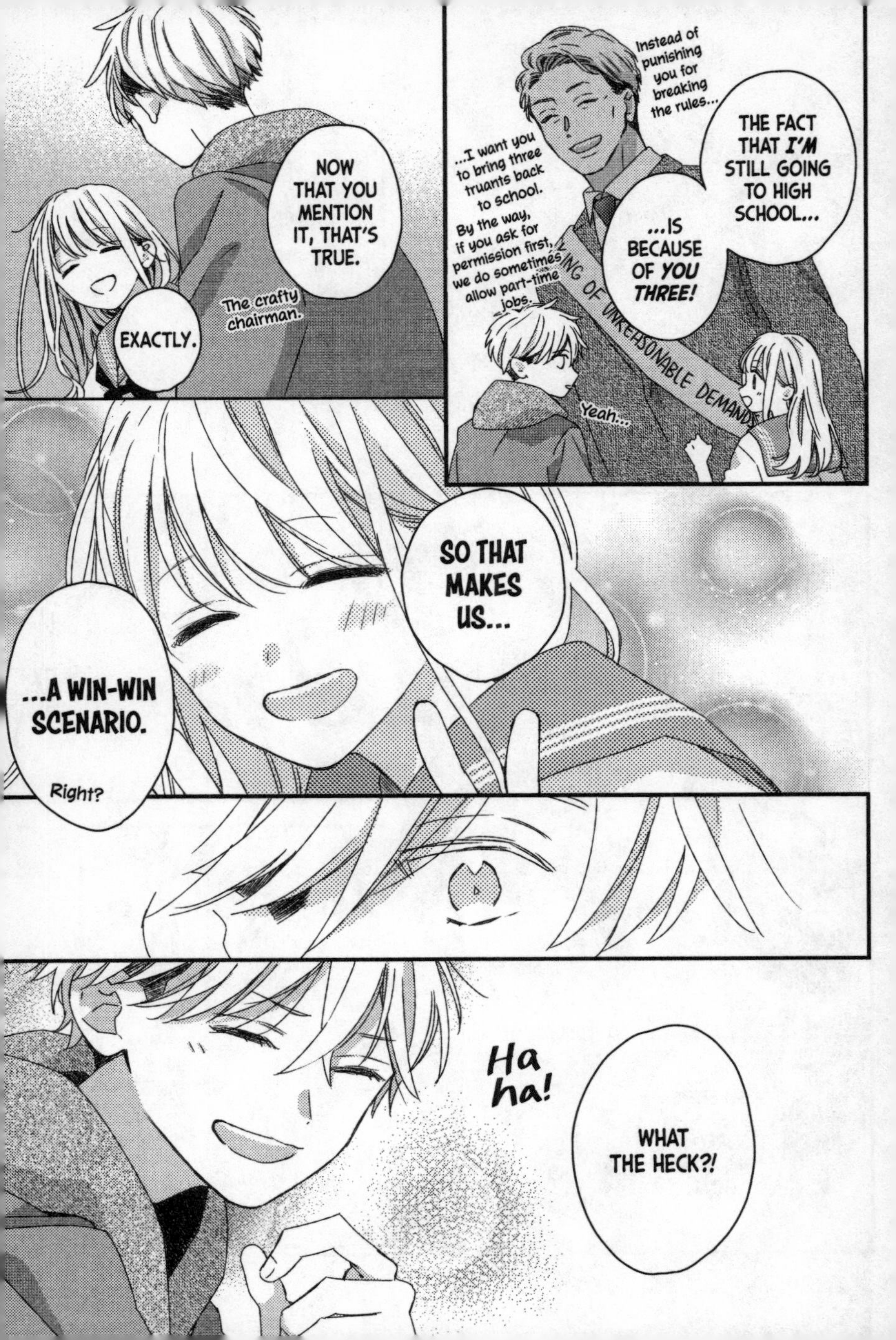
Instead of punishing you for breaking the rules...
THE FACT THAT I'M STILL GOING TO HIGH SCHOOL...
...IS BECAUSE OF YOU THREE!
...I want you to bring three truants back to school. By the way, if you ask for permission first, we do sometimes allow part-time jobs.
Yeah...
NOW THAT YOU MENTION IT, THAT'S TRUE.
The crafty chairman.
EXACTLY.
SO THAT MAKES US...
...A WIN-WIN SCENARIO.
Right?
Ha ha!
WHAT THE HECK?!

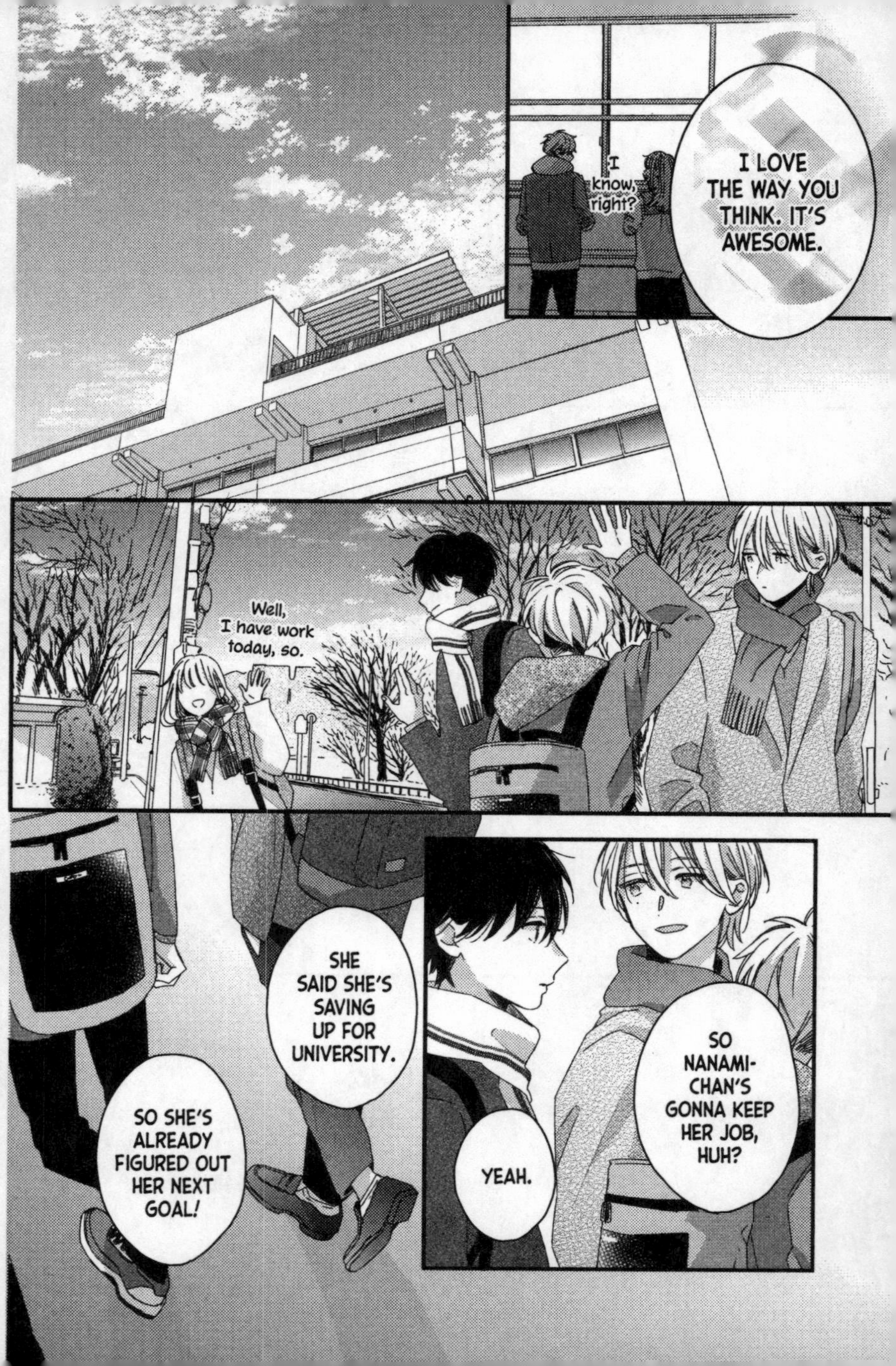
I LOVE THE WAY YOU THINK. IT'S AWESOME.
I know, right?
Well, I have work today, so.
SO NANAMI-CHAN'S GONNA KEEP HER JOB, HUH?
YEAH.
SHE SAID SHE'S SAVING UP FOR UNIVERSITY.
SO SHE'S ALREADY FIGURED OUT HER NEXT GOAL!

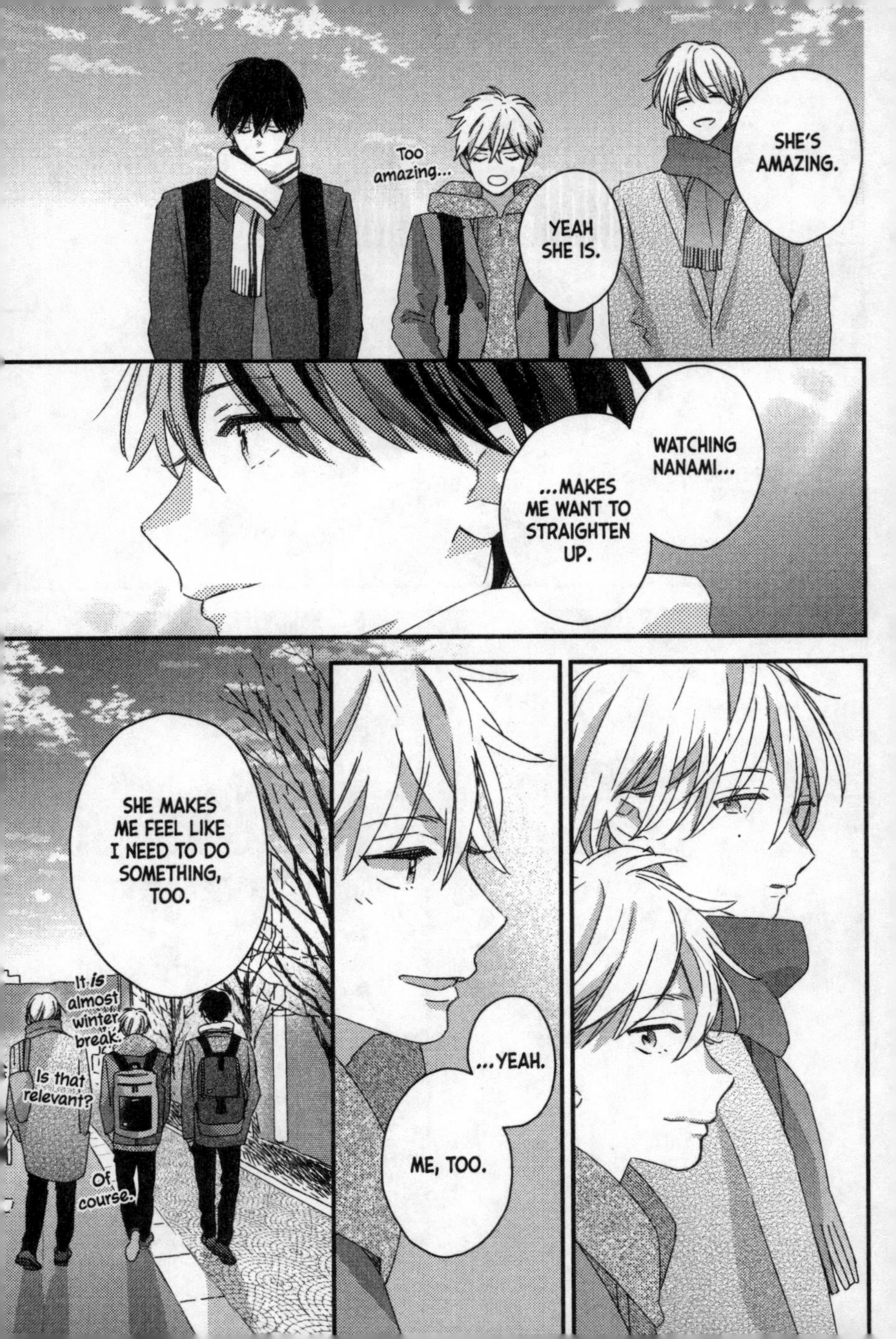
SHE'S AMAZING.
YEAH SHE IS.
Too amazing...
WATCHING NANAMI...
...MAKES ME WANT TO STRAIGHTEN UP.
...YEAH.
ME, TOO.
SHE MAKES ME FEEL LIKE I NEED TO DO SOMETHING, TOO.
It *is* almost winter break.
Is that relevant?
Of course.

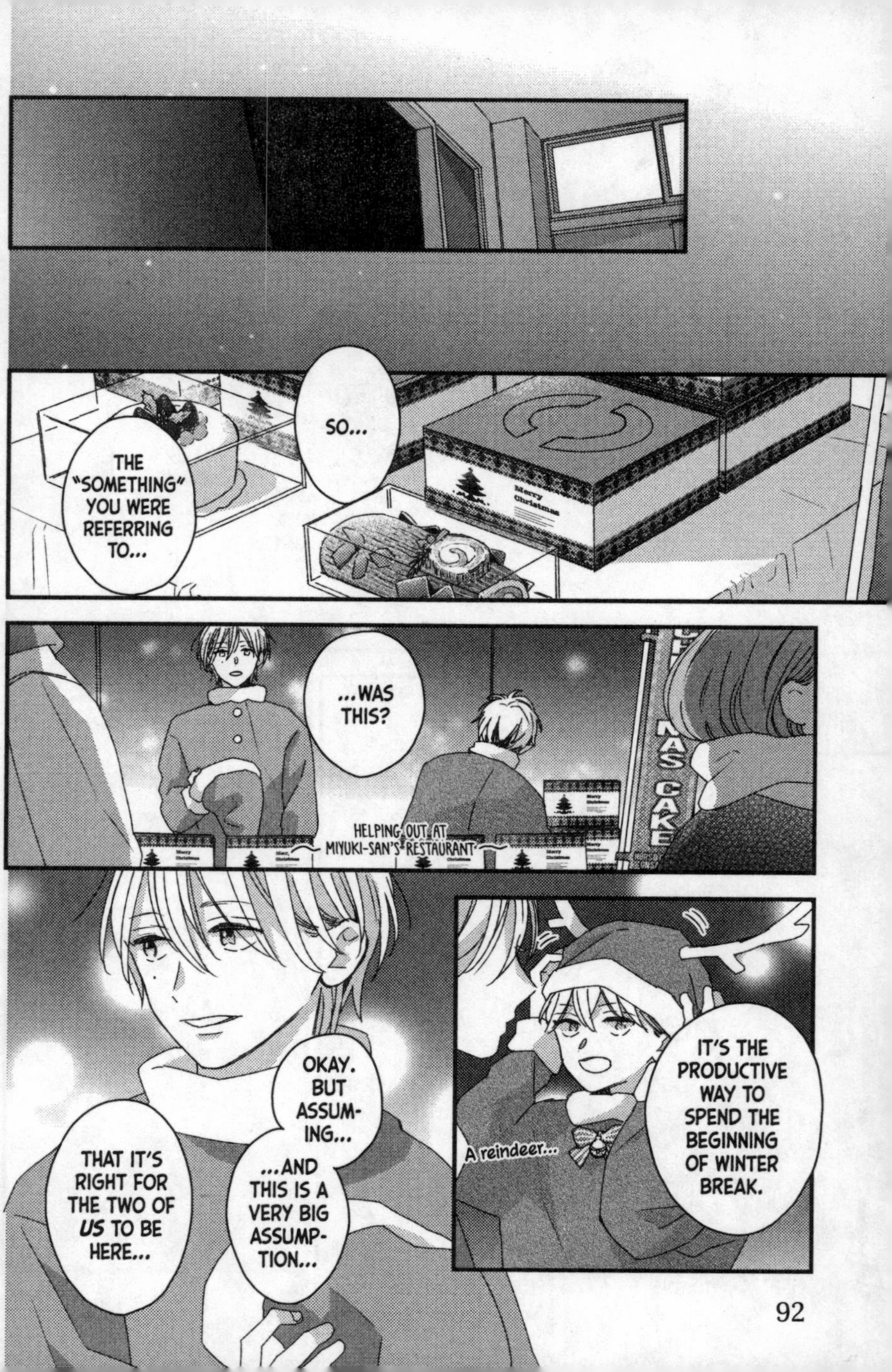
SO...
THE "SOMETHING" YOU WERE REFERRING TO...
Merry Christmas
...WAS THIS?
~ HELPING OUT AT MIYUKI-SAN'S RESTAURANT ~
IT'S THE PRODUCTIVE WAY TO SPEND THE BEGINNING OF WINTER BREAK.
A reindeer...
OKAY. BUT ASSUMING...
...AND THIS IS A VERY BIG ASSUMPTION...
THAT IT'S RIGHT FOR THE TWO OF *US* TO BE HERE...

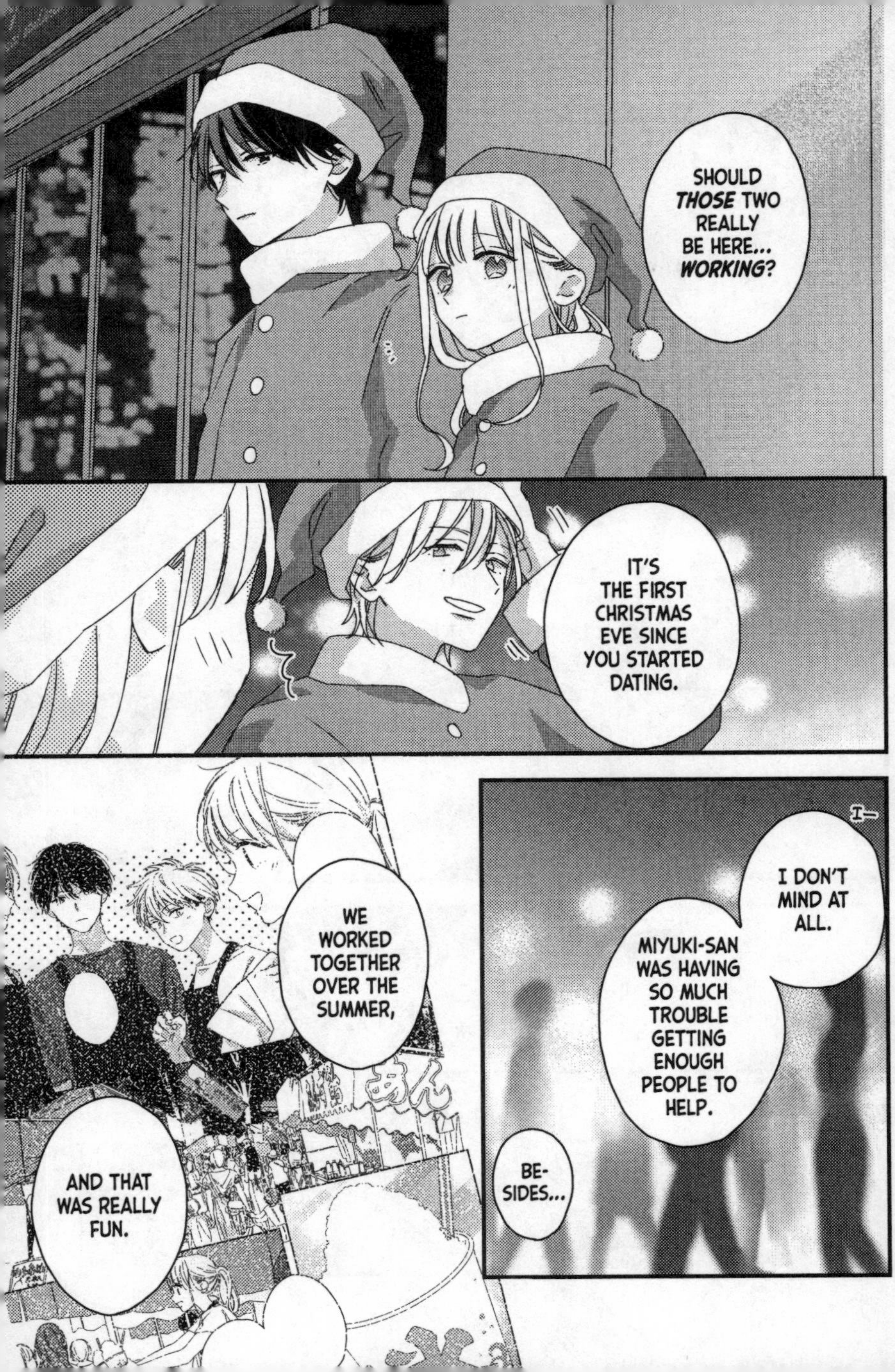
SHOULD *THOSE* TWO REALLY BE HERE... *WORKING*?
IT'S THE FIRST CHRISTMAS EVE SINCE YOU STARTED DATING.
I—
I DON'T MIND AT ALL.
MIYUKI-SAN WAS HAVING SO MUCH TROUBLE GETTING ENOUGH PEOPLE TO HELP.
BE-SIDES...
WE WORKED TOGETHER OVER THE SUMMER,
AND THAT WAS REALLY FUN.

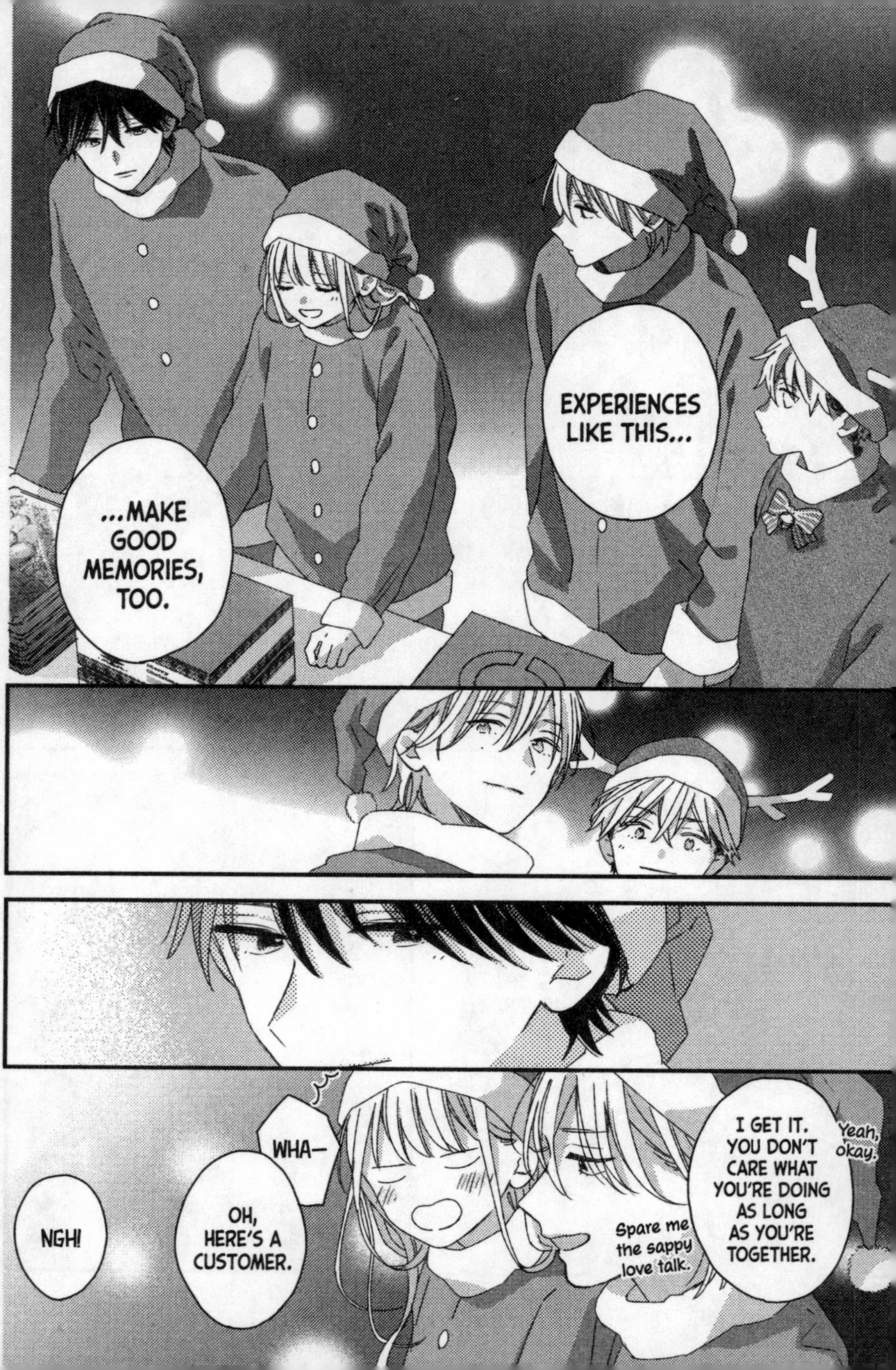
EXPERIENCES LIKE THIS...
...MAKE GOOD MEMORIES, TOO.
Yeah, okay.
I GET IT. YOU DON'T CARE WHAT YOU'RE DOING AS LONG AS YOU'RE TOGETHER.
Spare me the sappy love talk.
WHA—
OH, HERE'S A CUSTOMER.
NGH!

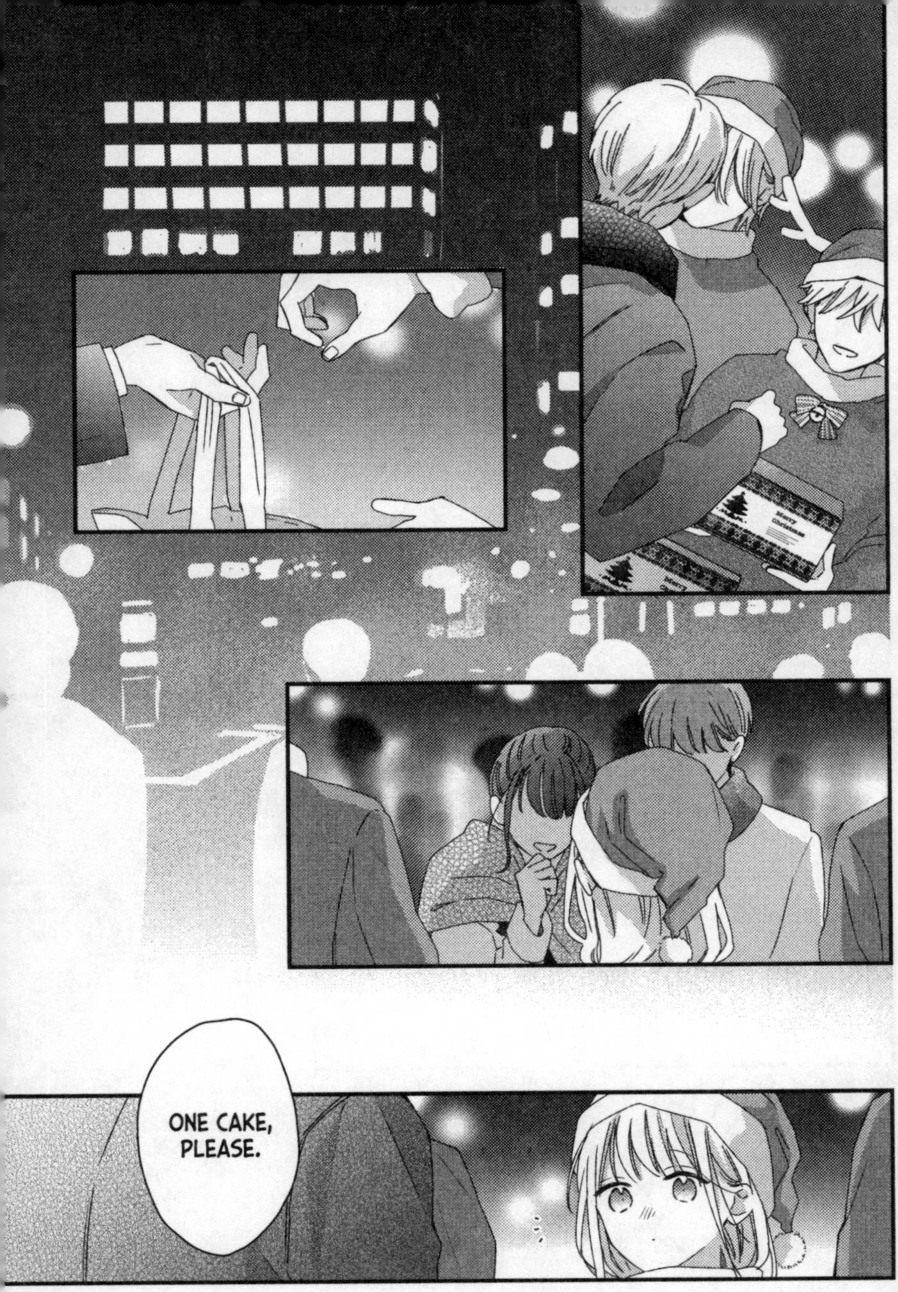
ONE CAKE, PLEASE.

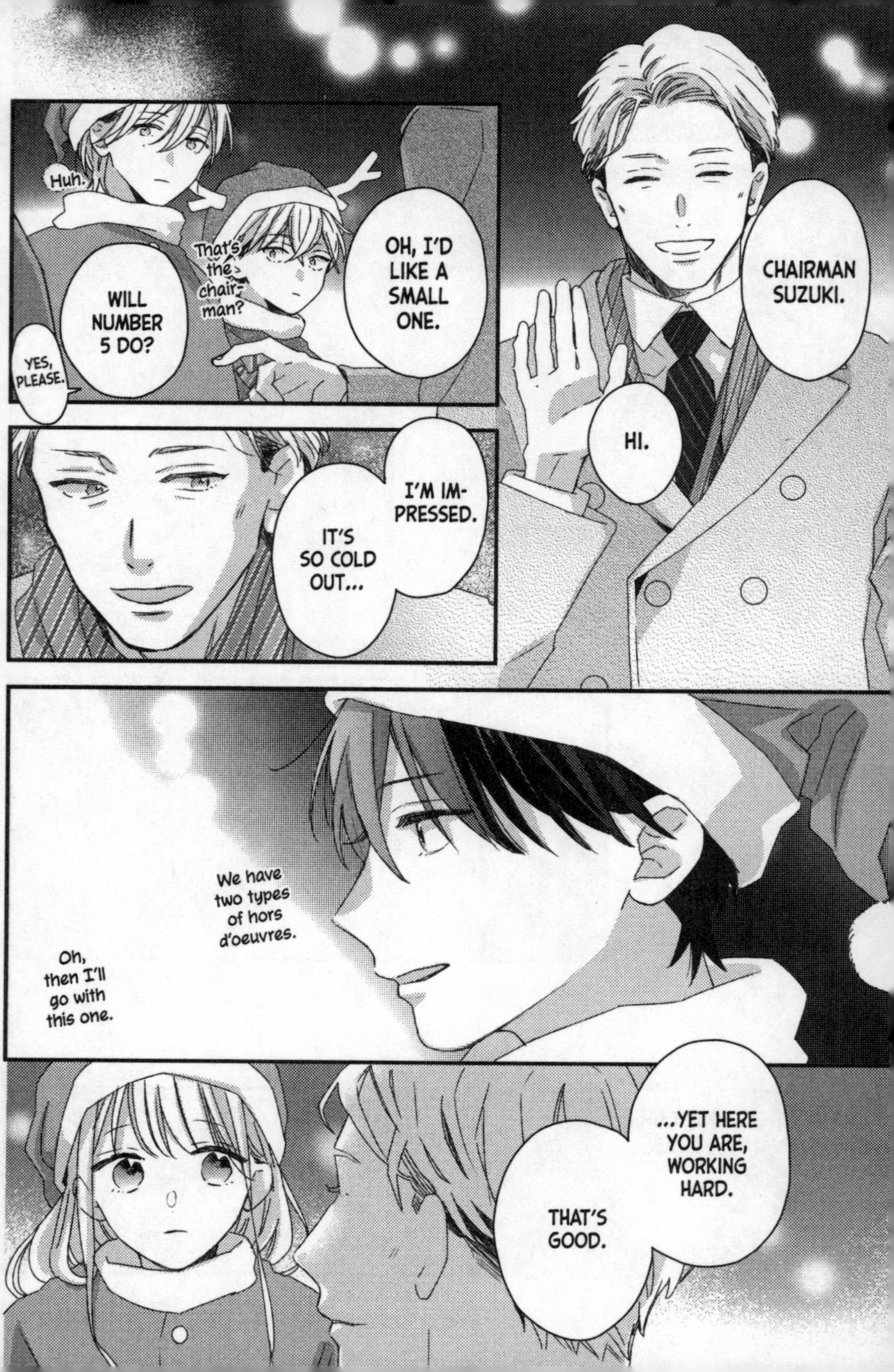
CHAIRMAN SUZUKI.
HI.
OH, I'D LIKE A SMALL ONE.
That's the chair-man?
Huh.
WILL NUMBER 5 DO?
YES, PLEASE.
I'M IM-PRESSED.
IT'S SO COLD OUT...
We have two types of hors d'oeuvres.
Oh, then I'll go with this one.
...YET HERE YOU ARE, WORKING HARD.
THAT'S GOOD.

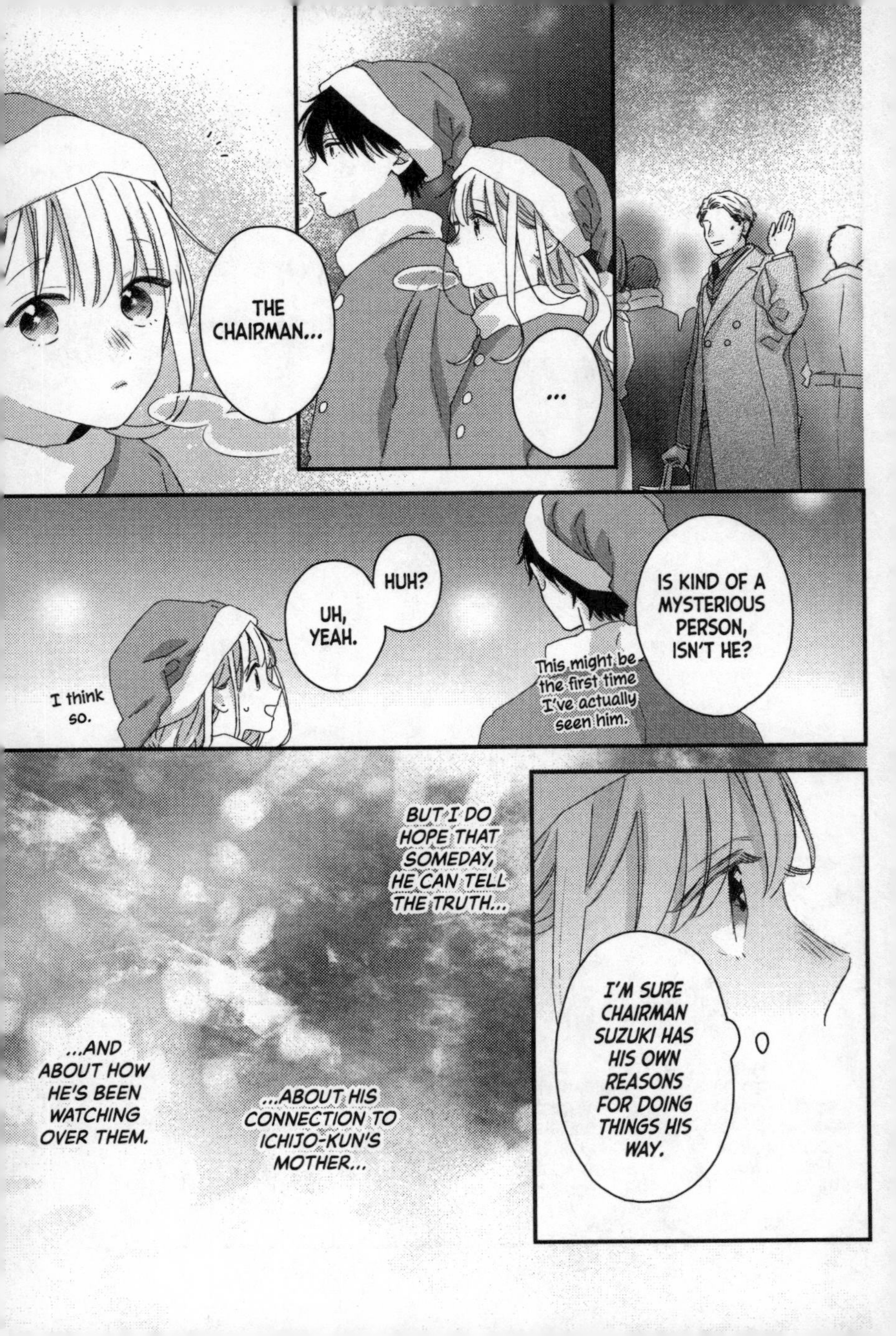
...
THE CHAIRMAN...
IS KIND OF A MYSTERIOUS PERSON, ISN'T HE?
This might be the first time I've actually seen him.
HUH?
UH, YEAH.
I think so.
I'M SURE CHAIRMAN SUZUKI HAS HIS OWN REASONS FOR DOING THINGS HIS WAY.
BUT I DO HOPE THAT SOMEDAY, HE CAN TELL THE TRUTH...
...ABOUT HIS CONNECTION TO ICHIJO-KUN'S MOTHER...
...AND ABOUT HOW HE'S BEEN WATCHING OVER THEM.

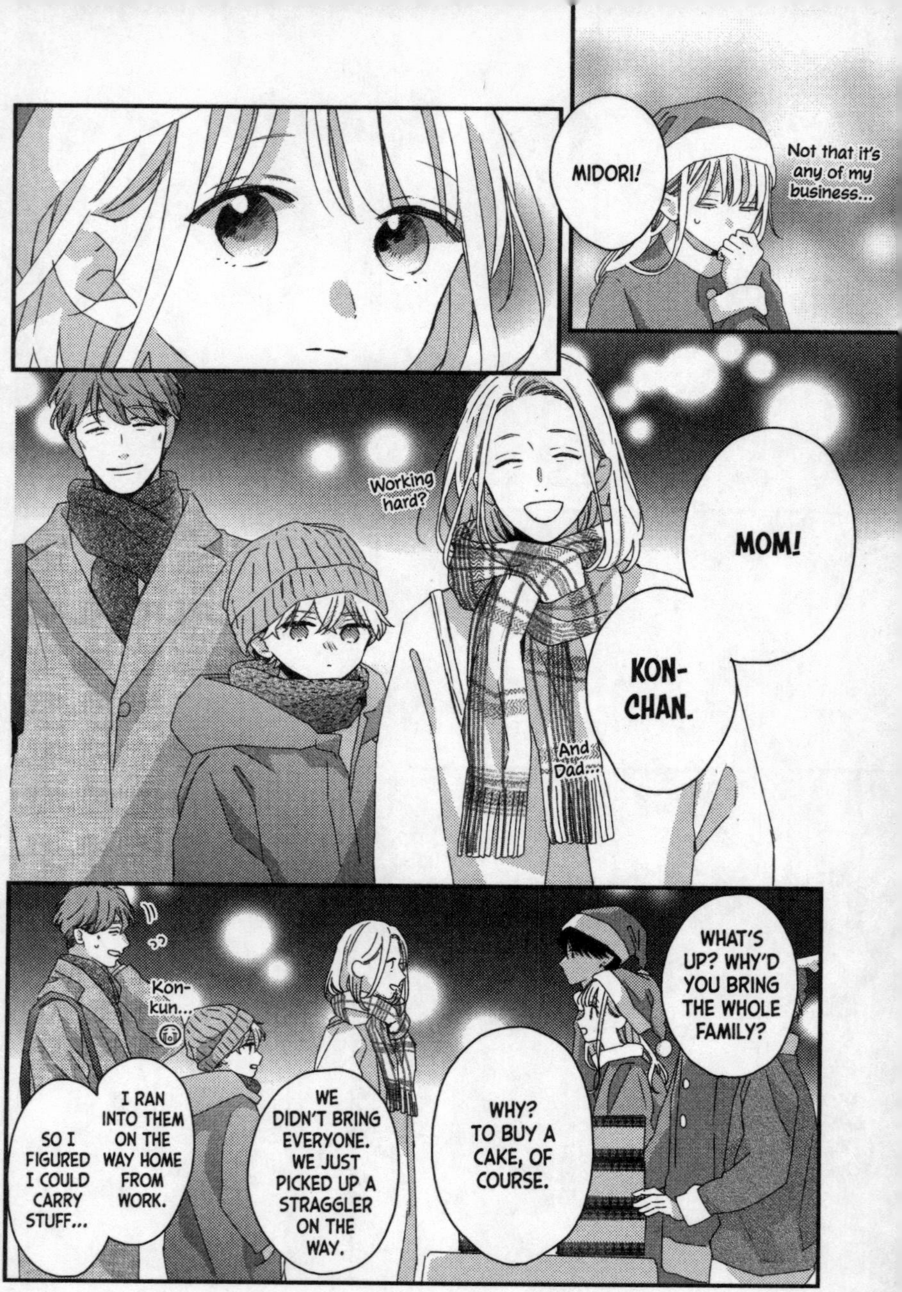
MIDORI!
Not that it's any of my business...
MOM!
KON-CHAN.
And Dad...
Working hard?
WHAT'S UP? WHY'D YOU BRING THE WHOLE FAMILY?
WHY? TO BUY A CAKE, OF COURSE.
WE DIDN'T BRING EVERYONE. WE JUST PICKED UP A STRAGGLER ON THE WAY.
Kon-kun...
I RAN INTO THEM ON THE WAY HOME FROM WORK.
SO I FIGURED I COULD CARRY STUFF...

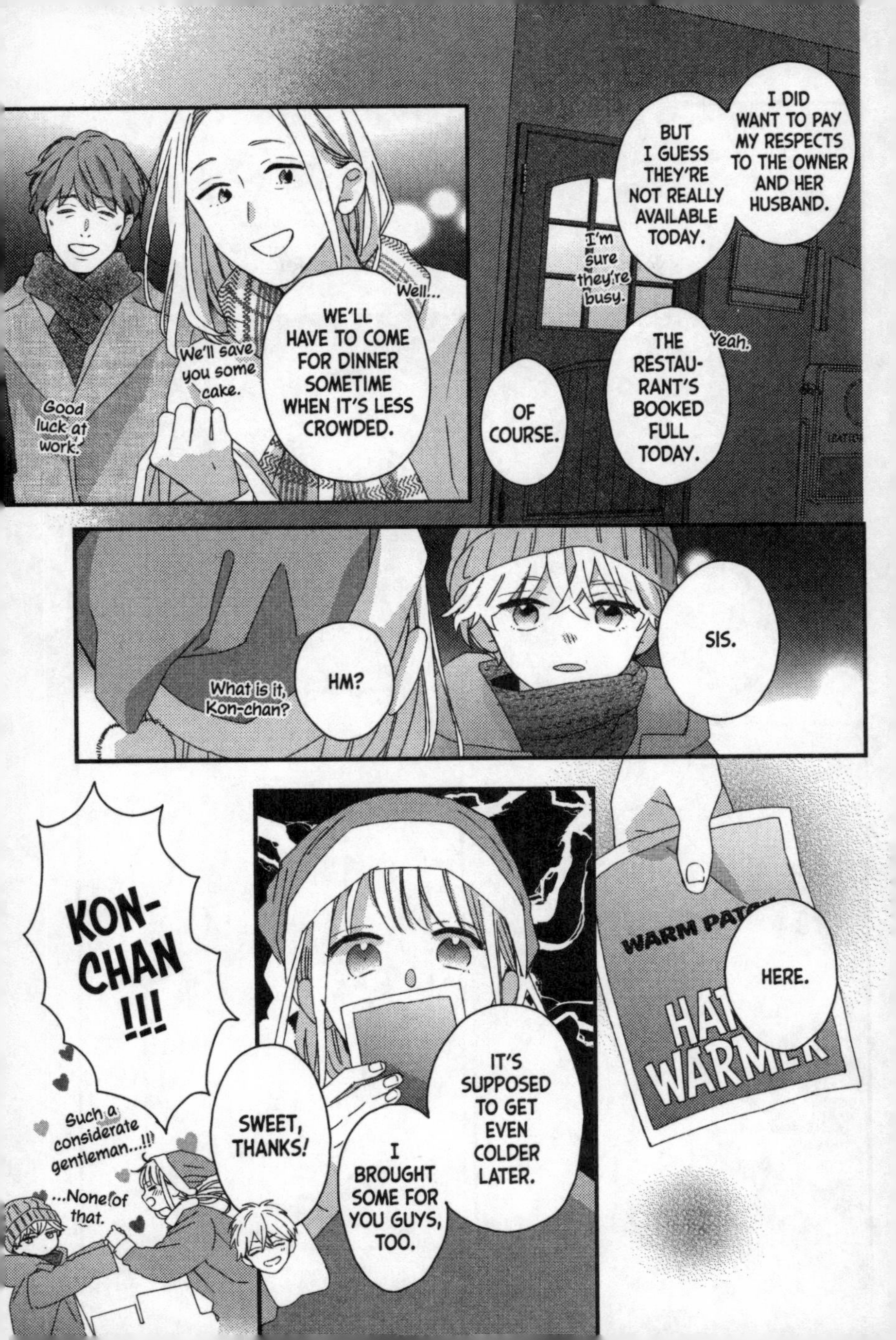
I DID WANT TO PAY MY RESPECTS TO THE OWNER AND HER HUSBAND.
BUT I GUESS THEY'RE NOT REALLY AVAILABLE TODAY.
I'm sure they're busy.
Yeah.
THE RESTAU-RANT'S BOOKED FULL TODAY.
OF COURSE.
Well...
WE'LL HAVE TO COME FOR DINNER SOMETIME WHEN IT'S LESS CROWDED.
We'll save you some cake.
Good luck at work.
SIS.
HM?
What is it, Kon-chan?
HERE.
IT'S SUPPOSED TO GET EVEN COLDER LATER.
I BROUGHT SOME FOR YOU GUYS, TOO.
SWEET, THANKS!
KON-CHAN !!!
Such a considerate gentleman...!!
...None of that.

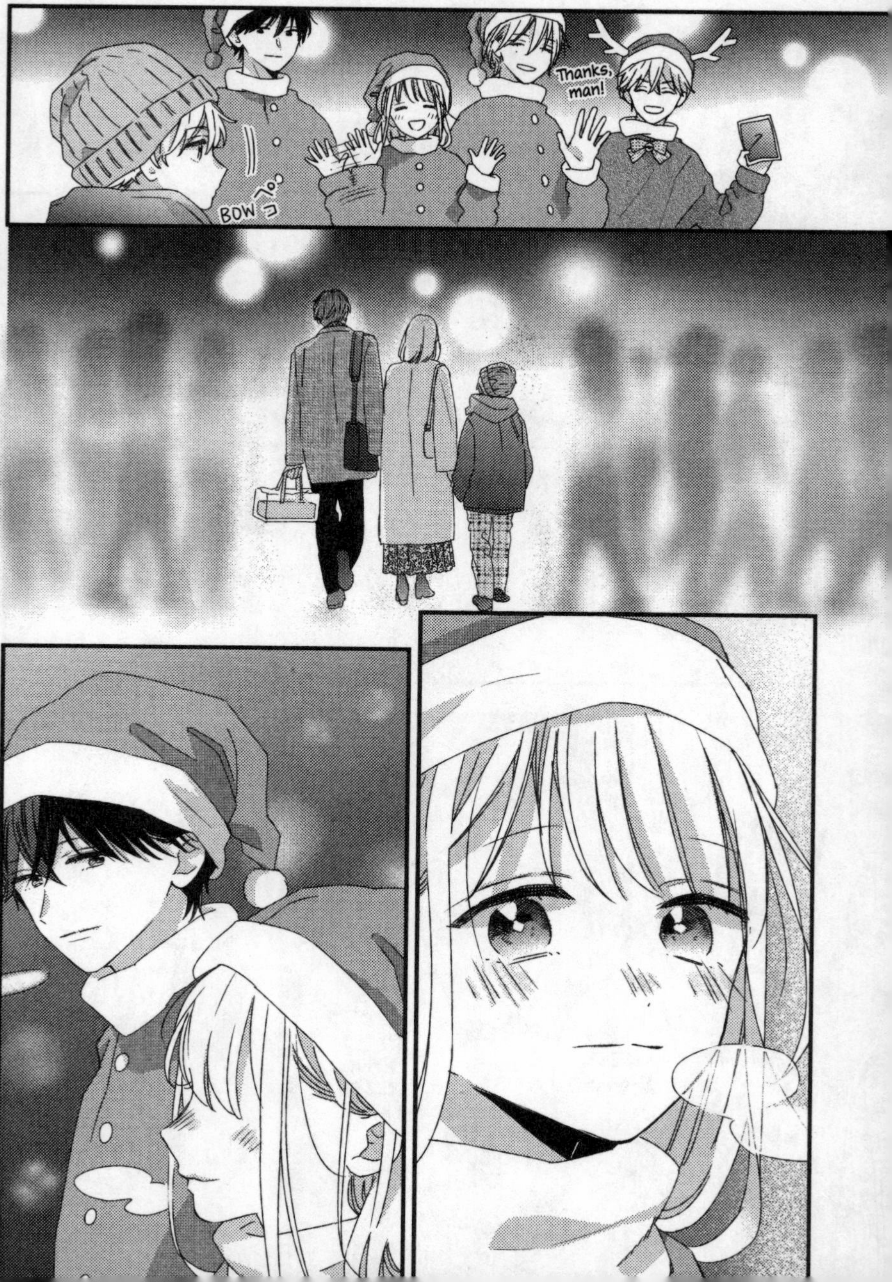
Thanks, man!
BOW ペコ

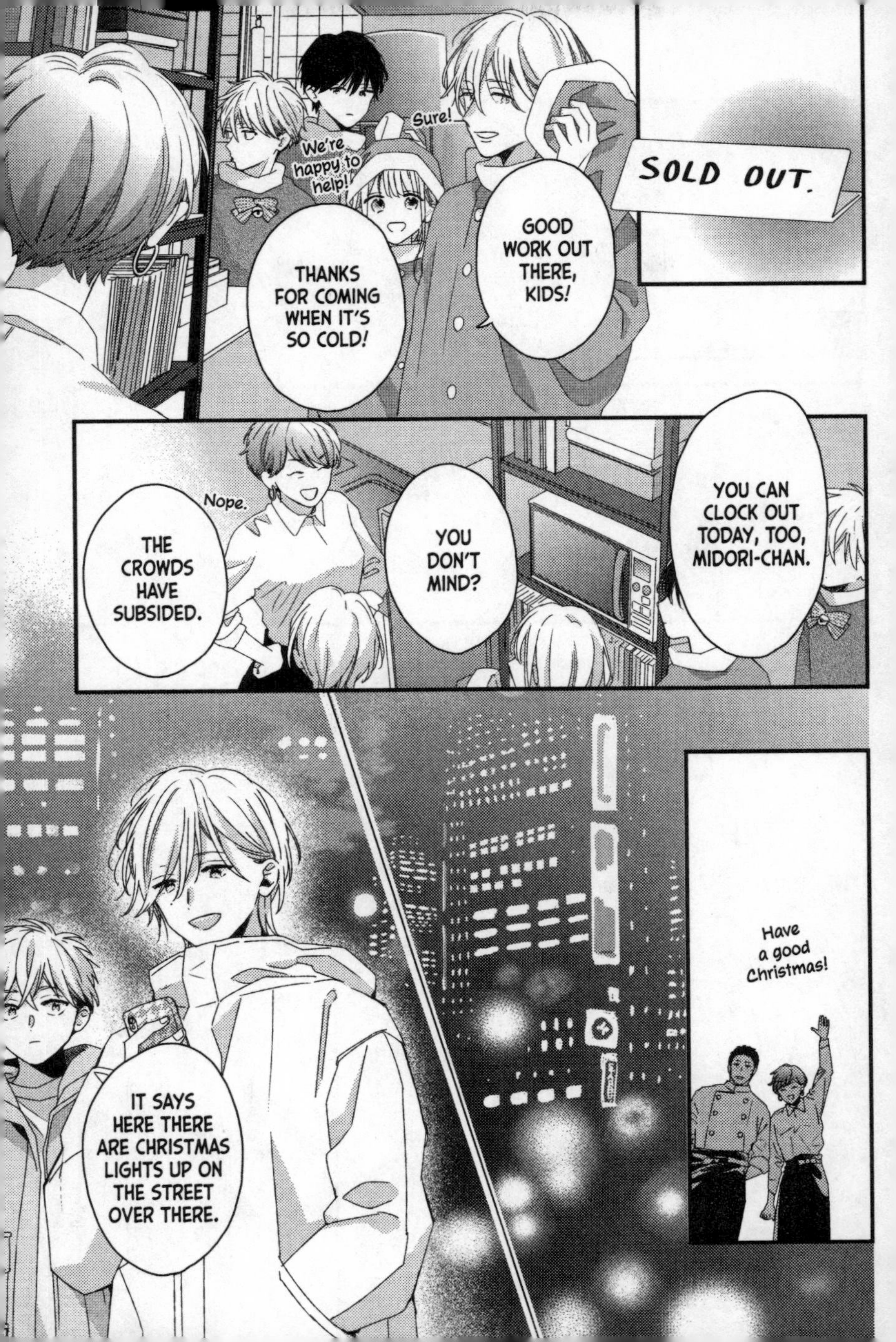
SOLD OUT.
GOOD WORK OUT THERE, KIDS!
THANKS FOR COMING WHEN IT'S SO COLD!
Sure!
We're happy to help!
YOU CAN CLOCK OUT TODAY, TOO, MIDORI-CHAN.
YOU DON'T MIND?
Nope.
THE CROWDS HAVE SUBSIDED.
Have a good Christmas!
IT SAYS HERE THERE ARE CHRISTMAS LIGHTS UP ON THE STREET OVER THERE.

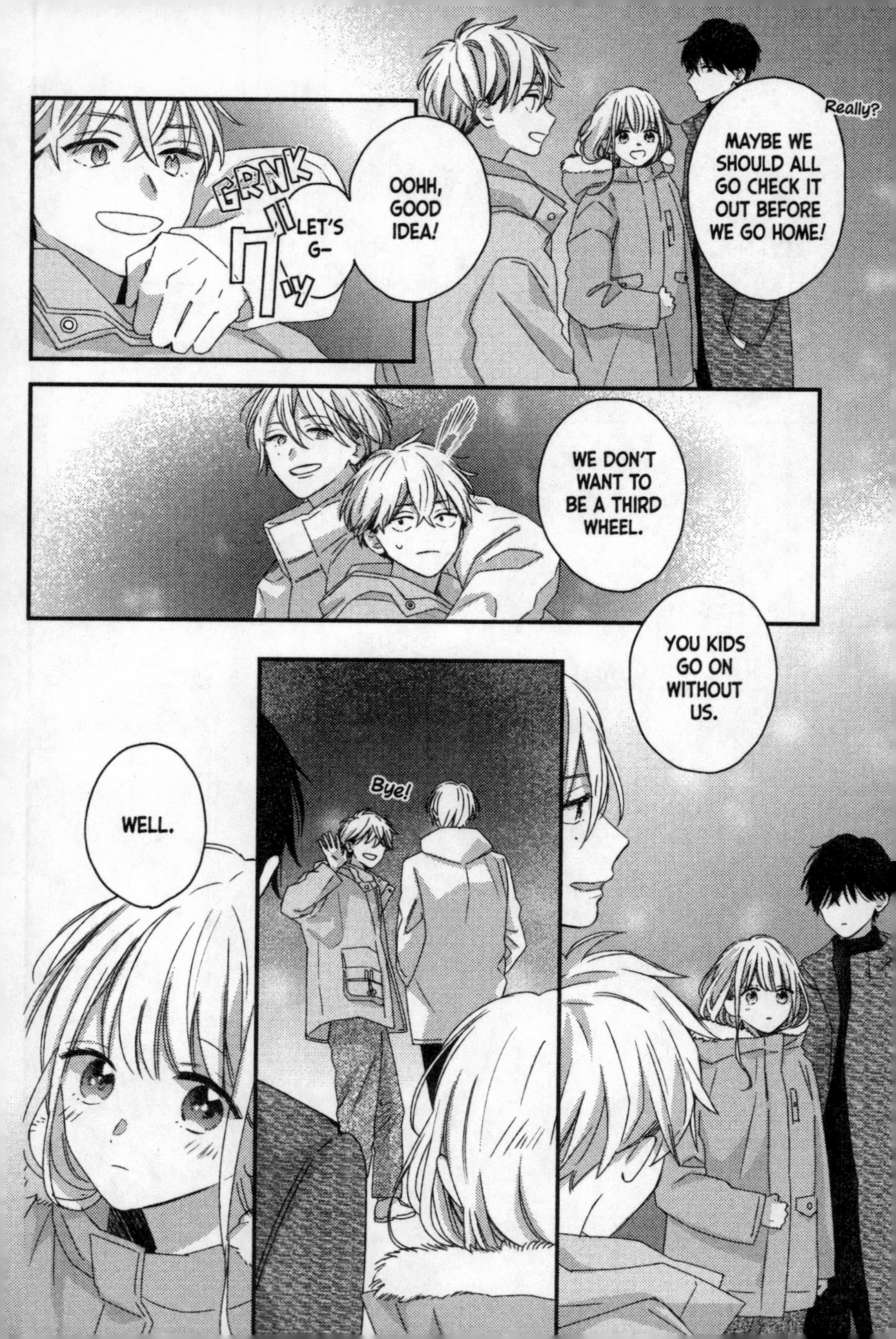
Really?
MAYBE WE SHOULD ALL GO CHECK IT OUT BEFORE WE GO HOME!
OOHH, GOOD IDEA!
GRNK
LET'S G-
WE DON'T WANT TO BE A THIRD WHEEL.
YOU KIDS GO ON WITHOUT US.
Bye!
WELL.

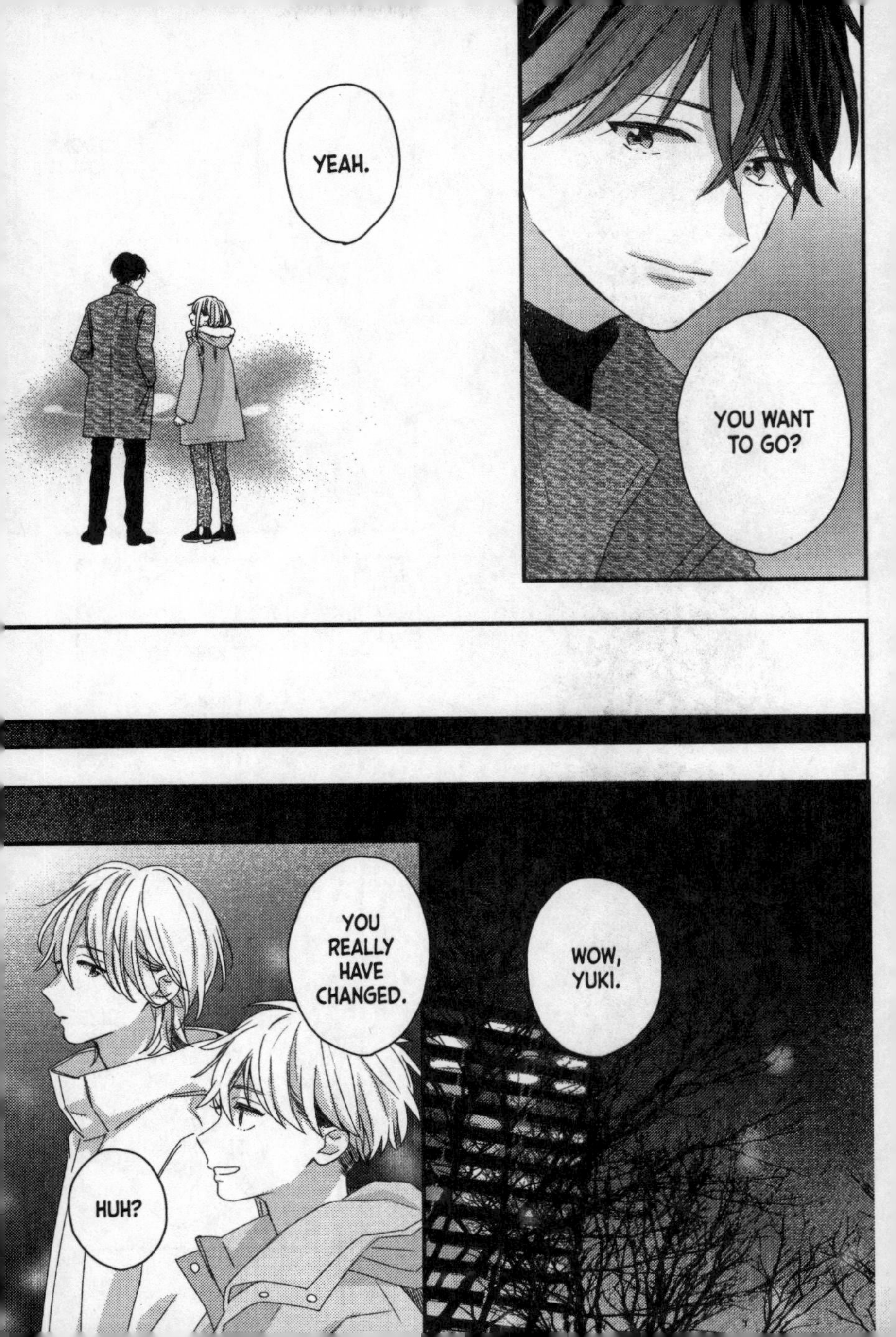
YOU WANT TO GO?
YEAH.
WOW, YUKI.
YOU REALLY HAVE CHANGED.
HUH?

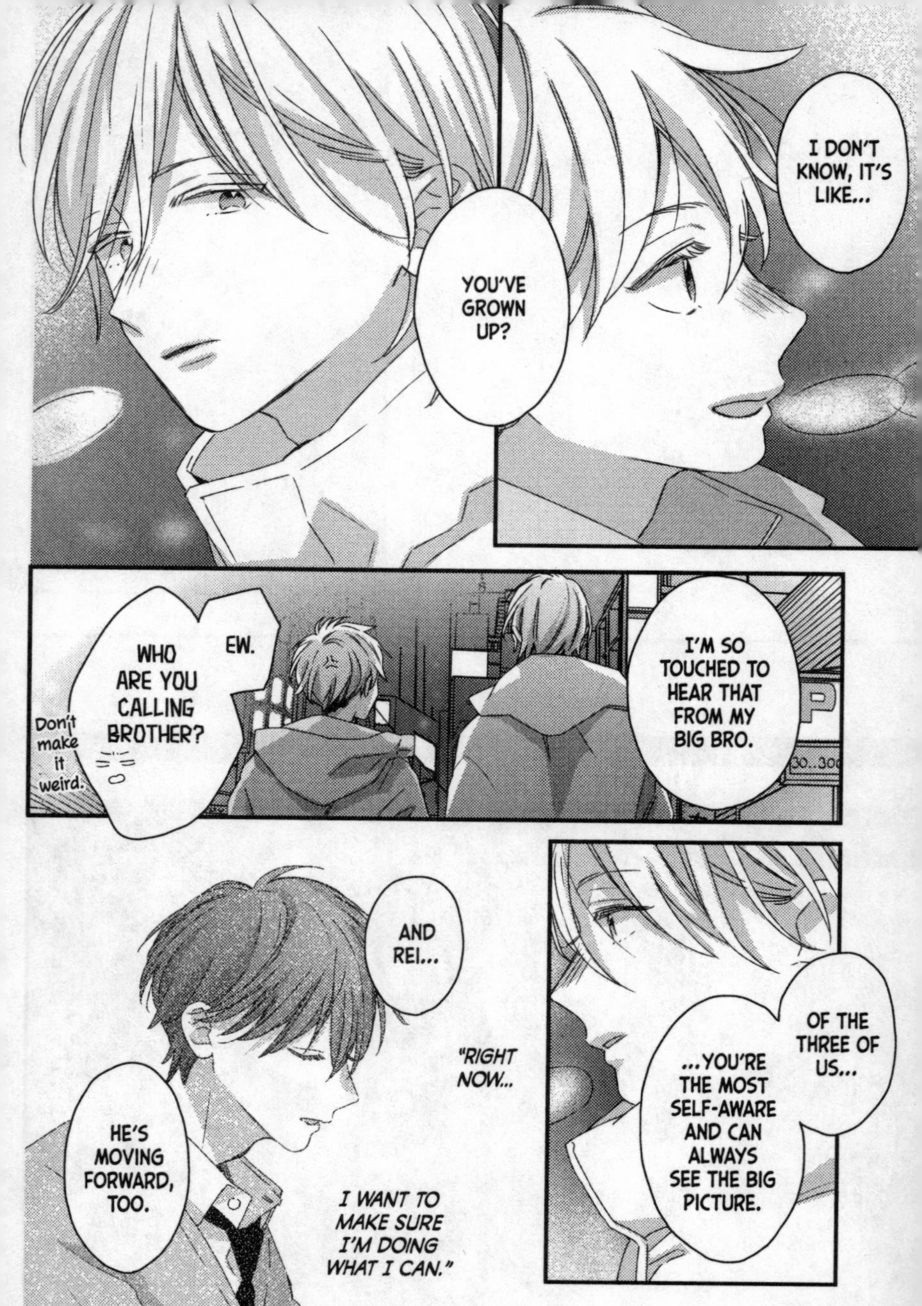
I DON'T KNOW, IT'S LIKE...
YOU'VE GROWN UP?
I'M SO TOUCHED TO HEAR THAT FROM MY BIG BRO.
EW.
WHO ARE YOU CALLING BROTHER?
Don't make it weird.
OF THE THREE OF US...
...YOU'RE THE MOST SELF-AWARE AND CAN ALWAYS SEE THE BIG PICTURE.
AND REI...
HE'S MOVING FORWARD, TOO.
"RIGHT NOW...
I WANT TO MAKE SURE I'M DOING WHAT I CAN."

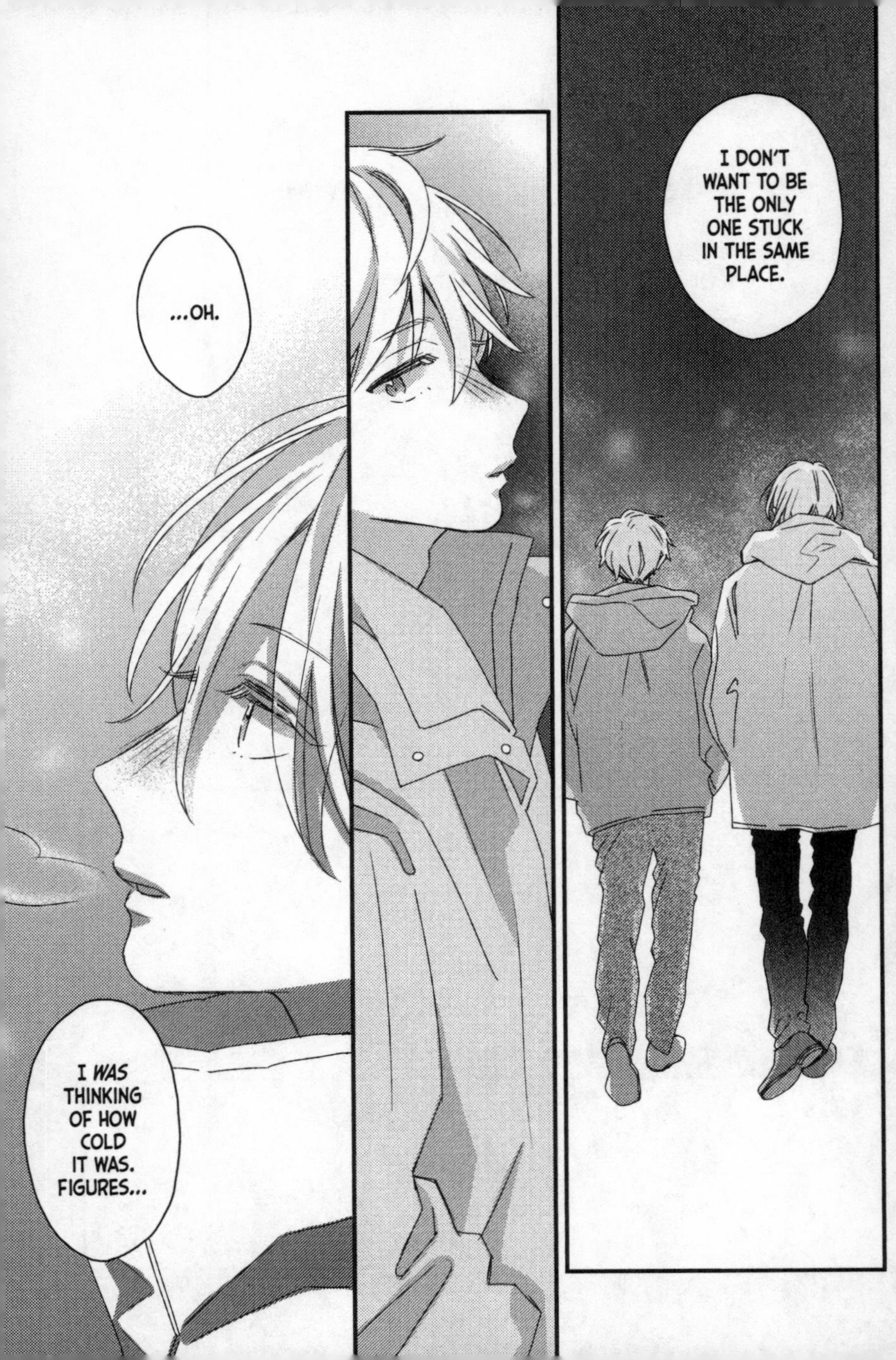
I DON'T WANT TO BE THE ONLY ONE STUCK IN THE SAME PLACE.
...OH.
I *WAS* THINKING OF HOW COLD IT WAS. FIGURES...

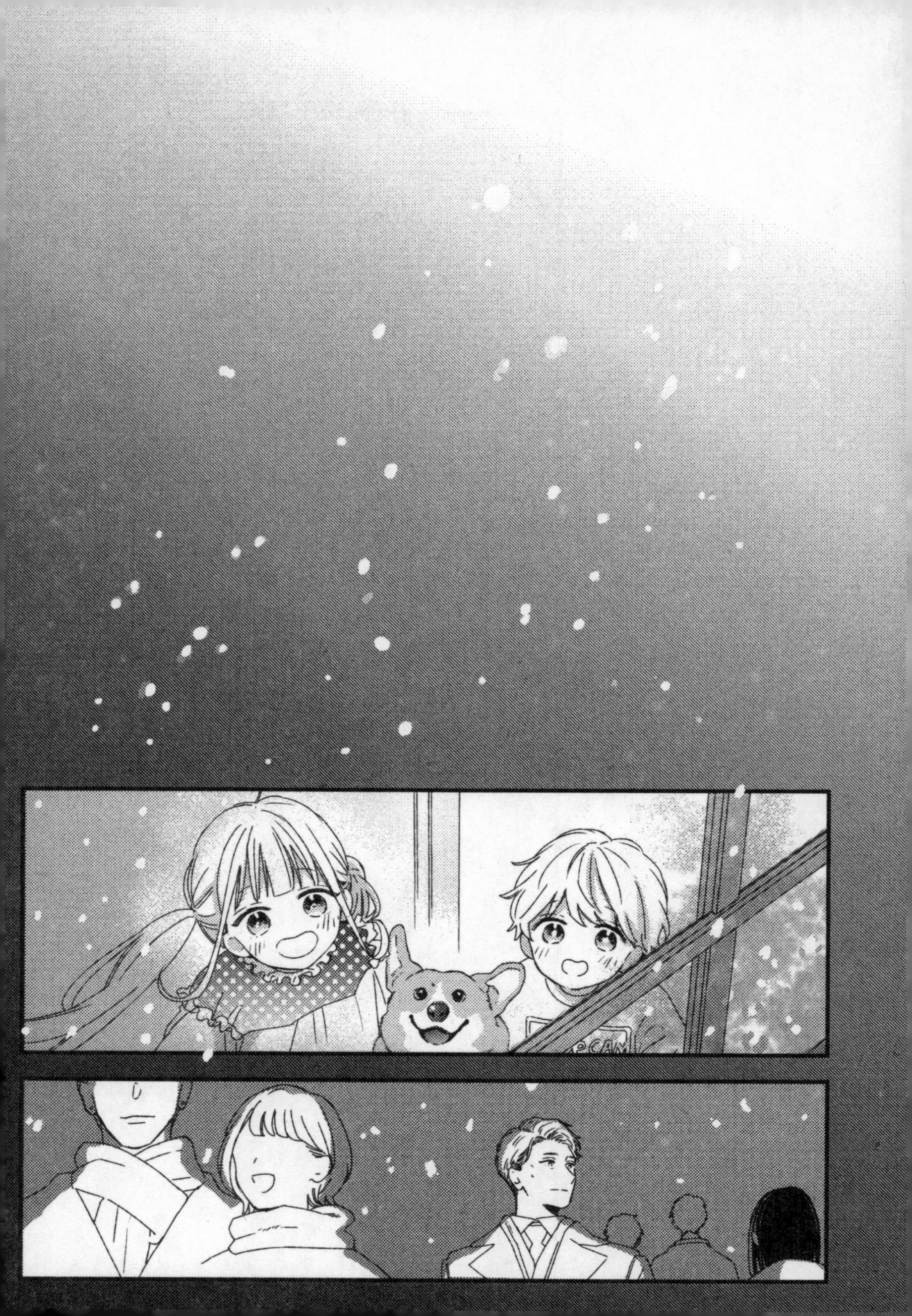

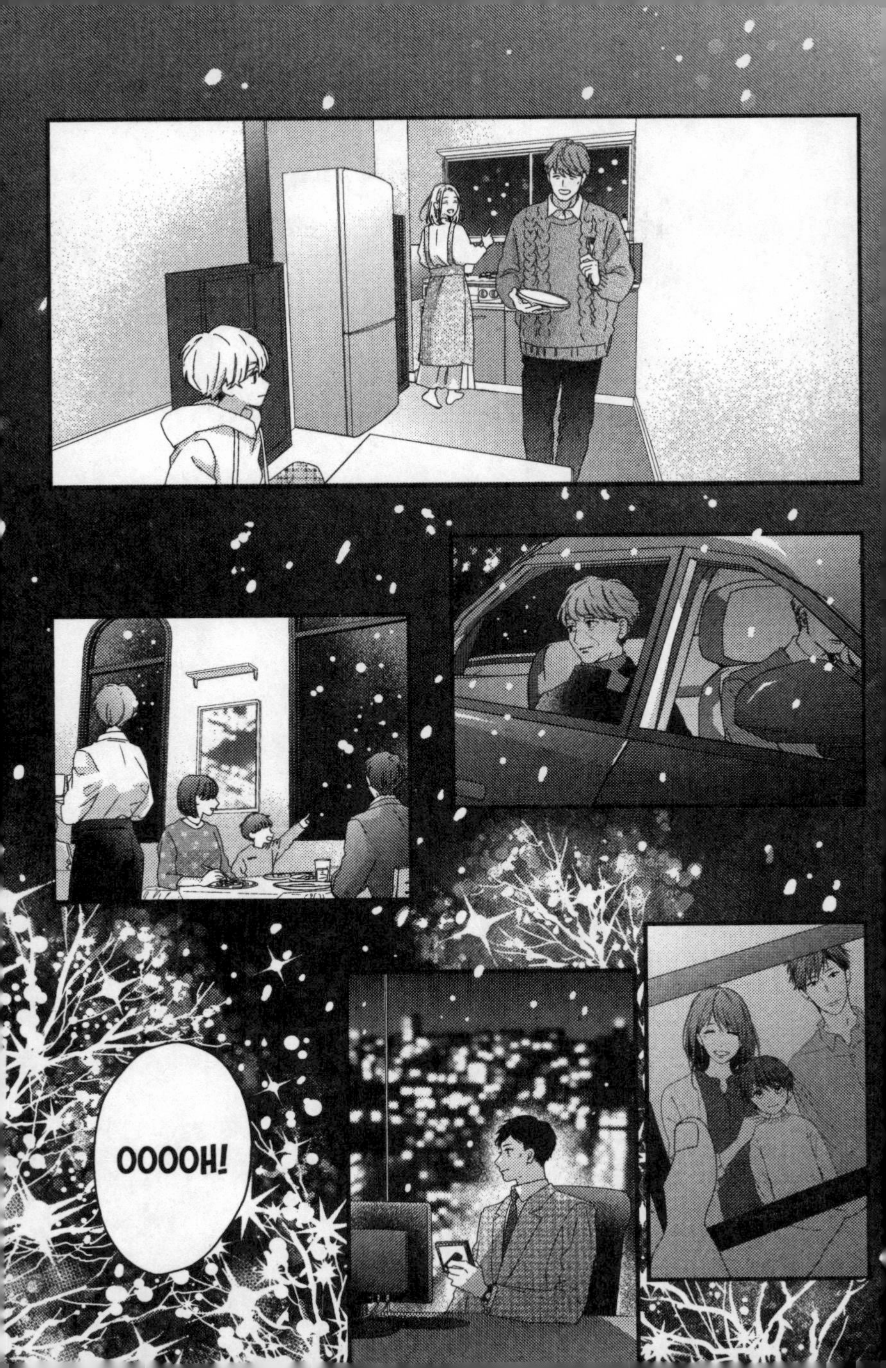
OOOOH!

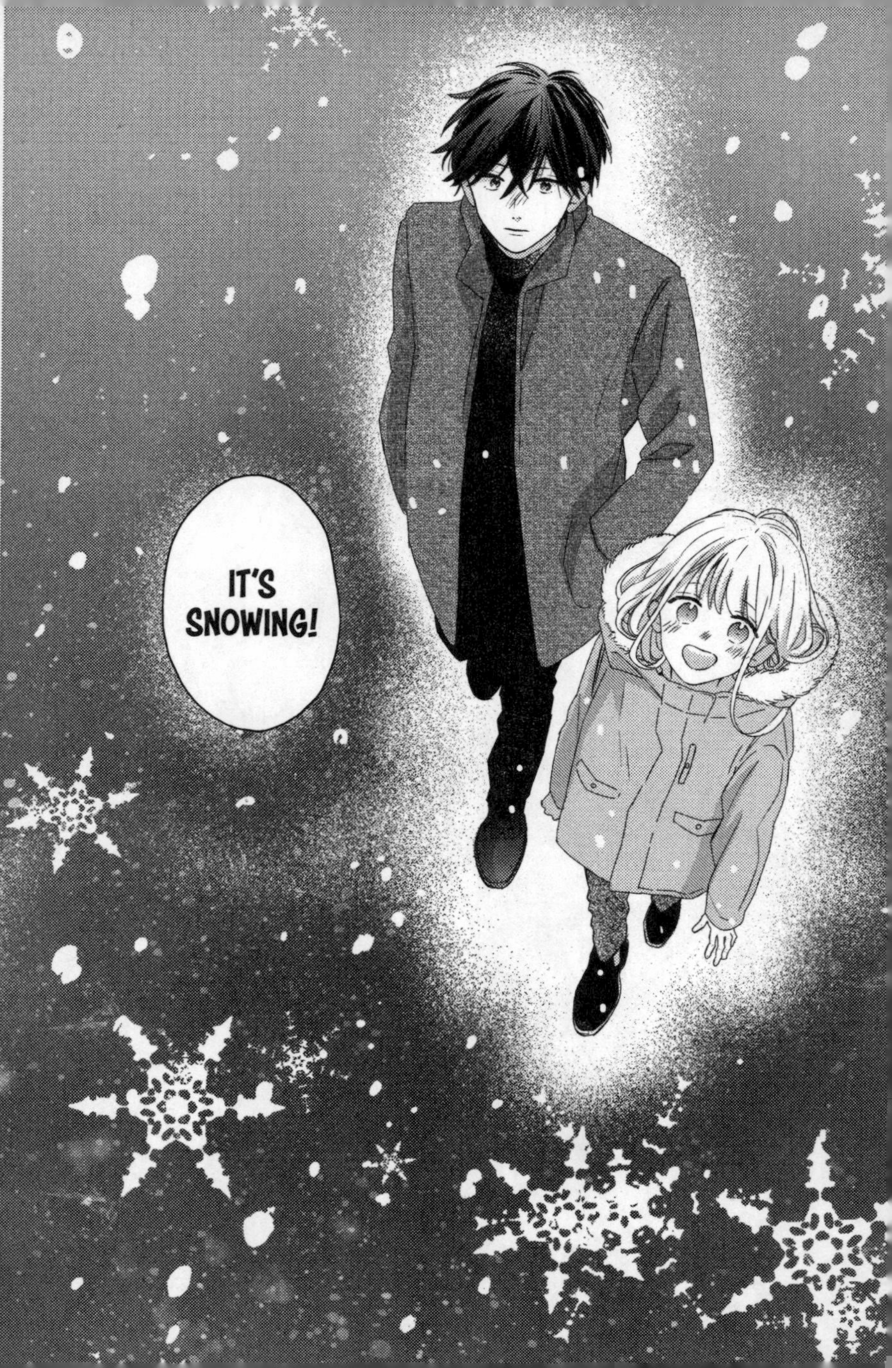
IT'S SNOWING!

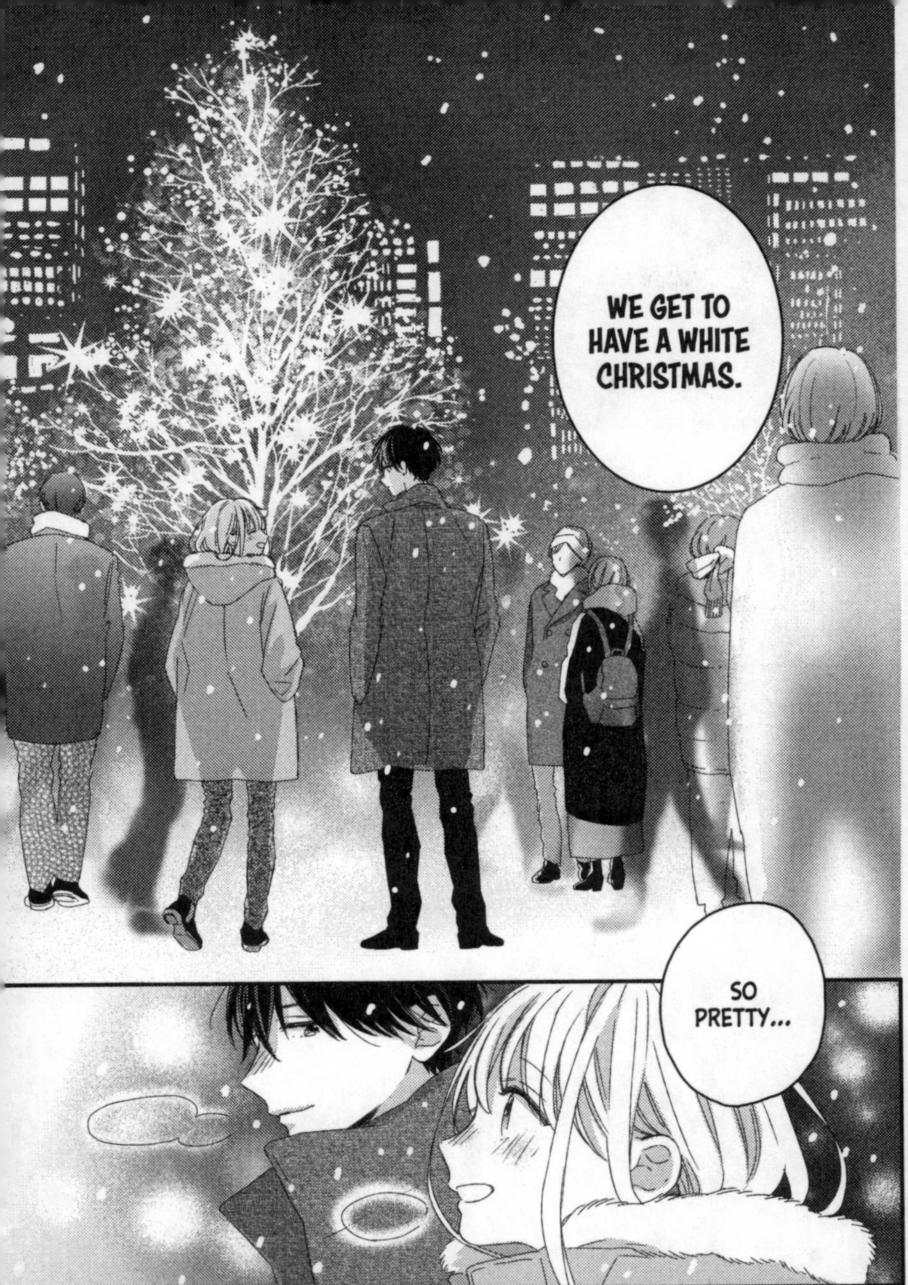
WE GET TO HAVE A WHITE CHRISTMAS.
SO PRETTY...

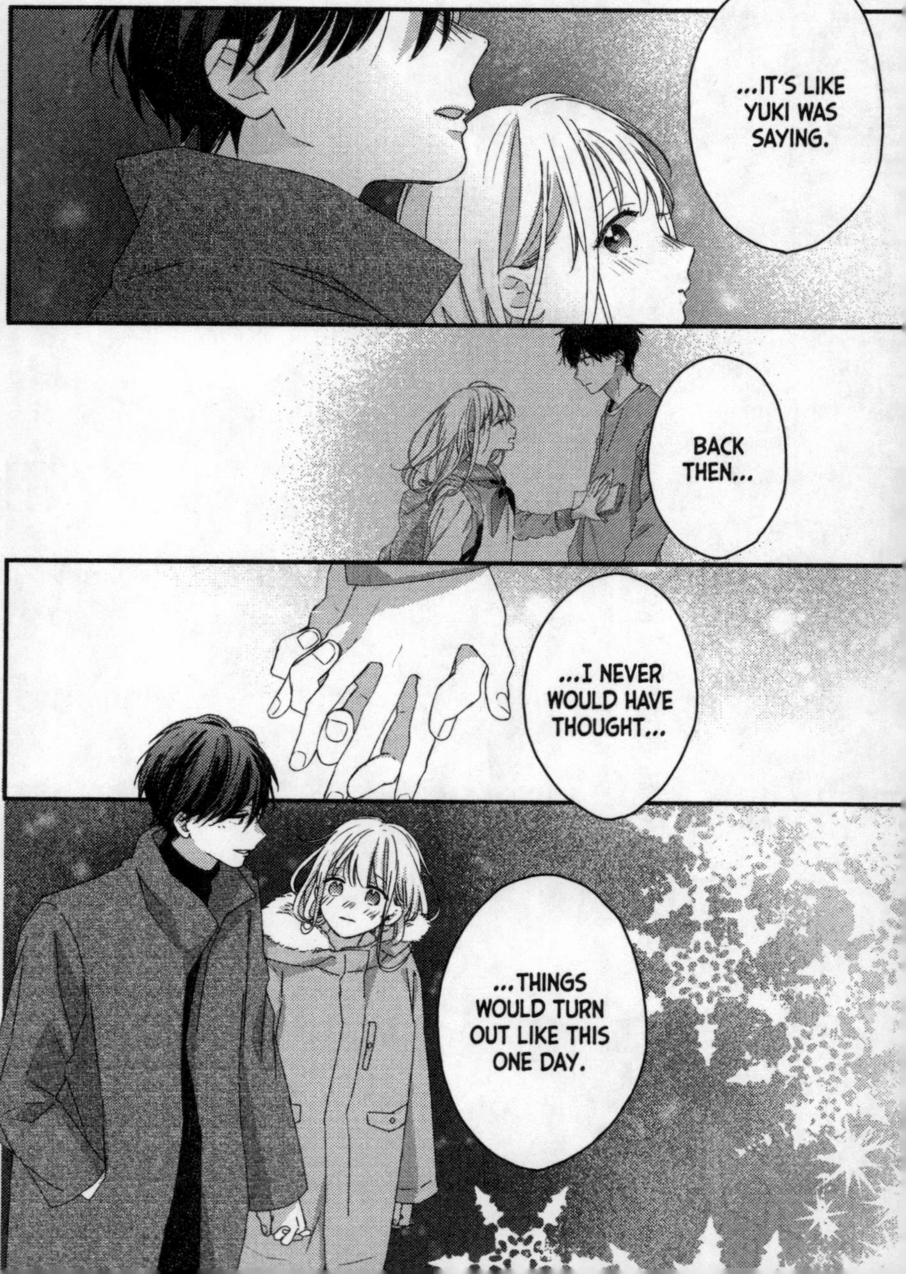
...IT'S LIKE YUKI WAS SAYING.
BACK THEN...
...I NEVER WOULD HAVE THOUGHT...
...THINGS WOULD TURN OUT LIKE THIS ONE DAY.

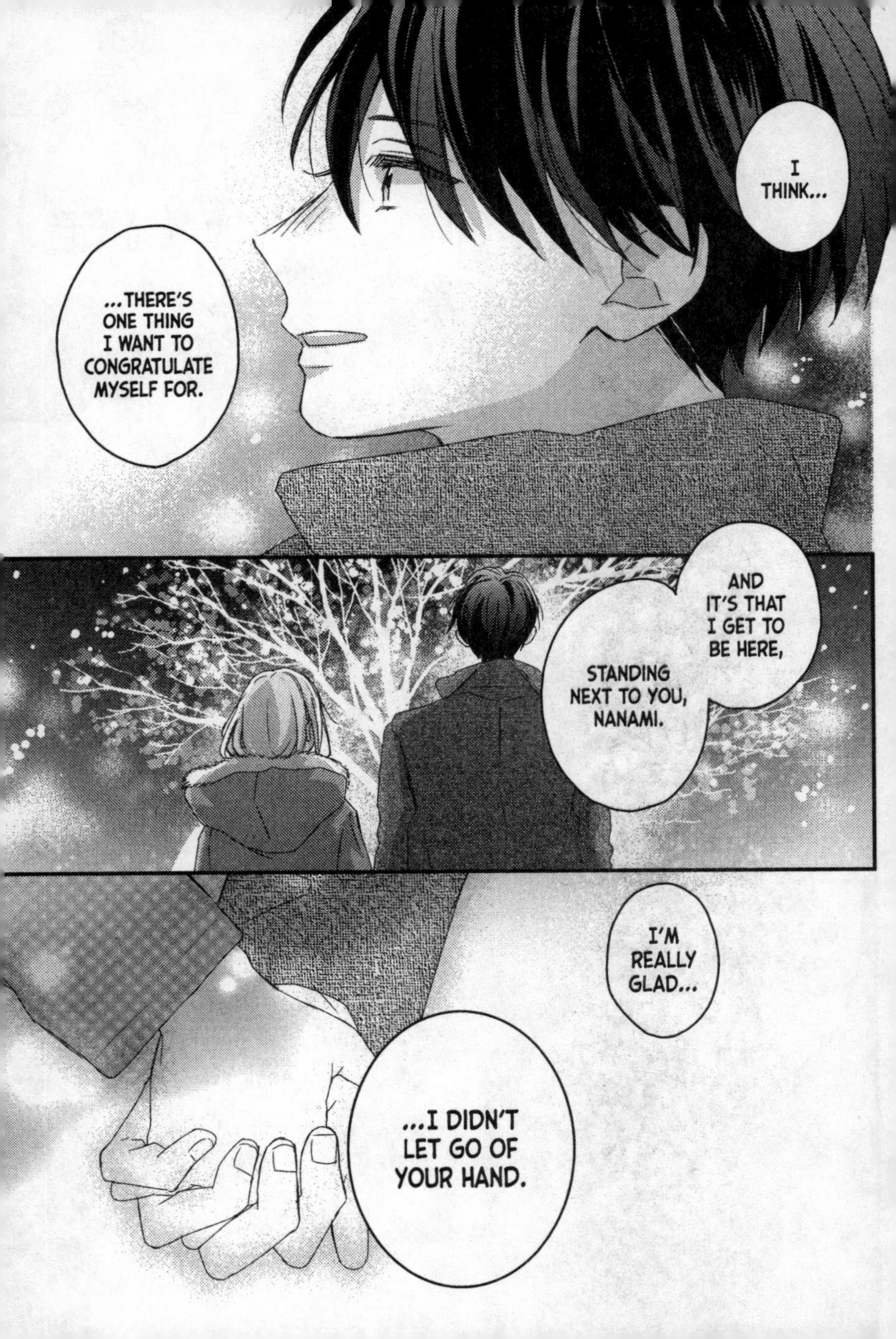
I THINK...
...THERE'S ONE THING I WANT TO CONGRATULATE MYSELF FOR.
AND IT'S THAT I GET TO BE HERE,
STANDING NEXT TO YOU, NANAMI.
I'M REALLY GLAD...
...I DIDN'T LET GO OF YOUR HAND.

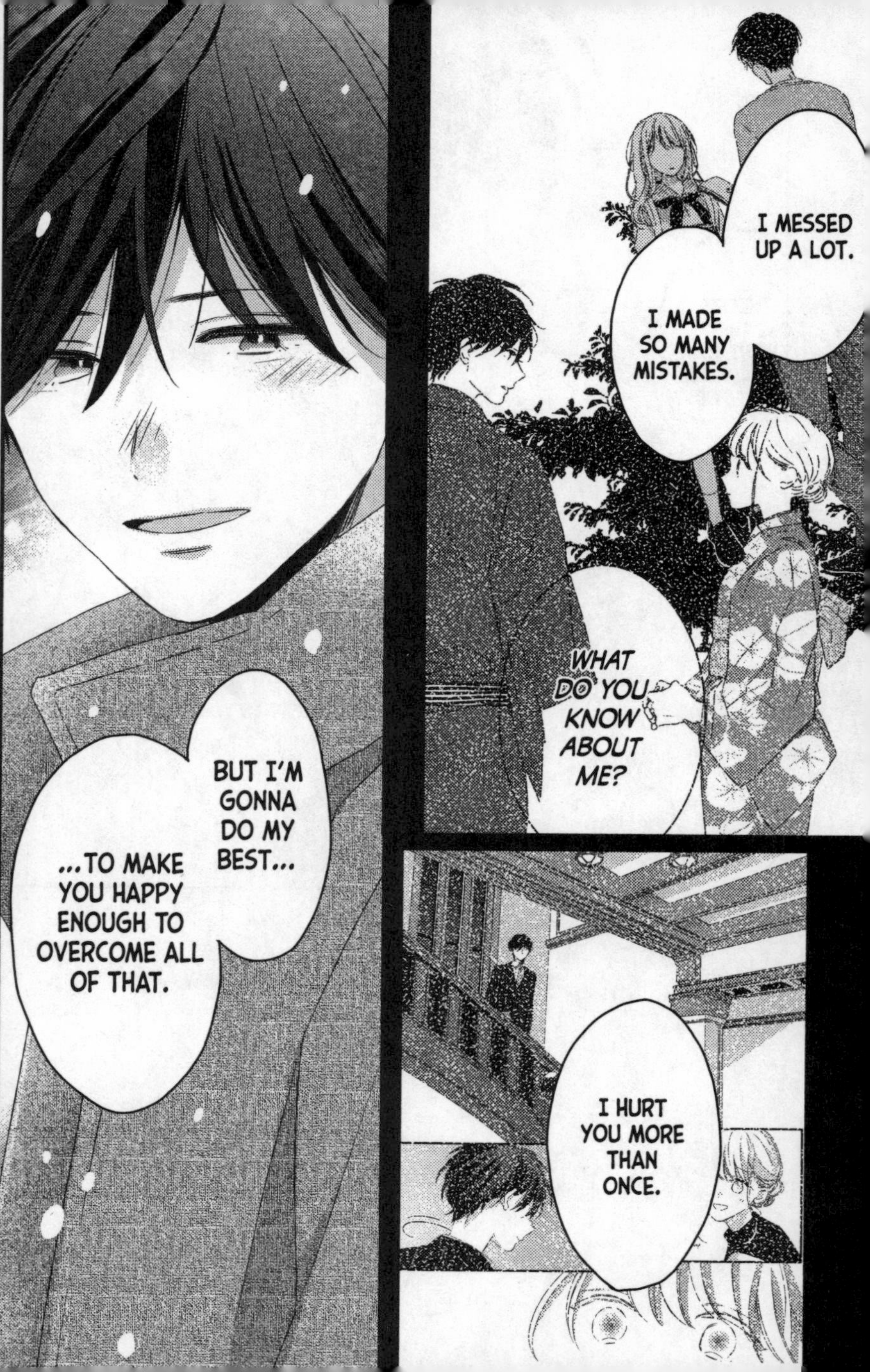
I MESSED UP A LOT.
I MADE SO MANY MISTAKES.
WHAT DO YOU KNOW ABOUT ME?
I HURT YOU MORE THAN ONCE.
BUT I'M GONNA DO MY BEST...
...TO MAKE YOU HAPPY ENOUGH TO OVERCOME ALL OF THAT.

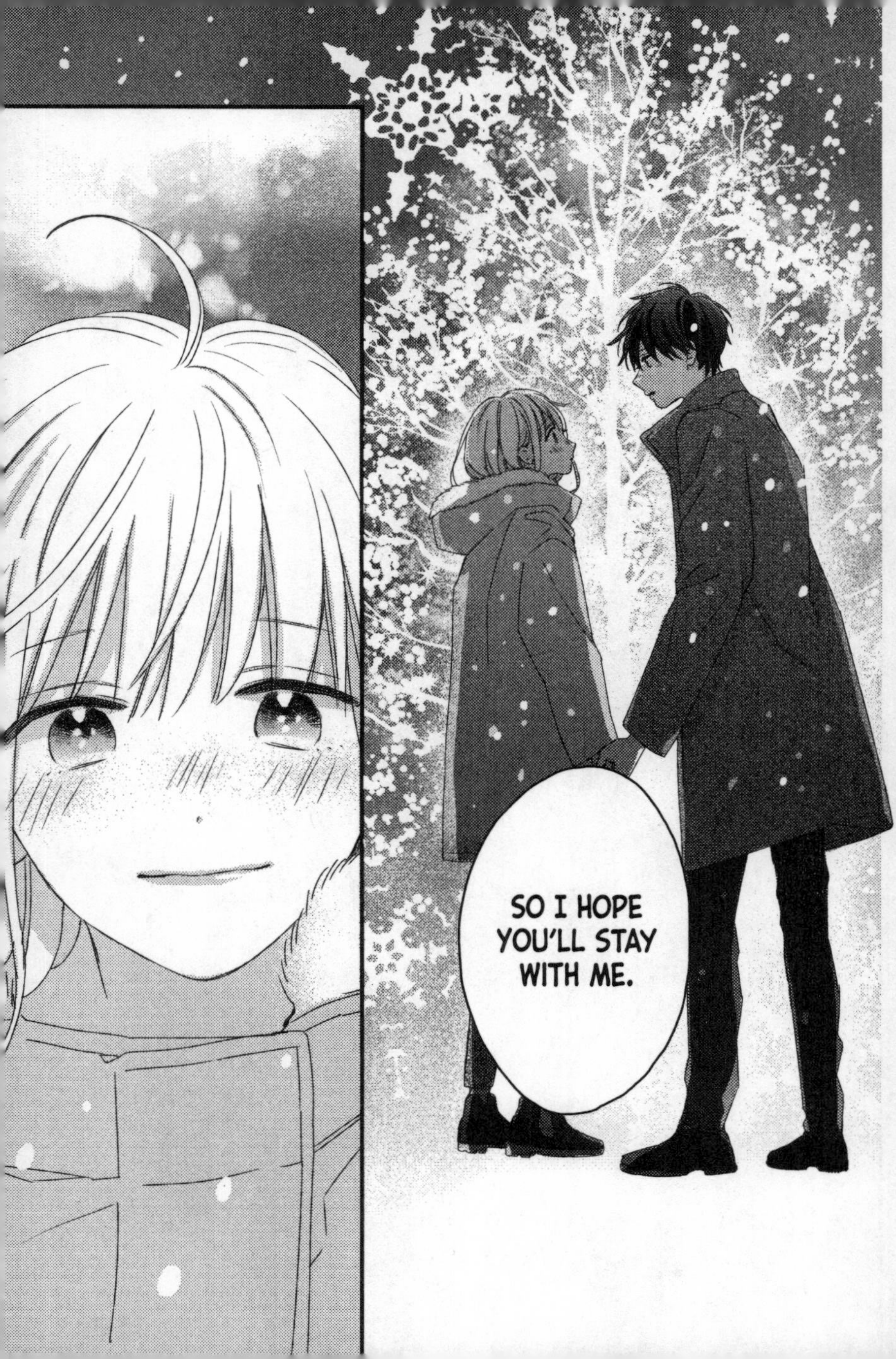
SO I HOPE YOU'LL STAY WITH ME.

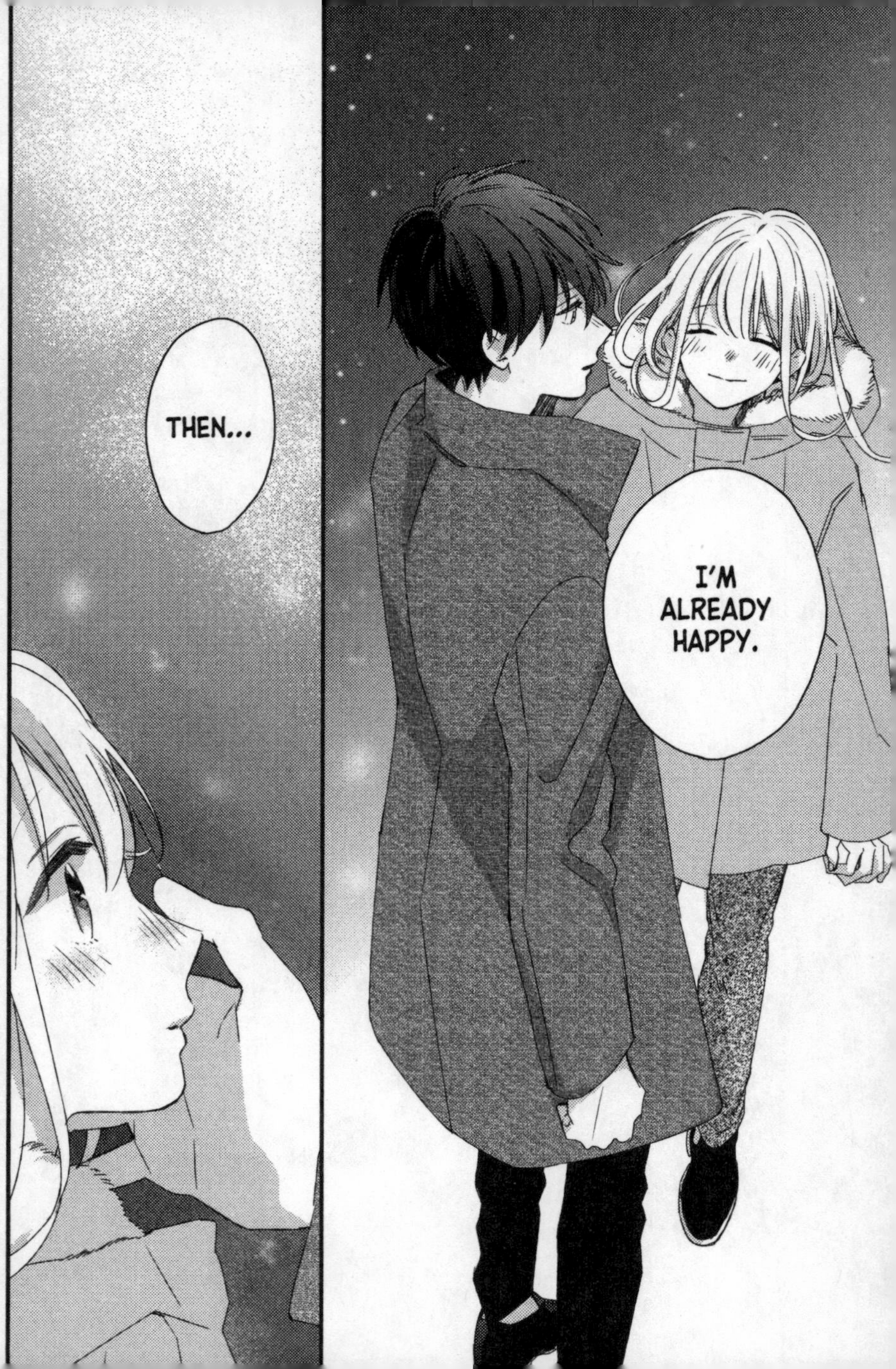
I'M ALREADY HAPPY.
THEN...

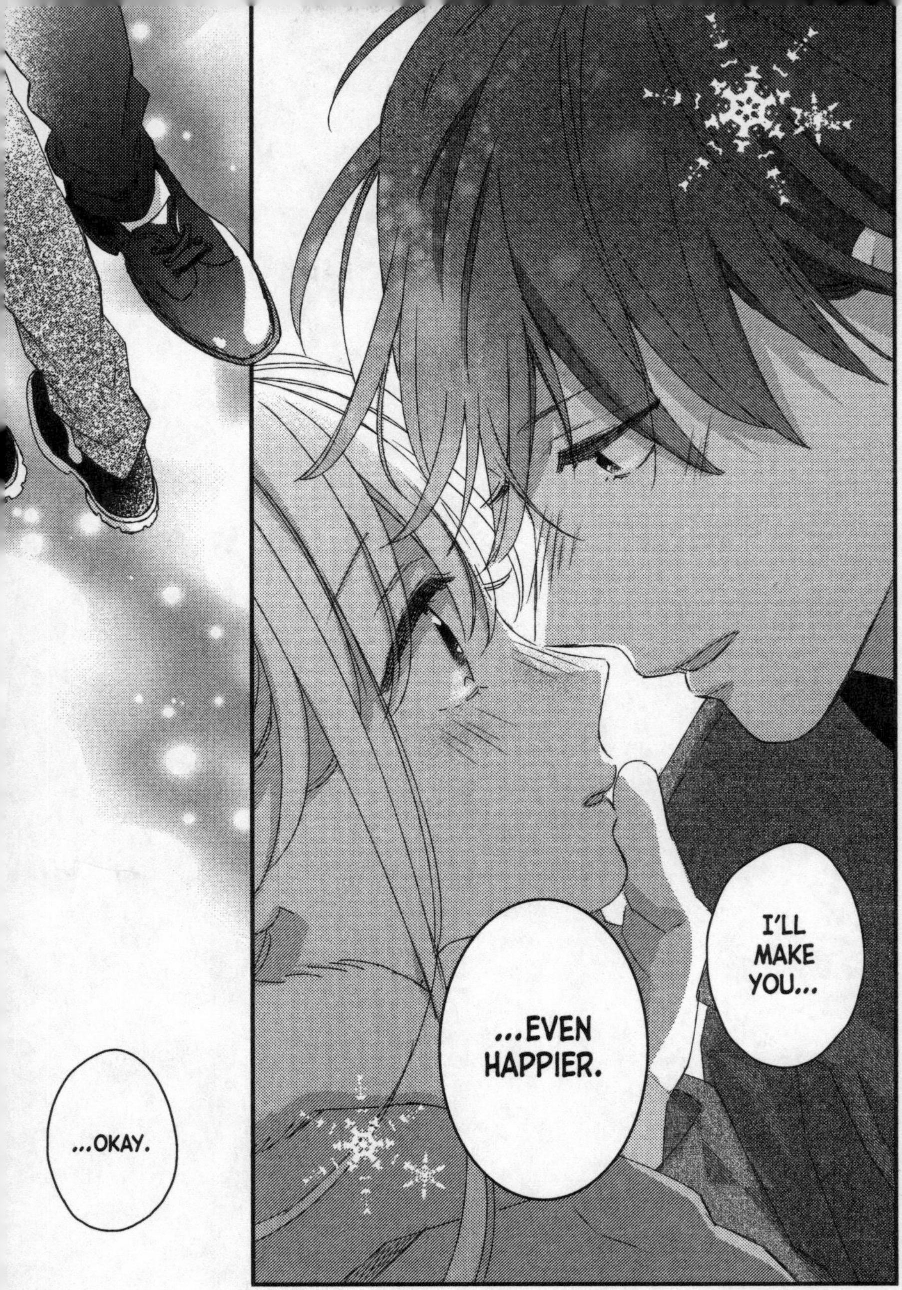
I'LL MAKE YOU...
...EVEN HAPPIER.
...OKAY.

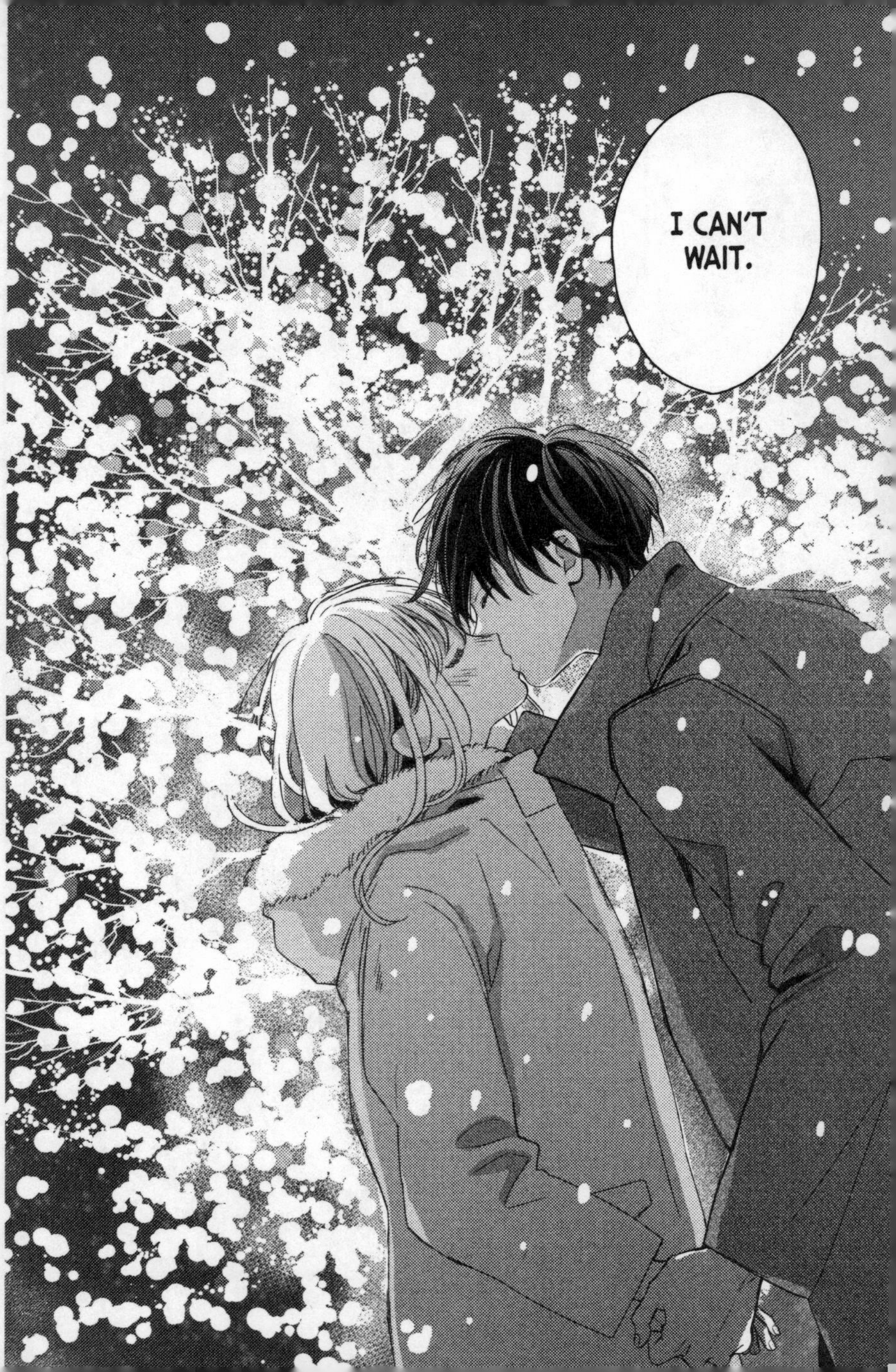
I CAN'T WAIT.

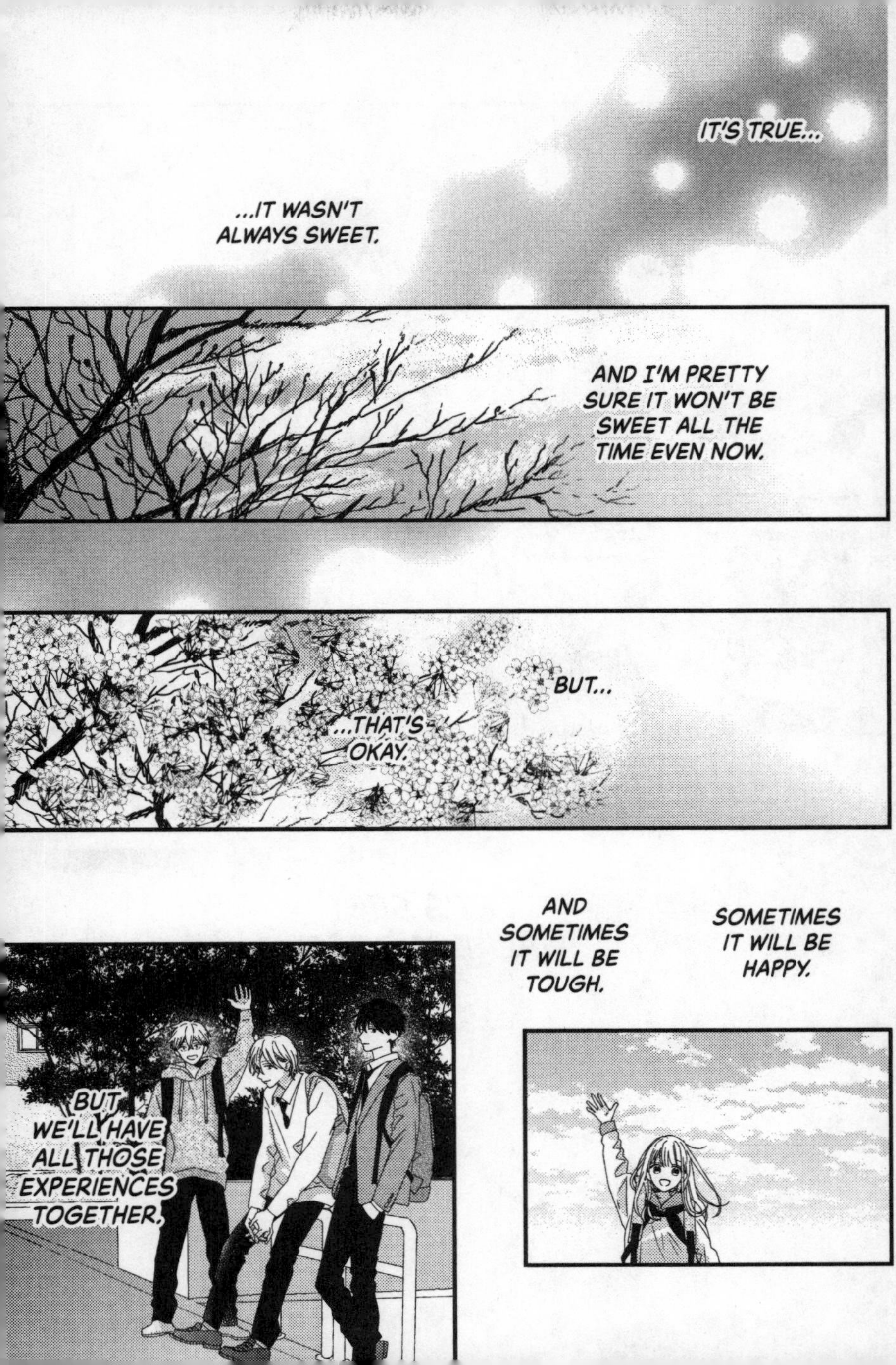
IT'S TRUE...
...IT WASN'T ALWAYS SWEET.
AND I'M PRETTY SURE IT WON'T BE SWEET ALL THE TIME EVEN NOW.
BUT...
...THAT'S OKAY.
SOMETIMES IT WILL BE HAPPY.
AND SOMETIMES IT WILL BE TOUGH.
BUT WE'LL HAVE ALL THOSE EXPERIENCES TOGETHER.

LET'S SEE
WHERE IT GOES.

THE END

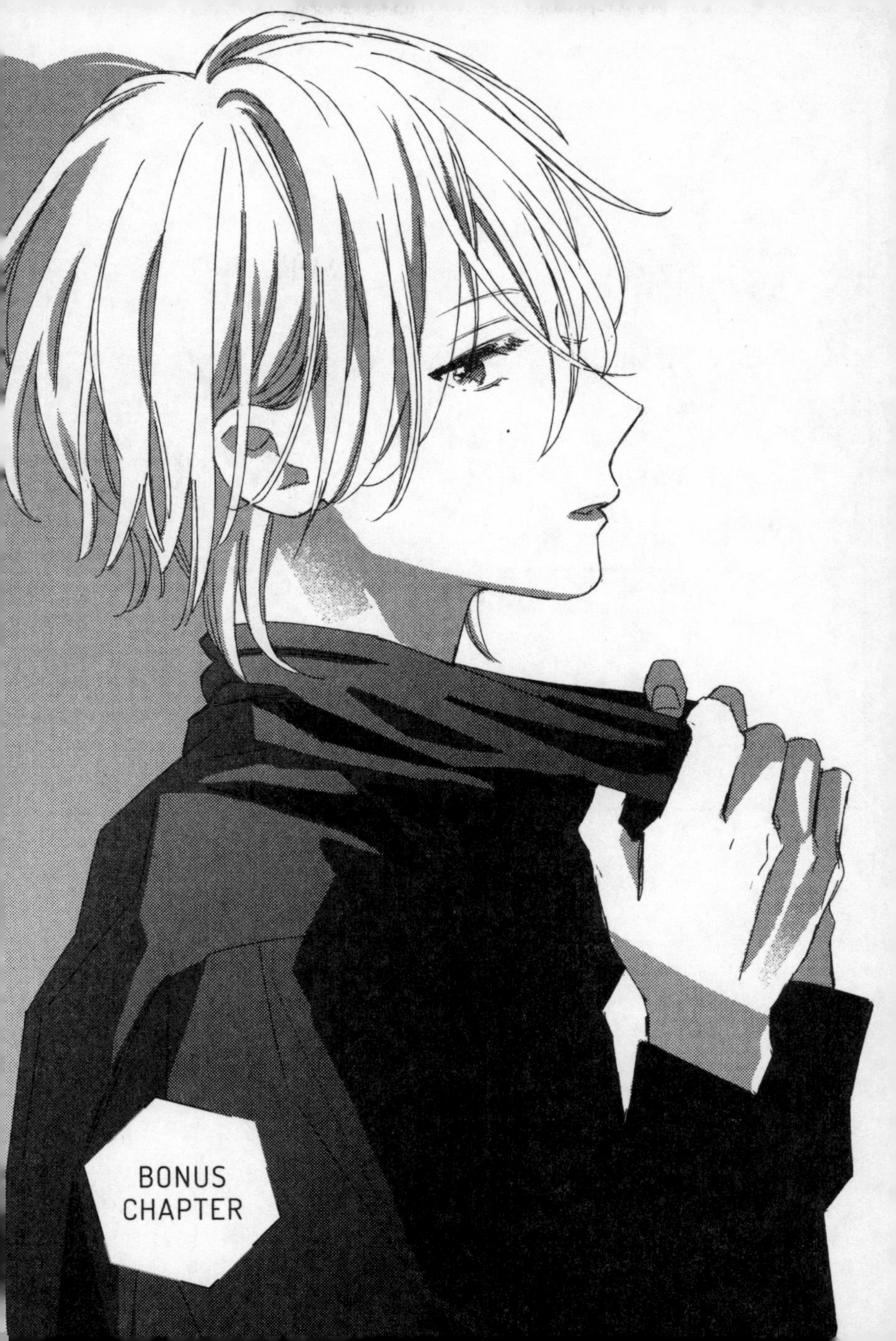
BONUS
CHAPTER

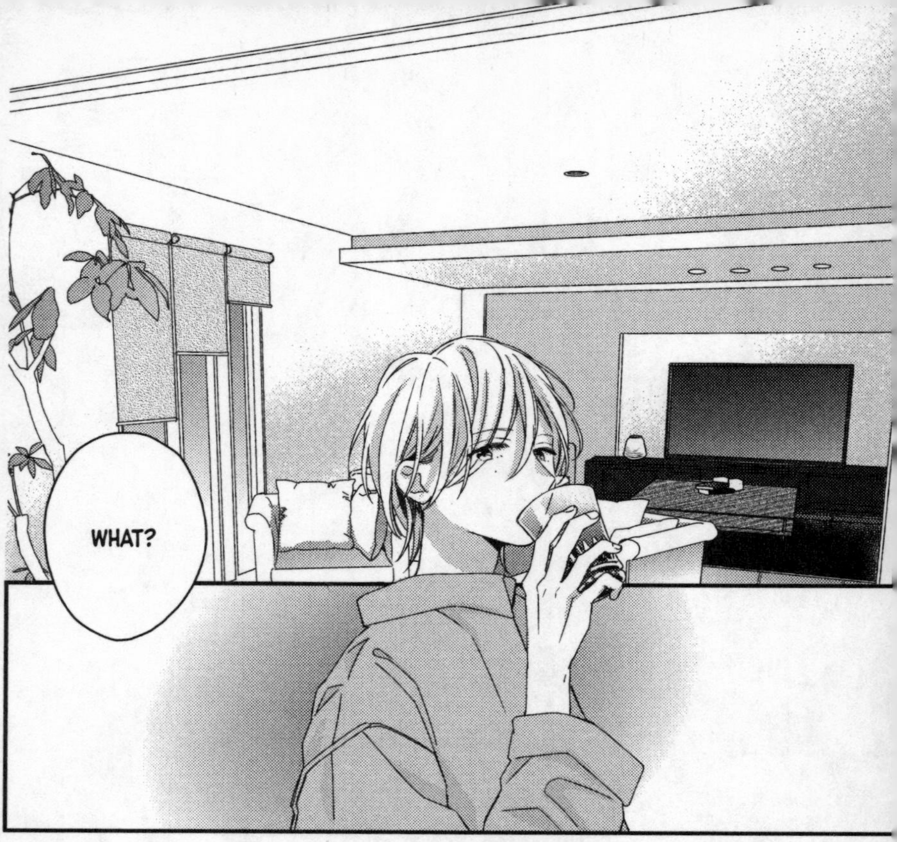
WHAT?
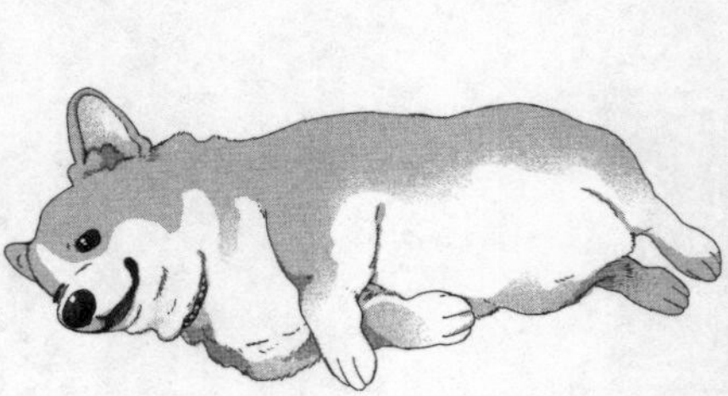

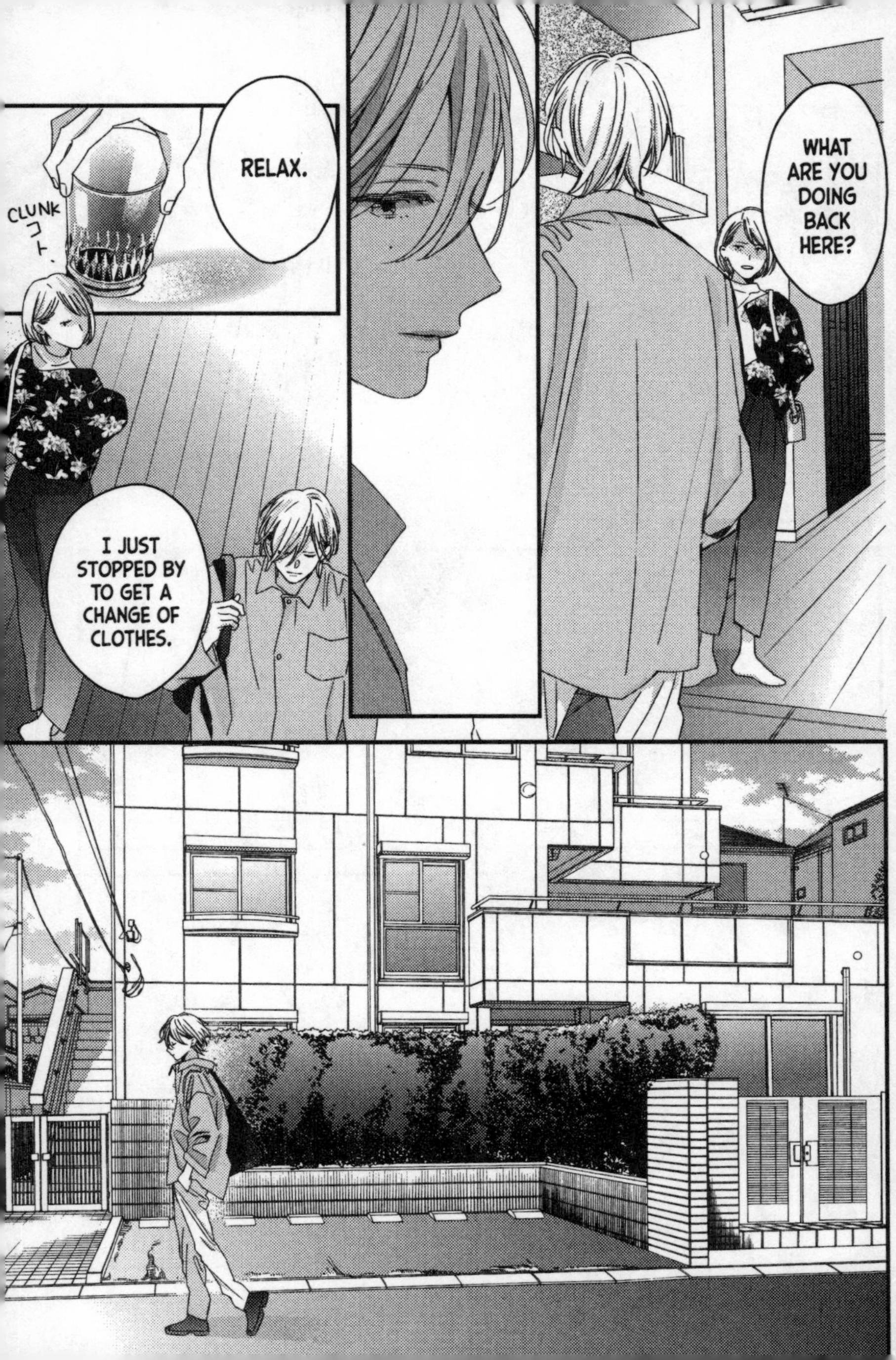
WHAT ARE YOU DOING BACK HERE?
RELAX.
CLUNK
コト
I JUST STOPPED BY TO GET A CHANGE OF CLOTHES.

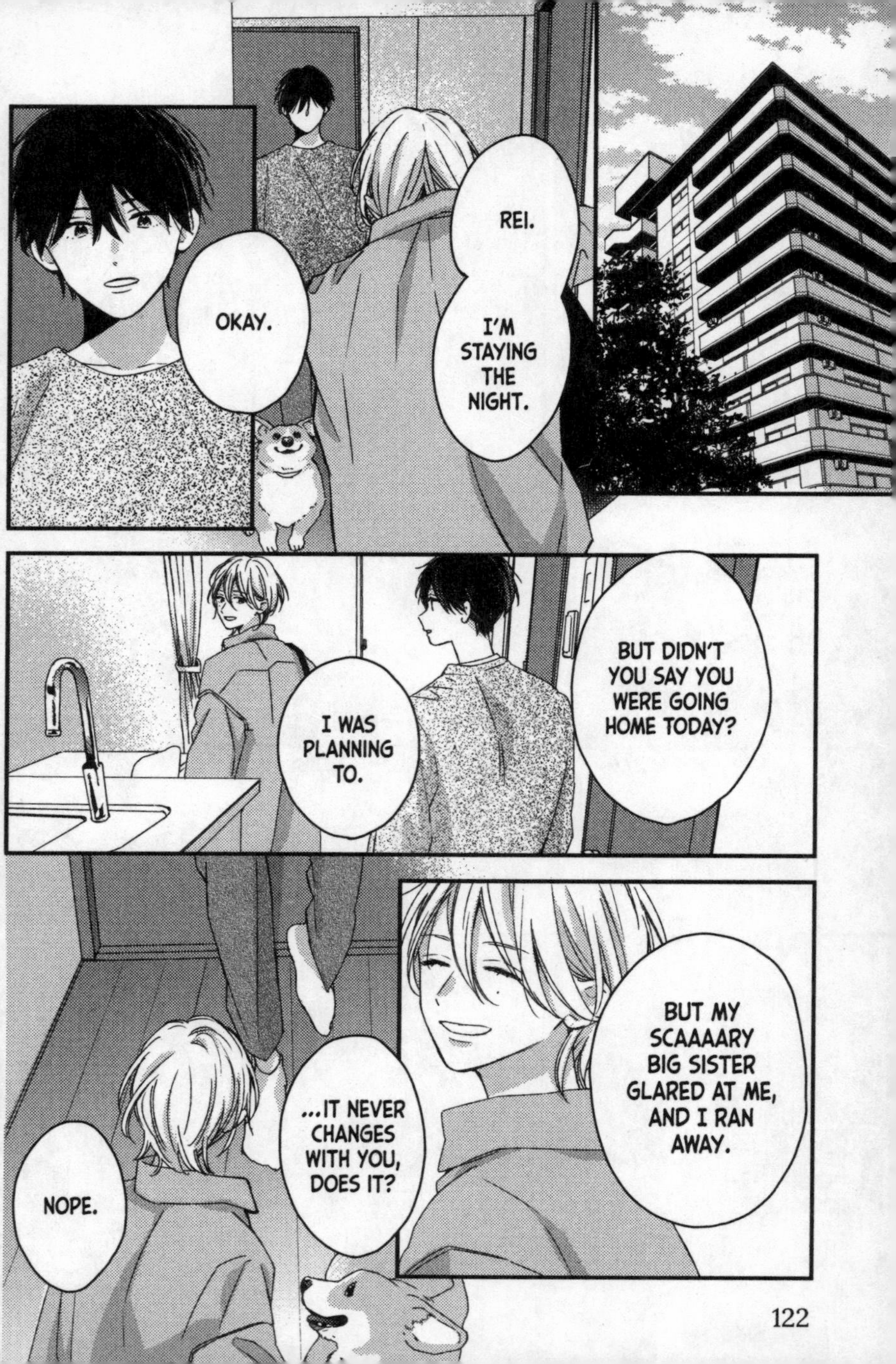
REI.
I'M STAYING THE NIGHT.
OKAY.
BUT DIDN'T YOU SAY YOU WERE GOING HOME TODAY?
I WAS PLANNING TO.
BUT MY SCAAAARY BIG SISTER GLARED AT ME, AND I RAN AWAY.
...IT NEVER CHANGES WITH YOU, DOES IT?
NOPE.

IT'S THE SAME AS EVER.

MY FAMILY IS DYSFUNCTIONAL.

THINGS FELL APART...

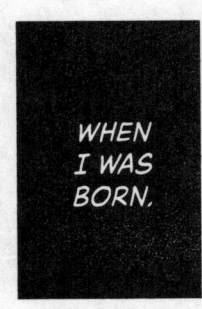

WHEN I WAS BORN.

"IEIRI-SAN'S LITTLE BOY, THE YOUNGER ONE.

"HE DOES HAVE A CUTE LITTLE FACE, DOESN'T HE?"

YUKINOJO-KUN."

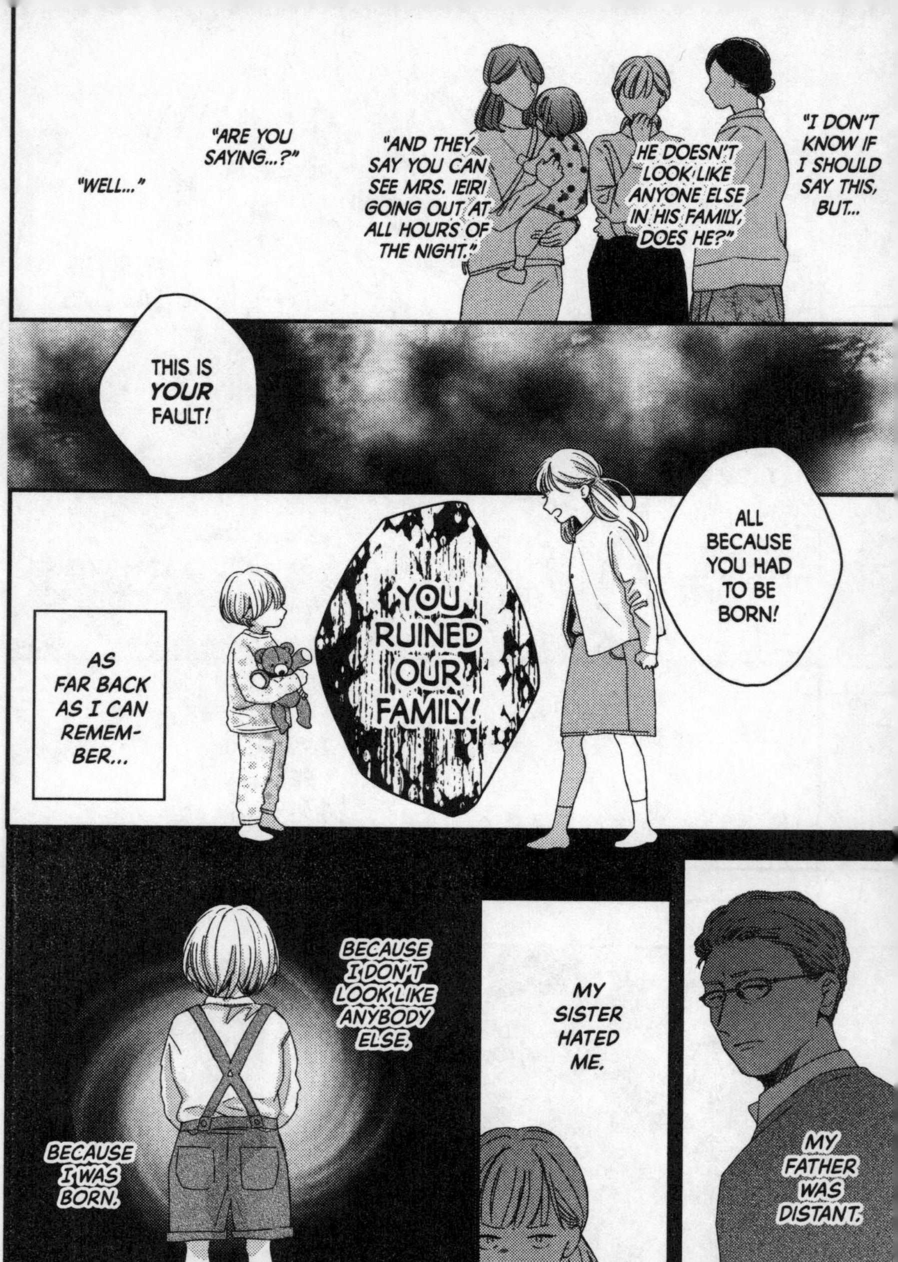
"I DON'T KNOW IF I SHOULD SAY THIS, BUT...
HE DOESN'T LOOK LIKE ANYONE ELSE IN HIS FAMILY, DOES HE?"
"AND THEY SAY YOU CAN SEE MRS. IEIRI GOING OUT AT ALL HOURS OF THE NIGHT."
"ARE YOU SAYING...?"
"WELL..."
THIS IS *YOUR* FAULT!
ALL BECAUSE YOU HAD TO BE BORN!
YOU RUINED OUR FAMILY!
AS FAR BACK AS I CAN REMEMBER...
MY FATHER WAS DISTANT.
MY SISTER HATED ME.
BECAUSE I DON'T LOOK LIKE ANYBODY ELSE.
BECAUSE I WAS BORN.

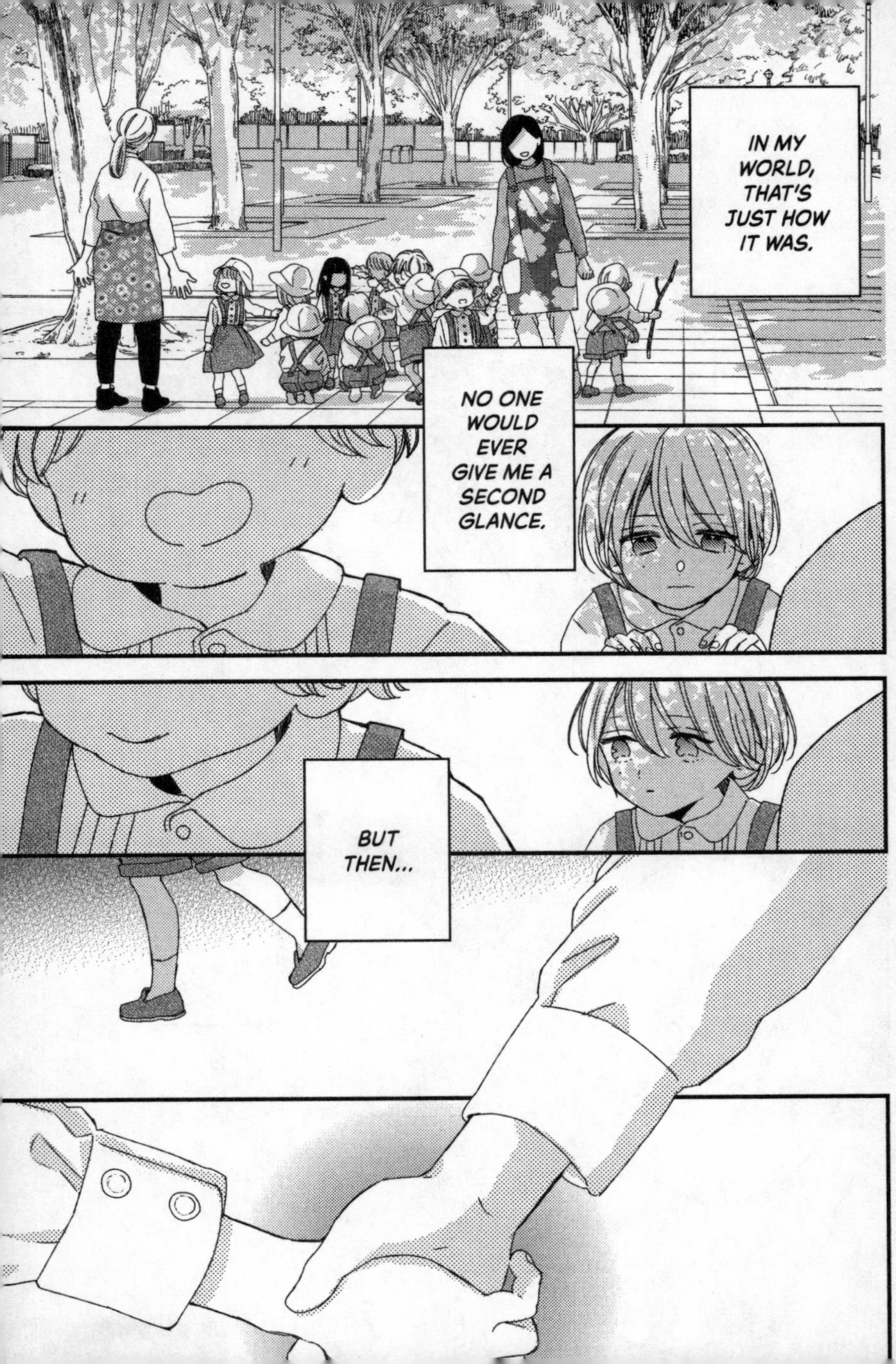
IN MY WORLD, THAT'S JUST HOW IT WAS.
NO ONE WOULD EVER GIVE ME A SECOND GLANCE.
BUT THEN...

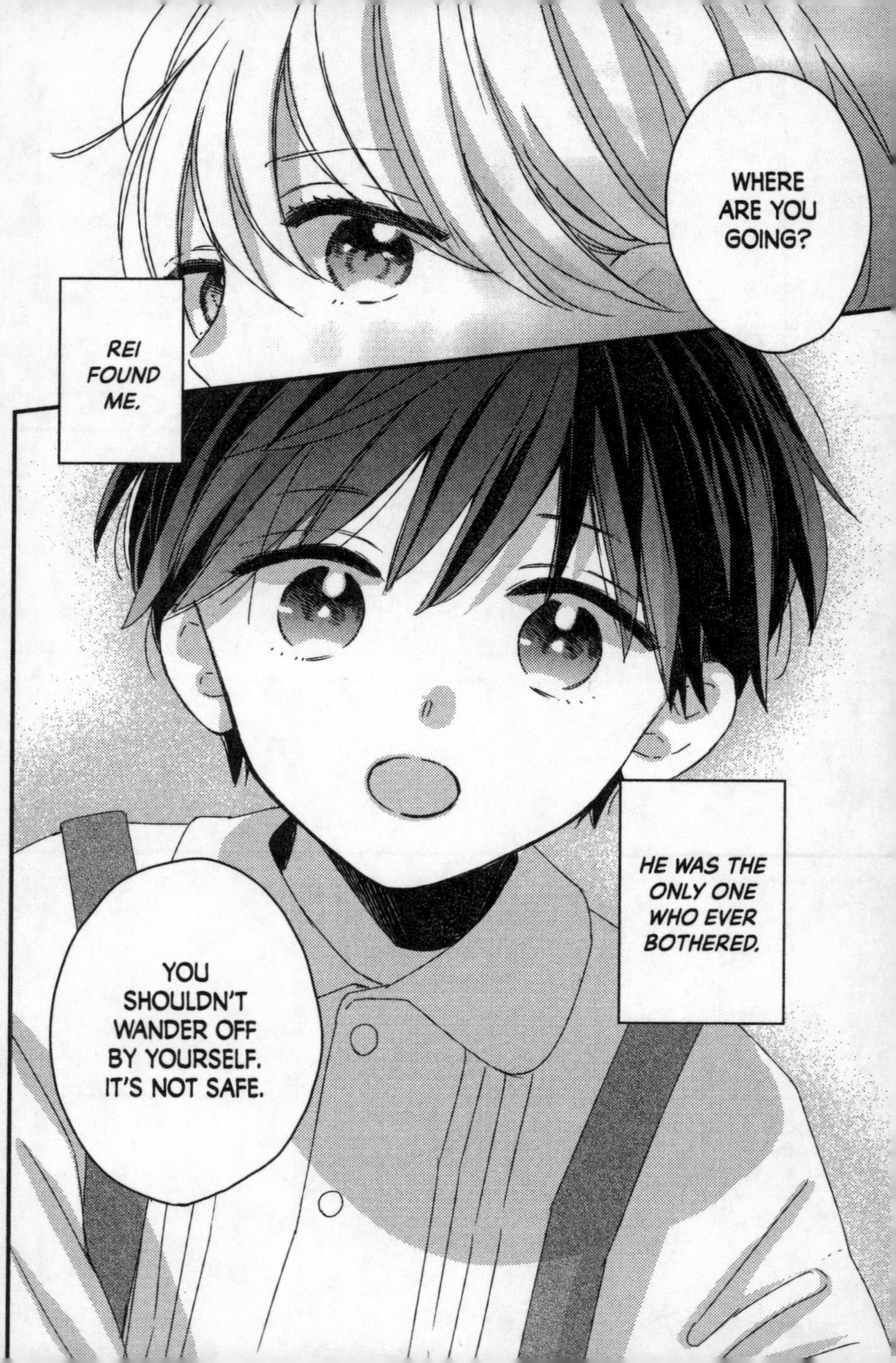
WHERE ARE YOU GOING?
REI FOUND ME.
HE WAS THE ONLY ONE WHO EVER BOTHERED.
YOU SHOULDN'T WANDER OFF BY YOURSELF. IT'S NOT SAFE.

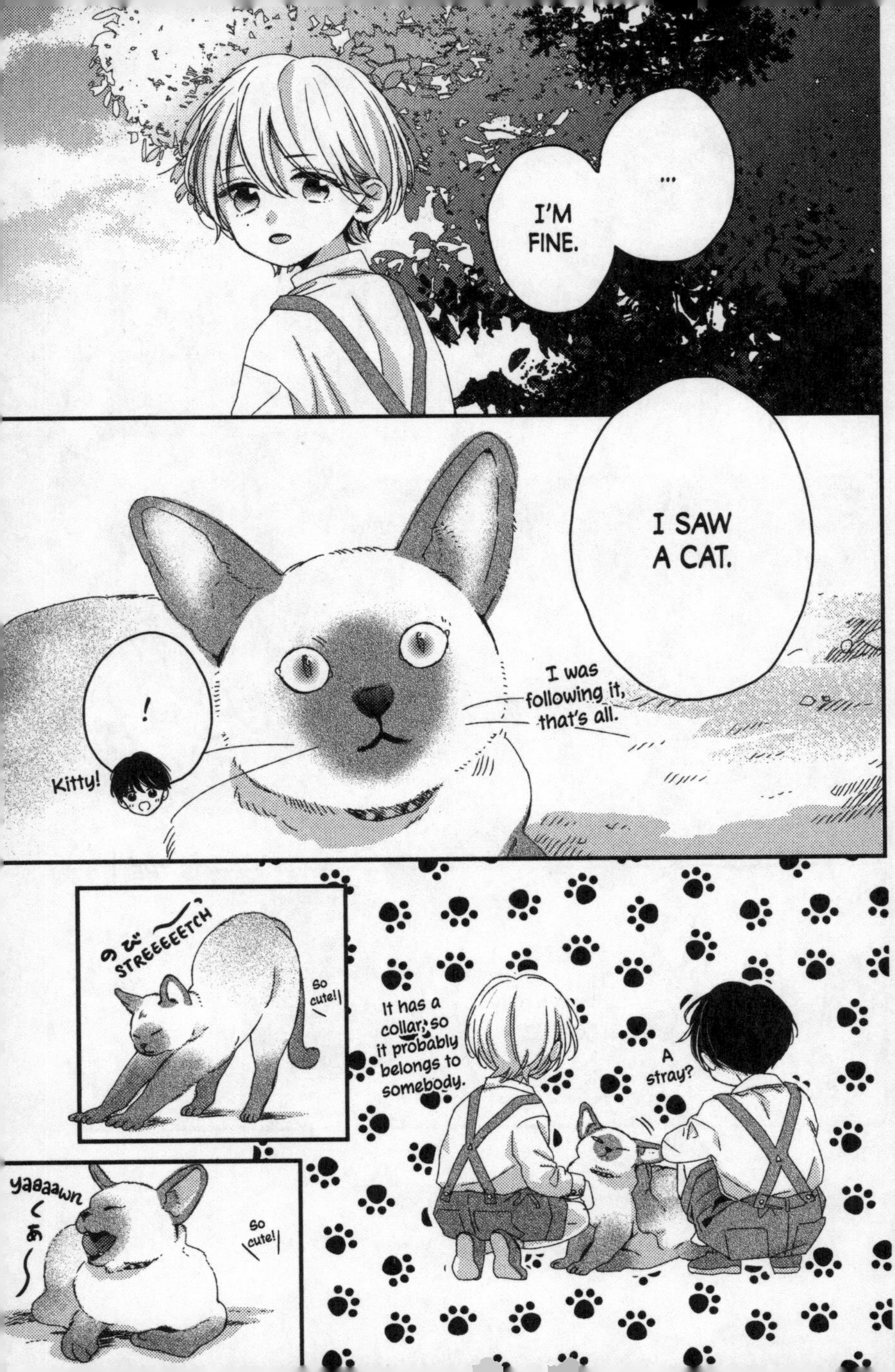
...
I'M FINE.
I SAW A CAT.
I was following it, that's all.
!
Kitty!
A stray?
It has a collar, so it probably belongs to somebody.
のび STREEEEEETCH
So cute!
くあ~ yaaaawn
So cute!

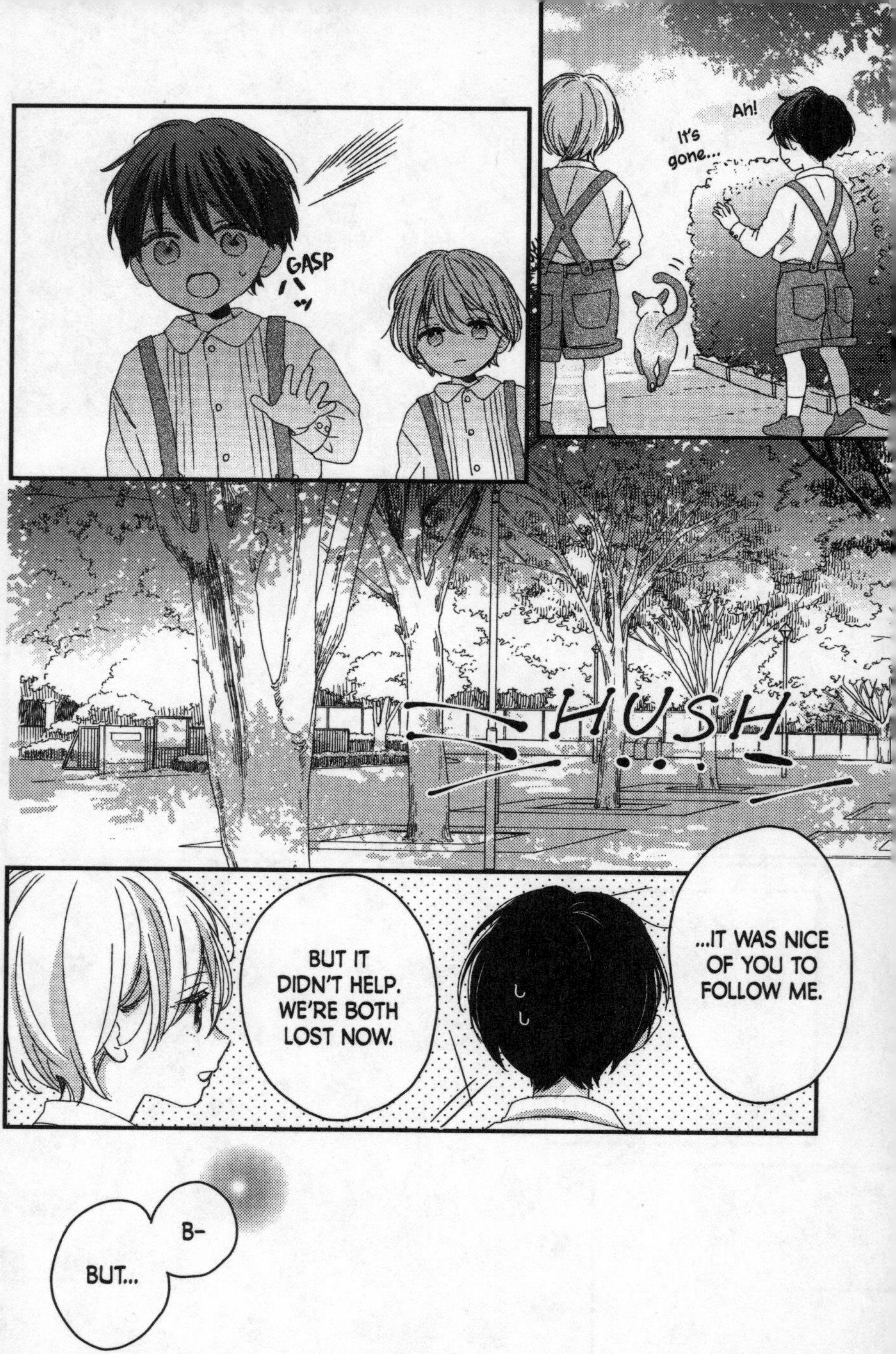
Ah!
It's gone...
GASP
ハッ
HUSH
...IT WAS NICE OF YOU TO FOLLOW ME.
BUT IT DIDN'T HELP. WE'RE BOTH LOST NOW.
B- BUT...

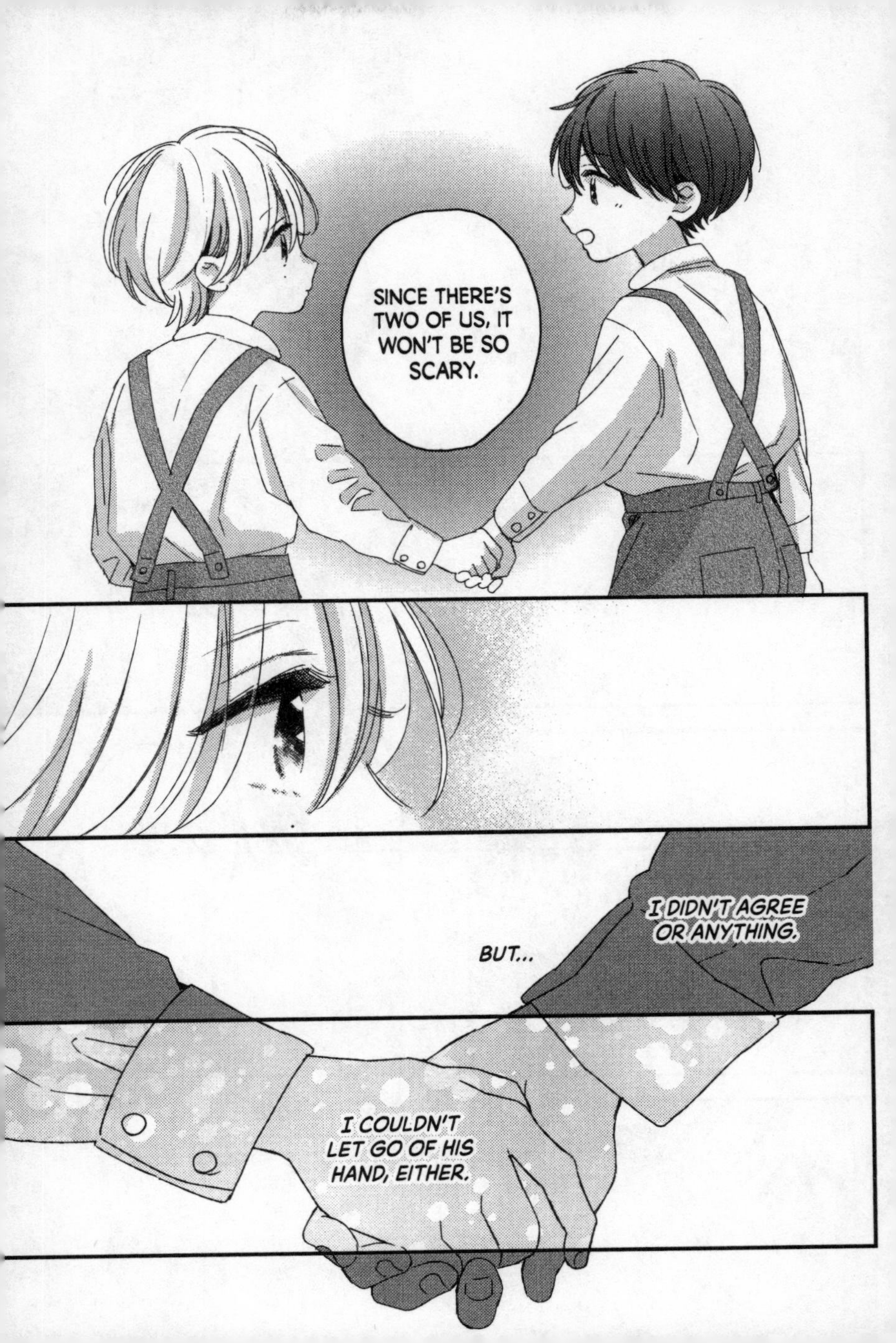
SINCE THERE'S TWO OF US, IT WON'T BE SO SCARY.
I DIDN'T AGREE OR ANYTHING.
BUT...
I COULDN'T LET GO OF HIS HAND, EITHER.

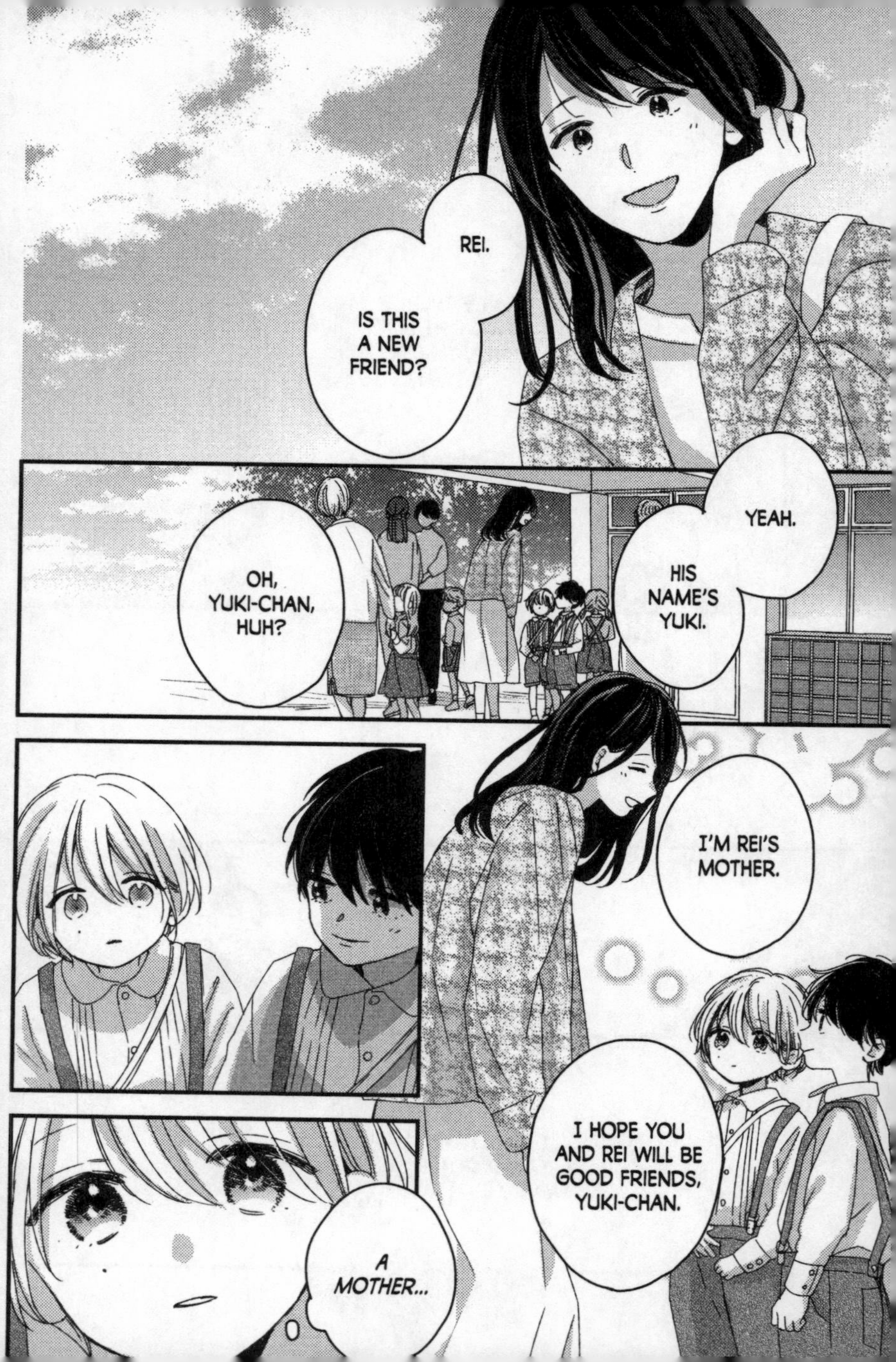
REI.
IS THIS A NEW FRIEND?
YEAH.
HIS NAME'S YUKI.
OH, YUKI-CHAN, HUH?
I'M REI'S MOTHER.
I HOPE YOU AND REI WILL BE GOOD FRIENDS, YUKI-CHAN.
A MOTHER...

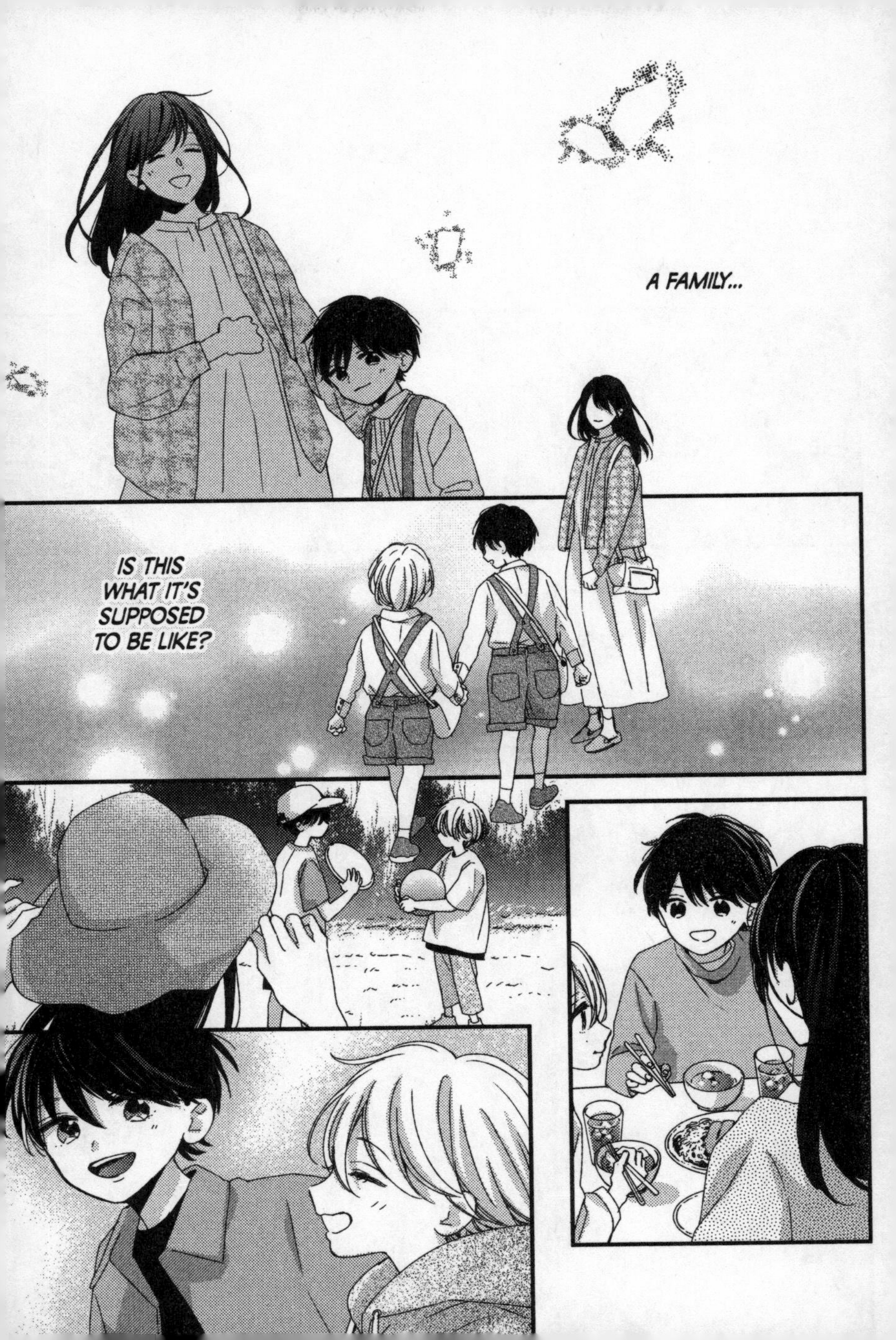
A FAMILY...
IS THIS WHAT IT'S SUPPOSED TO BE LIKE?

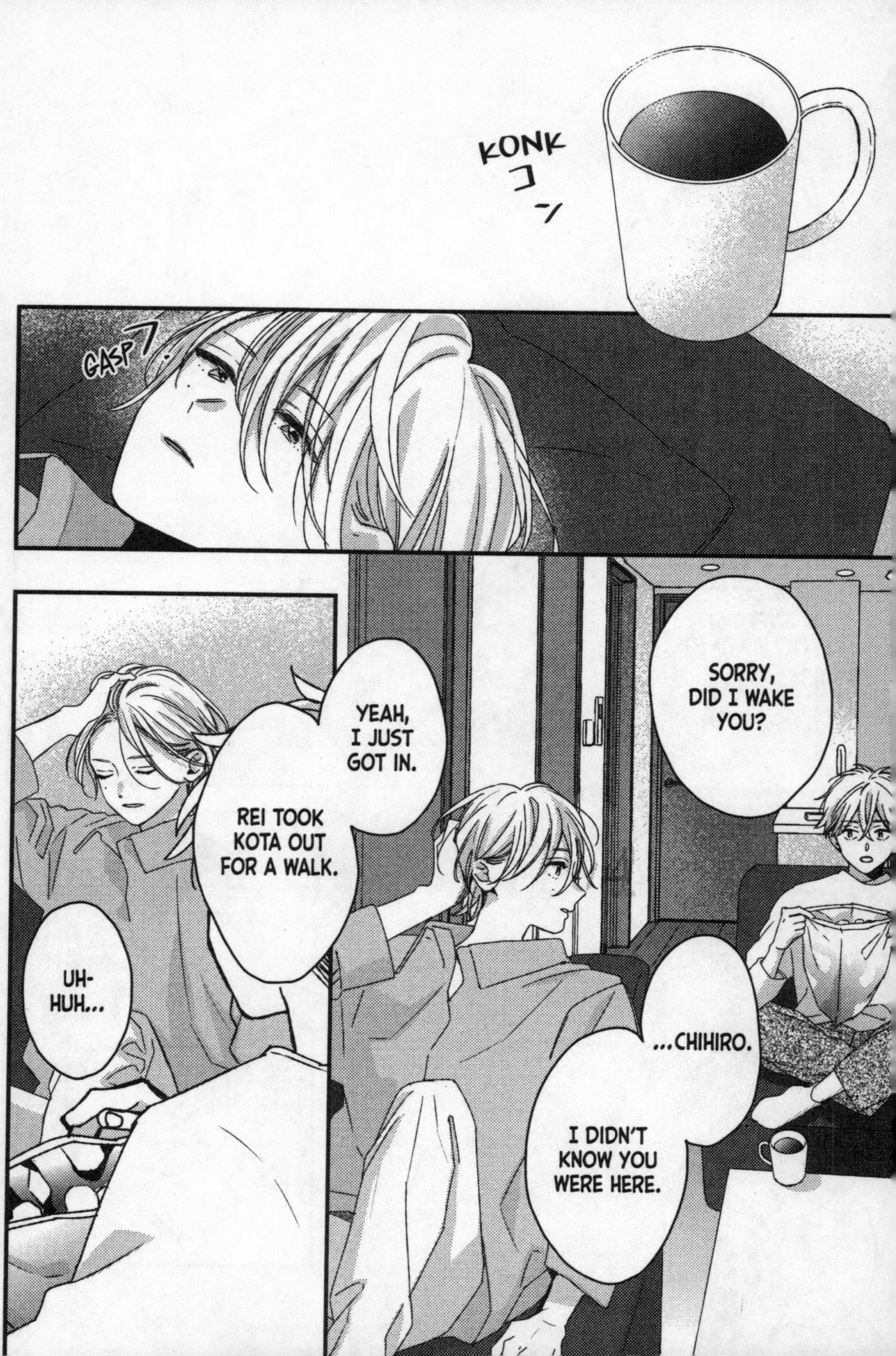
KONK
コン
GASP
SORRY, DID I WAKE YOU?
...CHIHIRO.
I DIDN'T KNOW YOU WERE HERE.
YEAH, I JUST GOT IN.
REI TOOK KOTA OUT FOR A WALK.
UH-HUH...

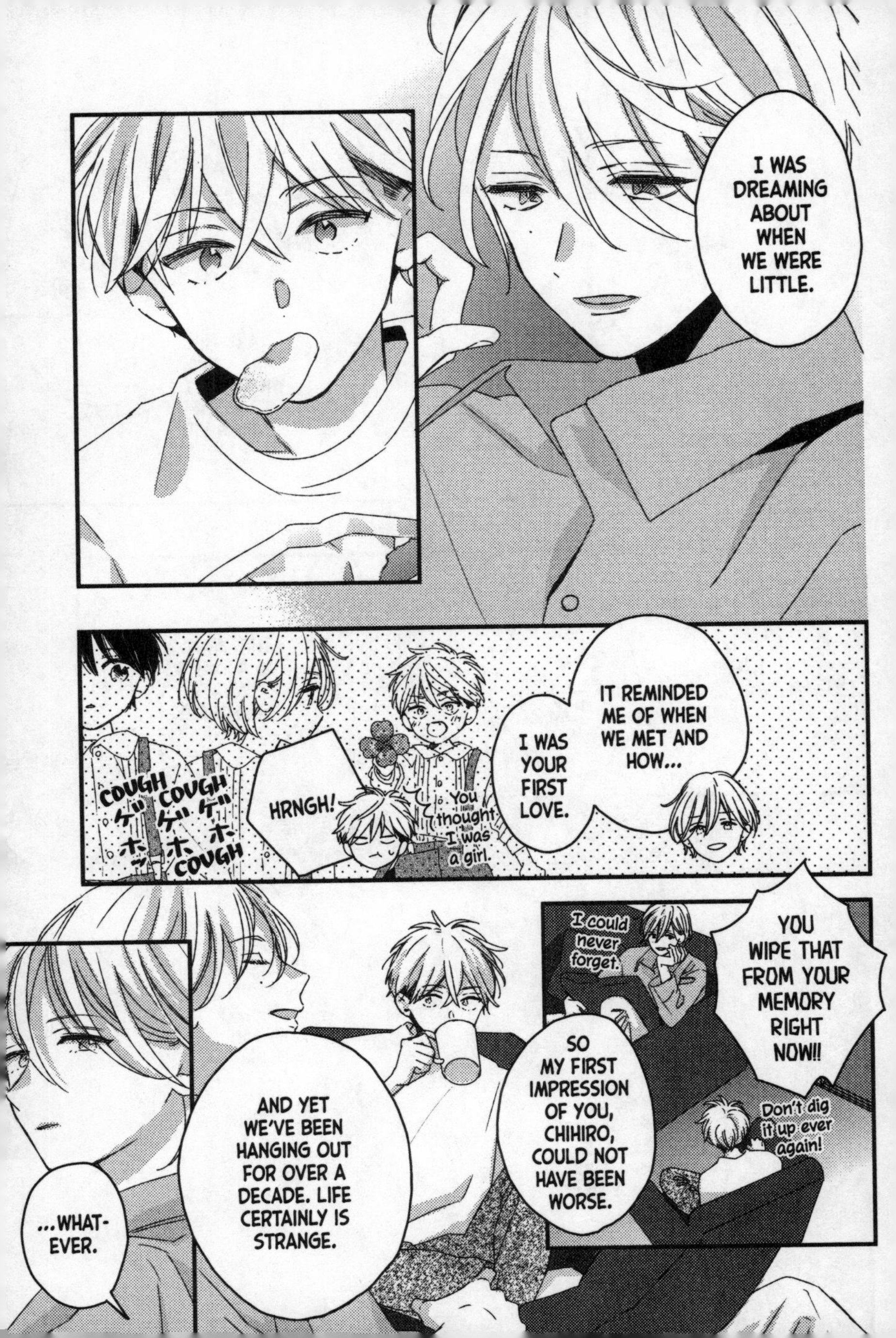
I WAS DREAMING ABOUT WHEN WE WERE LITTLE.
IT REMINDED ME OF WHEN WE MET AND HOW...
I WAS YOUR FIRST LOVE.
You thought I was a girl.
HRNGH!
COUGH
COUGH
COUGH
YOU WIPE THAT FROM YOUR MEMORY RIGHT NOW!!
I could never forget.
SO MY FIRST IMPRESSION OF YOU, CHIHIRO, COULD NOT HAVE BEEN WORSE.
Don't dig it up ever again!
AND YET WE'VE BEEN HANGING OUT FOR OVER A DECADE. LIFE CERTAINLY IS STRANGE.
...WHAT-EVER.

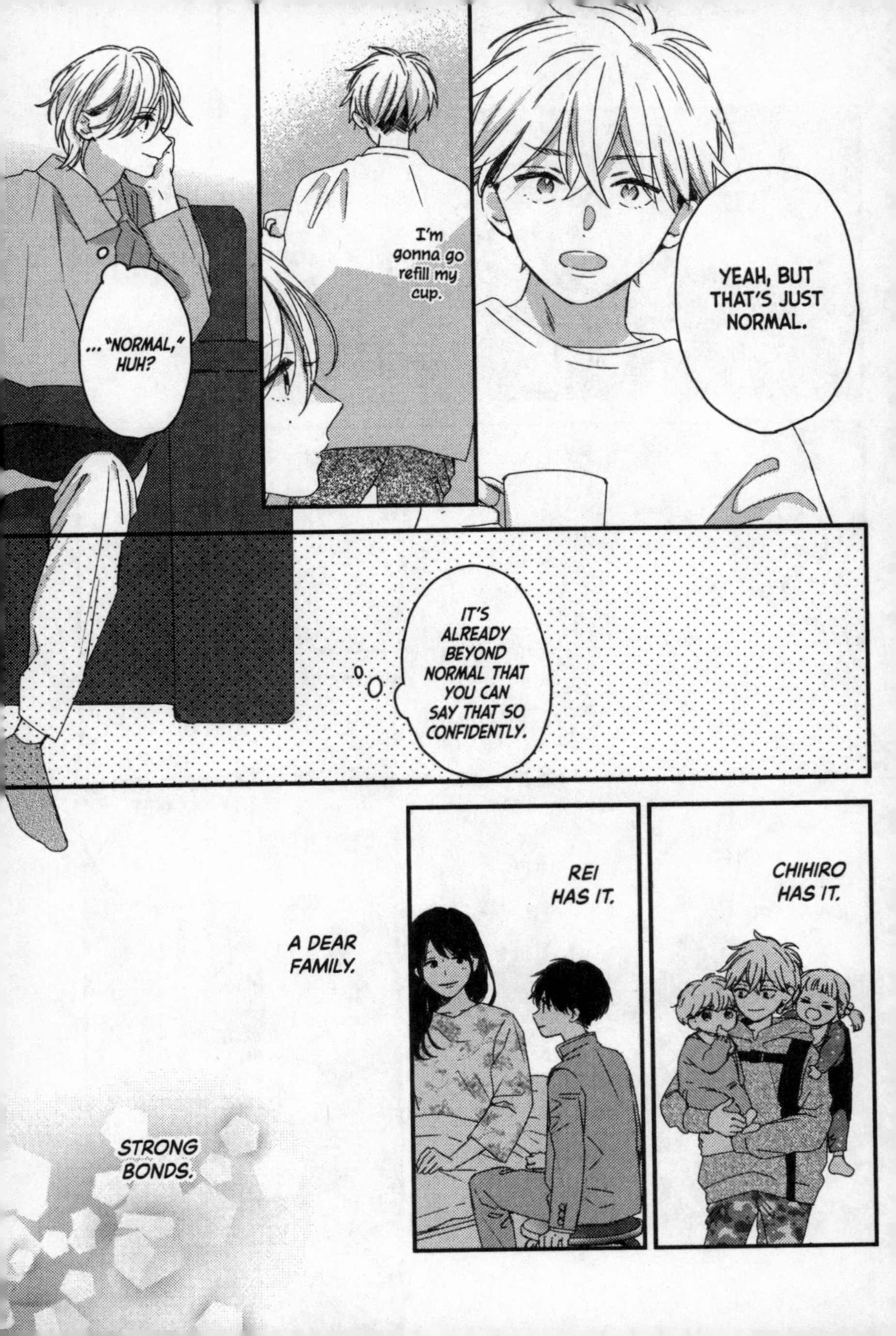
YEAH, BUT THAT'S JUST NORMAL.
I'm gonna go refill my cup.
..."NORMAL," HUH?
IT'S ALREADY BEYOND NORMAL THAT YOU CAN SAY THAT SO CONFIDENTLY.
CHIHIRO HAS IT.
REI HAS IT.
A DEAR FAMILY.
STRONG BONDS.

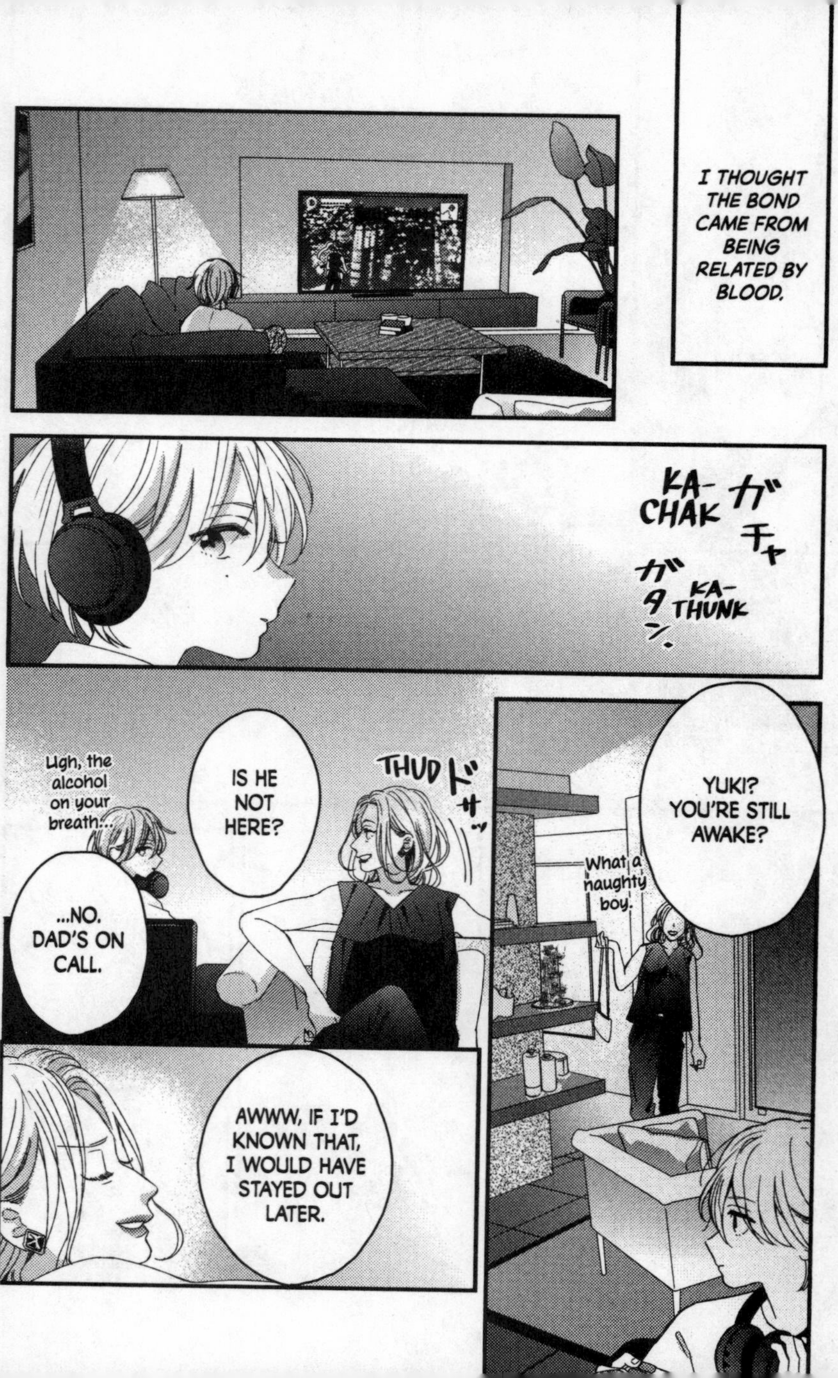
I THOUGHT THE BOND CAME FROM BEING RELATED BY BLOOD.
KA-CHAK ガチャ
ガタン KA-THUNK
YUKI? YOU'RE STILL AWAKE?
What a naughty boy.
THUD ドサッ
IS HE NOT HERE?
Ugh, the alcohol on your breath...
...NO. DAD'S ON CALL.
AWWW, IF I'D KNOWN THAT, I WOULD HAVE STAYED OUT LATER.

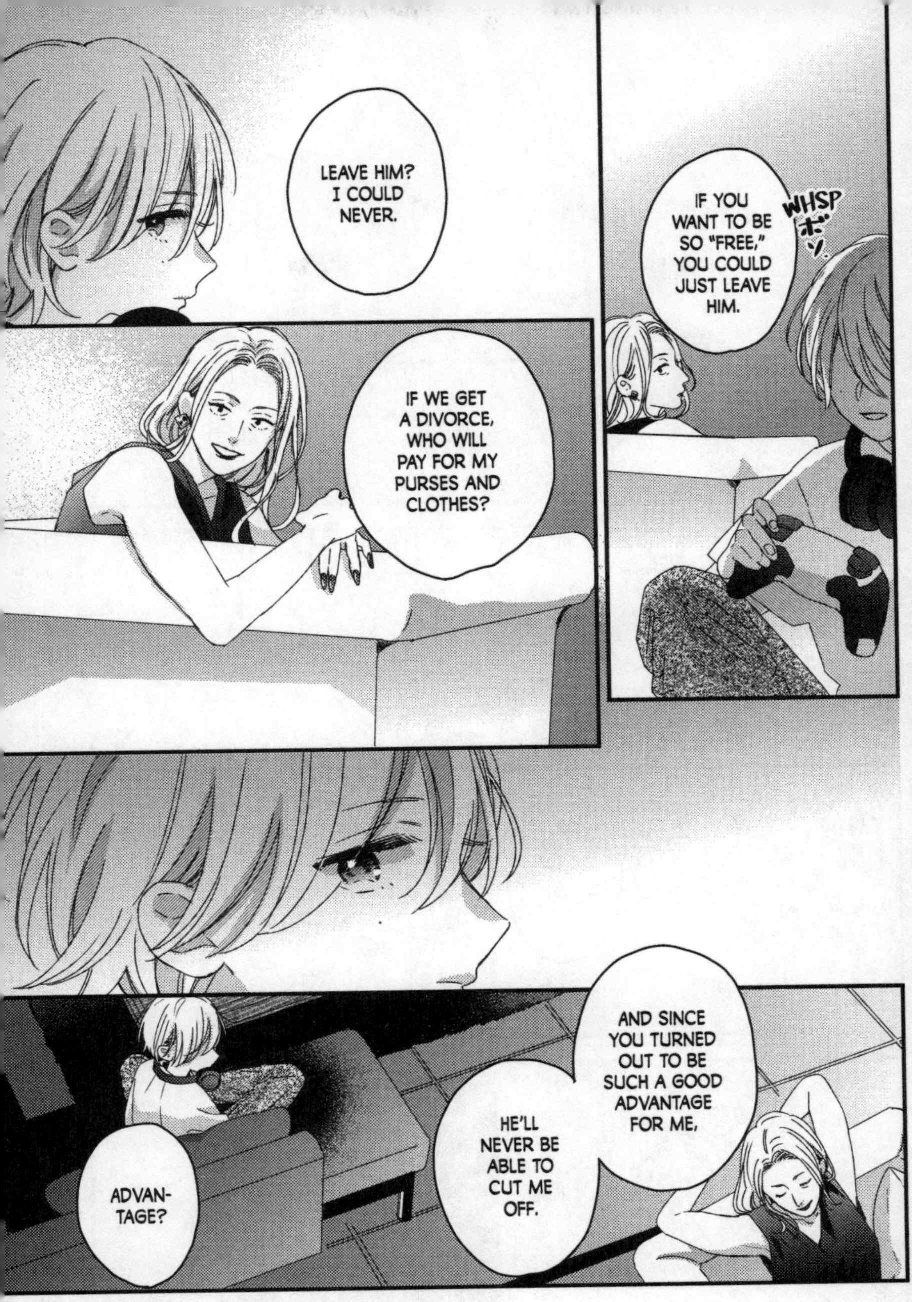
IF YOU WANT TO BE SO "FREE," YOU COULD JUST LEAVE HIM.
WHSP
LEAVE HIM? I COULD NEVER.
IF WE GET A DIVORCE, WHO WILL PAY FOR MY PURSES AND CLOTHES?
AND SINCE YOU TURNED OUT TO BE SUCH A GOOD ADVANTAGE FOR ME,
HE'LL NEVER BE ABLE TO CUT ME OFF.
ADVAN-TAGE?

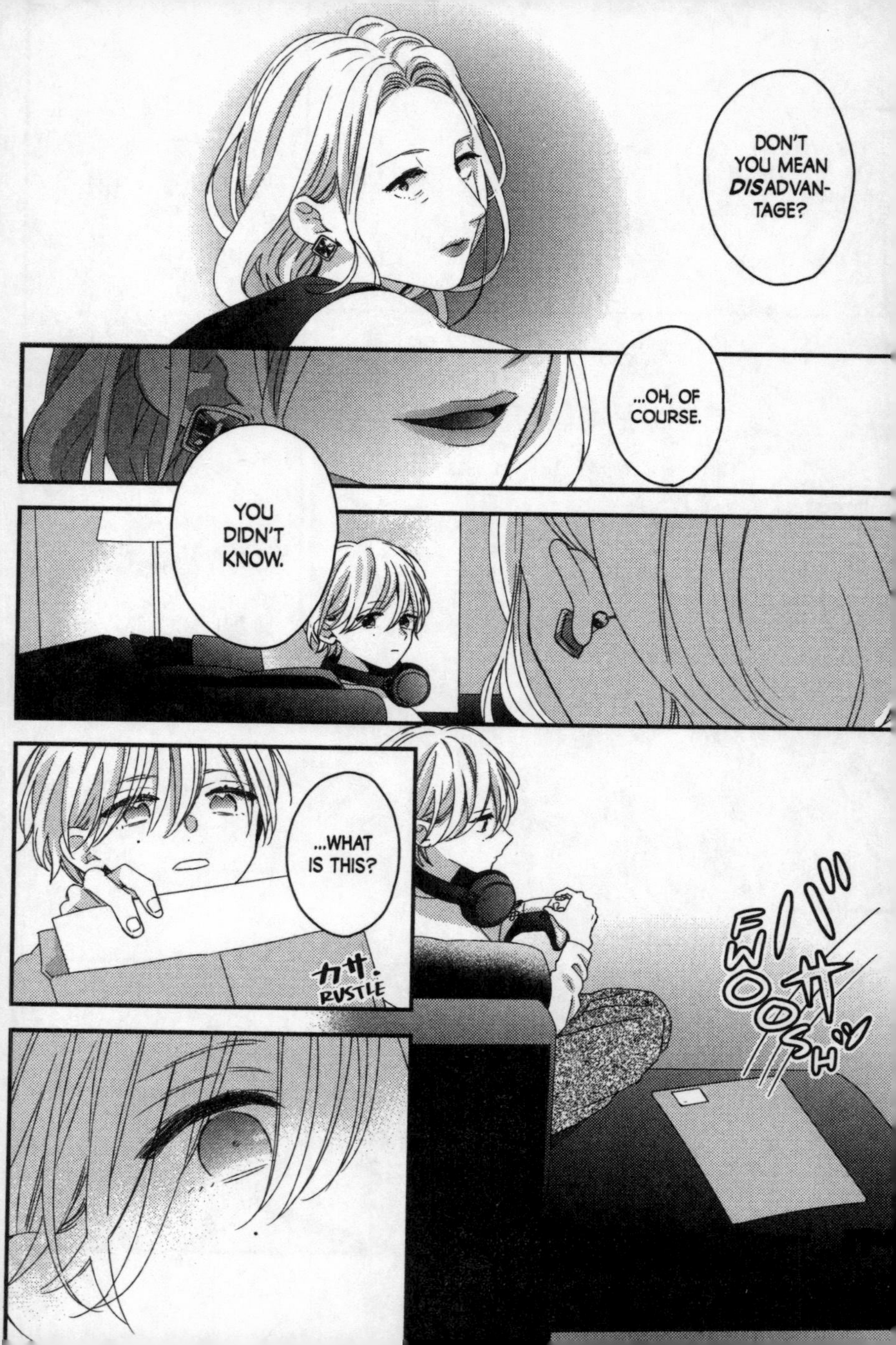
DON'T YOU MEAN *DIS*ADVANTAGE?
...OH, OF COURSE.
YOU DIDN'T KNOW.
バッ
FWOOSH
...WHAT IS THIS?
カサ
RUSTLE

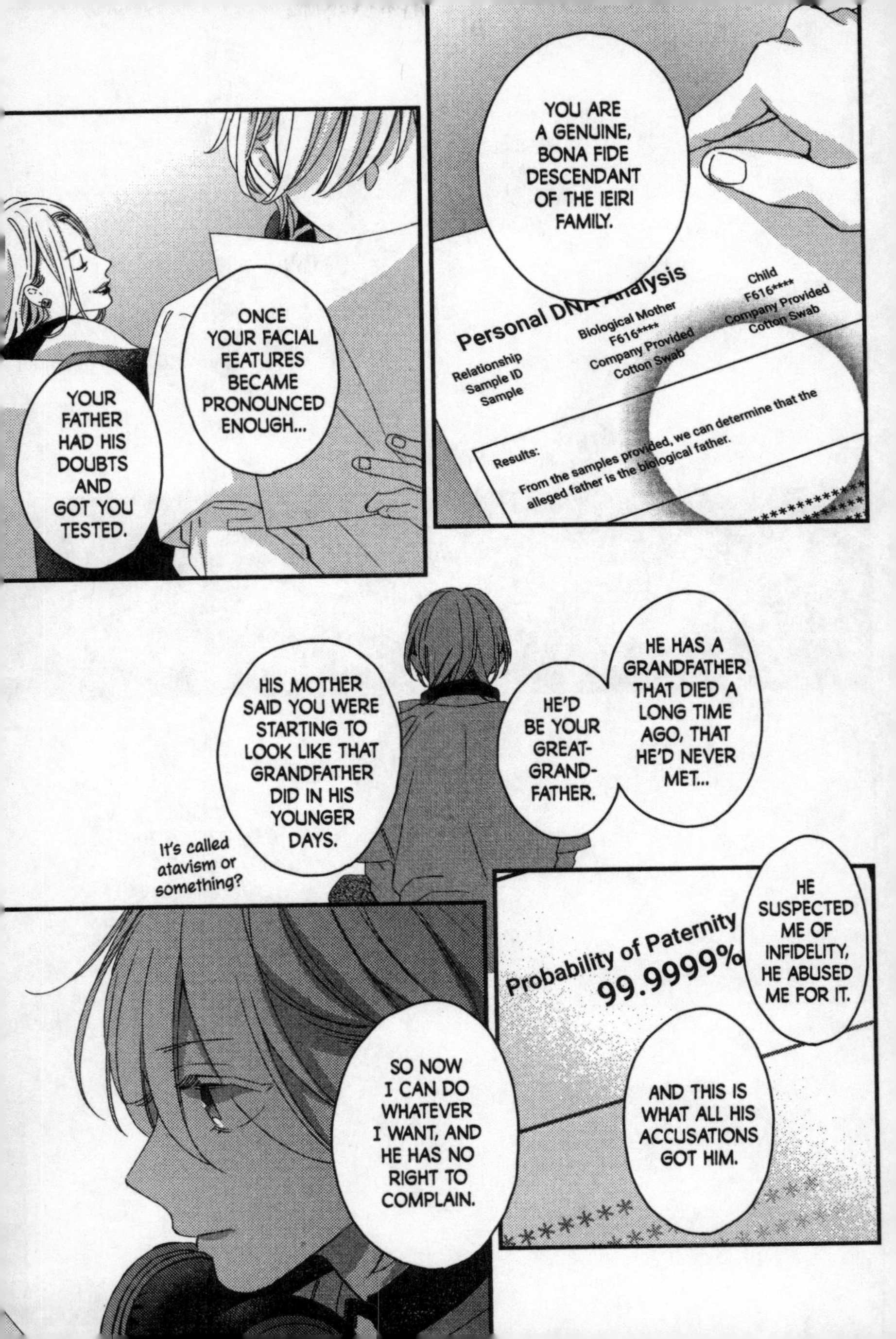
YOU ARE A GENUINE, BONA FIDE DESCENDANT OF THE IEIRI FAMILY.
Personal DNA Analysis
Relationship
Sample ID
Sample
Biological Mother
F616****
Company Provided
Cotton Swab
Child
F616****
Company Provided
Cotton Swab
Results:
From the samples provided, we can determine that the alleged father is the biological father.
ONCE YOUR FACIAL FEATURES BECAME PRONOUNCED ENOUGH...
YOUR FATHER HAD HIS DOUBTS AND GOT YOU TESTED.
HE HAS A GRANDFATHER THAT DIED A LONG TIME AGO, THAT HE'D NEVER MET...
HE'D BE YOUR GREAT-GRANDFATHER.
HIS MOTHER SAID YOU WERE STARTING TO LOOK LIKE THAT GRANDFATHER DID IN HIS YOUNGER DAYS.
It's called atavism or something?
HE SUSPECTED ME OF INFIDELITY, HE ABUSED ME FOR IT.
Probability of Paternity
99.9999%
AND THIS IS WHAT ALL HIS ACCUSATIONS GOT HIM.
SO NOW I CAN DO WHATEVER I WANT, AND HE HAS NO RIGHT TO COMPLAIN.

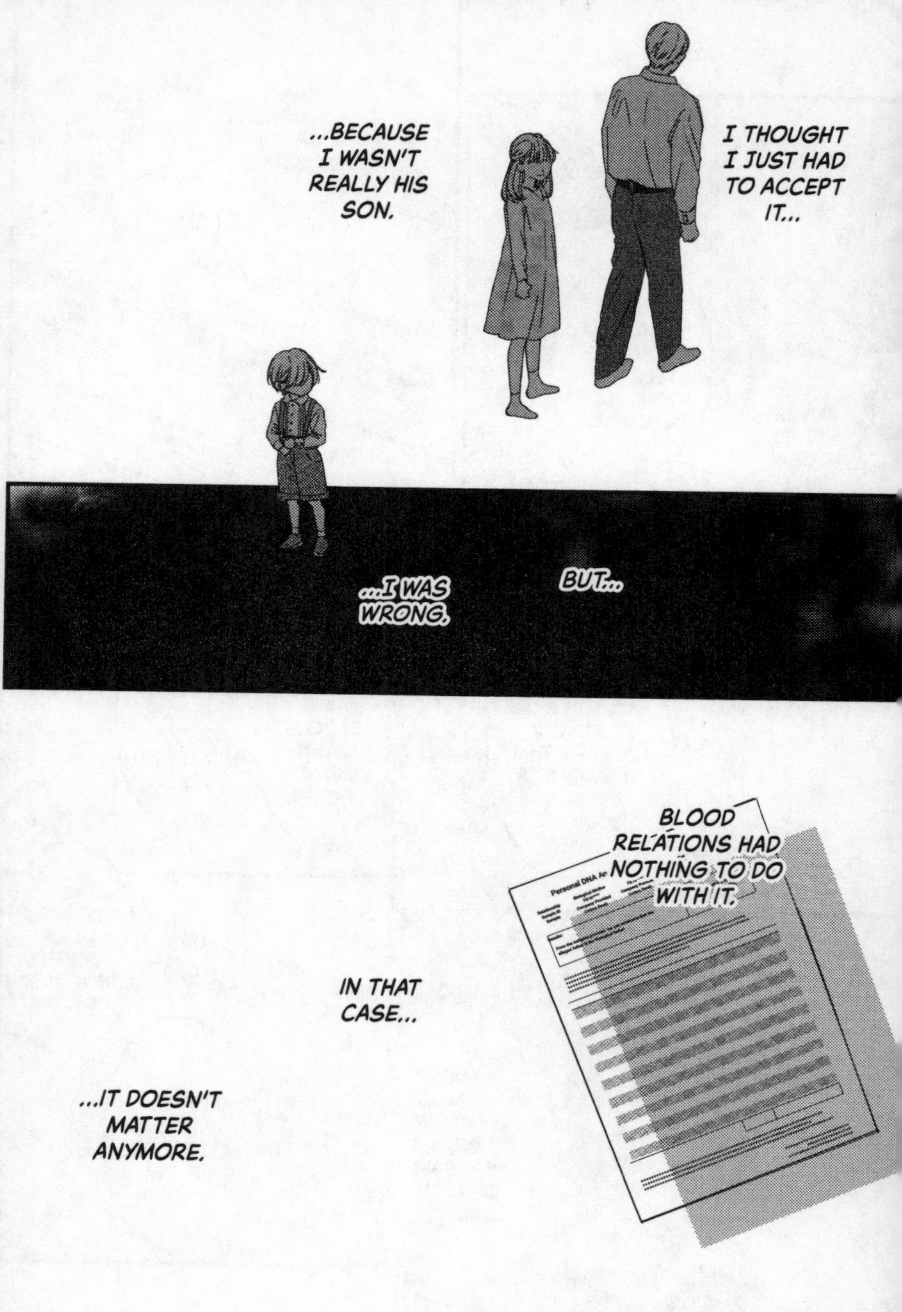
I THOUGHT I JUST HAD TO ACCEPT IT...
...BECAUSE I WASN'T REALLY HIS SON.
BUT...
...I WAS WRONG.
BLOOD RELATIONS HAD NOTHING TO DO WITH IT.
IN THAT CASE...
...IT DOESN'T MATTER ANYMORE.

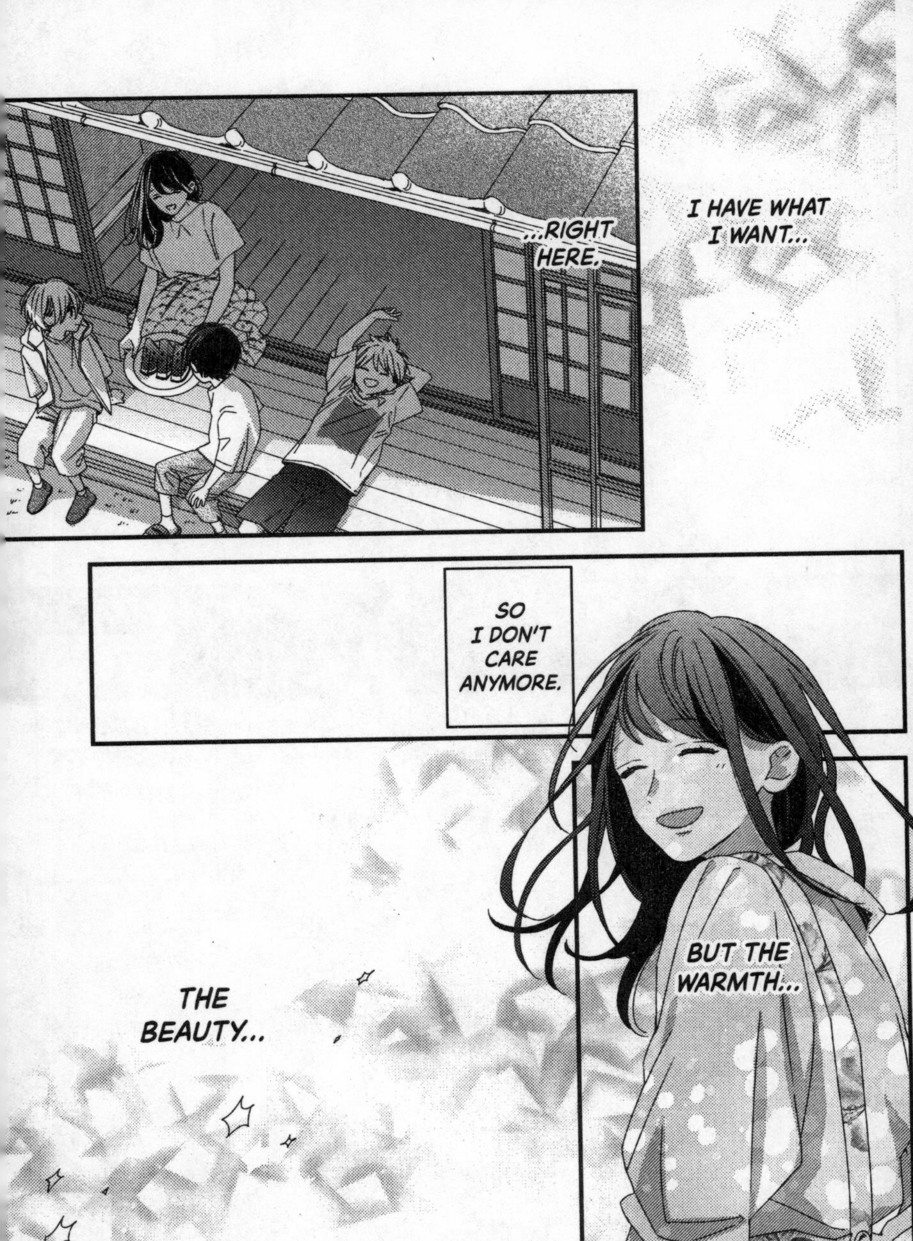
I HAVE WHAT I WANT...
...RIGHT HERE.
SO I DON'T CARE ANYMORE.
BUT THE WARMTH...
THE BEAUTY...

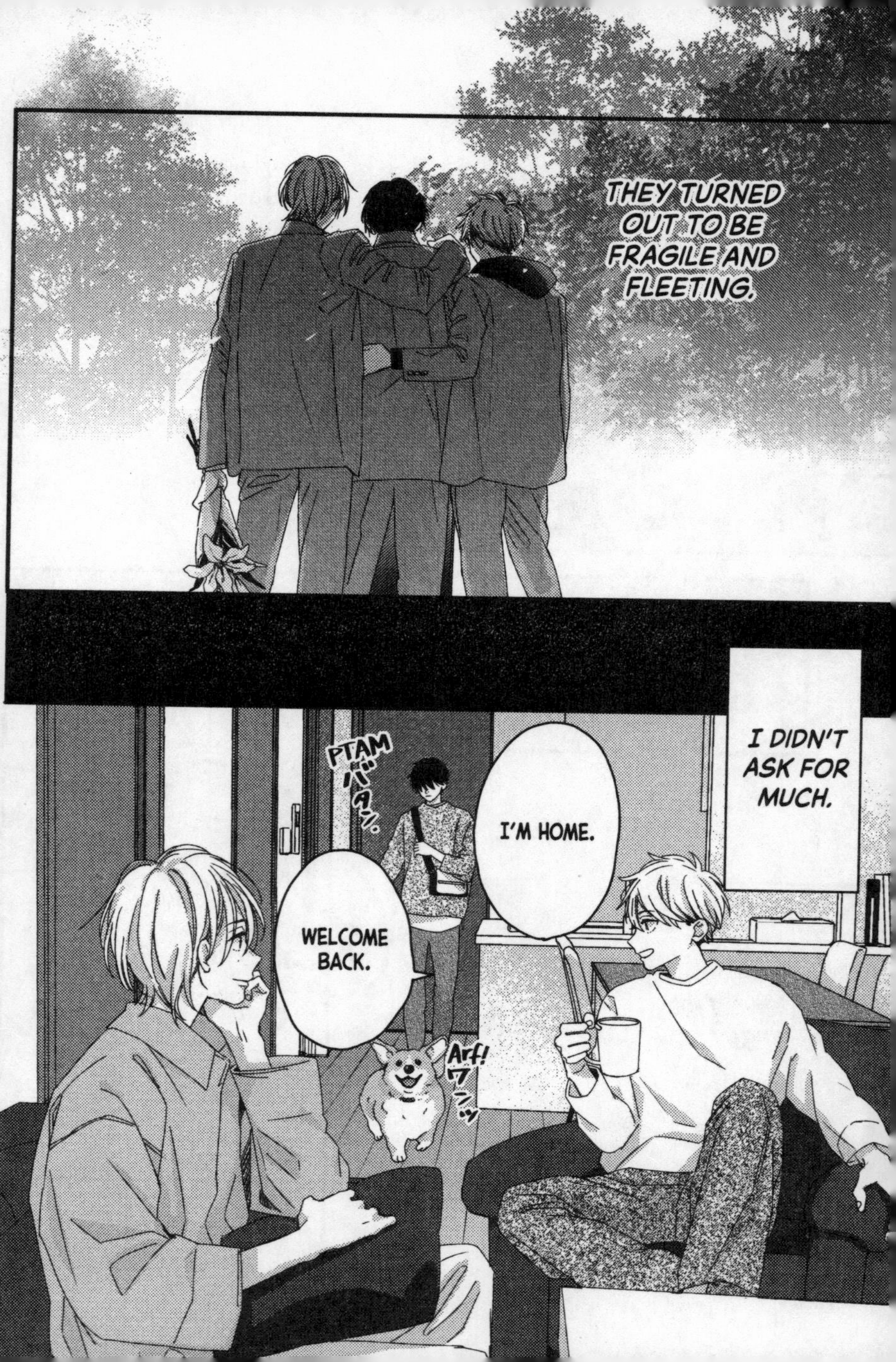
THEY TURNED OUT TO BE FRAGILE AND FLEETING.
I DIDN'T ASK FOR MUCH.
I'M HOME.
PTAM バタン
WELCOME BACK.
Arf! ワンッ

...RIGHT HERE.

I HAVE WHAT I WANT...

SO I DON'T CARE ANYMORE.

BUT THE WARMTH...

THE BEAUTY...

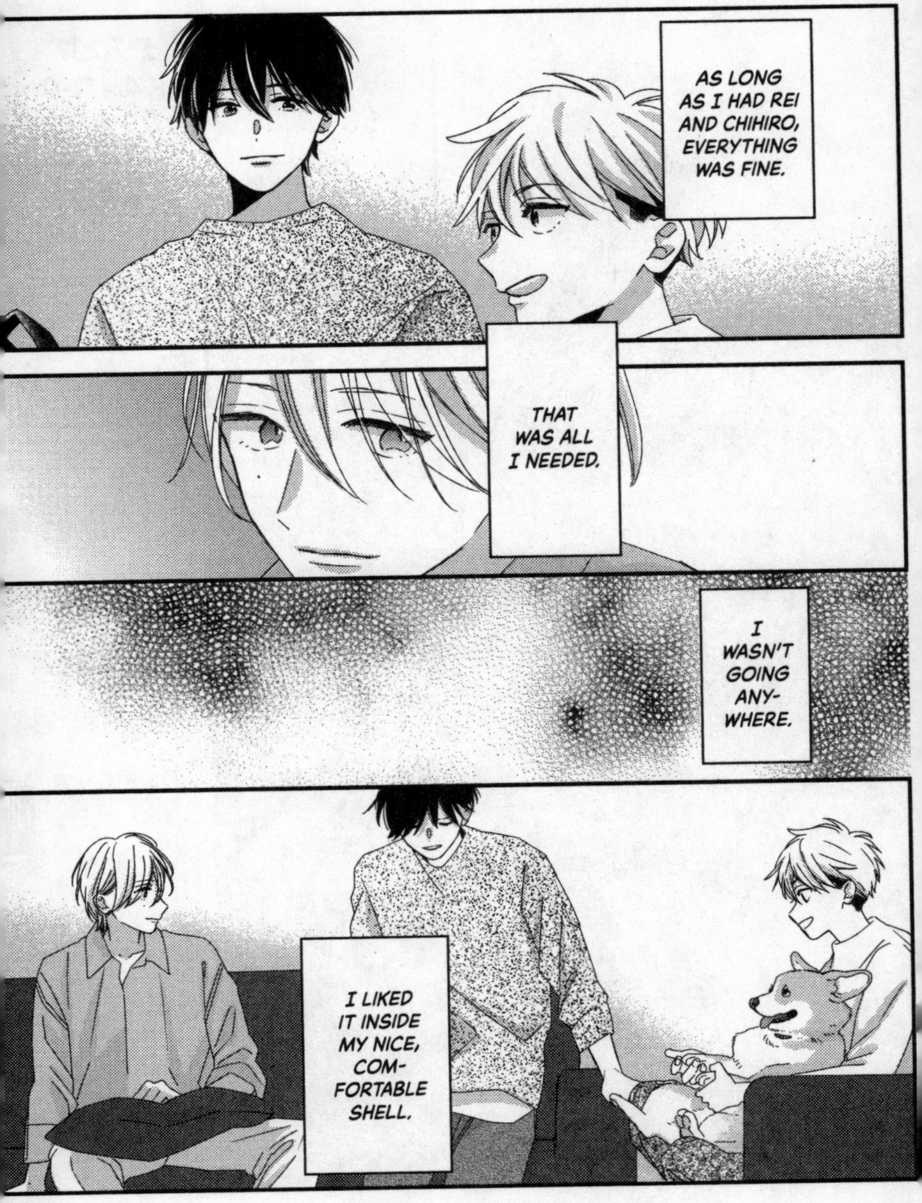
AS LONG AS I HAD REI AND CHIHIRO, EVERYTHING WAS FINE.
THAT WAS ALL I NEEDED.
I WASN'T GOING ANY-WHERE.
I LIKED IT INSIDE MY NICE, COM-FORTABLE SHELL.

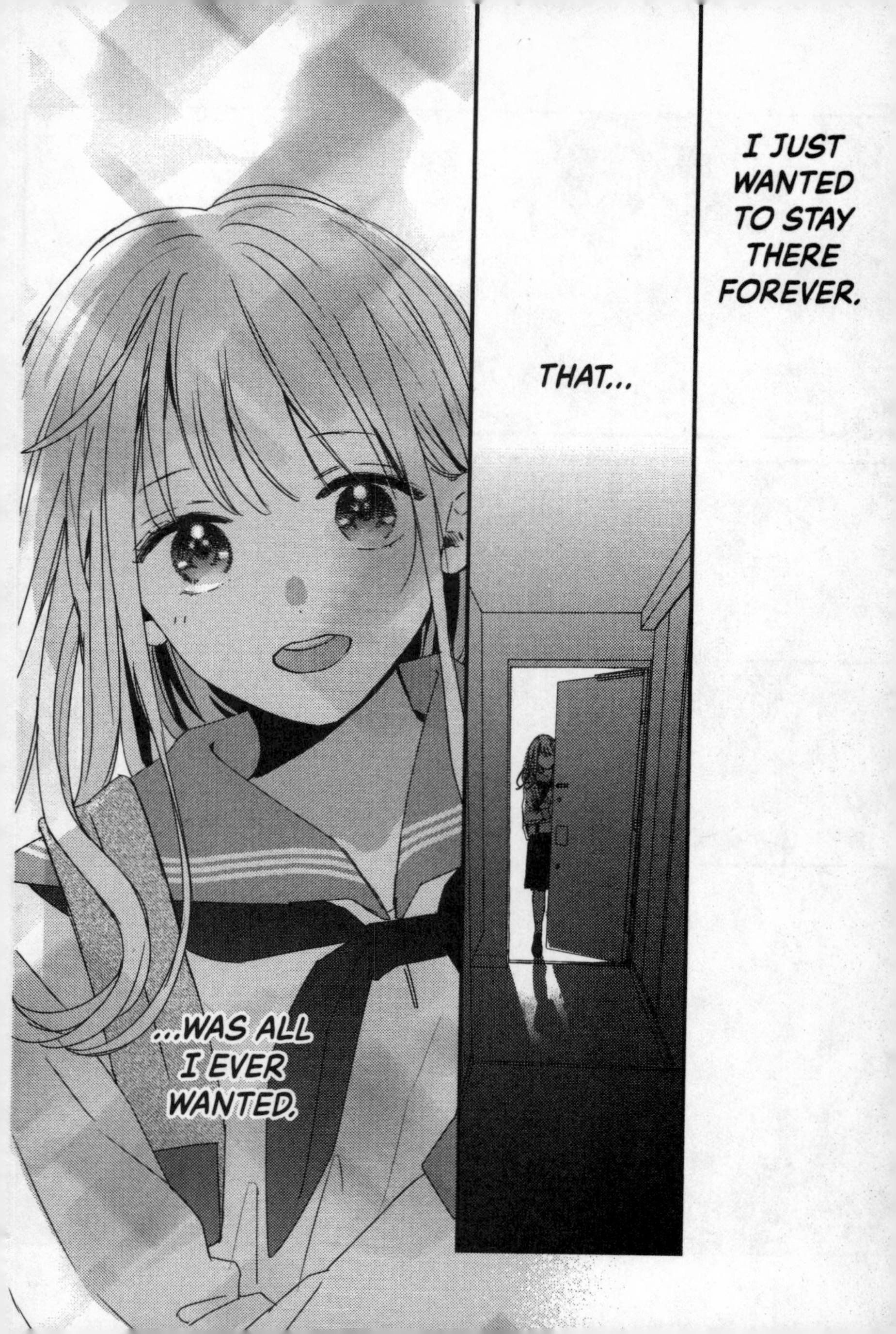
I JUST WANTED TO STAY THERE FOREVER.
THAT...
...WAS ALL I EVER WANTED.

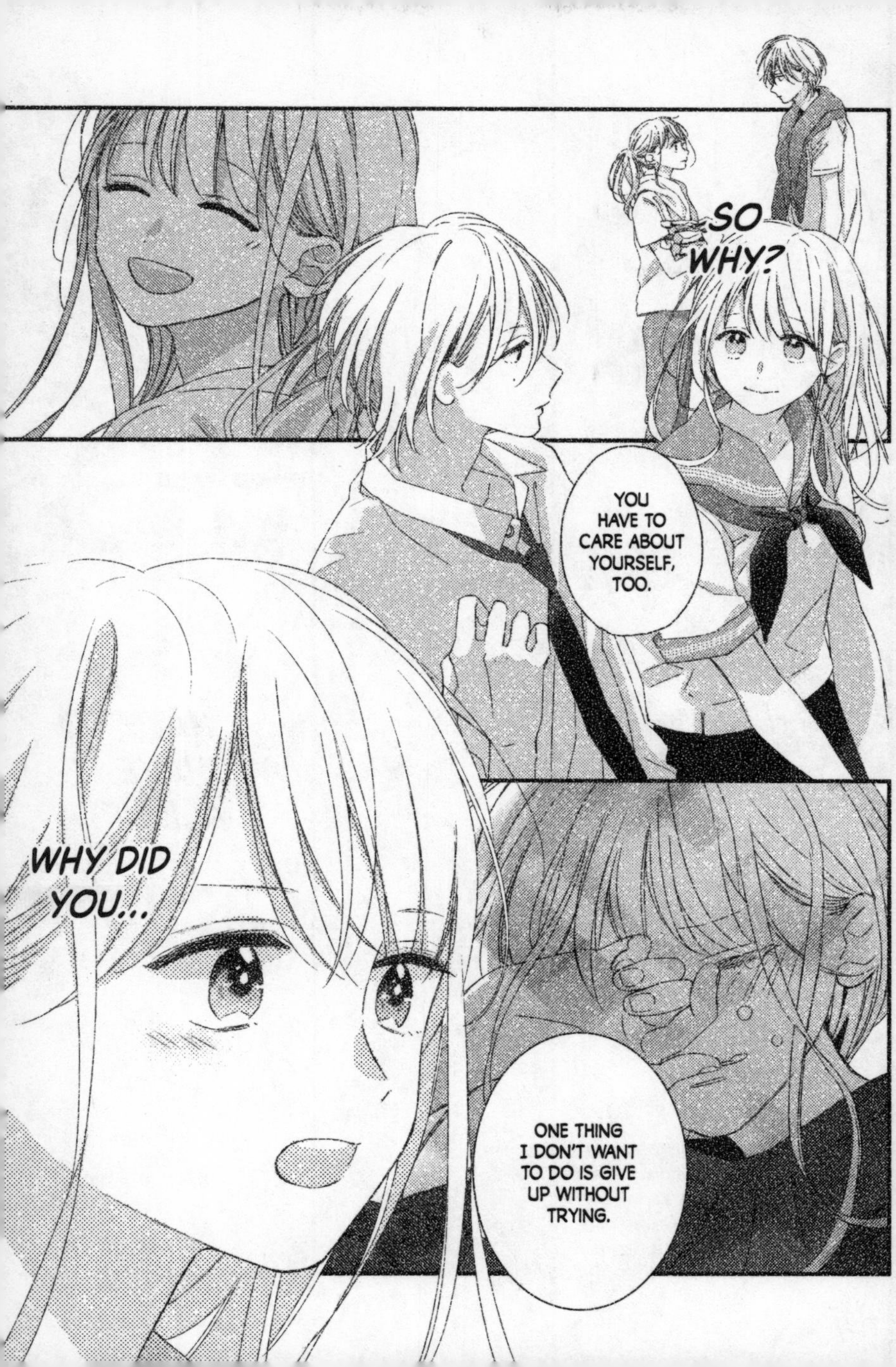
SO WHY?
YOU HAVE TO CARE ABOUT YOURSELF, TOO.
ONE THING I DON'T WANT TO DO IS GIVE UP WITHOUT TRYING.
WHY DID YOU...

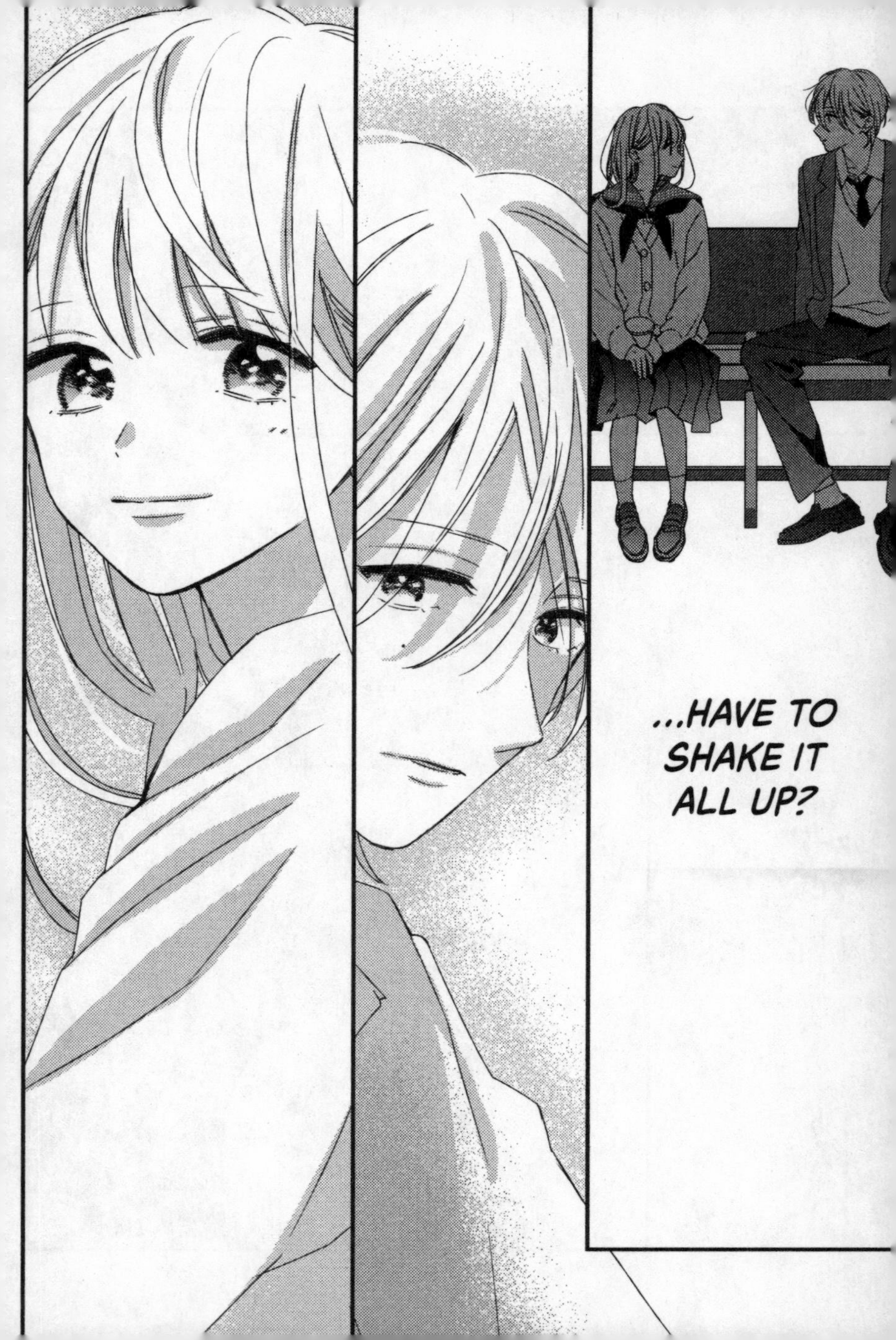
...HAVE TO SHAKE IT ALL UP?

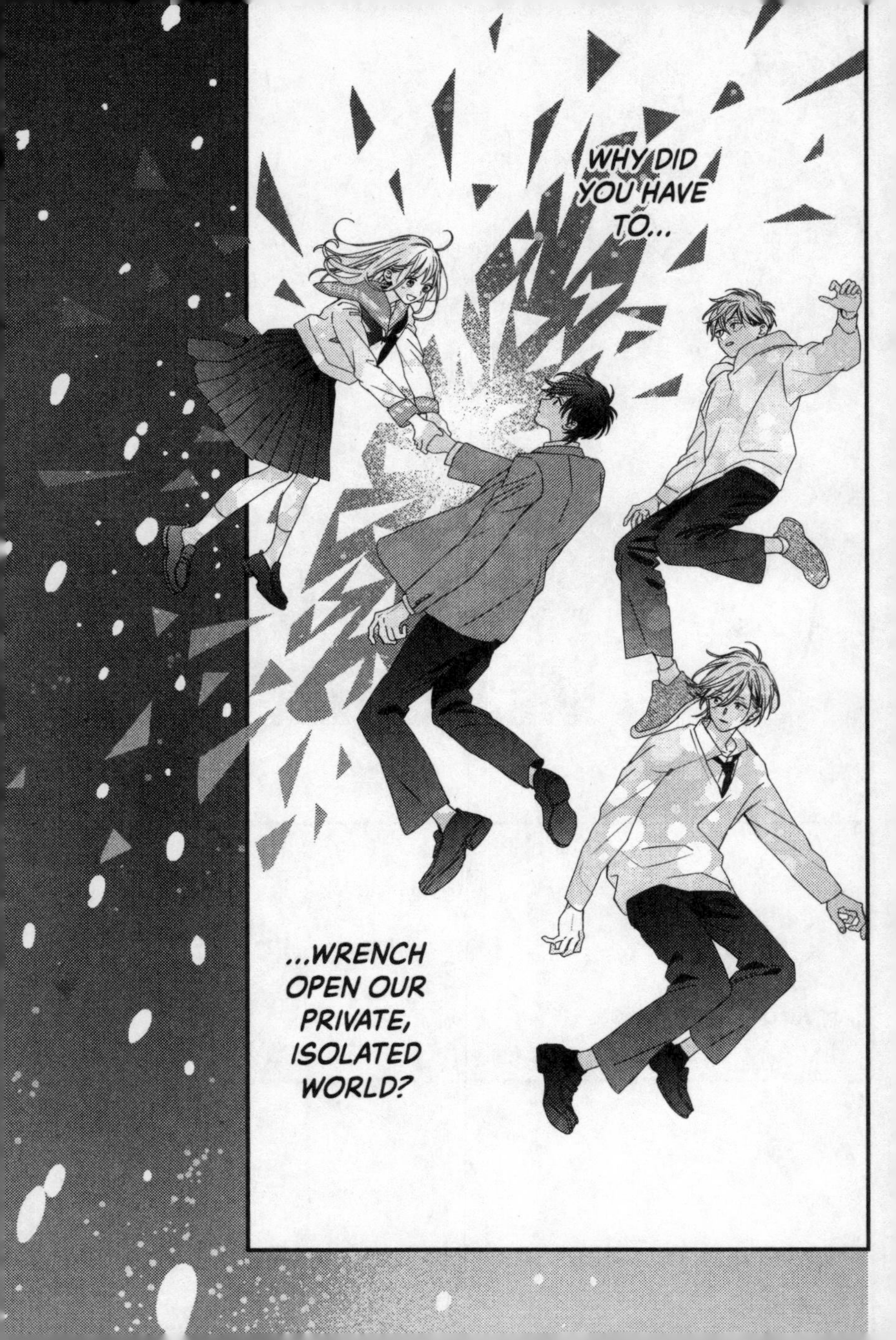
WHY DID YOU HAVE TO...
...WRENCH OPEN OUR PRIVATE, ISOLATED WORLD?

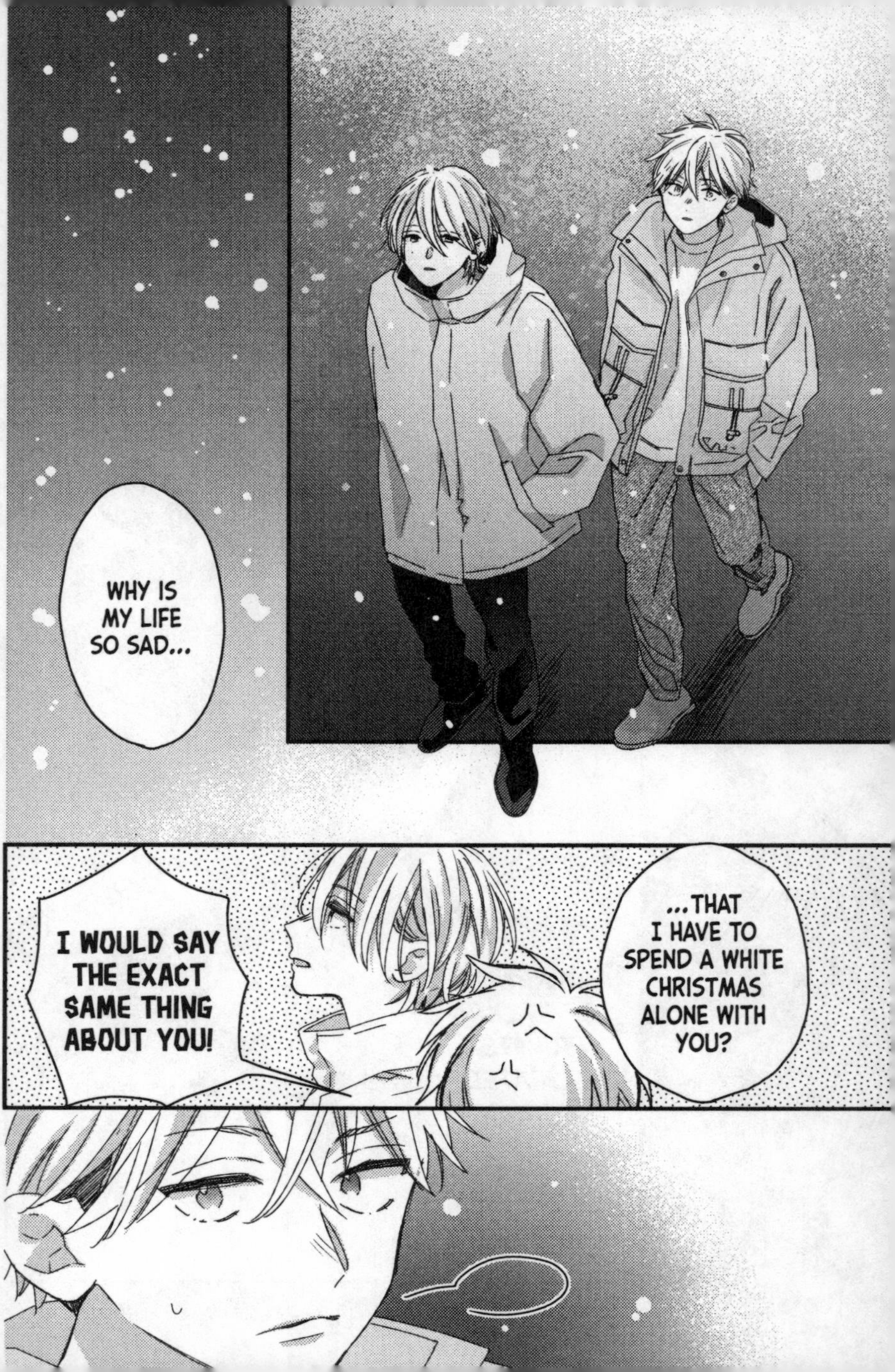
WHY IS MY LIFE SO SAD...
...THAT I HAVE TO SPEND A WHITE CHRISTMAS ALONE WITH YOU?
I WOULD SAY THE EXACT SAME THING ABOUT YOU!

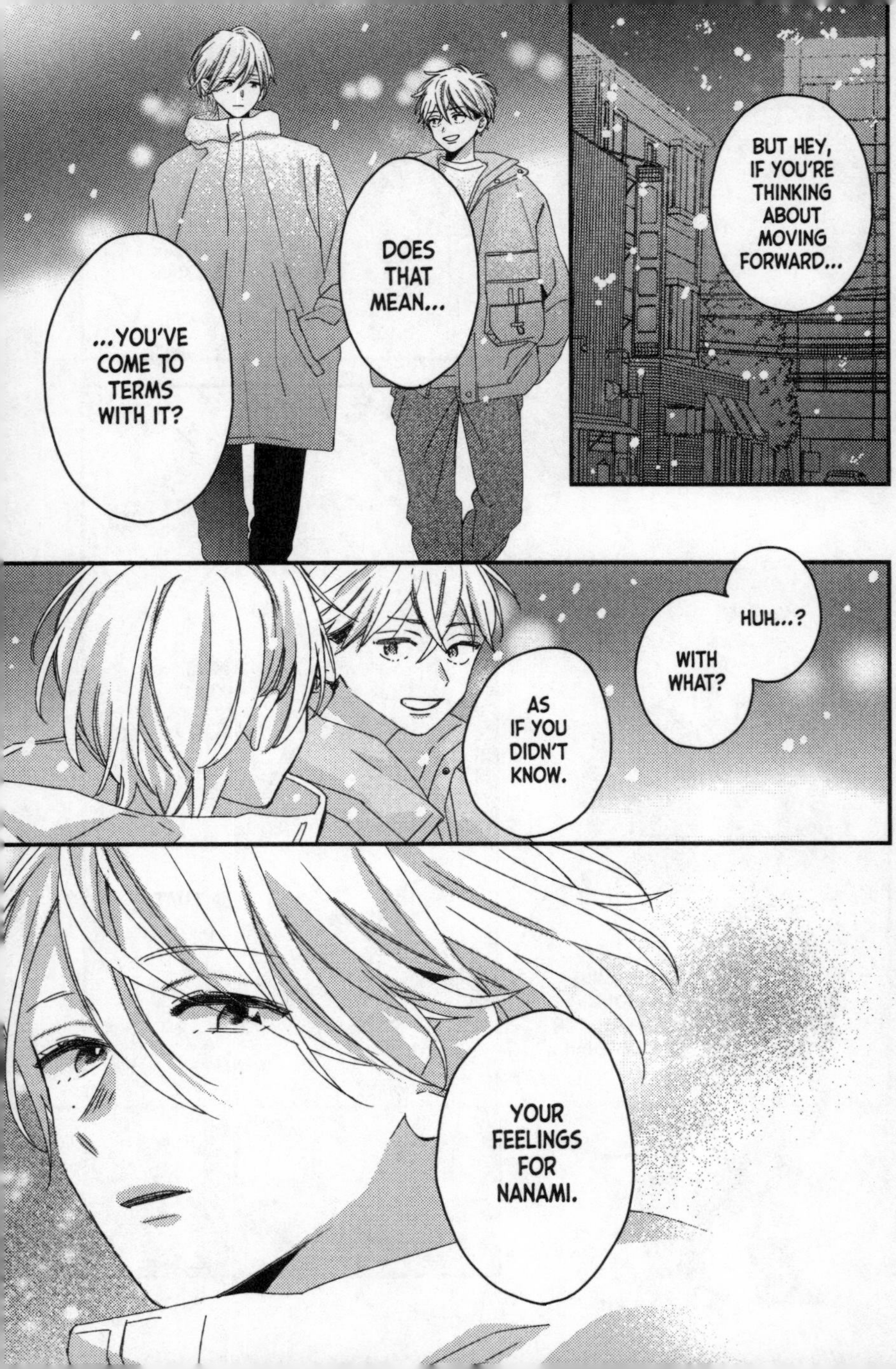
BUT HEY, IF YOU'RE THINKING ABOUT MOVING FORWARD...
DOES THAT MEAN...
...YOU'VE COME TO TERMS WITH IT?
HUH...? WITH WHAT?
AS IF YOU DIDN'T KNOW.
YOUR FEELINGS FOR NANAMI.

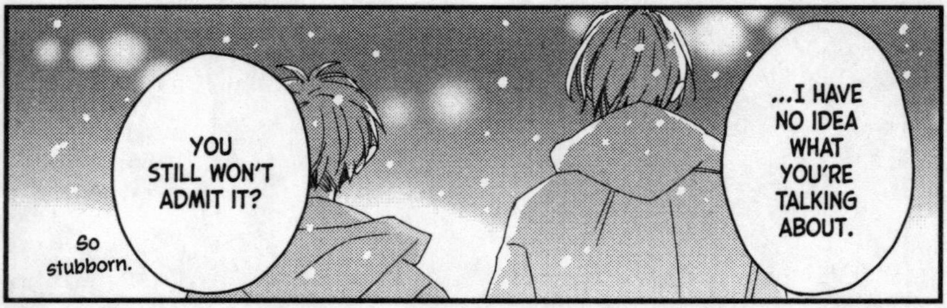
YOU STILL WON'T ADMIT IT?
So stubborn.
...I HAVE NO IDEA WHAT YOU'RE TALKING ABOUT.

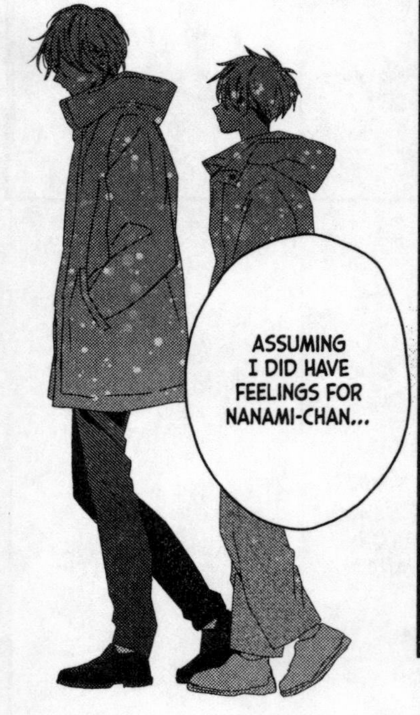
ASSUMING I DID HAVE FEELINGS FOR NANAMI-CHAN...

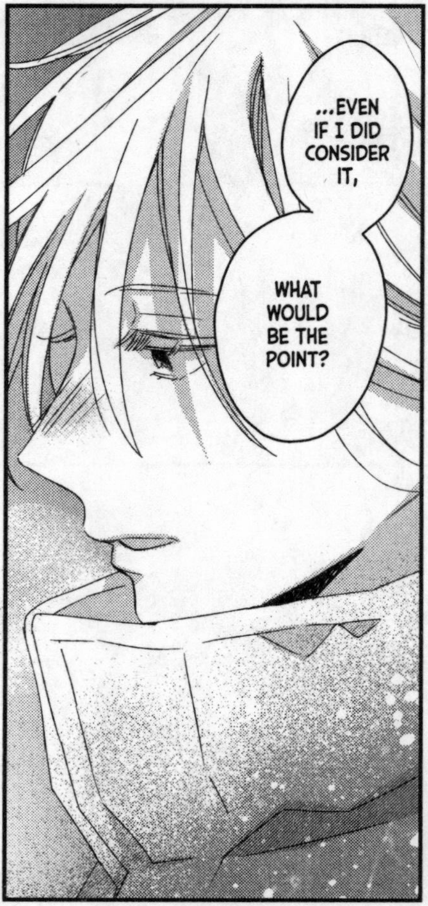
...EVEN IF I DID CONSIDER IT,
WHAT WOULD BE THE POINT?

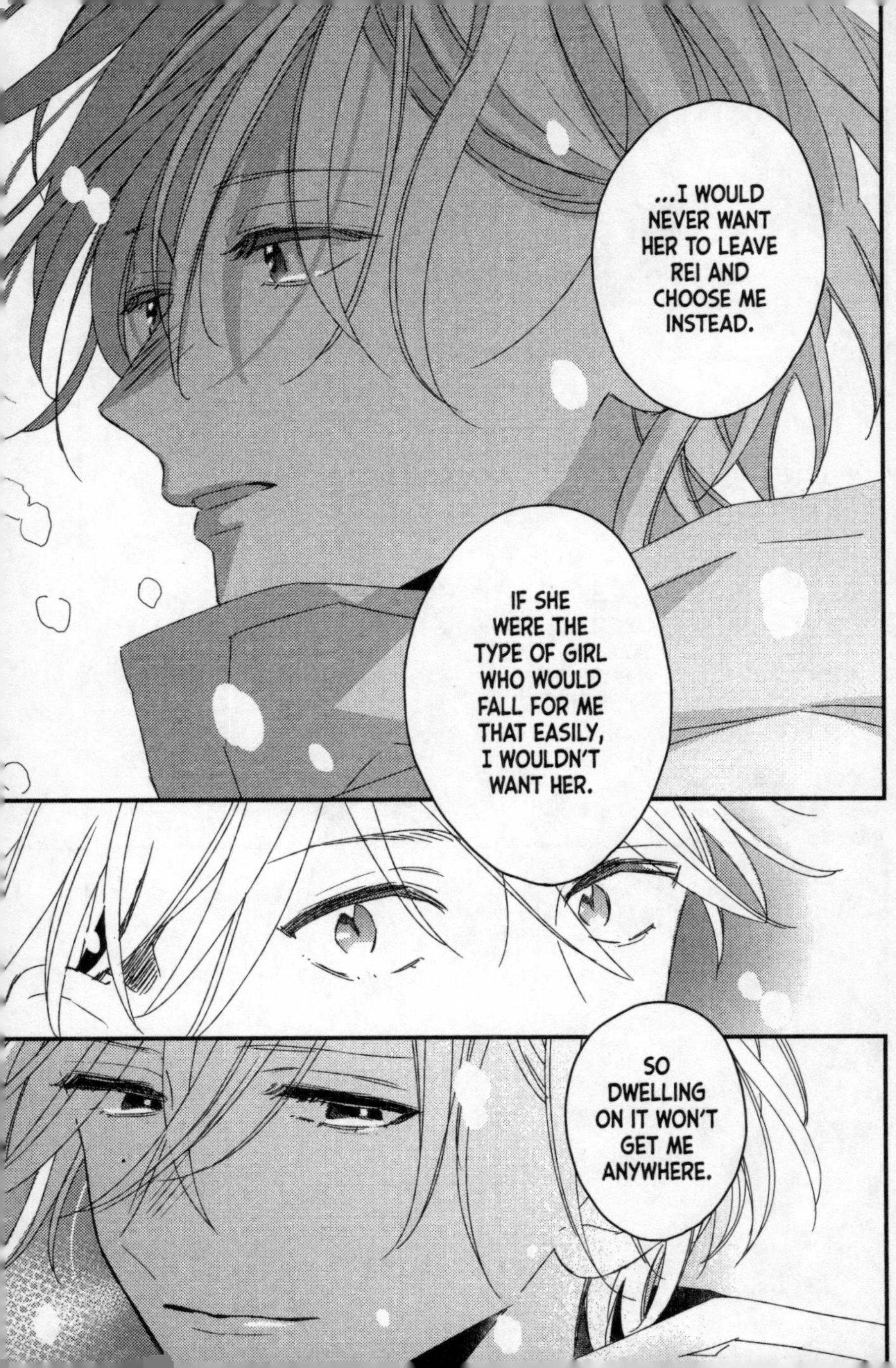
...I WOULD NEVER WANT HER TO LEAVE REI AND CHOOSE ME INSTEAD.
IF SHE WERE THE TYPE OF GIRL WHO WOULD FALL FOR ME THAT EASILY, I WOULDN'T WANT HER.
SO DWELLING ON IT WON'T GET ME ANYWHERE.

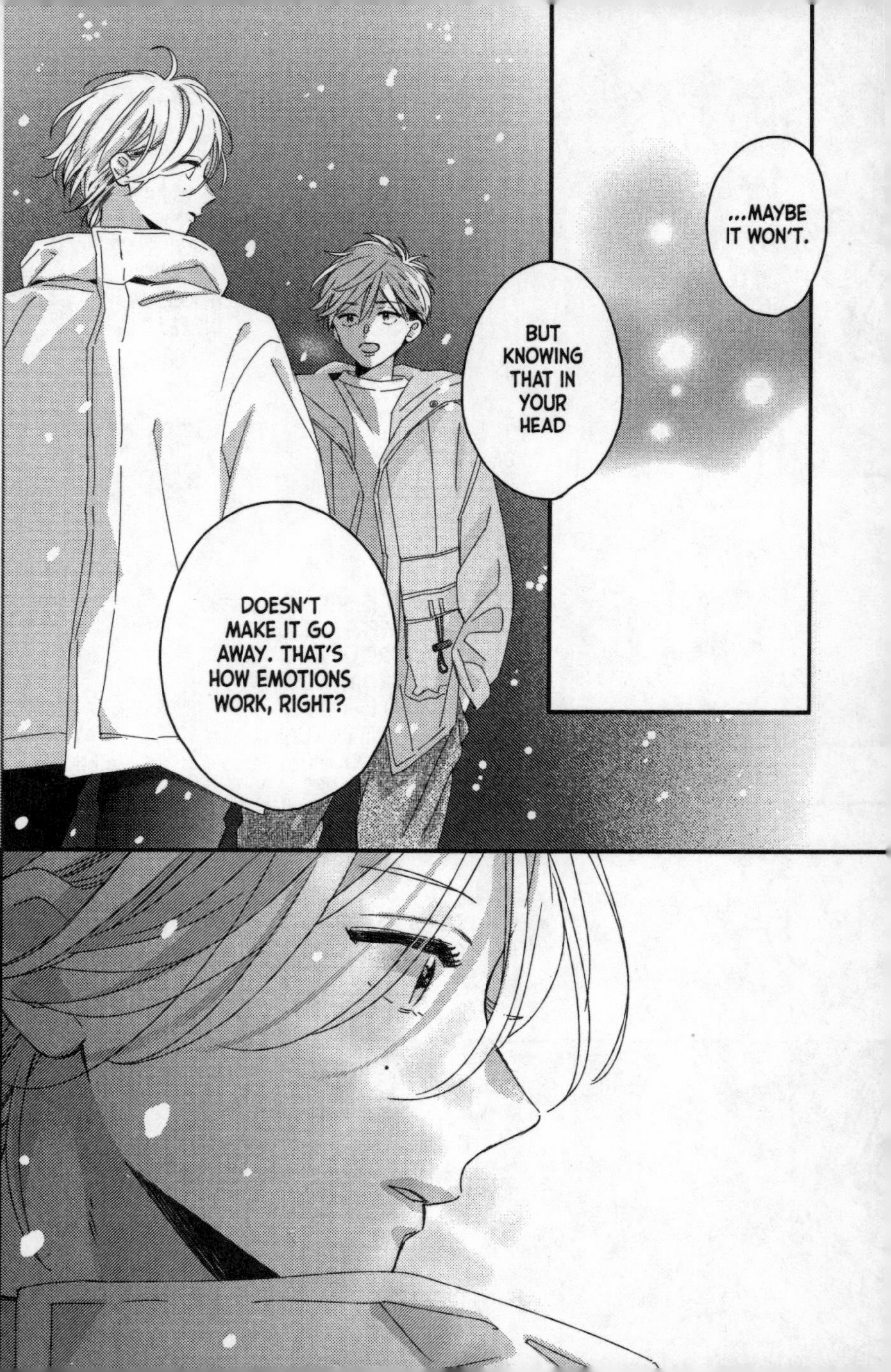
...MAYBE IT WON'T.
BUT KNOWING THAT IN YOUR HEAD
DOESN'T MAKE IT GO AWAY. THAT'S HOW EMOTIONS WORK, RIGHT?

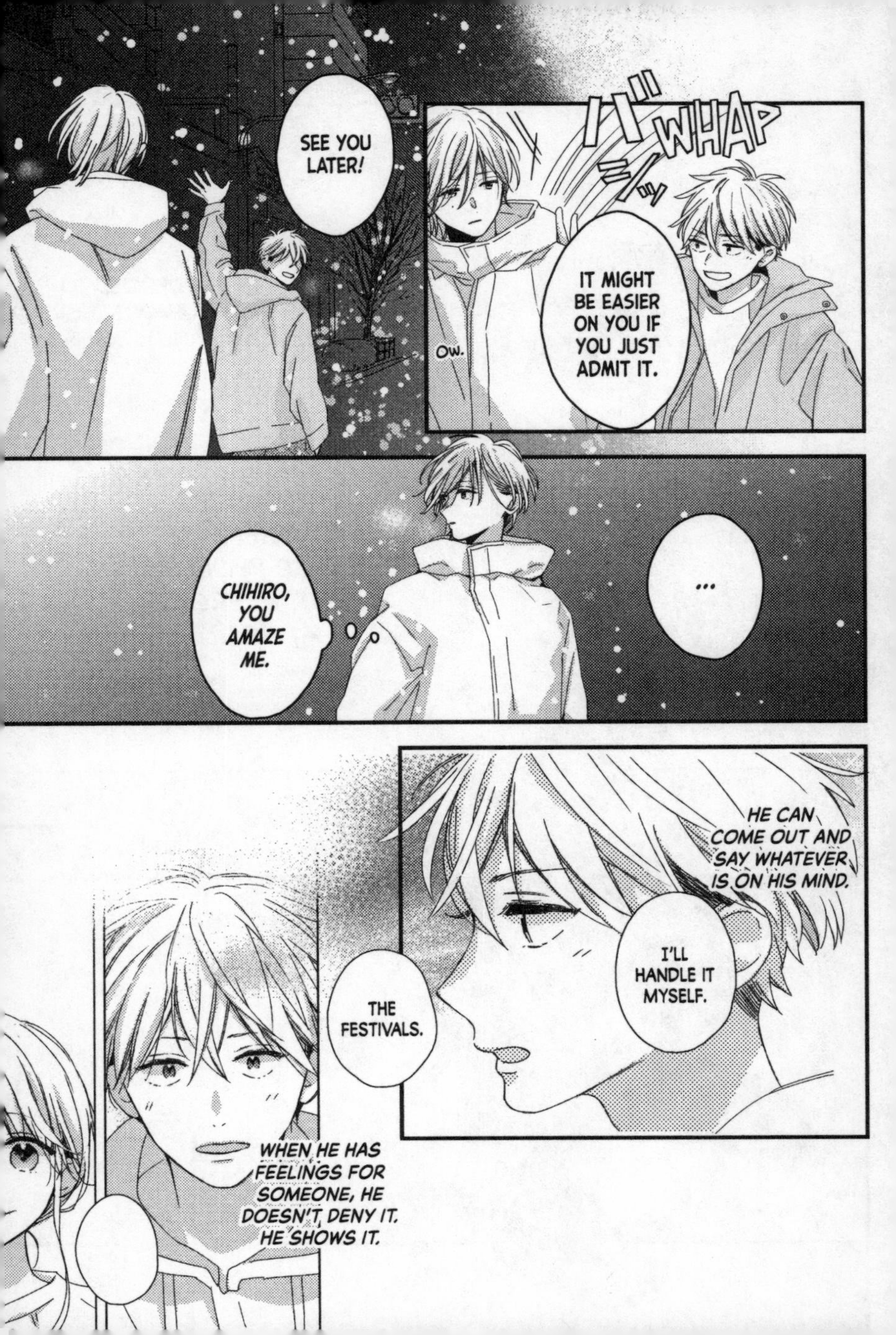
WHAP
IT MIGHT BE EASIER ON YOU IF YOU JUST ADMIT IT.
OW.
SEE YOU LATER!
...
CHIHIRO, YOU AMAZE ME.
HE CAN COME OUT AND SAY WHATEVER IS ON HIS MIND.
I'LL HANDLE IT MYSELF.
THE FESTIVALS.
WHEN HE HAS FEELINGS FOR SOMEONE, HE DOESN'T DENY IT. HE SHOWS IT.

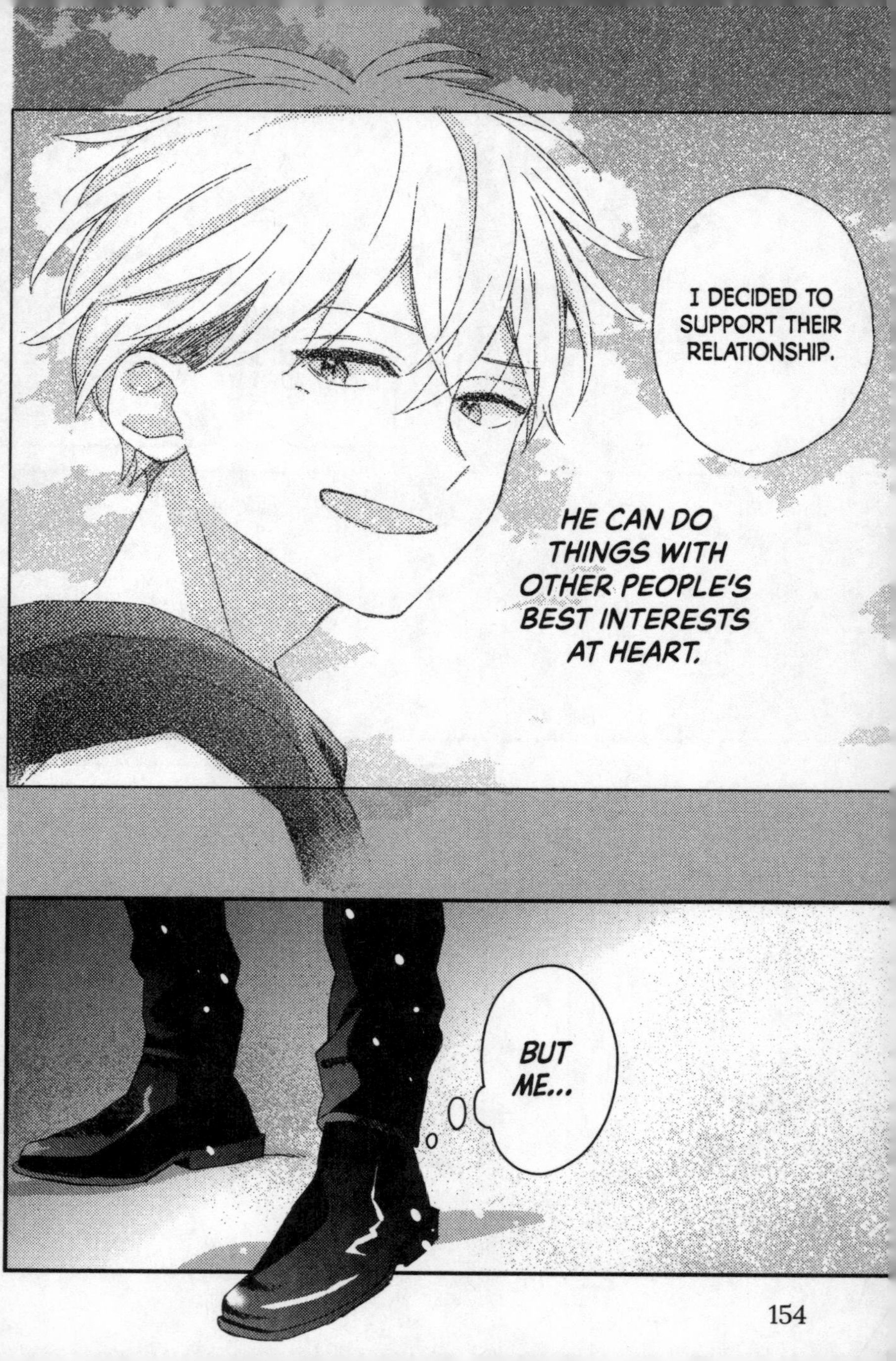
I DECIDED TO SUPPORT THEIR RELATIONSHIP.
HE CAN DO THINGS WITH OTHER PEOPLE'S BEST INTERESTS AT HEART.
BUT ME...

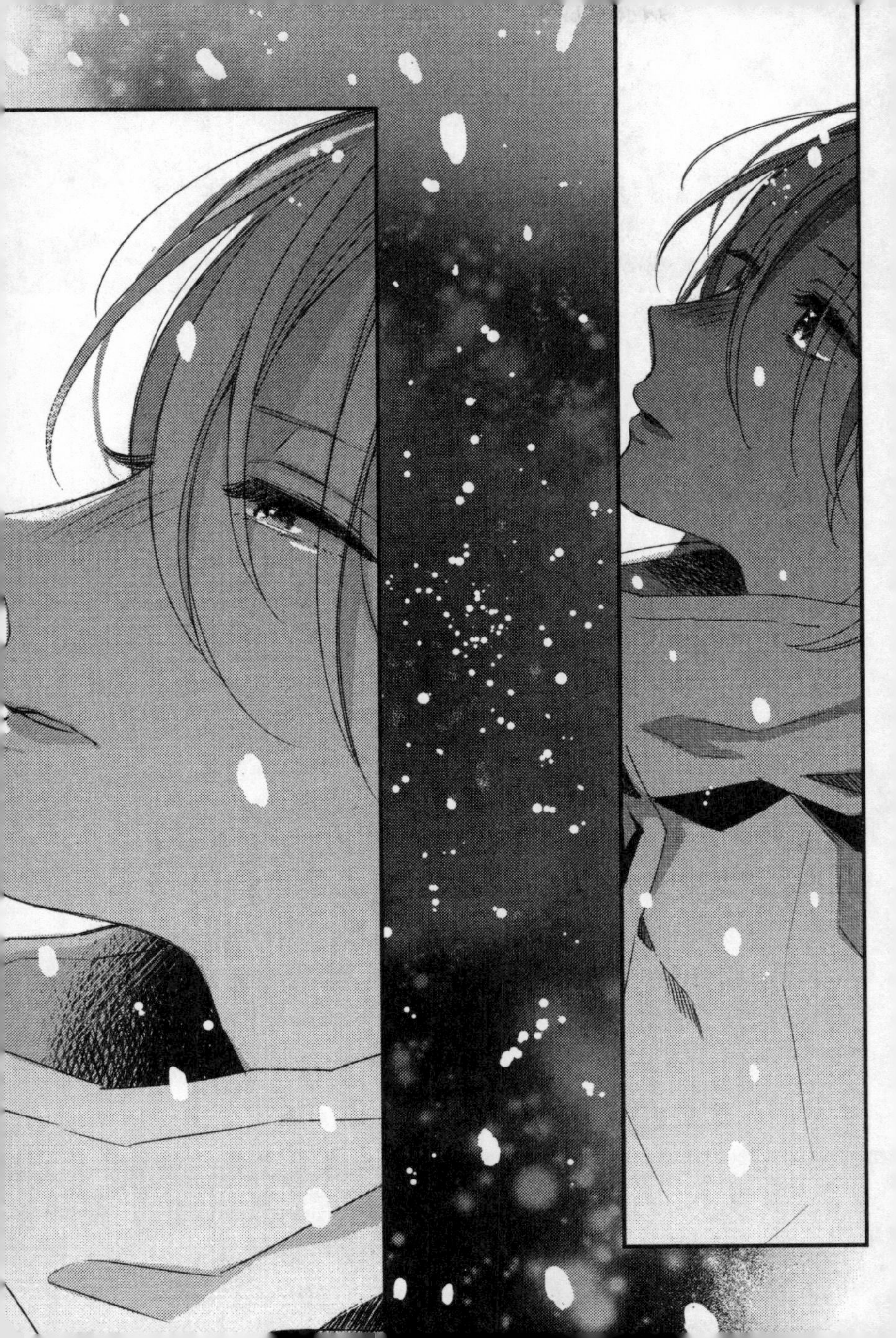

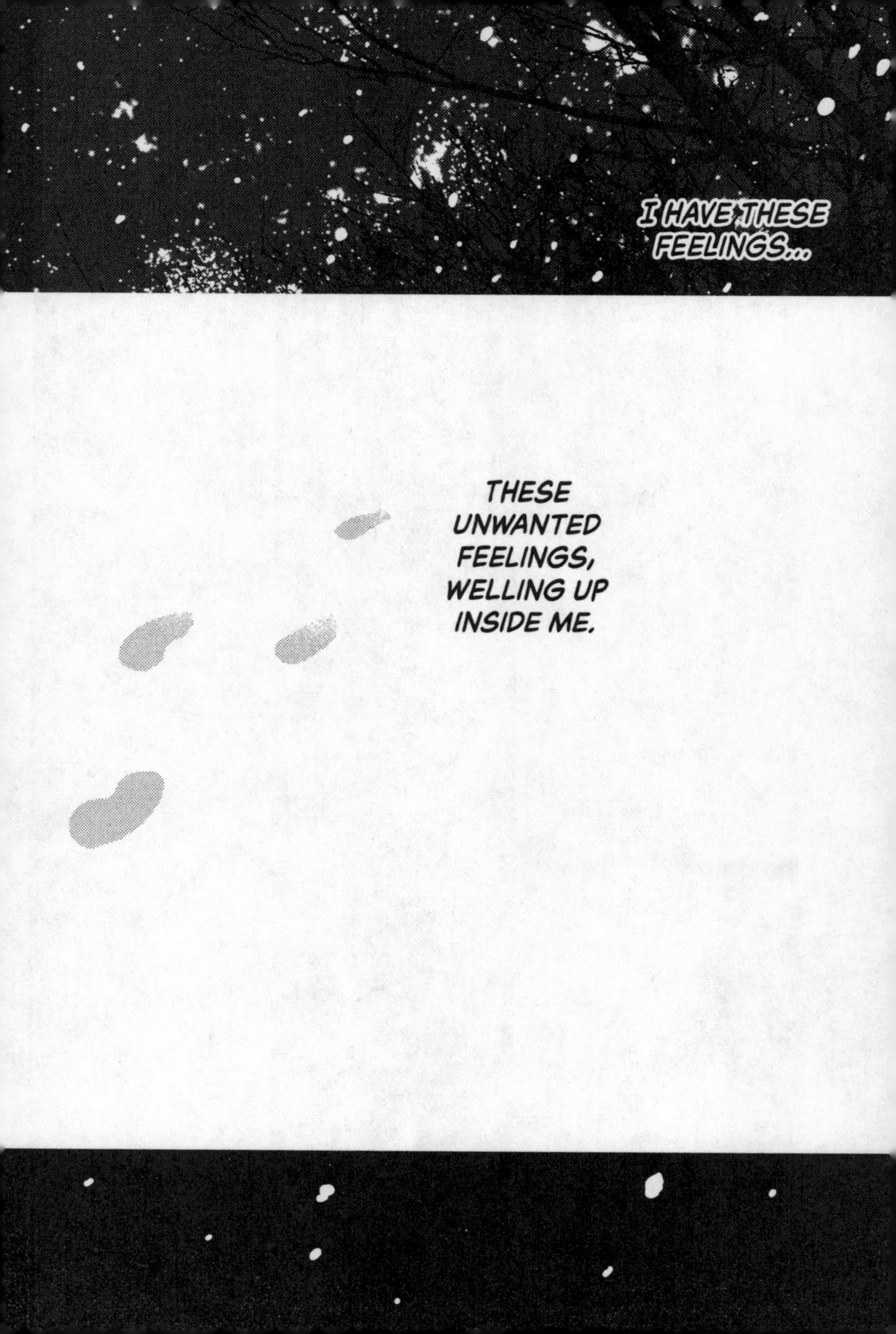
I HAVE THESE FEELINGS...
THESE UNWANTED FEELINGS, WELLING UP INSIDE ME.

AND I DON'T EVEN KNOW THE WORDS TO DESCRIBE THEM.

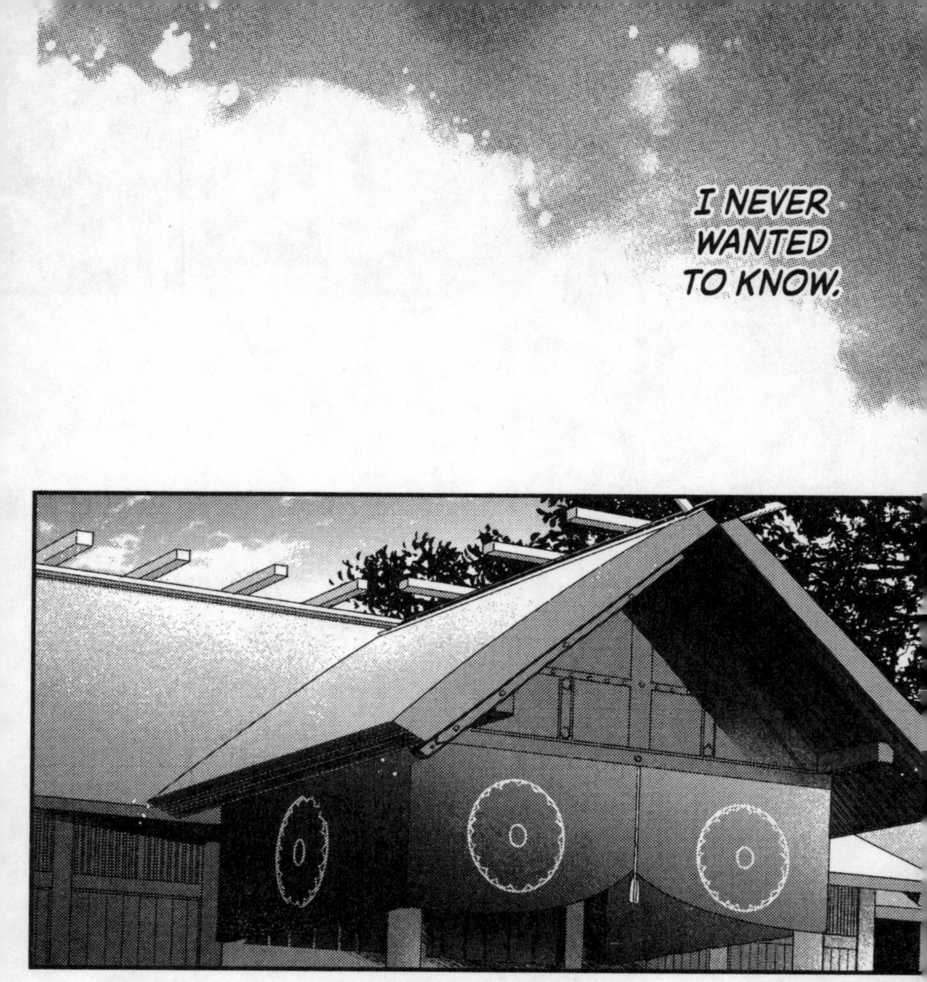
I NEVER WANTED TO KNOW.
CLAP
パン
CLAP
パン

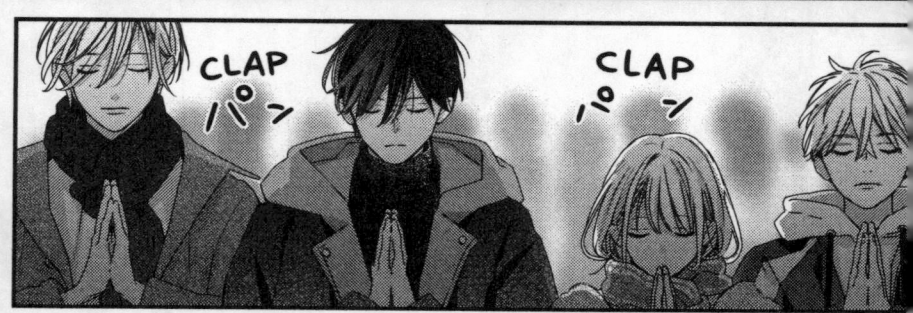

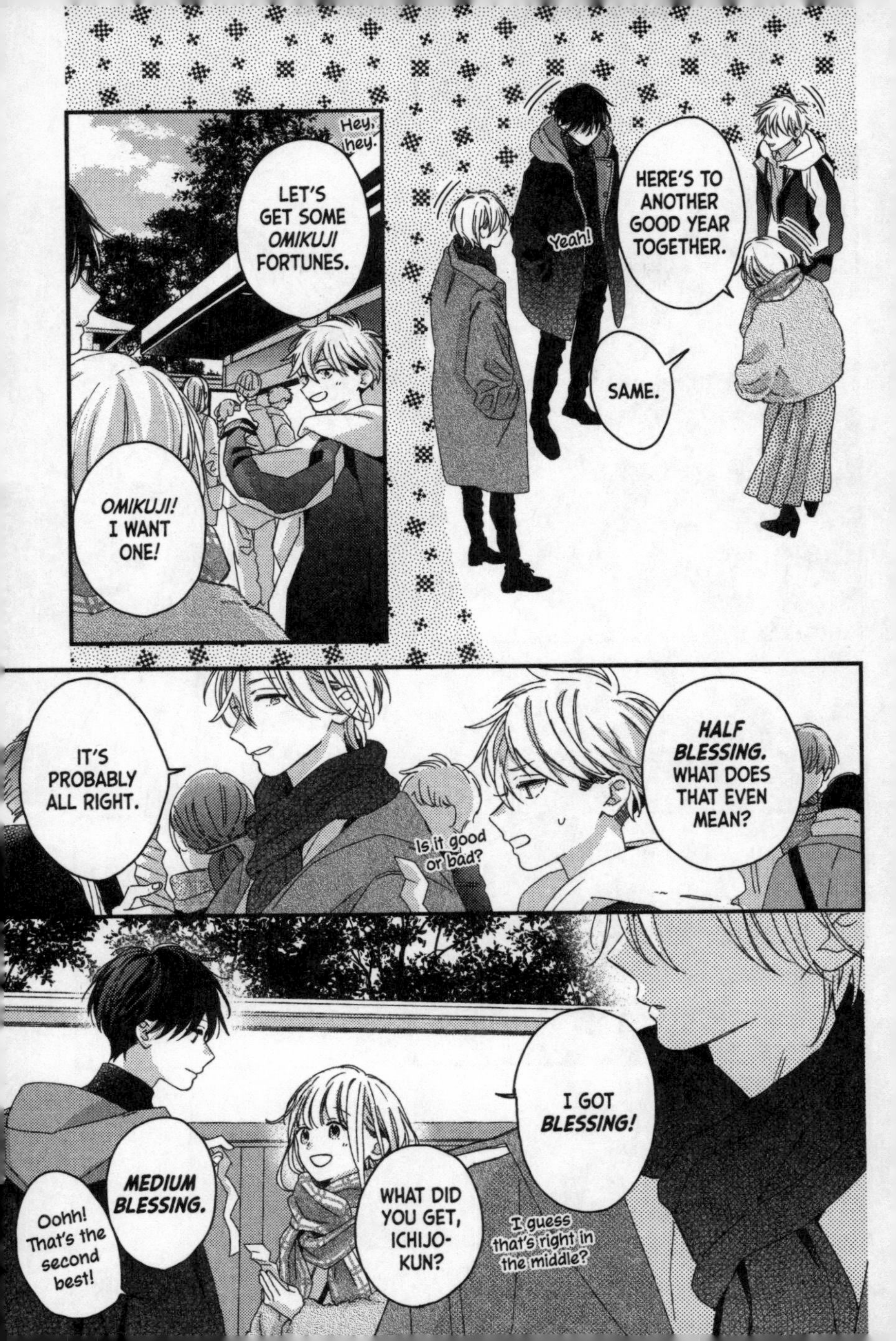
HERE'S TO ANOTHER GOOD YEAR TOGETHER.
Yeah!
SAME.
Hey, hey.
LET'S GET SOME *OMIKUJI* FORTUNES.
*OMIKUJI!* I WANT ONE!
***HALF BLESSING.*** WHAT DOES THAT EVEN MEAN?
Is it good or bad?
IT'S PROBABLY ALL RIGHT.
I GOT ***BLESSING!***
I guess that's right in the middle?
WHAT DID YOU GET, ICHIJO-KUN?
***MEDIUM BLESSING.***
Oohh! That's the second best!

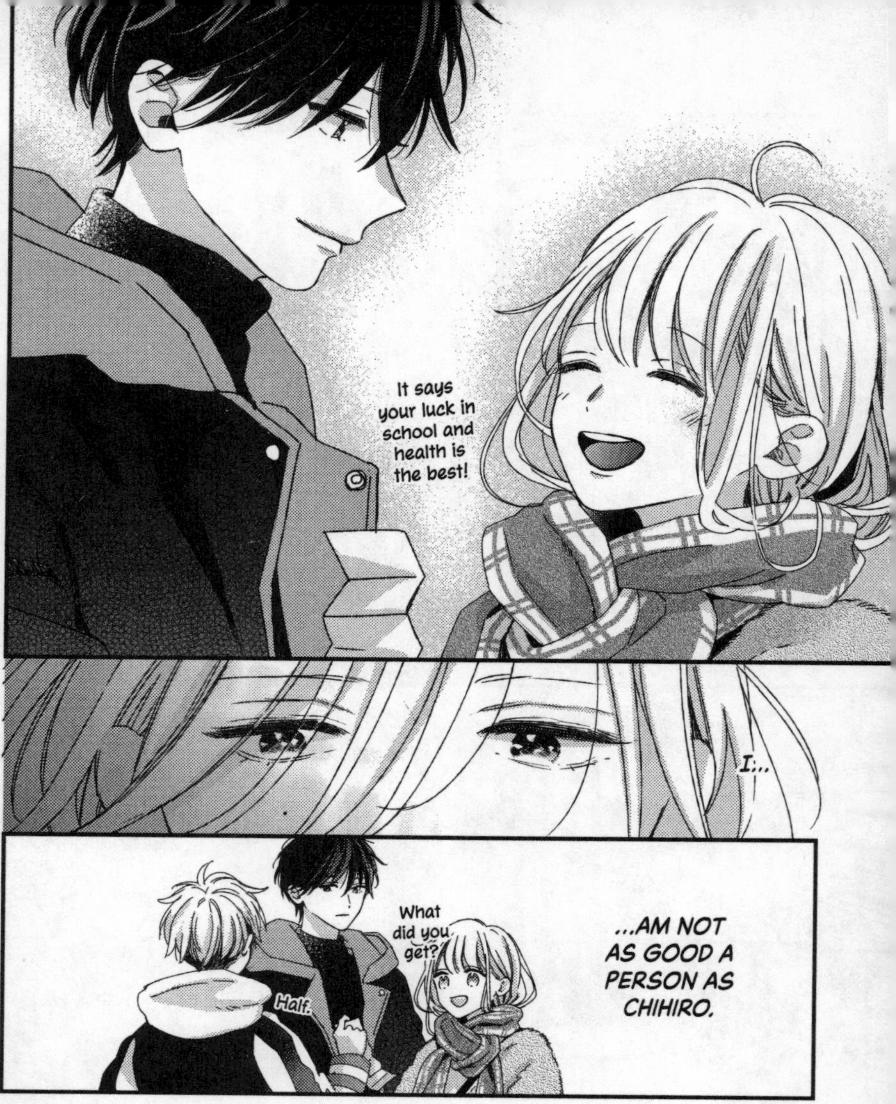
It says your luck in school and health is the best!
I...
...AM NOT AS GOOD A PERSON AS CHIHIRO.
What did you get?
Half.

SO I WON'T GIVE THEM MY BLESSING.

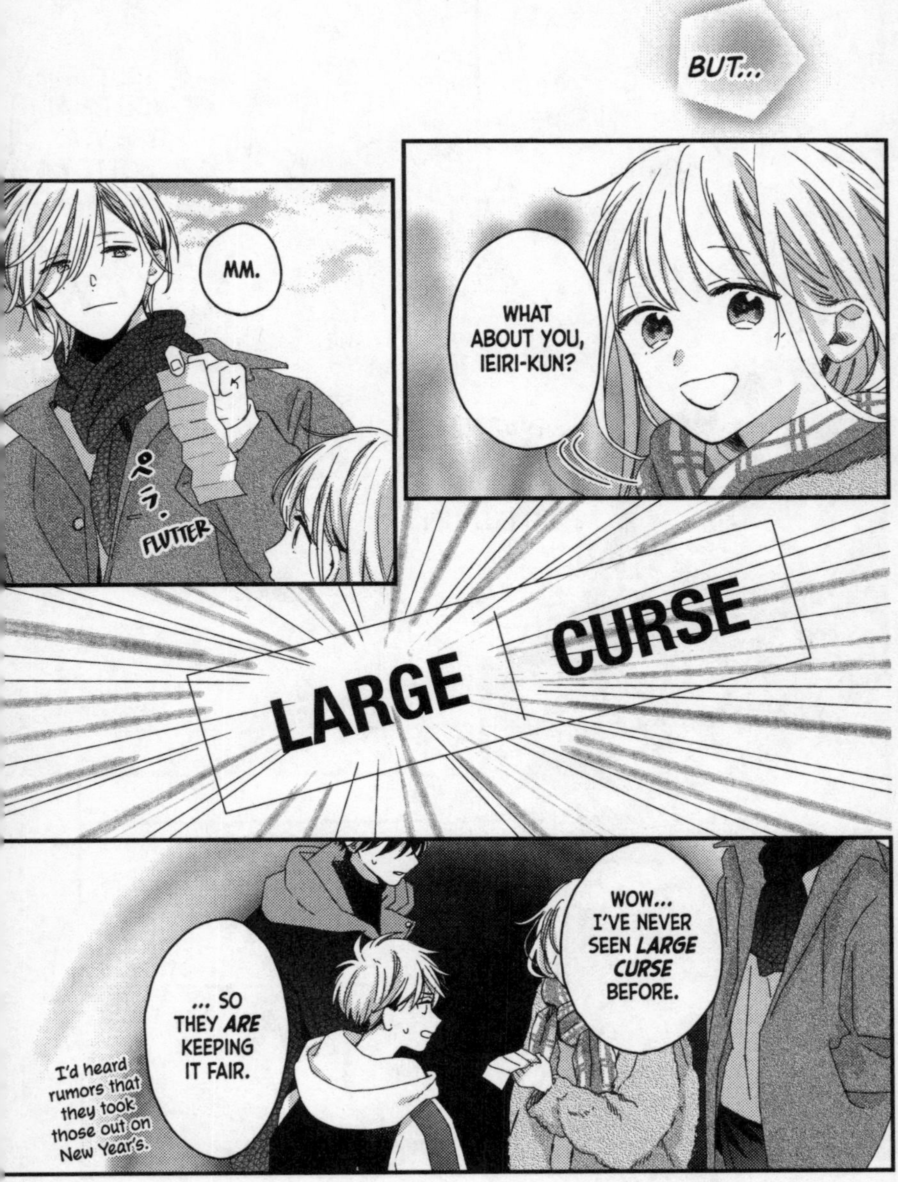
BUT...
WHAT ABOUT YOU, IEIRI-KUN?
MM.
ペラ・
FLUTTER
LARGE CURSE
WOW... I'VE NEVER SEEN *LARGE CURSE* BEFORE.
... SO THEY *ARE* KEEPING IT FAIR.
I'd heard rumors that they took those out on New Year's.

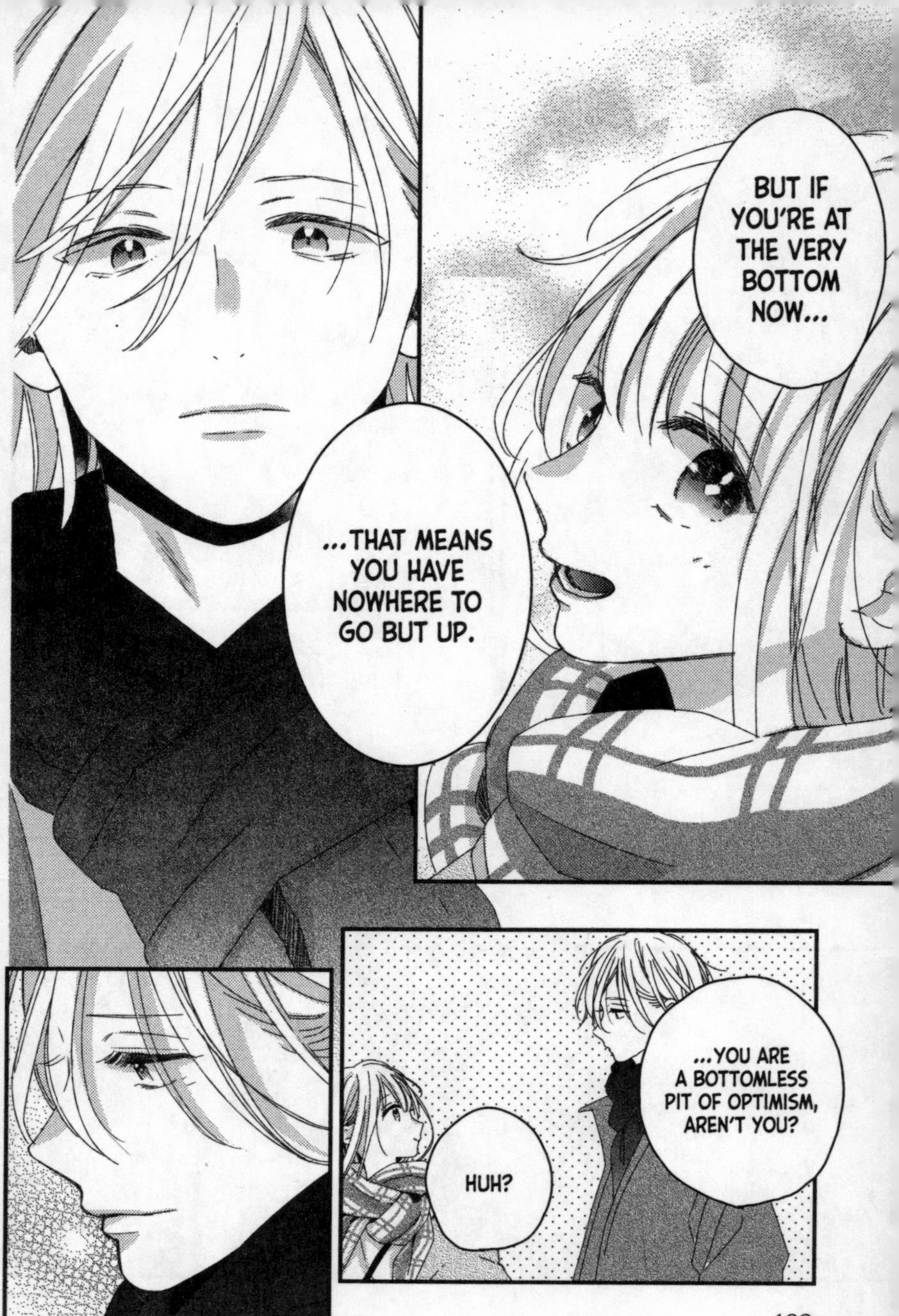
BUT IF YOU'RE AT THE VERY BOTTOM NOW...
...THAT MEANS YOU HAVE NOWHERE TO GO BUT UP.
...YOU ARE A BOTTOMLESS PIT OF OPTIMISM, AREN'T YOU?
HUH?

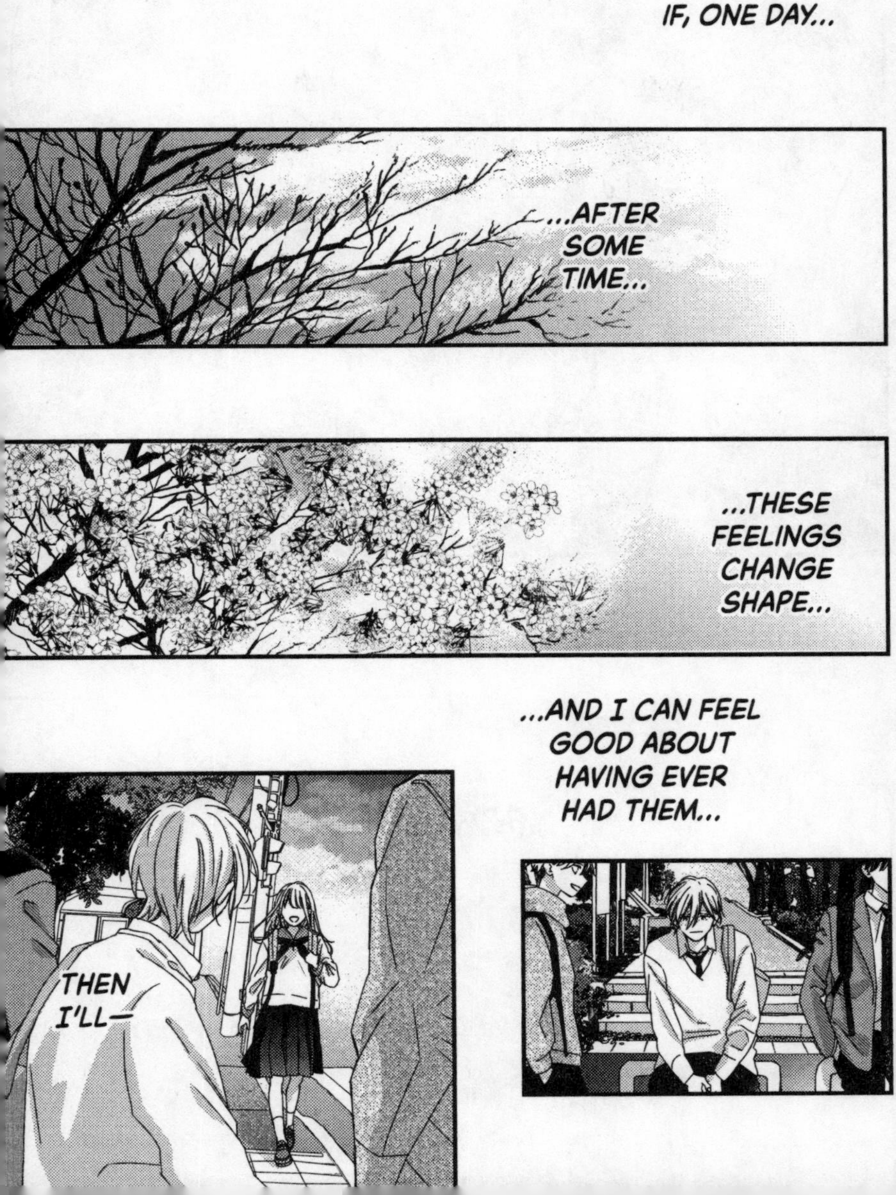
IF, ONE DAY...
...AFTER SOME TIME...
...THESE FEELINGS CHANGE SHAPE...
...AND I CAN FEEL GOOD ABOUT HAVING EVER HAD THEM...
THEN I'LL—

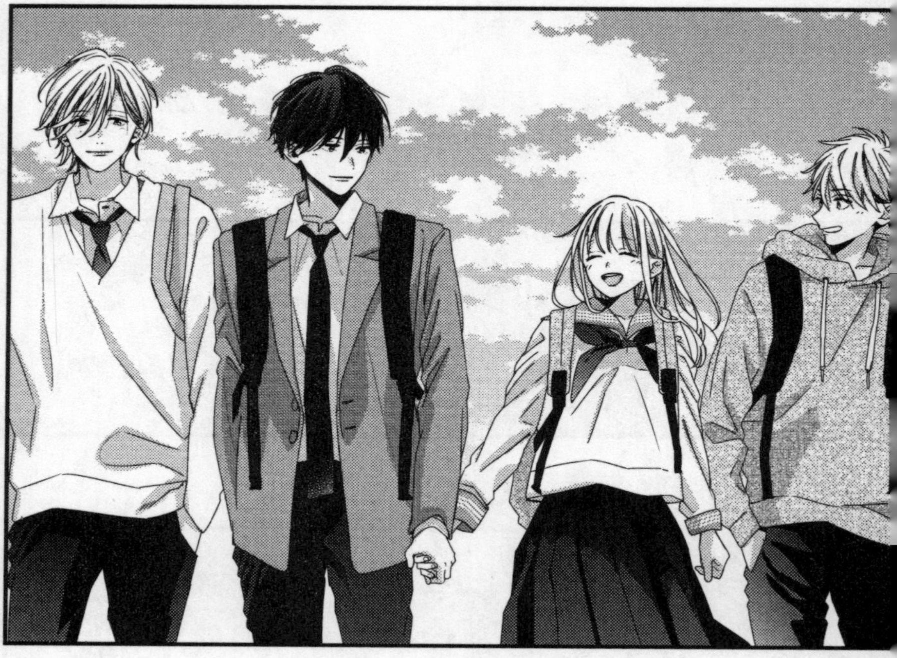

...SOMEDAY.

BONUS CHAPTER END

THANK YOU SO MUCH FOR PICKING UP VOLUME SEVEN!

IT'S THE LAST VOLUME.

I'VE MENTIONED THIS SEVERAL TIMES BEFORE,
BUT THIS IS THE LONGEST SERIES I'VE EVER DONE.

I WAS SO HAPPY TO GET TO DRAW THIS SERIES FOR SO
(COMPARATIVELY) LONG!!

THANK YOU SO MUCH FOR WATCHING OVER MIDORI AND THE
NOT-SO-SWEET BOYS REI, YUKI, AND CHIHIRO!

THANK YOU FOR ALL THE LETTERS
YOU SENT DURING THE SERIES! ♡

I'M VERY SORRY THAT
I CAN'T REPLY TO THEM...

THEY GIVE ME A LOT OF
ENCOURAGEMENT!

Special Thanks.

AKI NISHIHIRO-CHAN

FRIENDS, FAMILY

MY EDITOR

EVERYONE AT THE DESSERT
EDITORIAL DEPARTMENT

ARCO INC.

EVERYONE WHO WAS INVOLVED
IN THE CREATION AND SELLING
OF THIS WORK.

BONUS

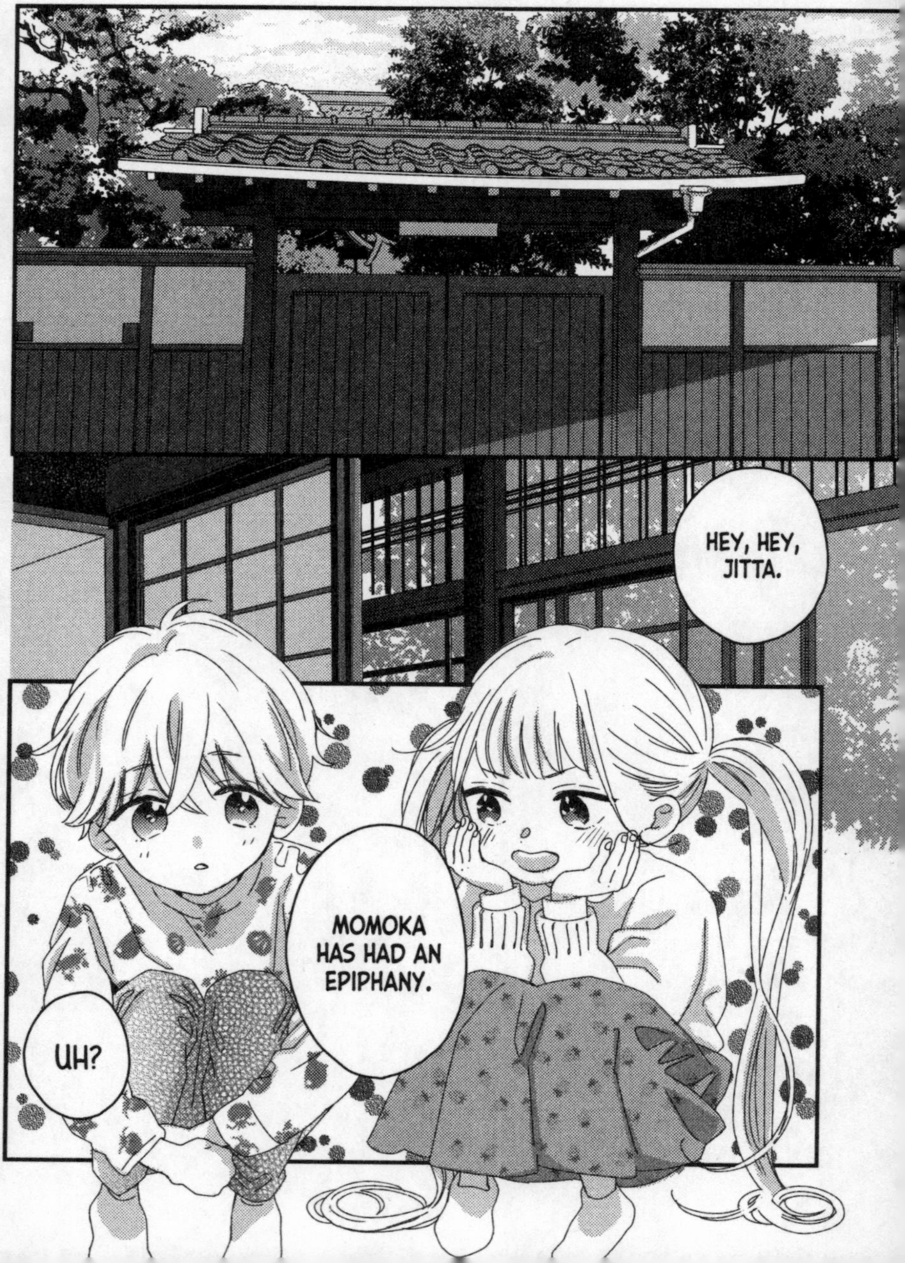
HEY, HEY, JITTA.
MOMOKA HAS HAD AN EPIPHANY.
UH?

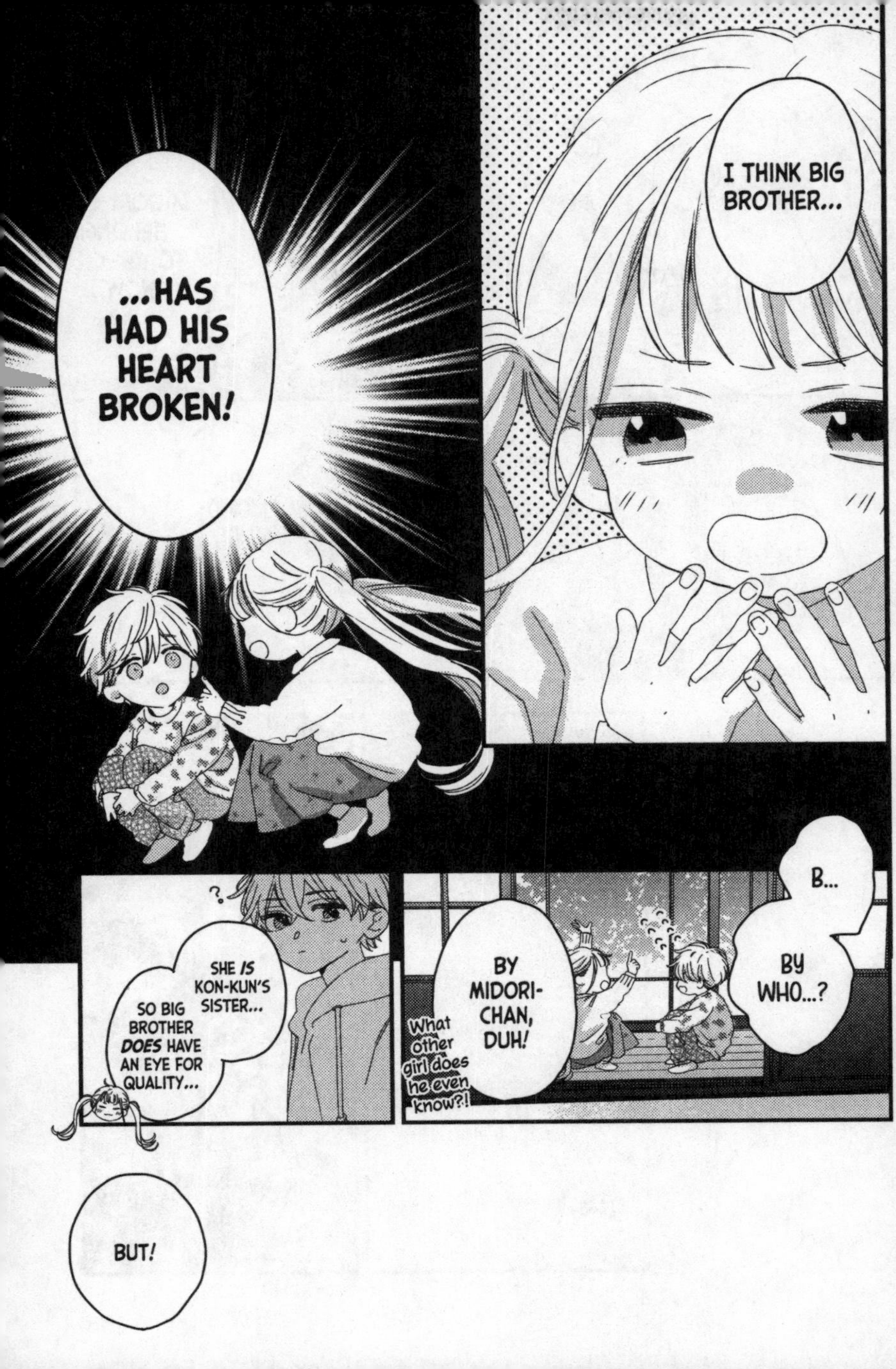
I THINK BIG BROTHER...
...HAS HAD HIS HEART BROKEN!
B...
BY WHO...?
BY MIDORI-CHAN, DUH!
What other girl does he even know?!
?
SHE *IS* KON-KUN'S SISTER...
SO BIG BROTHER *DOES* HAVE AN EYE FOR QUALITY...
BUT!

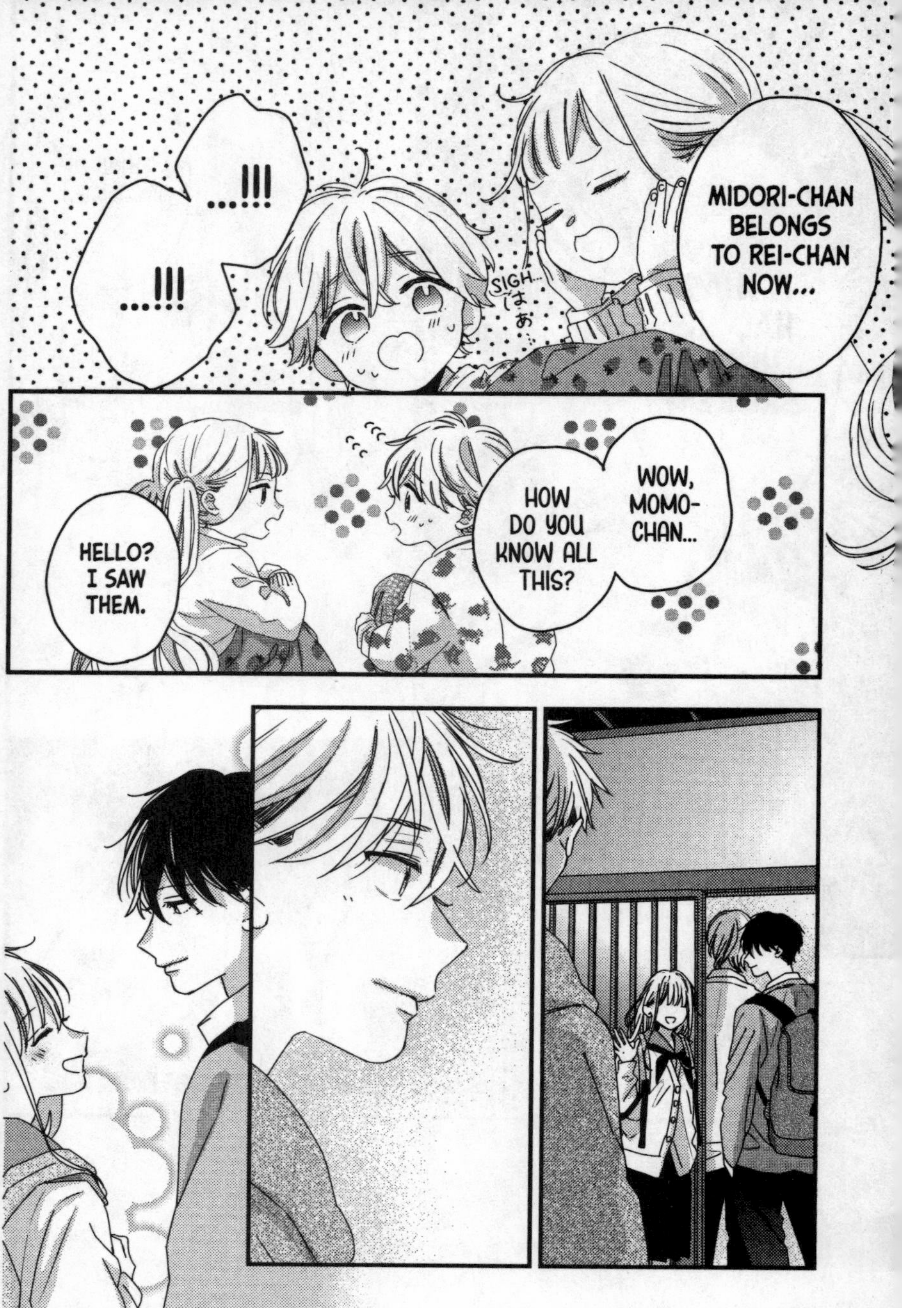
MIDORI-CHAN BELONGS TO REI-CHAN NOW...
SIGH... はぁ…
...!!!
...!!!
WOW, MOMO-CHAN...
HOW DO YOU KNOW ALL THIS?
HELLO? I SAW THEM.

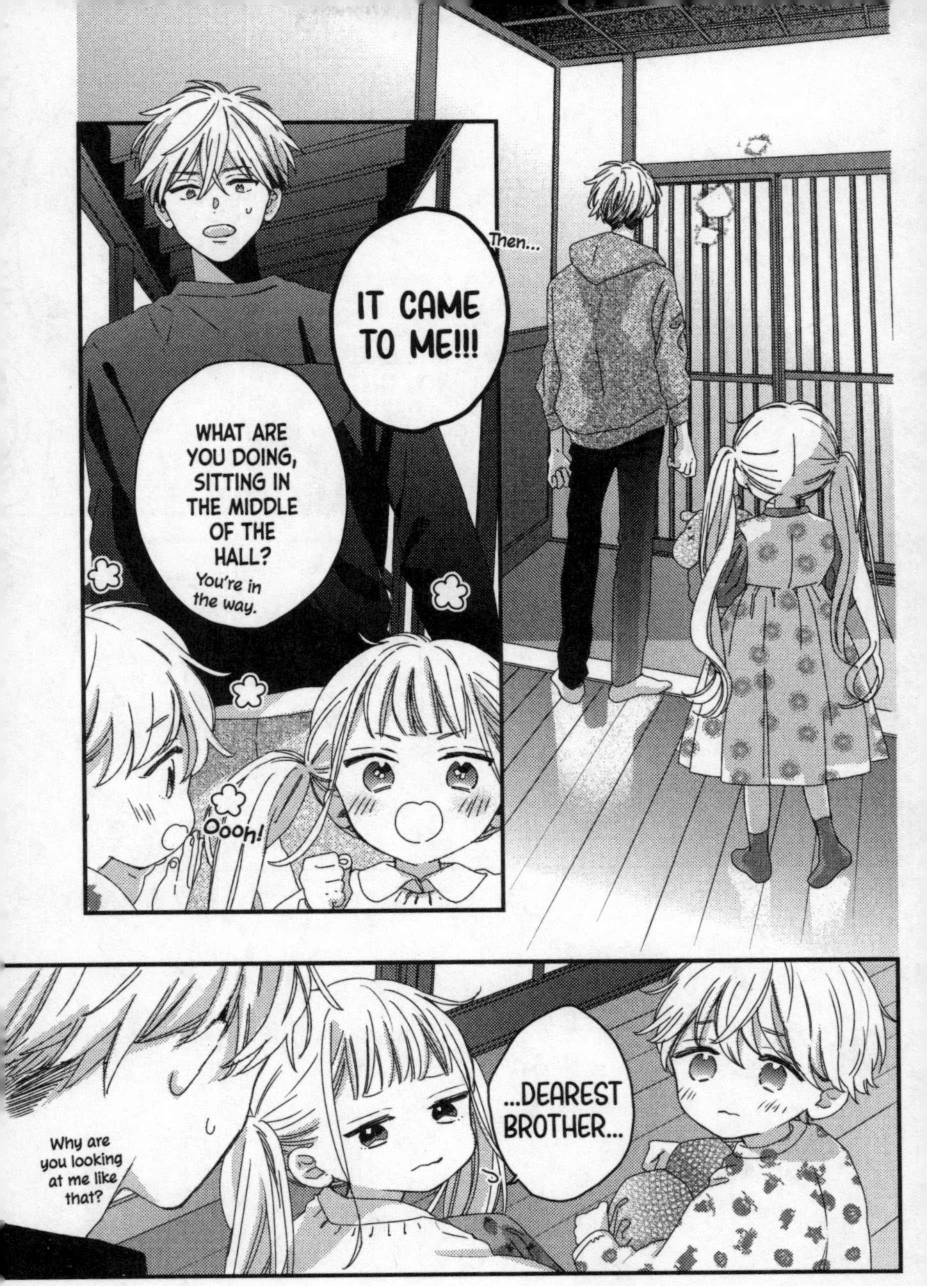
Then...
IT CAME TO ME!!!
WHAT ARE YOU DOING, SITTING IN THE MIDDLE OF THE HALL?
You're in the way.
Oooh!
...DEAREST BROTHER...
Why are you looking at me like that?

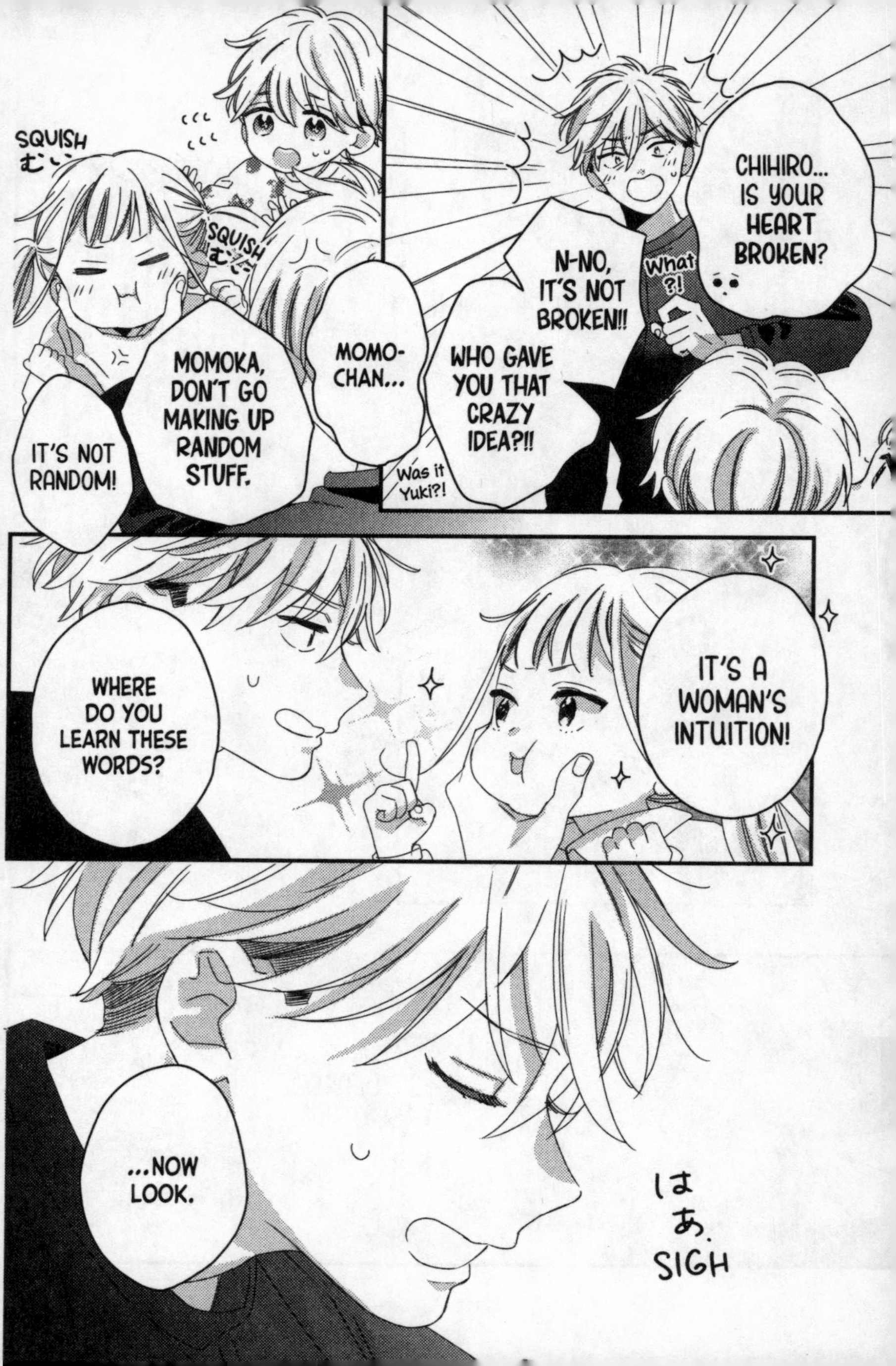
CHIHIRO... IS YOUR HEART BROKEN?
What?!
N-NO, IT'S NOT BROKEN!!
WHO GAVE YOU THAT CRAZY IDEA?!!
Was it Yuki?!
SQUISH むい
SQUISH むい
MOMO-CHAN...
MOMOKA, DON'T GO MAKING UP RANDOM STUFF.
IT'S NOT RANDOM!
IT'S A WOMAN'S INTUITION!
WHERE DO YOU LEARN THESE WORDS?
はあ. SIGH
...NOW LOOK.

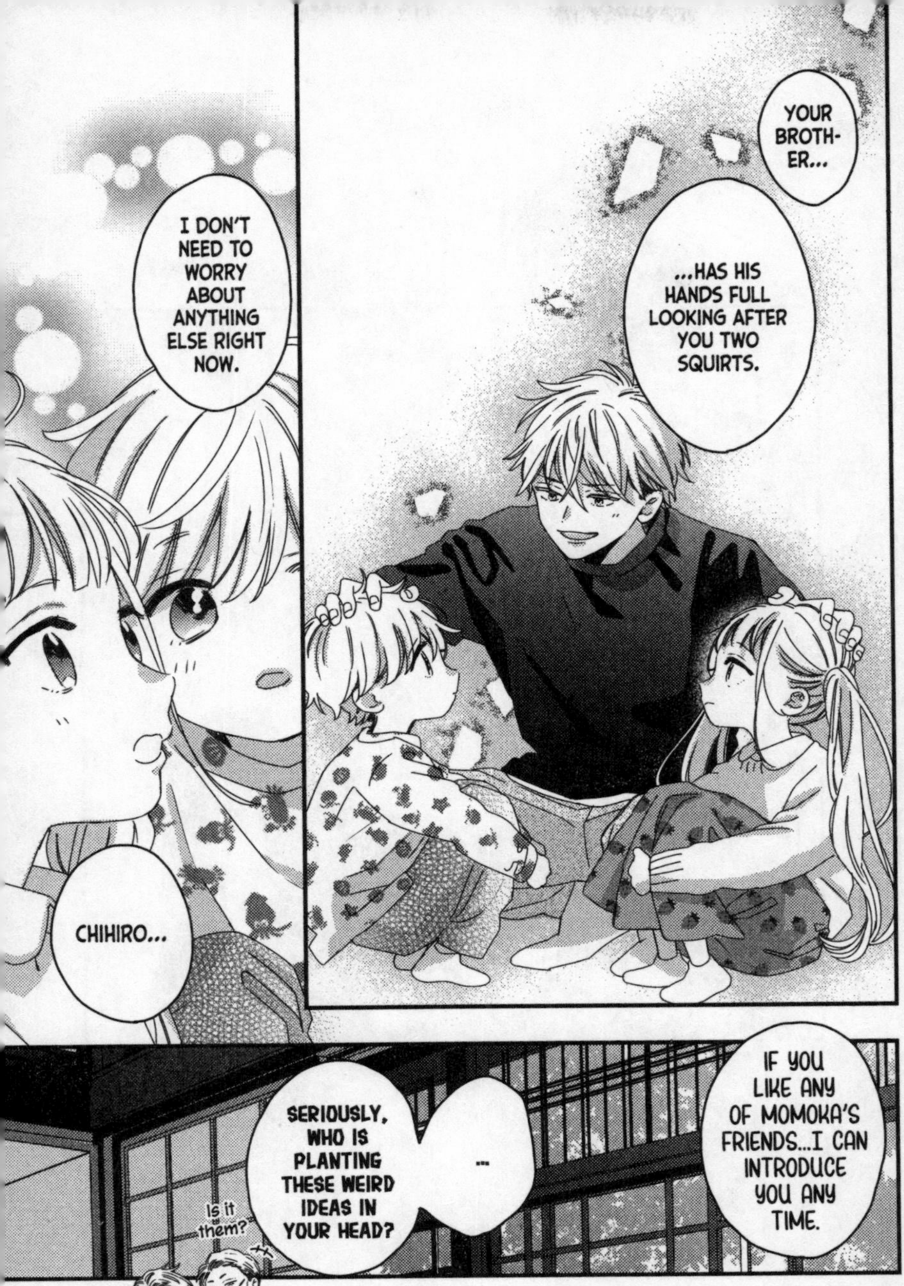
YOUR BROTH- ER...
...HAS HIS HANDS FULL LOOKING AFTER YOU TWO SQUIRTS.
I DON'T NEED TO WORRY ABOUT ANYTHING ELSE RIGHT NOW.
CHIHIRO...
IF YOU LIKE ANY OF MOMOKA'S FRIENDS...I CAN INTRODUCE YOU ANY TIME.
...
SERIOUSLY, WHO IS PLANTING THESE WEIRD IDEAS IN YOUR HEAD?
Is it them?

<THE END>

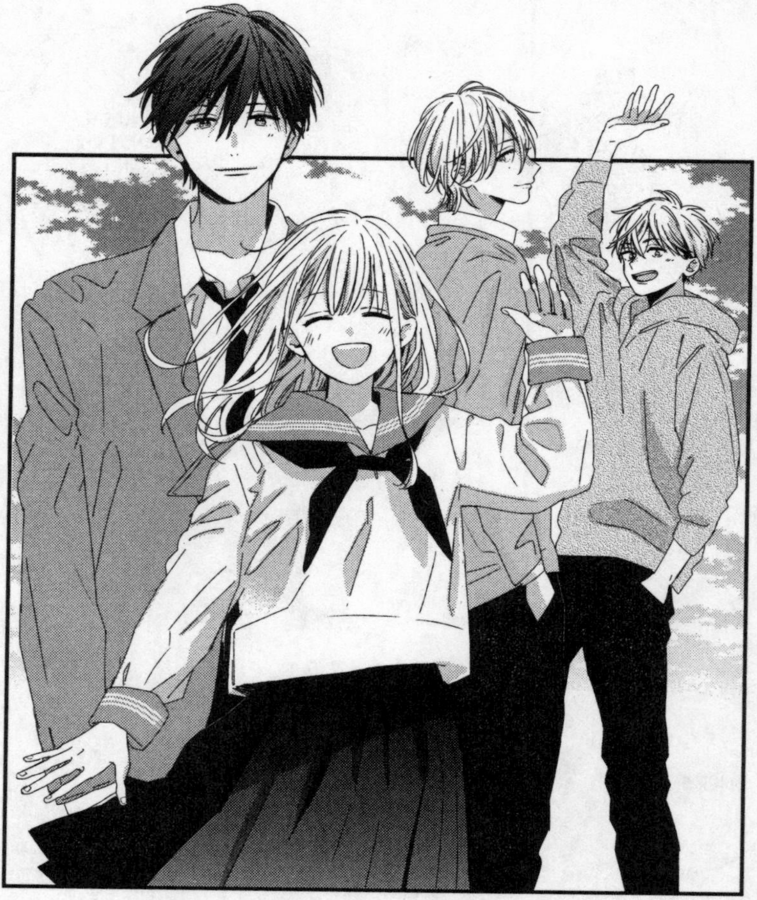

I HOPE TO SEE YOU AGAIN
IN MY NEXT WORK!!

野切耀子

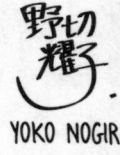

YOKO NOGIRI

# TRANSLATION NOTES

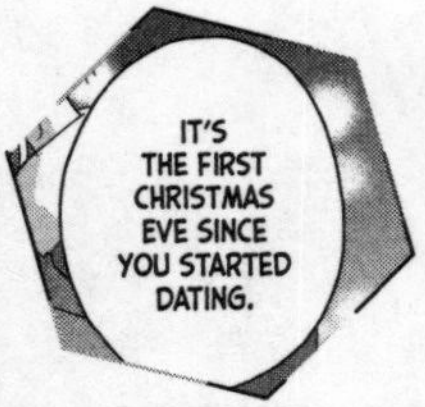
IT'S THE FIRST CHRISTMAS EVE SINCE YOU STARTED DATING.

**CHRISTMAS EVE, PAGE 93**
In Japan, Christmas Eve is celebrated as a romantic holiday, for people to spend a lovely evening with their significant others. It is also a family holiday with many traditions and feasts.

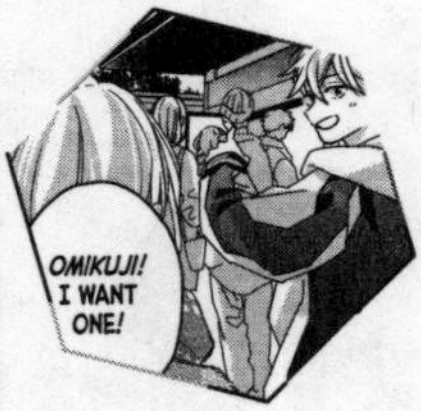
OMIKUJI! I WANT ONE!

***OMIKUJI* FORTUNES, PAGE 159**
An *omikuji* is a little strip of paper with a fortune written on it, obtained at Japanese Buddhist and Shinto shrines by making an offering and choosing one at random. Each strip lists the amount of luck the chooser is going to have, ranging from *dai-kichi* (great blessing, great luck), through lesser degrees of luck, and on through the degrees of curses or bad luck. If you get a bad luck fortune, you can dispel the curse by tying the *omikuji* strip of paper to a tree or a designated wire provided by the shrine or temple. Different temples and shrines sometimes use different rankings for the types of blessings or luck, so it's not always clear how fortunate your *omikuji* has made you.

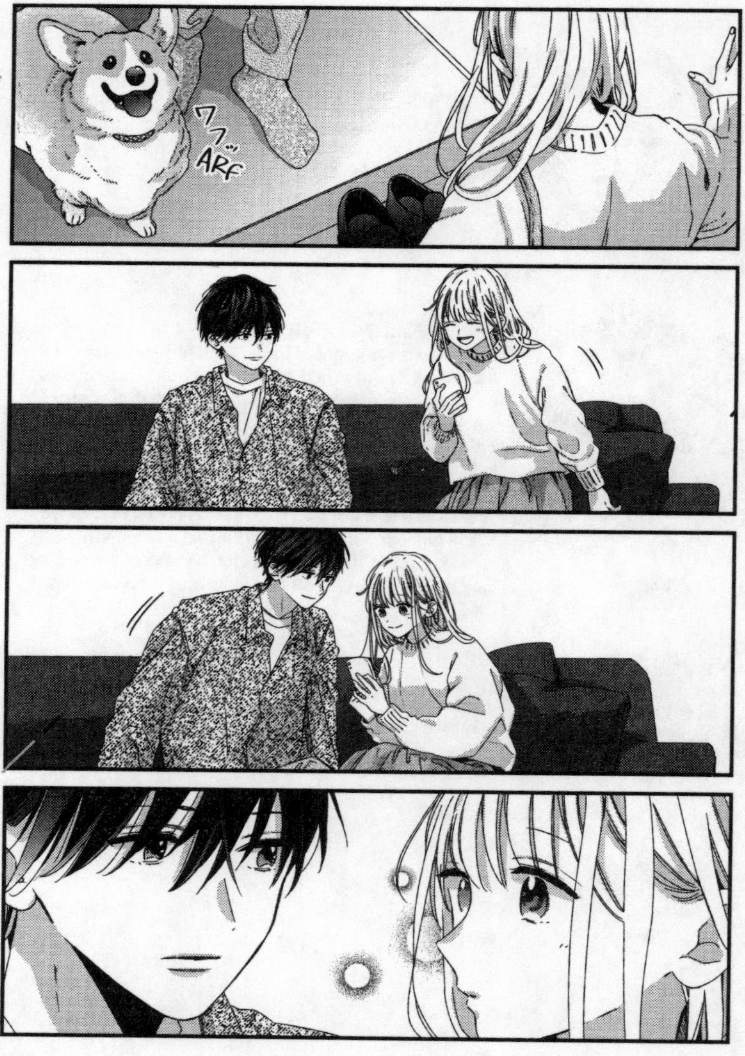
ワフッ
ARF

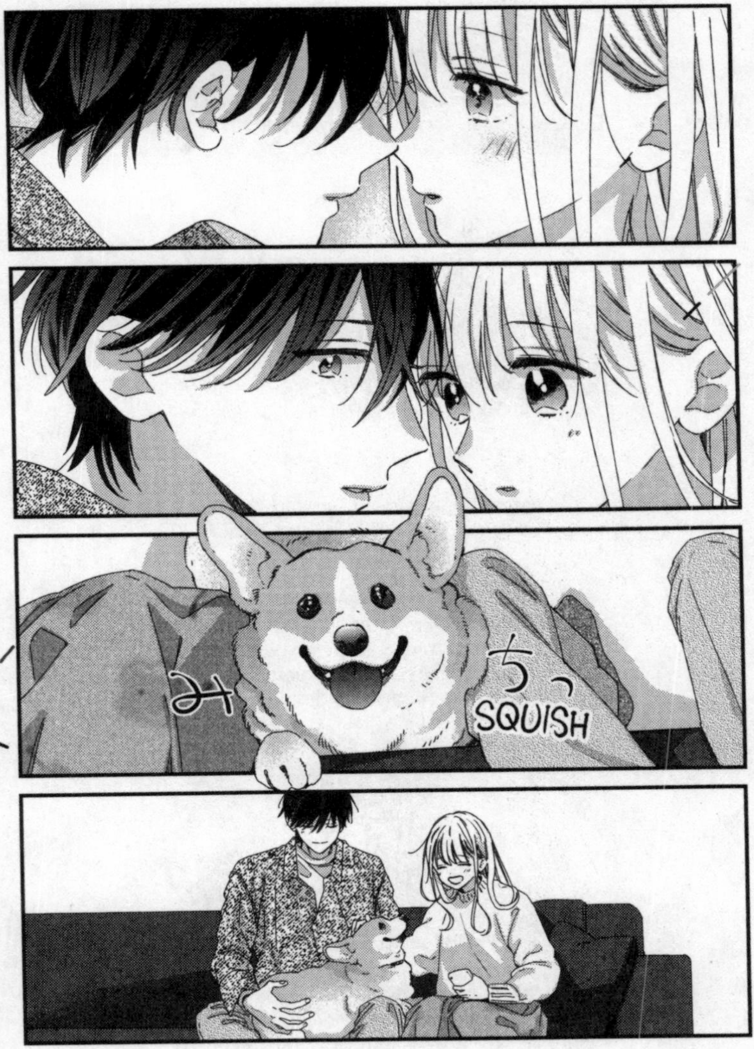

ちっ
み
SQUISH

A Kodansha Comics Trade Paperback Original
*Those Not-So-Sweet Boys* 7 copyright © 2022 Yoko Nogiri
English translation copyright © 2022 Yoko Nogiri

Published in the United States by Kodansha Comics, an imprint of
Kodansha USA Publishing, LLC, New York.

Publication rights for this English edition arranged through
Kodansha Ltd., Tokyo.

First published in Japan in 2022 by Kodansha Ltd., Tokyo
as *Amakunai Karera no Nichijo wa.*, volume 7.

ISBN 978-1-64651-441-0

Printed in the United States of America.

www.kodansha.us

1st Printing
Translation: Alethea Nibley & Athena Nibley
Lettering: Sara Linsley
Editing: Haruko Hashimoto
Kodansha Comics edition cover design by Phil Balsman

Publisher: Kiichiro Sugawara

Director of publishing services: Ben Applegate
Director of publishing operations: Dave Barrett
Associate director, publishing operations: Stephen Pakula
Publishing services managing editors: Madison Salters, Alanna Ruse
Production managers: Emi Lotto, Angela Zurlo
Logo and character art ©Kodansha USA Publishing, LLC